D0891946

THE WORKINGS
■ OF FICTION ■

BOOKS BY ROBERT BECHTOLD HEILMAN

America in English Fiction, 1760–1800 (1937)

This Great Stage: Image and Structure in King Lear (1948)

Magic in the Web: Action and Language in Othello (1956)
(The Explicator Prize)

Tragedy and Melodrama: Versions of Experience (1968)

The Iceman, the Arsonist, and the Troubled Agent: Tragedy and Melodrama on the Modern Stage (1973)

The Ghost on the Ramparts and Other Essays in the Humanities (1974)

The Ways of the World: Comedy and Society (1978)
(The Christian Gauss Prize of Phi Beta Kappa)

The Southern Connection: Essays (1991)

The Workings of Fiction (1991)

THE WORKINGS
■ OF FICTION ■

Essays by Robert Bechtold Heilman

UNIVERSITY OF MISSOURI PRESS
Columbia and London

5   4   3   2   1   95   94   93   92   91

Library of Congress Cataloging-in-Publication Data

Heilman, Robert Bechtold, 1906–
    The workings of fiction : essays / by Robert Bechtold Heilman.
        p.   cm.
    Includes bibliographical references and index.
    ISBN 0–8262–0787–1 (alk. paper)
    1. English fiction—History and criticism. 2. American fiction—
History and criticism. I. Title.
PR823.H45   1991
809.3—dc20   90–29184
                                                                  CIP

Designer: Elizabeth K. Fett
Typesetter: Connell-Zeko Type & Graphics
Printer: Thomson-Shore, Inc.
Binder: Thomson-Shore, Inc.
Typeface: Elante

To

CONTENTS

vii

PREFACE

IN COLLECTING SOME of one's own essays one may unconsciously beg the question of their ability to stir interest and seem useful. One probably relies more on hope than on reason. I have tried, however, to eliminate essays that belong essentially to the time of their publication or are addressed to a purely professional audience, and to reprint only those that seem to survive their times and those addressed to a general audience. I do include one essay of a somewhat technical character, the account of euphuism that opens the section on style. I take this risk because euphuism, as I argue later, is not merely a curiosity of a past era but a survivor that we run into, perhaps unexpectedly, in other times.

The continuing vitality of some of the essays is suggested by their appeal to anthologists. Nine of the essays in this volume have appeared in various collections, from one time for several of the essays to twelve times for "Innovations in Gothic: Charlotte Brontë." As for anthological resurrections, the essay on the picaresque has had an odd fate: though I think it has enough life to justify its opening position in the volume, it has escaped the attention of some five activists in the field, identified by a scholar kind enough to allude to my "important observations." On the other hand, it has been anthologized twice in America and translated into German for a third anthology.

The majority of my essays are about English writers. I taught the English novel and of course was constantly thinking about how the novelists managed things; some of the essays originated in classroom discussions. Other essays originated in casual reading: those on Mann, Dürrenmatt, and Lampedusa, and several of those on American novels. Some essays began life as commissioned reviews. The essay on *Silas Marner* (originally entitled "Return to Raveloe") was part of a series in a journal that decided to take a new look at old standbys in high-school reading. Hardy is more amply represented than other novelists; that is because I happened to be asked to edit several of his novels and hence got interested in various Hardy problems.

One writes for different kinds of publications, and the habits of a journal have some impact, perhaps on what one says, but more obviously on how one presents what one has to say. In writing for literary quarterlies one assumes the voice of authority; one's own perceptions and style have to make the case. In writing for scholarly journals one tends to engage in a partly collaborative enterprise, carrying on a kind of dialogue with other workers in the field, claiming their support where one can, noting parallels of thought, acknowledging anticipations, or even, in a reckless mood, pointing a finger at apparent error. Ordinarily two insignia identify the scholarly mode: an in-house vocabulary, with a more or less recondite style, and a forest of footnotes that establish irrefutably one's insidership. In writing for either type of journal I have tried to avoid a dense technical style and to rely, instead, on a public vocabulary and syntax. But in essays for scholarly journals I have sometimes presented a formidable apparatus, with a rich assemblage of footnotes, cross-references, dialogues with other critics, and so forth. In reprinting such essays, however, I have mercilessly eliminated most of the evidence of this "knowledge of the field." May my colleagues forgive me for doing away with them; I offer the comforting thought that elimination from footnote life is one of the more survivable forms of experienced homicide. Mostly I have wanted my essays to look the same throughout, to avoid an oscillation between different ways of doing things. Besides, documentation, if it is to have character, needs to be complete and up-to-date; there is no point in identifying all the relevant criticism of a novel for a period from thirty to ten years ago. And even if one greatly enlarged the mass by adding on another decade of scholarly references, one's 1990s up-to-dateness would soon be out-of-date again. Nothing ages, or even dies, like documentation. One must leave it to the formal bibliographies and rely on one's text rather than on its relationship with other critical exercises.

In doing without references to other opinions that may strengthen one's case, one assumes, as it were, the privilege of assertion. Still, it is assertion within limits. I like to have the authority of evidence, and so I rely heavily on quotation, especially when I discuss style. The risk of being burdensome in this way seems preferable to the risk of relying on pronouncement in lieu of proof. I generally identify quoted passages by chapter, since most of the novels are available in too many editions to make one pagination preferable to the others. I do use page references in discussing a text likely to be found only in one basic edition such as the Everyman. Whether by chapter or by page, references appear only when they were appropriate in the publication in which the essay originally appeared (that is, in scholarly rather than literary quarterlies). Hence in discussing a novel in different essays, as I do once or twice, I may provide local identification of passages quoted in one but not in the other. The difference of procedure has seemed preferable to various devices of consistency.

The essays appear essentially in their original forms. I have made a few minor changes that reflect my sense of a changed situation. When I wrote "'Intentions' in *The Mayor*," for instance, the air was full of debate about the importance or irrelevance of the author's formal intentions, and various statements of mine reflected the currency of the issue. So it makes sense to minimize these references to discussions of that time. The issue itself, naturally, does not die, and I believe that this is true of most of the matters dealt with in these essays. One hopes, of course, not to be too scarred by anachronisms inevitable in the flux of years. One essay represents another kind of change from the original form. The discussion of D. H. Lawrence belonged to a review of a book about Lawrence by Eliseo Vivas, and in revising I have eliminated the passages that dealt with Vivas rather than with Lawrence. I have tried to cut out all passages in which one essay repeated another one, and I have made a few additions meant to establish connections between essays.

When one has not attempted a comprehensive study of a field but writes about subjects that have come into view almost accidentally as it were, a collection of his essays, even centered in one major topic (here, "the novel"), is likely to have only what used to be called "the unity of the author." I hope that the term, insofar as it fits this volume, implies some consistency of point of view. The consistency lies, perhaps, in starting with apparently standard positions and trying to see how accurate they are. Take Hardy, for instance. One thinks of all the talk about his "pessimism," as if it meant an imposition of the author's personal view of life upon his characters and their fates. The conclusion is inaccurate. What one finds in the novels is less a philosophical stance than a tragic sense; that is, what happens to Hardy's men and women comes out of their own characters rather than out of set ideas of their creator, however much Hardy may bandy his views about in the editorial passages to which he is addicted. One's point of view, then, is marked by skepticism of some going generalizations. But one may be skeptical and confirmatory. Many critics talk about the inconsistencies of Hardy's art and his style, but few choose to spell things out. The issue seemed worth a detailed look, and the detailed look does confirm the more or less standard opinions of the commentators.

On the other hand, in the general world of writing about books, it is almost standard to use *picaresque* as if it meant only a "rambling tale." One flinches at the apparent looseness and superficiality of this usage. Detailed inspection of an actual picaresque narrative reveals that, while ramblingness may indeed be present, it is a derivative characteristic, and not an identifying one, since it often appears in narratives that are in no way picaresque. Likewise, most people who know something about English fiction will take it for granted that "euphuism" died aborning in the sixteenth century. But when one looks at actual practices of euphuists, one finds in their mechanical, convoluted, and relentless practices certain basic stylistic procedures that long survive in later styles, some purified to become the instruments of a logical mode, and others debased as the once recondite falls into that singular modern mode, the popular-pretentious (descending through Hardy in his autodidact's fanciness to advertising, business English, and some journalism). Charlotte Brontë has become so much a cause célèbre on other grounds that one may hardly think of her as a stylist and indeed a quite remarkable one: a somewhat driven recorder of intense romantic passions with a diversity of stylistic tools, one of which would indeed ally her with Samuel Johnson. Nor, again, would many readers think of her as engaging, as she does, in a lifelong battle between Reason and Imagination (words which she often capitalizes).

All this is to say that "unity of the author" may mean a consistent point of view, one partly determined by critical attitudes that are in the air. One examines these with skepticism—steady but not preset, energetic but not belligerent; a persistent but dispassionate looking at the object. One reads not to contradict and confute, but to weigh and consider. One may challenge or confirm. One may decide that prevalent opinion is vague and imprecise, or quite wrongheaded, or accurate but not supported by evidence. Or in specific fashions one may detect larger implications that are worth exploring. One will be thorough when it seems appropriate, and as lively as one can. If one is fortunate, his words may seem revealing.

■ I ■
GENRES AND THEIR WAYS

■ 1 ■
Variations on Picaresque:
Mann's *Felix Krull*

i

THERE IS A SENSE in which it is not surprising that Thomas Mann, having begun a picaresque story at the age of thirty six and left it unfinished when the special demands of its style became burdensome, should never be able to dismiss it wholly from his mind, should at the age of sixty-eight debate with himself whether to take up again the tale of a rogue or to begin work on the great Faustus theme, should in the eighth decade of his life return to the "artistic jest," as he once called it, and at seventy-nine publish a continuation which was still not a conclusion, and should plan to go on from there. This persistent attachment to the story of Felix Krull is understandable if we remember Mann's tendency not to forget themes that had once got into his imagination, his delight in facing new technical problems, his zest in the unexpected or the daring, and, of course, that sense of the playful and the comic which we may lose sight of when, as may happen to the philosophic novelist, adulation focuses only on the portentously vatic.

Yet that Mann, after *Magic Mountain*, the Joseph series, and *Dr. Faustus*, should at eighty be going on with an apparently trivial tale—think of Shakespeare after the tragedies returning, say, to *Taming of the Shrew*—will, somehow, evoke a question. And surely the basis of the question is the fact that the picaresque tradition is a relatively thin and discontinuous one, with few great works and fewer great practitioners. On the whole it seems meant for the writer, like the Byron of *Don Juan*, who will not or cannot encompass experience in its densities. If it be argued that *The Transposed Heads* and *The Holy Sinner* raise the same problem, or else eliminate the problem entirely by showing that Mann periodically tried a jocular hand at slight and slender forms, the answer must be that *The Transposed Heads* and *The Holy Sinner*, however far they go or do not go in themselves, nevertheless belong to the realm of fable, fairy tale, and fantasy where all depths are possible; while *Felix Krull* is in a mode that is not only "realistic" but deliberately limited in its realistic scope.

3

ii

In picaresque a "rogue" is "hero," and we may define rogue as one who lives by his wits. The word *rogue* suggests such other words as *scamp* and *rascal,* the family of terms by which we designate the person who lives partly, though not threateningly, outside communal standards of responsibility. It is, of course, part of his way of life to simulate insideness; when he achieves a partial insideness, not by a specially designed façade, but by aspects of personality that elicit a spontaneous warmth of response, he is likely to be called "lovable rogue"—a term that, though it suggests some actual paradoxes of human makeup, is likely to denote a sentimental stereotype. "Lives by his wits," popular phrase though it is, has substantial defining value. For one thing, it suggests the wit that characteristically belongs to the picaro—the instant readiness of mind, made evident in repartee, manipulation of ideas, or extemporization of apt words or actions. More important, it states affirmatively his central modus vivendi, and thus it simultaneously implies the lopping off of those elements of personality characteristically lacking in the picaro. Living by wits implies knowledge of "the world," a sharp insight into responses that may be played upon advantageously, a mastery of the techniques of playing upon them, the ready appraisal of life by what Charlotte Brontë might have called "the organ of computation"—in a word, the apparatus of a "lightning calculator." Since in the life of "wits" certain functions of the mind dominate, this life also means a diminution, if not total elimination, of emotional depths and moral concern. The rogue is without conscience or superego or the inhibitions created by the community's sense of right and wrong; not so much that he is the enemy of these or falls short of an expectable standard by which we judge him, as that he lives in another world from them. He lives outside the "ordinary" feelings of the community: his hypertrophy of practical intelligence replaces a full emotional development. Not that the picaro is entirely "heartless" or without feelings; it is aesthetically necessary that he be not a monster. His self-love gives him some link to the rest of mankind; he can fear; he may have transient fidelities. But if he is afraid, his fear does not deepen into terror. He may experience disgust, but not horror. He is likely to be well endowed with sex, but he hardly experiences passion or serious jealousy, and least of all love. He may find people difficult, objectionable, or annoyingly skeptical, but he does not hate.

The key is shallowness, which in this case is to be seen not as a defect but as a fact, like the size of feet, and understood to have both advantages and disadvantages; in shallowness lies the clue not only to the degree but also to the direction of his feelings. Ordinarily, rather than earning an emotional identity by experiencing a complex of rejections, acceptances, and modifications, he simply takes over available patterns of feeling, and these are most likely to be conventional or orthodox (in the presence of the articulate, energetic off-center sexuality of Diane Philibert, Felix Krull sounds almost like a proper young man). In their different ways, Jack Wilton and Moll Flanders are unprincipled conservatives, who automatically identify with lords or dominant classes; a Communist picaro, though a private entrepreneur in his roguery, would be Marxist in feeling. As a wearer of old school ties the rogue is still the shallow man, responsible for nothing and free to act as unconservatively as he pleases—for instance, to pick the pockets of his tie-brothers. If the picaro tries unpicaresquely to discover an individual order of feeling, his shallowness leads him into a foamily sentimental outsiderism (if this is not a redundancy) in which we can see resemblances, at a great distance, to bohemians, Robin Hood, and the like.

In looking at the man who lives by his wits, we do not use words such as *villain, revenge, cunning, malice, bitterness,* or *troublemaker,* for these imply a profundity of feeling or an intensity of commitment foreign to this kind of schemer. Words like *crook* or *scoundrel* vary with context and intonation; they may denote either a picaro or a serious attacker of the moral order. *Criminal* seems to me not to belong to the vocabulary of picaresque, though I say this with some diffidence, since the word is used by good critics of Mann, and even by Mann himself, to apply to the Krull-world. True, criminal and picaro both break laws, and there are other subtler affiliations which we must observe later. But *criminal* implies earnestness, the will to disturb, seize, and violate; deliberateness or "engagedness" in an attack on the will of others or on the public order; ruthlessness; illness. *Picaro,* on the other hand, implies flippancy; harassments rather than serious attacks; the trick-or-treat prankster; seduction rather than rape; the securing of and playing upon the victim's consent; a relish of the game as such; in Dantean terms, less the perversion of right feeling than a nonfunction of right feeling. Let us say that both are "psychopathic personalities," one with a distorted soul, the other with a rudimentary one. The picaro is the literary equivalent of that familiar abnormal type that must use talents, which are often extraordinary, not for murder but for masquerade; who must take by trick what he could earn by effort; who must dazzle rather than seek respect; to whom the world is a theater rather than a school; who by spectacular fakery can get by as a physician or even surgeon, but who would never take a medical degree. Though many variations, degrees of development, and overlappings are possible, the criminal has kinship with Iago, the picaro with Falstaff.

So much for the rogue as such; now for the rogue as "hero." The picaresque writer has the interesting technical problem of securing, for an extralegal operator, "sympathy" and even "identification." He can do this by giving the picaro certain generally admired qualities—good nature, charm, an ironical view of himself. Or he can do it, as in *Lazarillo de Tormes* and *Guzmán de Alfarache* and initially in *Moll Flanders,* by making the rogue somewhat a creature of necessity, maltreated by others and by circumstances; though here the scent of the "problem" story, the bouquet of pathos, and the perfume of the sentimental threaten the true picaresque mode. A sounder fictional method is negative: giving no place, or at least no prominence, to other characters who, by being larger or nobler people and thus having a stronger claim on our "right feelings," might usurp the sympathy due the picaro. One way of "protecting" the picaro is to endow representatives of right feeling and "right thinking," if these get into the story, with disagreeable personal traits—pretentiousness, complacency, and so on. But in this method the danger is that the work may slide into satire, which, though it may have a role in picaresque, is, as a mode, a different thing, generically related to melodrama and therefore calling upon another area of aesthetic responsiveness. Though neither picaresque nor satire is essentially unstable, either one may, if the tone is not skillfully controlled, lapse into the other. Sinclair Lewis's Elmer Gantry, intended as an object of satire, is treated with so little depth and thrust into such a frenzy of misdeeds that the moral critique is somehow transformed into a tale of adventures inviting a relish of successful rascality. Becky Sharp, conversely, is transmuted from picaresque heroine to object of satire: this happens when sympathy for her piquant gamesmanship is allowed to shift to her victims, who are shown fully enough to draw us in on their side (Rawdon as father, for instance). For the most important method in picaresque is to keep the victims out of sight, lest they threaten our alliance with the rogue (thus we never see the candy-store owner whom Felix robs). Or the victims can deserve what they get, through graspingness, or foolish pride, or a gullibility that is an affront to all good sense—the area in which satire may transiently enter picaresque. Or most subtly the writer can, as I believe Mann does, convey a sense of the positive satisfaction accruing to the "victim" in his experiences with the rogue. Here analysis of picaresque would take us close to the general realm of that singular victim—dupe, seducee, or even murderee—who must unknowingly convey his unknown readiness to the trickster or evildoer who will fulfill him.

The rogue-hero determines not only the treatment of other characters but also the scene and structure. Such a hero precludes extensive analysis of a situation: while retention of sympathy for him means a cursory treatment of other characters, his own shallowness forestalls prolonged study of his own nature. Instead of depth and rigor we have speed and multiplicity: since without "character" a story cannot indefinitely be spun out of one set of circumstances, one situation must soon be replaced by another; and since living by wits alone is not conducive to long residence, one scene normally gives way to another without much delay. Picaresque is naturally cinematic and episodic. However, the familiar use of *picaresque* as if its basic meaning were *episodic* is quite inaccurate, for, while it is virtually impossible to be picaresque without being episodic, it is entirely possible to be episodic without being picaresque, as in *Joseph Andrews*. Though in criticism *episodic* has usually a pejorative sense, nonetheless the continual change of scene inherent in picaresque has compensations: the form is made for the travelogue-novel. Mann may well have had this sense of the picaresque, for Felix Krull loved "the world" and was evidently intended to explore a good deal of it. In the end the potential of the episodic travelogue-fiction depends on the endowments of the world-tourist. The man who lives by his wits can have any amount of wits the author chooses, any amount of descriptive and analytical intelligence; he can be a brilliant mirror of life in the world. Often Mann confers upon Krull the gifts of his own recording and exploring, even of his searching, mind; indeed, even a measure of his creative imagination. Among his exploits in this book he must indeed have enjoyed making the charlatan something of a philosopher, the masquerader an exemplar of his own industrious, even cataloging, encyclopedism.

iii

The form that cuts off the larger dimensions of human reality appeals by affording a relief from responsibility. For the reader it bans scruple and passion, offering aesthetic pleasure freed of the moral concern or emotional trials that are, in whatever way, a part of the aesthetic pleasure of "great" fiction. The writer of picaresque enjoys, apparently, freedom from the most severe imaginative demands; his mind can roam like a picaro, commenting where and as he will. He need reconcile the free flow of observation and opinion with only slight demands of structure and with the most easily obtainable consistencies of character. Mann can have a free hand here without our impugning his sense of form as we are inclined to do in his other novels.

But since picaresque is not the only fictional holiday from the full self, we must seek its uniqueness in another function. This, I suggest, is the catharsis of rascality—catharsis, certainly not as purification; perhaps as elimination; but primarily in the sense that it gives free "play" to certain human impulses. Or we might shift to the opposite metaphor and say that it permits these impulses to "work," and even, if one should want to argue for that end result, to "work off." (The end result, the psychic and moral residue of aesthetic experience, is outside the scope of this paper.) Through the picaresque hero a seamy side of man, the tricksy side, has a fling—that persistently present, though conscientiously kept under, side, where there lurks a universal impulse to escape the shadows of guilt and to put things over on others or the world, to be nimble of foot, and hand, and head. One need not be a wit to feel the charm of living by wits: in the rogue world every deed is a repartee of action. The reader put off by the gay libertinism may find a comparable satisfaction in the "success story," for Algeresque is really picaresque transposed into another key: a fragmented personality still gets the booty, but now he is an insider operating by the latest edicts of the central rules committee. Since now there are no reckonings, Algeresque is a much more misleading imaginative exercise.

In picaresque another quality has a fling, the quality that I will call the "instinct for episodes." The very episodic structure which, as we have seen, derives from the nature of the picaresque hero, shows us something about the aesthetic functioning of the form: it appeals to a longing to reduce the muddled continuum of life to episodes manageable by cleverness alone. And here we run into counterimpulses called into play by an apparently simple literary genre: for that control of life by ingenuity which is offered by picaresque is secured by a reduction of reality, and that reduction itself implies a yielding, a going-under. For the "instinct for episodes" means a secret inclination to discontinuity, to hit-and-run raids on life, the impulse to shun the long and exacting unity, to live instead by episodes. If this "instinct" for the episodic becomes dominant, that is, gets out of balance with counterforces in our psychic equipment, it produces the "episodic character": he may find, within the norms of society, a way of life marked by many breaks and shifts, each perhaps eliciting a momentary burst of energy; or, outside the lines of conventional esteem, become a rolling stone, a gypsy or a "floater," or find some other style of "life by episodes."

At this point the orbit of the picaresque comes fairly close to another attribute of Everyman that is less likely to be recognizable because it is more held out of sight and rendered inoperative—namely, a certain vague proneness to degradation (perhaps a variant of the death wish). This appears normally in an impulse to relax the guards that give form to life or even in a taste for polite humiliation that is not restricted to eccentrics; radically in the life of the *clochard* or "bum" or in pursuits of a psychopathological sort; even sentimentally in certain flattering disguises—for instance, when dirtiness appears to its possessor to be an incisive critique of the falsities that may accompany cleanliness. But in what is necessarily a very oblique tapping of this element in the psyche, picaresque could very easily slide over into scatology or satire or a simplistic cynicism.

Finally, though I have argued that rogue and criminal must be distinguished, it may be profitable to consider the rogue a kind of denatured or sterile criminal, for we could then understand picaresque as releasing even the radically rebellious impulses. Since the conscious rebel finds all the direct voices he needs, the liberating picaro would speak only for those who in ordinary consciousness would take for granted their own unreserved sympathy with legal and moral order. The criminal, as it were devitalized in the picaro, could evoke the responses of the "good man" like an expressionistic symbol that passes through consciousness to engage other nonconscious powers. An exponent of catharsis doctrines might argue, from the tolerance of the picaro, for an analogous permissiveness of criminality by the social order generally, a "consent" through need, a letting-go to be followed by the imposition of penalties that are also self-punishment. The analogy doubles us back again to fiction: in picaresque the nonmoral holiday always comes to an end; the picaro is reformed or is jailed; and in the aesthetic experience the rascal after his play period retreats within the citizen.

The operating hypothesis of picaro as residual criminal (true outlaw passion neutralized, as in the making of a serum) has another utility. The man who lives by his wits has usually a vigorous instinctive life; he somewhat paradoxically combines natural man and the sophisticated schemer. In this he is cousin, in however attenuated form, to some of the great embodiments of evil in literature—Goneril and Iago: the union of animal passion and exorbitant craft of mind.

iv

Though living by wits suggests immediately sleight-of-hand and verbal skill, it should also suggest the older meaning of *wit*, that is, mind or intelligence in a general sense. For the picaro is in his way a creature of "mind"; his family tree is that of Ulysses rather than that of Prometheus or Hercules or Roland or Romeo. The picaresque experience is in one sense an exercise of mind, really a reveling in the mind as conqueror, a relishing of power through purely mental rather than physical or political or social means. The picaresque hero, a solitary victor with weapons of intelligence, corresponds to a desire in Everyman, a desire essential enough to insure, even in an anti-intellectualist atmosphere, endemic dreams of mastery by brain-power, that is, "control of nature." When, in ruminating about the picaresque mode, I first thought of the picaro as an imaginative representation of the instrumental intelligence, I felt immediately that there must be another artistic version of the dream of power—a version in which the impulse was not transposed into terms of playful rascality or seen in the intermittent flash of episodes, with the habitual picaresque flight closing off the full potential of energy in the idea only partly tapped by the fractional rogue-figure. In the other version, the theme would have to be, not living by wits alone, but living by brains alone, an earnest, total commitment to the exercise of power through the operations of mind. To complete the formulation was to identify the imaginative form of it: the Faustus myth. And to spot this cousinship, these divergent developments from a common starting point, was also to see further into the contrasting aesthetic experiences of picaresque and tragedy: in the picaresque, the free tasting of private power, easily summoned and applied as occasion came; in the Faustian, living in power while discovering the consequences of acquiring and regularly wielding it; in the former, indulging some of the self but happily cut off from the parts whence self-awareness and guilt would come; in the latter, being thrust by the fable of total self-indulgence into the depths of self where total knowledge is the final burden.

At this point I came across Mann's *Die Entstehung des Doktor Faustus,* and in it his account of his hesitating, after the completion of *Joseph* in 1943, between two possible subjects for his next work. It now seemed extraordinarily significant, more than a simple uncertainty between unconnected alternatives, that his choice lay between the Faustus theme and a continuation, after many years, of the Krull story. Then comes his climax: he reread the Krull materials—"with singular result," namely, "insight into the inner relation of the Faust-material with it (depending upon the solitariness-motif, here tragic-mystical, there humorous-criminal)." In this exploration of the picaresque it seems to me worthwhile to record these independent conclusions, very close despite the difference of emphasis, on the affinity, illuminating as I hope it is, between the picaresque theme and the great tragic theme, or at least between the Mann versions of the two. One cannot note the bond without wondering whether Mann, in giving Krull the name Felix, of the meaning of which much is made, happened to recall that the Latin adjectives *felix* and *faustus* are synonyms. And one remembers, inevitably, the theory that in Hamlet and Falstaff a common theme is explored in different styles.

In all the literature that deals with the wit-conducted life there is, ultimately, ambiguity. Perhaps only detective stories naively exploit the passion for the mind's control of existence. Tragedy and picaresque set this passion in play; yet, though tragedy endows it with all the dignity of which it is capable in the completely presented human being, and picaresque lives by exercising the human delight in this control, both are penetrated by a sense of the failure of mind alone. Oedipus finds mysteries he cannot solve by taking thought; Faustus learns the destructive price of power by knowledge. Picaresque heroes, at their best almost infinitely clever, nonetheless fall prey to sex, covetousness, prodigality, carelessness, vanity, in a word, to the irrationalities of human nature, and to accidents, the irrationalities of circumstance.

v

Within the limits of picaresque a novelist can do little or much. As one would expect of the writer who saw in Felix Krull a version of the Faustian solitary, Mann used his form very richly. Compare Georges Simenon, also of international fame: his nondetective fictions have a great air of searching the soul, but in the end we have only psychological mechanisms and banalities; whereas Mann, with the air of one intent only on a literary gambol, convinces us that more is going on than meets the eye—which is precisely what does not happen in most picaresque. Not that Mann does not observe the basic conventions of his form: Felix's career falls into episodes, and we know that the law was to puncture his felicity. Yet the episodes are developed with unusual fullness, they have certain dramatic interconnections, and Felix periodically finds in one experience a reminder of something earlier, a linking image or concept or feeling; in these ways the book moves toward a unity that itself suggests complications beyond the picaresque. Felix's fall is long postponed; the moral guardian always hovering fretfully over traditional picaresque is less present; and in this increase in picaresque "purity" we sense an original amplification of the rogue tale. Felix's own intelligent perceptiveness drives us to seek the intentions behind the mask. We find, too, a sense of character that goes beyond picaresque habits: Susanna Kuckuck, for instance, is in several ways quite reminiscent of Aglaya Yepanchin in Dostoyevsky's *Idiot*.

A stylistic mode of enrichment is self-evident—a grandioseness that is a parodic reminder of serious autobiography. So it is not surprising to find Mann describing the "fantastic intellectual charm in the burlesque idea of taking a much loved tradition—self-portraiture in the Goethe manner, the introspective 'Confessions' of the born aristocrat—and transferring it to the criminal sphere." That Mann found an immediate stimulus in the memoirs of a living confidence man makes an enlightening parallel between him and Fielding. Fielding found in the life of the criminal Jonathan Wild the genesis of a fiction ironically employing traditional ideas of greatness; Mann found in the autobiography of George Manolescu the genesis of a fiction ironically employing the traditional manner of great autobiography. But whereas Fielding was at heart an angry homilist who fell into laborious irony, Mann's method is akin to that of Joyce: placing the heroic and the contemporary in an ambiguous juxtaposition marked more by ironic interplay than by satirical undermining.

In amplifying picaresque Mann took another Joycean tack. Felix is not an isolated Mann character but is another figure in the study of rascality with which Mann was infatuated; Felix has some kinship with Joseph. Mann says that he wrote the Joseph story because of an interest in "the eternally-human, eternally-recurring, timeless, . . . the mythical." It is clear, I think, that the Krull story was taking on a mythical dimension, and that in some way it would have continued the Joseph theme. Joseph is many things, Mann says, "but then he perceptibly slides into a Hermes part, the part of the mundane and skillful business man and the intelligent profit producer among the gods." It is fascinating to see how Hermes persisted in Mann's imagination, for Hermes comes into the Krull story as the patron deity of Felix as thief, and his name is repeatedly mentioned. Indeed, it is not only by being a thief that Felix is a Hermes-figure: he is identified with luck, travel, theft and trickery, priapism, eloquence, and the arts—over all of which Hermes presided. Mann was clearly infusing into picaresque something of the mythic that absorbed him; indeed, we might say that he was constructing "the picaresque myth."

Goethe had noted the possibilities in the Joseph materials, Goethe was the model and rival in the use of the Faust materials, Goethe was, if not exactly the target, at least the figure that contributed some of the meaning to the amiable joke in *Felix Krull*. There is some complication in Mann's attitude to Goethe; beside the *"imitatio Goethe,"* as it has been called, there is a sly impulse to twitch up the prima donna's skirts in front of the audience—not to expose but to get a laugh from dignity undone. Mann says that *Felix Krull* represents "my attitude toward tradition, which is at once kindly and destructive" (elsewhere, "sympathetic and detached"). How true, we feel. But another meaning intrudes here: since Mann "identifies" with Goethe and tradition, the words "kindly and destructive" also imply something of his attitude to himself. Indeed, in the same sentence from which I have just quoted, Mann says that *Felix Krull* "may be the most personal" thing he has done. These words written in 1930 have a peculiar applicability to the whole work, the fragments already written and the major additions of almost twenty-five years later: Mann's most daring exploitation of picaresque is to model the hero partly on himself. In *Felix Krull* are his own fantastically jocular *Dichtung und Wahrheit* and *Wilhelm Meister* (Wilhelm's son, incidentally, was named Felix).

Nor is it too hard, keeping in mind the necessary reservations, to conceive of *Felix Krull* as autobiographical. Critics often allude to the elements of self-portraiture in Mann's works, and Mann himself speaks of an artistic work as "a realization . . . of our individuality," even as "the sole and painful way we have of getting the particular experience." But if, even after Mann himself says, "A work must have long roots in my life," Mann-as-picaro seems inherently improbable, we can at least note the parallels between the Krull story and the Mann story as Mann himself traces it in *A Sketch of My Life*. Mann reports that he was an indifferent student, given up by the school, but condescending to his fellows, becoming a young man of "indolence, bad civic conscience, and the sure and certain feeling of latent powers." Felix hated school, played truant skillfully, and always felt superior to others. The elder Mann died when Thomas was fifteen, the elder Krull committed suicide when Felix was eighteen. Mann says that the family business had not been going well, the Krull business had gone bankrupt. Thomas went to Munich and worked in an insurance office directed by a friend of his father, Felix went to Paris and took up a hotel job secured for him by a family friend. Thomas hated the army (his "determination to free myself was prompt, deadly and in the event irresistible"), developed an ankle inflammation in which there appears to have been at least a psychosomatic ingredient, and thus through medical connections secured a discharge after three months. To Felix, military service was an "unpleasant problem" that "weighed heavy on my heart"; his godfather "did not have any sort of connection with army doctors" (as Mann's family did); but he succeeded in having himself declared unfit by faking an epileptic attack. While working in the insurance office, Thomas "secretly . . . wrote my first tale"; from his secret life, of course, sprang his career. While working at the hotel, Felix had also his secret life as "gentleman"—the beginning of his basic way of life. An untried author, Mann persuaded the hesitant Fischer firm to take *Buddenbrooks* on his terms, and this was good for both. Felix, a novice thief, persuaded a receiver-of-stolen-goods to give him something like his own price, and both profited. It is most difficult not to see the autobiographical in Felix's comments on the expatriate's feelings about his native land—his tendency to sentimentalize it, to give it an undue authority, "especially when one's homeland has behaved unkindly, unjustly, and obtusely toward one," and eventually to "yield to the temptation" to return and "show himself to its narrow view in all the glitter he has gained abroad," and, "with mixed anxiety and derision in his heart," to "feast upon its astonishment—just as, in due course, I shall report of myself."

And so on. Beyond the discovery of factual parallels, which I suspect could be carried into greater detail, the most interesting quarry for the biographer would be the oblique self-revelation by the author. What, for instance, is to be made of the fact that Felix's Lisbon friends, his tutors in diverse ways, are in one striking way reminiscent of Mann's parents: the husband is German, and the wife Portuguese? The difficulty arises when Felix makes love to the wife (as well as her daughter), but this difficulty is no greater than that of dismissing the German-Portuguese marriage as a coincidence, since Mann was not the writer to stumble into such patent resemblances of fable to life. Though biographical interpretation is not my object, it might be helpful to work from Henry Hatfield's proposal that *Buddenbrooks* is "a sort of reckoning with the father image by the young man who has broken with family tradition" and treat Senhora Kuckuck's passionate embrace of Felix as an establishment of Thomas in the maternal approval, whether the mother symbolize the family tradition or the artistic impulse sometimes said to have been transmitted to Thomas through his mother. But this would be only part of it. What of Kuckuck, whose name fittingly suggests both "cuckold" and "rote," and who embodies something of Mann's own encyclopedism? Again, Felix is an alter ego for the Marquis of Venosta, who is also something of a Mann-figure: just as Mann's long visit to Italy was the symbolic break with family tradition, so Venosta breaks with, or at least resists, his family by *not* taking the grand tour planned for him. Mann here reverses the family history in much the same way as he does in transmuting the splendid funeral of his father into the paltry rites for Felix's father. The Marquis (the insider who wants to get out) and Felix (the outsider who wants to get in) are in part opposing sides of Mann, complementing each other somewhat as do Serenus Zeitblom and Adrian Leverkühn, the contrasting masks of the author of *Dr. Faustus*, that sober twin of *Felix Krull*.

If we look for "oblique self-revelation," we must face the tantalizing question of Mann's motive in rendering some phases of private history in picaresque, of the "secret connections," as Mann himself puts it, that "must lead from it [a work of his] to earliest childhood dreams, if I am to consider myself entitled to it, if I am to believe in the legitimacy of what I am doing." For one thing, picaresque would be the least expectable mode of autobiographical fiction; it would permit surprise, it would be new and daring, it would be ironic and vastly playful—all ends that Mann valued. It would disarm the audience, and, as an antidote to self-love, it would be an extraordinary means of securing detachment, of providing a wonderful distance and even freedom. The most convincing guess about Mann's leaving *Felix Krull* long unfinished would rely on his remark that *The Magic Mountain* could not have been written ten years earlier, since for that work he needed certain experiences which had "to ripen within him." Surely this would be true for *Felix Krull,* in which the severely limited view of man would be possible to an artist of profound perceptions only when long experience would enable him to restrict his total vision, and of which the comically disillusioned perspective, held serenely rather than with querulous cynicism, is possible only to an artist of the mature assurance conferred by long personal and professional growth. Through such control he might give voice to self-criticism or guilt, perhaps effect a catharsis. If, as Hatfield says, "Werther and Aschenbach die in order that their creators may live," it may be that Felix had to live on in order that his creator might live with himself. Might not the disillusioned artist large enough to include himself in his own disillusionment say, "How like a rogue's life mine looks!" Within the capacious irony of the rogue's tale there lies, we may conjecture, humility· partly an oblique confession, partly an assumption of Everyman's rascality, a discovery of the heart masterfully transfigured into an urbane jest.

vi

In his remarkable expansion of picaresque Mann, ever "novarum rerum cupidus," as he put it, altered tradition most strikingly by making *Felix Krull* "the story of an artist." This interpretation by Mann is not inconsistent with the other readings that I think the book requires—with the Hermes myth suggested by the textual evidence, with the Goethe parody that delighted Mann, and with the variations on autobiography that it is difficult not to infer. And if the picaro is, as I define him, one who lives by his wits, this definition also reflects much of the artist's professional modus vivendi—his skill, ingenuity, working with head rather than body, with individual artifice rather than group planning.

Mann's public wrestling with the problem of artist versus bürger has shaped a large body of criticism. In the *Krull* chapters long available for study Mann's view of the artist strikes critics as denigratory. Though this view is open to argument, I wish less to debate than to distinguish two critical problems, both legitimate: one concerns the relation of a given work to the history of the writer's opinions on a given subject; the other concerns the kind of illumination of the theme by the unique work. The former problem belongs to biography; the latter, on which I want to work, to literary analysis. The assumption here is that the author is less recording an attitude, which may change tomorrow, than he is exploring a theme in the terms provided by the chosen form. This does not deny that he is recording an attitude, but it proposes that what is said is more than an attitude, and less impermanent. We might argue that *Felix Krull* says, "The artist is only a picaro," or, conversely, "The picaro is really an artist." The problem, however, is less one of contending for the deflation of one character, or the exaltation of the other, than of seeing what steady light is shed by the insistent pursuit of the analogy.

Mann's statement that Felix is an artist-figure is documented by many aspects of the story that need only be quickly mentioned: Felix's love of and skill in make-believe, costuming, and acting; his precocity and sensitivity; his flight from school to dreams; his sense of audience, whether he is staging scenes or doing daily jobs; his identification of himself with the "artists" at the circus; his taking on diverse roles with such ease that priest and soldier would claim him, and a whore thinks him "predestined for the service of love." Mann's technique is no less striking but goes deeper when he raises a serious problem of the artist. Early in the book Schimmelpreester complains that though they admire talent people never want to accept the "oddities that are always associated with it, and perhaps are essential to it," and shortly afterward Felix himself is shocked when, after being charmed by a talented actor, he meets him without benefit of makeup and finds his face repulsive and his back covered by "horrible pustules." For the theme of the discrepancy between artist as artist and artist as person, the picaresque is an ingenious choice: the hero's rascalities are a vivid comic symbol for all the "oddities" that accompany talent. Mann never forgets the duality of the artist, but, with characteristic novelty, he fuses two versions of the duality: the maculate man behind the charm of art, or, conversely—and more emphatically—the specialized conscience behind the consciencelessness in ordinary life.

This novelty is a key to the book, which Mann surely wrote with the love of novelty to which he refers more than once. For him the subject was old, but the method a total innovation. Early in the book Felix uses the words "as one should see everything—that is, with a fresh eye undimmed by habit," and near the end he elaborates: "One should always try to see everything, even the most commonplace, the most completely matter of fact, with new, astonished eyes as though for the first time. In this way it wins back its power to amaze, which has faded into matter-of-factness, and the world remains fresh."

Take the traditional view of the artist as lonely, isolated, outside the community. This can become a romantic or sentimental truism. But exhibit this solitariness in the man who lives by his wits, outside the ordinary responsibilities and reciprocities, who never settles down but always travels, and it begins to take fresh outlines in a hard, untouched-up light. Show this solitariness as at once instinctive and finicky, calculated and prudential, vain and protective, the aloofness of a rascal who in his felt superiority schemes against the world. Combine an almost racketeering toughness with a constant aesthetic awareness. Paint the picaro despising the majority, fearing that if "[I] spent myself in a loose sociability—I should literally do violence to some secret part of my nature," separating himself from the circus crowd and feeling that he belongs to the "profession" of "entertainer and illusionist." To picture loneliness without sloppy clichés, let the picaro study the circus "artists"; have him ask, "Are they really human at all?"; have him deny that they can love, lest the lions revolt and the acrobats "pitch headlong toward the ground into disgrace and death." Have the Marquis of Venosta tell the picaro: "You always hold something back. . . . You seem to me the type who is more loved than loving." Here are the outsider and his essential unresponsiveness, but also the devotion evoked by art and the artist.

Yet this solitary astonishingly seeks not pure contemplation but power, power in the very world withdrawn from. True to the picaro type, Felix is a lover and pursuer of things found only in the world—material things, physical comforts, society and high places; he even has a "natural instinct for good form." The solitary as man of the world—an inconsistency? Mann faces right into this, maneuvering his comic tale toward the inherent contradictoriness of all serious things. Felix says at one time that his basic "withdrawal from the world" can go "amiably hand in hand with an eager delight in the world"; at another time that my "Basic attitude toward the world and society can only be called inconsistent." What we see in the dramatic action is the paradox that withdrawnness is often an attribute of the power-holder, that art must succeed in the world, that the artist is despite himself a strange marriage of bohemian and bourgeois.

How freshen up the fact that as technician the artist works through the concrete, that unlike the hermit he must cling to the immediately perceived and felt surfaces of life? Again make him a lover of the world, of all palpable and visible reality; make him an amorous observer and recorder of sensory surfaces, an embodiment of visual and olfactory and tactile passions. Let him stare into shop windows and lust after pastries and jewels, carpets and clothing; let him exclaim, ". . . the enticing, educational aspects of the world, . . . O scenes of the beautiful world!"

To fulfill himself as artist he must possess that world, take what he can as he can. But of course. How give life to a copybook maxim for the aspiring writer? Let Felix be a thief—of bonbons, jewelry, money; even of the life and family history of another, at once ornamenting it and himself and so delighting an audience. The "ruthlessness" of the artist as artist appears with equal originality when Felix sharply rebuffs "honest Stanko" by refusing to join in a projected robbery, since he "was not born to be anybody's accomplice." Mann refines upon the artist's acquisition of materials in the two "robberies" from Diane Philibert: in the first, with a minimum of active effort, Felix takes what chance has offered; in the second, he takes what she offers herself; in each case what he gets is used shrewdly, not thrown away prodigally. When Diane insists that he "steal" from her for her own singular pleasure, in effect she is the individual begging the artist, "Use me."

In a well-known sense the artist must "love" all people, for hate leads only to polemics. So let the artist appear as the picaro Don Juan: let Felix love Genovefa the maid, Rosza the prostitute, Diane Philibert the bluestocking writer, both Senhora Kuckuck and her daughter Zouzou—old and young, arrogant aristocrat and "prickly" Puritan. Then a double reverse: let each bed-affair be a growth, a learning, even a symbolic statement. Let the prostitute be praised for giving her lover "refinement . . . *through* love." Let Diane, in that wonderful erotic scene in the hotel, embody at once the ambivalence of parental and sexual relations, a Jocasta candidly seeking youth (richer far than Cocteau's querulous neurotic), the "intellect [that] longs for the delights of the non-intellect," "spirit" yearning to glorify "beauty" and to be at one with the elemental, a highbrow humanity romantically possessing, in an "eternal instant," through the ageless art of which the ingenious youth is a symbol, the potency and completion not offered in everyday life. Let Zouzou, a remarkable character, be no less than a character, but attach to her the chill odor of literalist common sense, scientific reductionism, and Puritan squeamishness: art must woo even this, striving to release its underlying, though incomplete, inclination to be at one with art. Thus Felix breaks inevitably into the home where "order, reason, and intelligent planning prevail"—breaks in, not to court but to seduce, for with none of them can he live after they have served him, and he them.

Felix does not merely use others; he gratifies them. From beginning to end he never loses the intent to give pleasure or the pleasure of giving it. Mann's view of art is Horatian, but here again he is entirely original. Don't show Felix as an insipid allegory of benevolent sweetness, but let him be seen blissfully inhaling applause for successful costumings, mimings, masquerades; report with satisfaction how much everyone likes him, even when he despises them; boast of the extraordinary pleasure he gives in sexual intercourse; let him have charm, not the Grandisonian kind, but the kind that charms men out of jobs and money, and women out of their clothes; have him please people not only by courtesy and attentiveness, but by funny stories, an "agreeable voice," a beautifying pronunciation of names, by flattery, and even pimping. But combine all this with indispensable self-restraint: like a Machiavellian prince, Felix must use all means that serve his end but cannot deviate into private self-indulgence. Excessive sexuality "impoverishes our capacity to charm, since only he who desires is amiable and not he who is satiated." But the art of pleasing is at once narcissistic and altruistic: "I loved myself—in a way that is really socially useful, self-love turned outward as amiability." No sonorousness here of "self-respect" or "integrity." Yet what is dramatized is a stern, demanding, anti-romantic view of the artist, disavowing the crabbed hermit who writes or paints only to gratify himself, contemptuous of an unresponsive public.

Mann paints the artist as nonmoral man; then he completes the storyteller's "double twist" by painting the morality of the nonmoral man. If the artist always "shapes himself to please," nevertheless playing to the public on its own terms will not do; again Mann might have come from a reading of Horace to write that "a performance . . . had to be masterly if it was not to be ridiculous." Not only must art "work," it must have a kind of excellence which is found in what it communicates beyond itself; Felix has contempt for "every deception which fails to have a higher truth at its root and is simply a barefaced lie." In this we do not see him as either smirking or self-deceptive, any more than we do when he keeps emphasizing the necessity of "discipline." He has a sense of vocation, and he talks repeatedly of avoiding the cul-de-sac, the "shortcut to happiness." He rejects the love of wealthy Eleanor Twentyman and that of Lord Strathbogie, who by bribery would possess the artist personally, for he "rebelled against a form of reality that was simply handed to me and was in addition sloppy" in favor of a life "dependent . . . only on imagination." "The way" is virtually a basic metaphor with him, and his "reason" calls masquerading as Venosta a "by-path" and a "dangerous road." But he is won by the "charm of the adventure, an adventure that would call upon all my talents"—a response to a challenge that Mann as artist might have used of himself; besides, he feels a connection between this great disguise and his boyhood costumings and games of imagination, so that we are to see here not a detour but the main line of vocation.

But let us suppose that to serve his sense of excellence the artist must have something else besides Horatian learning and discipline and studiousness to please, that is, the je ne sais quoi, the mysterious spark, the nonrational gift of Ion—how give it a new, untrite phrasing? Let a worldly priest and a lustful woman independently praise Felix for an "agreeable quality of . . . voice," and an army doctor attribute to him "astounding hyperacuity of hearing." Let him assert that what he did, in acting an epileptic fit, "happened as though without my cooperation . . . to my own momentary amazement." Let him show "natural adroitness" in hotel work, know a waiter's skills "by instinct," make an impressive report on unseen architectural beauties, and show an "amazing and mysterious" gift for languages, chattering in virtually unknown tongues with an "almost ecstatic feeling of being possessed by a foreign spirit." Let him burst into a highly articulate rhapsody on love and "swear" that "it just came to me," that he was "inspired." Let him plunge recklessly into tennis, a new game to him, and through sheer daring and bravado balance his "hopeless errors" by "occasionally performing feats of pure genius"—the doctrine of "inspiration" in joking understatement.

Besides the fine comic representation of inherited ideas about art—the morality of vocation, the union of imagination and discipline, snatching a grace beyond the reach of art—there are exciting inquiries and speculations. More than once Mann grapples piquantly with the sensations of imaginative life. When the "starry-eyed" Kuckuck talks of cosmic space and time, Felix has a "feeling of significance and vastness"; Kuckuck's tale of origins produces a "feeling of expansion that almost burst the limits of my nature." This strange excitement Felix goes on to declare "identical with" what as a child he called "The Great Joy," a "secret formula" of vague meaning but "soon endowed with an intoxicating breadth of significance." He had first mentioned an "incomparable expansion of my whole being" in describing the robbery of the candy store ("the carrying over of my dream treasure into my waking life"), and this in turn he identified with a "nameless sensation," "a yoking of emotions and fancies" that he called "The Great Joy." Though this is in some way connected with sex also, he insists that the sex act is only "the grosser part" of The Great Joy. Mann suggests links among childhood imaginings, theft, sex, and new knowledge. Whatever the center of the ultimately undefined association—mysterious transformation, initiation, creation—what is unmistakable is the groping for the symbolic continuity among diverse experiences.

The finding of links, the quest of oneness, is an insistent theme, announced plainly or given imaginative, even strange and puzzling, forms. If art is "universal," the artist is a unifier; he has something in common with all. Felix is to travel, it appears, to many countries; he is a master of many tongues; but our attention is more caught by the fact that, although his active maleness is not questioned, he has a delicate attractiveness that puts him aesthetically between the two sexes ("And I was," he says, an "extraordinary being in between"), so that he excites homosexual impulses in the hotel owner and other men and infatuates Lord

Strathbogie—a bold symbolic way of attributing to the great artist the human inclusiveness that lies behind the universality of his work. If Felix is equally attractive to all, he himself feels a singular attraction, not to one person or even to a succession of persons, but to pairs of persons, to what he regularly calls the "double image"; this appears first in a brother and sister whom he sees on the balcony of a Frankfurt hotel and who strangely excite his imagination; then in the mother and daughter Kuckuck, who remind him of the Frankfurt pair; and near the end Felix tells us of a Lisbon toreador who was to reappear later in his life "as part of a double image." It would be unfair to the spirit of Mann to see in Felix's fascination with doubles, given fantastic form in his simultaneous wooing of mother and daughter, anything less than a double meaning: say, the sexual overlapping of apparently discrete experiences, as well as the artist's need to be at one with, to win, men and women, old and young; or possibly a reflection of the artist's own duality. But overlying all other meanings is the quest of oneness; in the kinship of different beings is a clue to unity. In Felix's mind the mother-daughter pair is imaginatively allied with the brother-sister pair, and he ultimately concludes that in the "double" of which he dreams there is "a significant whole blessedly embracing what is beguilingly human in both sexes." The "esemplastic" quality of Felix's imagination, striving to put two things into one, the "significant whole," or at least to discover unifying analogies, carries him even outside the "beguilingly human." In Kuckuck's lectures Felix is aware of the impulse to find unity in vast reaches of natural history; he hears that "men and animals are closely related," that man and nature are analogous, that in "playfully crossing the line from one domain into another" (organic and inorganic) nature "was trying to teach us that she was one," and that "All's well when Being and Well-Being are in some measure reconciled." When he praises love to Zouzou, Felix argues climactically that the kiss is "the pledge of that marvelous release from separateness" and that love always tries to "raise it [closeness] to the actual oneness of two lives." The story moves toward more paradoxical intimations of unity when the aristocratic Senhora Kuckuck, who a little later will accept Felix as lover, undergoes a mounting passional excitement as the bull is fought and killed at the corrida. Felix glances "from her surging breast to the living statue of man and animal" and concludes: "more and more the stern and elemental passion of this woman seemed to me one with the game of blood below." In the "game of blood" life, death, and art have a strange nexus; and in the same game, what is more, the professor traces links between Christian beliefs and practices and those of a rival blood-worship cult in which the god lived both in the bull who was sacrificed and in the man who killed him—a teaching that joined believers "in life and in death; and its mystery consisted in the quality and identity of slayer and slain, axe and victim, arrow and target."

What *Felix Krull* dramatizes is the working of a Joycean artist, if not finally putting all things into one, at least pursuing with fascination all the subterranean connections that reduce the multiplicity of the phenomenal world. The artist as artist does many things, but universality is his need, and unity his obsession. Such is the oneness ironically concealed behind the narrative disunity of the picaresque, the acquisitive and amatory episodes of the mobile rogue; these are the wonderfully original design for that part of the old *ars poetica* traditionally assigned to the *poeta*.

vii

The story was to end conventionally: the picaresque hero exposed and jailed. A romantic might argue that this would be society's inevitable rejection of the artist, a positivist that society eventually got its feet on the ground and rejected illusion; but both of these would be foreign to Mann, above all to the Mann of this book. It is safer to guess, I think, that imprisonment would have been a symbol of some failure of Felix's own—perhaps too great a fondness for "high life" in the "man of the world," a decline from that use and mastery of the world which are legitimately his into an unpermissible worldliness, such as tasteless pandering, being corrupted by material things, choosing local glory instead of moving on alone—or perhaps a nobler failure, an attempting of that ordinary humanity, of those personal devotions, which at the circus Felix theorized might mean the destruction of the artist. Or there is another possibility, and a more tempting one, that even within the confines of rogue comedy Mann might have explored another kind of flaw, such as vainglory and pride: for Mann did see Krull as a counterpart of Faustus, and one can imagine this audacious experimenter attempting a comic and yet not unheroic version of another artist who undertook too much. At one time Felix believed he "had improved upon nature, realized a dream," and with "strange and dreamlike satisfaction" he rested from his "creative task."

Here we have to look at the raison d'être of the confidence man, who is distinguished among outlaws in that he requires the consent of his victims. Though we must not discount entirely the profit motive in the victims, it would account only in small part for confidence men, since there are better—safer or more intoxicating, as the individual's nerves require—ways of seeking gain. What we must postulate, I am convinced, is a basic need to confide, to show faith, to yield belief: in a word, a debased religious feeling (one would expect confidence men to flourish in skeptical ages). Here is a distant secular echo of *credo quia impossible,* or, as a practicing Christian put it to an outsider hesitantly sticking a toe into Jordan, "I believe because I want to." We must also theorize that, whatever the eventual disillusionment and outraged outcries, the relation with the confidence man (the ritualistic exchanging of wallets, which is just what Venosta and Felix literally do) exists because the actions that constitute it are in some way satisfying or fulfilling in themselves. Now traditionally the writer of picaresque puts us on the side of the "con man" or "false god"; and this enjoyment of power becomes aesthetically possible because, as we have seen, the victims are not shown. But a greater writer of picaresque, who understood all the implications of "confidence," would surely mediate between the man of wits and those who believed in him, between the man of wits who not only took but in some way gave, and the faithful who were not only taken in but in some way fulfilled. Now is not this precisely what Mann does in *Felix Krull?* We see Felix energetically striving for, and eliciting, confidence, but whatever his ends, we also see his believing followers in some way rewarded or satisfied, finding, whatever the discrepancy between appearance and reality in Felix, a physical or psychic fulfillment—all the people for whom he works, Diane Philibert the novelist, the Marquis of Venosta, Luxembourg ambassador and Portuguese king, lecturing professor, and, on the evidence of an unfinished story, presumably his wife and daughter whom Felix strives to seduce. We see less victims than seekers and finders, tricked, yes, but served.

Now if the picaro is also thought of as artist, this theory of the confidence man is plainly relevant. Like the confidence man in real life and the picaro in fiction, the artist must win assent or confidence; the former must find the will to believe, the latter a comparable state of mind—namely, the willing suspension of disbelief. How boldly Mann puts it as he has Felix describe an audience's response to a skillful actor: "What unanimity in agreeing to let oneself be deceived! Here quite clearly there is in operation a general human need, implanted by God himself in human nature." Picaro and artist serve this need analogously, and for the "deceived" there is clear profit. When the actor left the stage, Felix reports, "shoulders slumped, and virtue seemed to go out of the audience." "Confidence man" and "audience" supply a need for each other: what happens between them is, in Mann's words, "a mutual fulfillment." What is here put theoretically is expressed dramatically in all the episodes of Felix's life.

In the foreground, we see an analogy between picaro-victim and artist-audience; and in the background, if my analysis is sound, a third rela-

tionship analogical to these two—that of deity and mankind. Does
Mann, in all his kindly yet ironic speculations on the need for belief and
the fulfillment of believers, bring these ultimate terms into play? I believe that in part he does. When, in a childhood feat of imitative artistry,
Felix delights his audience, he is called "an angel child and an amazing
little devil." The casual terms of praise suggest the "inspiration" in
which Felix always believes, and on another occasion this is emphatically construed as noncelestial; as an artist in epilepsy Felix suggests
that he must have been under "a satanic influence and impulse"—a theory to which he devotes a half-page discussion that is a joke and yet not a
joke. The intimation of the more-than-human comes in most strongly in
the account of Andromache, the circus artist. Was she "really human,"
he asks several times. He "worshipped" her, the crowd "worshipped
her"; their "lust for her was transformed into awe"; she was a "solemn
angel," the vision of whom was "painful and uplifting at once." Though
man was closer to the animals, she "was a chaste body, untainted by
humanity, and stood much closer to the angels." This thoughtful contemplation of the circus divinities, with whom Felix identifies himself,
seems entirely earnest, uncolored by the deadpan ambiguities so characteristic of the book. The tongue-in-cheek treatment of the more-than-
human appears with greatest verve when Diane Philibert pours forth
raptures as Felix undresses and joins her in bed: ". . . catch sight of the
god . . . *prêt pour la chapelle* . . . your divine limbs . . . The holy breast . . .
you angel of love . . . you young devil." Her "intellect longs for . . . the
divinely stupid, it kneels before it, it prays to it." For her, "the divine, the
masterpiece of creation" is Hermes, "*le dieu voleur*," and thus she confers upon Felix a new identity that he never quite forgets. To him,
Kuckuck praises Hermes as "an elegant deity" whose brain-cell fabric
"must have assumed especially artful forms."

Thus in a jest, and on one occasion less gamesomely, Mann gently
pushes the picaro-artist a little way toward the analogous divinity-figure.
And there, perhaps, he would have dropped it. But a tempting possibility comes to mind: suppose the rogue attempted the ultimate deception,
the confidence man got too much confidence, the artist set out to provide fulfillments beyond the reach of art? Suppose the master-builder
aspired to too great heights in his "creative task," or the herald of the
gods mistook himself for Apollo or Zeus? This might have been the climax of "picaresque tragedy"; it would have been entirely consistent
with the complex terms of the story as far as Mann has taken it; as a
"kindly-destructive" reflection on the religion of art, it would have been
of a piece with the philosophical jesting of the work; and the jail where
we know Felix was to land would have been the right purgatory for a

hero whom, despite some divinity in the dimensions, the author was determined to hold in a fresh picaresque perspective.

"Only the episodic," Mann has Kuckuck say to Felix, "only what possessed a beginning and end, was interesting and worthy of sympathy because transitoriness had given it a soul." Mann has taken a standard episodic form, one very likely to be tedious, and discovered in it a soul: not an allegory, but, beyond its outer liveliness, an inner continuity and vivacity that encourage speculation about its generic form and about the artfulness of its fabric.

■ 2 ■
Two-Tone Fiction:
Nineteenth-Century Types and
Eighteenth-Century Problems

i

BY "TWO-TONE FICTION" I mean novels in whose impact we sense some inconsistency or discrepancy or variation or departure from the expectation established by the apparently controlling devices employed by the novelist. I avoid the term *ambiguity* because it has been excessively called upon and because, if used precisely, it means an unresolved semantic doubleness, which is not my subject here. Hence, also, I do not use *doubleness*; besides, it inevitably reminds a reader of "the double vision," that is, a quality of creative consciousness which also is not what I am talking about. I have thought of *duplicity*, which might do in literal terms, but which would seize attention in the wrong way by pointlessly setting up moral vibrations and then ignoring them. *Duality* could be the key term, but it has a faint aroma of criticism-factory jargon. Thus, by process of elimination, *two-tone*. At the risk of oversimplification I use "two" rather than "three" or "poly" because in my experience the split or discord (if it comes to that) is characteristically between two tonal qualities rather than more. (It might be theoretically argued that a work of multiple tonal currents is an impossibility because the consciousness out of which it would have to come would lack the degree of integration needed for the labor of composition. But that is another issue.)

Two other notes to chart the drift of this essay. "Two-tone" does not allude to traditional combinations of different generic effects denoted by such terms as *tragicomedy* and *romantic tragedy*. With these two-genre or mixed-genre works we live easily, and if we do not immediately grasp a central coherence, we take it to be there and we feel obligated to search for it. "Two-tone" implies rather a problem or difficulty, not necessarily an irreconcilable disunity, but at least a divergence that excites inquiry. Second, "two-tone" is not the same as "two-meaning." This is of course a ticklish issue, and I don't imply that "tone" and "meaning" are easily separable. Talk about "tone" has to do with the "feeling" of a work, and this may be related to meaning in several ways: because we "feel" in such-and-such a way about a work, we may attribute such-and-such a meaning to it; or, conversely, we may be detecting a certain meaning, which automatically elicits one feeling rather than another. It may be that we "feel" differently about *The Turn of the Screw* if from the beginning we believe either that the governess is destroying good children or that she is failing to save bad ones. But need we? In either case the tone is one of horror and of the sinister, and no reader mistranslates this into, say, the romantic or the comic. If there is ambiguity of sense in *The Turn*, there is no evasiveness or oscillation of tone. But when both uncertainties are present, I want to deal with the tonal problem, be it one of wavering, of alternation, or of persistent doubleness. This is a slightly different enterprise from the more frequent critical labor, the exegesis of nonexplicit meaning. If I do not talk about "what the author is saying," it is that it seems irrelevant to, or else implied by, the discussion of tone.

If there is a question of tone, one may just describe it, or one may speculate about the reason for it. The issue may arise from a not wholly lucid or consistent communication of the narrative substance, possibly the case in Thomas Pynchon's *V.* It may arise because the author has, so to speak, different "intentions" that are in control at different times, or because he is overtaken, half unawares, by a subtle change in attitude. It may arise because he has unstable responses to a character or situation, or, at a deeper level, has emotional contradictions that express themselves in fictional elements of not wholly congruous impact. It may be that he is operating within conventions that we do not understand and that can accommodate tonal results in which only we of another era or culture see disparities. Lady Murasaki's *Tale of Genji,* for instance, appears (as it comes through in Arthur Waley's translation) to alternate between a fairy-tale manner (wonder at the glory and magnificence of characters and occasions and trappings, always hyperbolically described) and a social realism wholly conversant with the emotional and psychic traumas of insecure amatory and courtly life (such as appears in a lesser fictionist like Aphra Behn or a greater one like Proust). Murasaki can even reach a plane of fine moral realism. On one occasion the hero, Prince Genji, laments his illicit passion for Fujitsubo, the consort of the Old Emperor (his father). He cries out against "foeman fate" and the "bonds" that "would hold him back from Paradise." Fujitsubo quietly replies, "If to all time this bond debars you from felicity, not hostile fate but your own heart you should with bitterness condemn" (part 2, ch. 1). But after such plunges into the heart of the matter Murasaki easily reverts to the alternate practice of letting Genji glow with the fused talents of Don Juan, Frank Merriwell, and John Kennedy. We do not know whether this two-tone effect emerges from an inherent disjunction in the tale, or whether an eleventh-century Japanese, spontaneously applying the conventions of his day, would have felt a congruence that I believe is not available to a modern Western reader.

There may be various sources, then, for two-tone fiction. Though cause-hunting is too uncertain a business to be the central occupation here, I will try some speculations about the origins of certain shifts. If such hypotheses make sense, they may shed a little light on novelists or their processes or products.

ii

The novels that I think deserve the fullest treatment are *Moll Flanders* and *Pamela*. The problems that they present, however, will be most meaningful if we can see them in a context of what happens in a number of other novels; besides, even a brief account of these will develop the theoretical framework a little further.

The two-tone effect may be incidental, cardinal, or pervasive. Several examples of each will be enough to make the distinctions clear.

In Scott's *Rob Roy* the effect is incidental but recurrent; though it is not characteristic of the novel as a whole, it appears in a number of episodes. Morris the government agent characteristically sets Scott off in different directions. We first see Morris as so fearful a traveler toward Scotland that he is totally ludicrous, a "humor" in the old sense; he creates the tone of farce. But then we are told that he is carrying both money to pay the troops in the North and "despatches of great consequence" (7; all references are to chapters)—an assignment inconceivable for such a character as Scott has created. Our responsiveness to him is balked by colliding pieces of fictional evidence. Then we are given the wrong kind of shock when Morris, a prisoner, is brutally drowned by the order of Helen MacGregor (31): a tale cannot jump from hilarity to horror unless such gross reversals are its main burden. Bailie Nicol Jarvie, also a prisoner of Helen's, "could not so suppress his horror, but that the words escaped him in a low and broken whisper,—'I take up my protest against this deed, as a bloody and cruel murder—it is a cursed deed, and God will avenge it in his due way and time'" (32). Thus Scott commits Jarvie to unqualified moral outrage. Fifteen lines later, when Helen asks Jarvie what he would say about the drowning if she were to free him, Jarvie replies, "Uh! uh!—hem! hem! . . . I suld study to say as little on that score as might be—least said is sunest mended." While Scott accurately perceives the inconsistency that flows from self-interest, he puts this in such gross, pell-mell fashion that we have another kind of farce—that of coarse automatic action—and hence a violent leap from horror back to hilarity (so blatant that on the next page Scott even makes a mild effort to mitigate it). One other case, partly comparable: in order to reward his hero Frank with Osbaldistone Hall, Scott has to kill off Frank's five male cousins, all young men presumably in good health; so on a page or so he rips off five fatal accidents (37). Here again is the farce of automatism—the row of routine knockdowns, here irreversible, but still pratfalls in spirit. Yet we are then to take seriously the shattered state of the surviving father, and to applaud the justice of Frank's becoming lord of the manor.

Repeatedly Scott is unable to forgo farce, though it clashes with some other effect that he does not regard as trivial. He will play for horse laughs at any time, without concern for tonal congruence. He is an entertainer, a Dickens who can clown or cry at will in a series of readings. A rather fancy theoretical approach would be to attribute to Scott's work a "unity of entertainment": entertainment always means change, novelty, diversity, so that a sequence of tonally disparate passages might seem to embody a Platonic idea of entertainment. But this would confuse the art of the novel with the art of the vaudeville program. Still, it puts a brake on facile charges of inconsistency.

It is a temptation to think that a novel with the "unity of entertainment" reveals as much about the audience as about the author. But it is too easy to condescend to audiences that for a century, most of it post-dating Coleridge's provision of a more rigorous concept of unity, included readers of literary sophistication and critical acumen. Better, perhaps, to assume in the humanity of the nineteenth century a wide spontaneous responsiveness to the Scott fare—and then to postpone the question of why this has been considerably narrowed down in our day, which can hardly be thought to have a greater proportion of knowledgeable and skeptical readers.

The two-tone effect is "cardinal" when we can see a hinge at which the novel apparently swings from one kind of effect to another. This may happen rather late in the game: witness the arguments over whether the main substance of Lawrence's *Rainbow* sustains the buoyant ending. There are significant, more central instances of the cardinal two-tone effect in Thackeray's *Vanity Fair* and Meredith's *Ordeal of Richard Feverel,* and here we can hardly help speculating about what led the authors into these striking swings.

Becky Sharp lives by her wits, untroubled by conscience or consequences; she puts things over on others, schemes, calculates, gets ahead, advances opportunistically from one game to another. We rejoice in her successes and are sorry when she doesn't pull it off; that is, the rogue is heroine, and the tone is picaresque. But this is true for only half the novel or a little more. The tone changes when Becky makes victims of the innocent, whom we are compelled to respond to as victims and who therefore compel us to yield to them the sympathy that once flowed naturally to Becky. When Becky deceives her husband, ignores her son, and fleeces the landlord Raggles and the servant Miss Briggs, she is no longer the amiable rogue profiting from the follies of others or beating them at their own game but a merciless cheater of nice guys. Thackeray did not have to do it this way: he might have kept Rawdon and the boy Rawdie out of sight or made them into a rascal and a brat whom we couldn't like. But he either rejected this way of keeping to the picaresque, or didn't think of it. Instead, he turned on Becky.

When Becky changes from charming gameswoman to gravely dishonest operator, the picaresque gives way to a sharply satirical tone (this is really a change in genre, too). Maybe Thackeray was not altogether comfortable with the picaresque; maybe the homilist or moralist in him nudged him toward a judgment-making form; maybe the cultural atmosphere in which he wrote (if it is safe to make any assumptions at all about it) or his sense of readers' expectations pulled him away from the amoral picaresque mode.

We can make two critical judgments of this tonal swing, but neither is wholly satisfactory. If we call it a failure, we risk the pedantry of going by rule in a somewhat Rymeresque way, and of ignoring a considerable history of imaginative responses that seem to have had no difficulty with the tone (any more than they have had with lack of unity or decorum in Shakespeare). One needs to be aware of this danger. Still he may regret the loss of the picaresque, with its particular delights, and feel that Thackeray turned unnecessarily against Becky and thus used her to support the moral judgments to which he was inclined. The other approach is to justify the tonal swing by arguing that Thackeray grasped the inevitable implications of the picaresque and carried the mode into the depths into which it has to lead if the writer does not arbitrarily stop short. In this view, the nonmoral has at its heart the immoral, the rogue is only the smile upon the villain's face, and responsible art must go all the way to the bottom of things. Though this theory is not implausible, unhappily it would commit every work to a kind of metaphysical relentlessness that would eliminate not only the diversity of appeal inherent in a diversity of modes but also the specific satisfaction proper to each mode, which can exist as a mode only by accepting conventional boundaries instead of essaying a universal inclusiveness or ultimateness. Picaresque, we may assume, pleases by making possible a vicarious exercise (or catharsis, perhaps?) of everyman's rascality (taste for slick profits, sleight of hand, the opportunism of wits, effrontery, and so forth), of his need for interludes of nonmorality. Traditional picaresque art, of course, ritually acknowledges the insufficiency of the picaresque way of life by having the hero end up in jail. It seems a pity that, with Becky, Thackeray should have transubstantiated the ritual acknowledgment into a flesh-and-blood demonstration of moral culpability.

The cardinal alteration in tone is very evident in *The Ordeal of Richard Feverel,* in which Meredith regrettably drifts away from his métier, comedy, and into satirical melodrama. In comedy the protagonist is perceived ironically in his inconsistency, his self-deception, or his folly, and potentially he has the grace to understand them; in satire his failings persist and may assume the tinge of vice; in melodrama we see his ill-doings and his victims. These modes may of course be combined, but Meredith does not commit the *Ordeal* to a combination. Instead he creates a superb comic tone which we expect to hold throughout, and then loses his grip on it: we see his detachment yielding to a sharp animus. This first appears when Mrs. Doria Forey, rebounding from Richard's marriage, forces her daughter Clare, whom she had trained to fall in love with Richard, into a substitute marriage with a man twice her age. This totally incredible marriage kills or helps kill Clare, and Meredith hangs on to the pathos by postmortem readings from Clare's diary. Up to this disaster the novel views Mrs. Doria with gentle irony as a marrying mother with "a System" of her own (38), an amusingly straightforward practical contrast to Sir Austin's elaborate theoretical scheme for educating Richard. Now she becomes a monster. Meredith simply loses his grip on his point of view. We may theorize that he got angry at Mrs. Doria and felt the need to denigrate her by making her guilty of involuntary manslaughter. (A little later, in a second burst of sentimental haste, he puts her through a second conversion, this time into a remorseful and suddenly wise woman.)

It is difficult to avoid the conclusion that Meredith lets himself get angry several times and hence falls into the change of tone that puts us off. First, two small protective steps. I am not coming up with the mawkish cliché that an author must "love" his characters; his obligation is rather detachment and thoroughness, which are undermined by anger (as by "indignation" and "compassion," those other social virtues that are often mistaken for literary virtues, though they are appropriate only to the narrow mode of satire). Second, it has been argued that Meredith prepared for a "tragic" ending by some early verbal, imagistic, and symbolic hints; but these in no way counterbalance or even modify the comic tone which is masterfully established by language and event in the first half of the book and which makes a comic conclusion seem obligatory. Meredith is truly brilliant in spotting the nexus between love and egotism, between benevolence and love of power; the paternal love that animates Sir Austin's "system" is fused with an *amour propre* that takes over when his love-and-power seems rejected. The loving dictation of another's welfare contains the love of dictation; the subtle but persistent images of deity define the role into which Sir Austin instinctively falls; and the balked father becomes the offended divinity "trying" (39), in this case punishing, the child who follows another love and thus comes under another power. This development is psychologically and morally right. The problem is whether the situation that he has created compels Meredith to keep Sir Austin so rigid in feeling offended and in probing for a surrogate power that disaster is inevitable. I am sure not. Meredith reveals the comic way out of the impasse when Sir Austin is trying to dissuade Richard from an excessive response to his adultery and to the man who had engineered it: "Sir Austin detained him, expostulated, contradicted himself, made nonsense of all his theories." He is even "seized with unwonted suspicion of his own wisdom; troubled, much to be pitied" (48). This is the true comic solution, and Sir Austin might have been brought to it before it was too late, before his love of power had minimized the power of his love to deflect Richard from melodramatic follies. Meredith has also endowed Richard with a faculty for occasional ironic self-criticism that might have checked his romantic extremism, deep as this is in him. But Richard is a victim, not only of his and his father's folly, but of Meredith's apparently growing need to do Sir Austin in. After having potentially rescued Sir Austin from humorless rigidity, Meredith again turns on him aggressively and in the final chapter belts him around unmercifully. Either through anger or through a misinterpretation of his own role he has surrendered the almost magical comic tone that he might have maintained triumphantly to the end.

iii

I hope that all this does not sound picky, for my intention is not to find fault but to give some accounting of certain felt dissonances in fiction. The discussion of the two-tone situation that is "pervasive," the final topic, is less likely to sound captious, for here one cannot point to specific incidents or great divides that encourage the sketching of alternatives. When bitonality is pervasive, it is a given, and one can only identify it and seek just ways of coming to terms with it. First, several preliminaries to set up the immediate context, and then the main subjects, *Moll Flanders* and *Pamela*.

One quick example: the two-tone effect moves toward pervasiveness in parts 1 and 2 of *Gulliver's Travels,* in which Lilliput and to a greater extent Brobdingnag figure principally as parodies of Europe but also as utopian constructs. The effect is truly pervasive in part 4, in which initial and persisting sympathy with Gulliver must increasingly compete with the sense of him as disturbed and unreliable. Yet here we should probably refer the basic problem less to duality of tone than to ambiguity of sense.

Representative cases of pervasive two-tone effect without the intellectual equivocalness that begets continual counterexegeses (as with Gulliver and the Houyhnhnms) occur in three of Hardy's major novels—*The Mayor of Casterbridge, Tess of the D'Urbervilles,* and *Jude the Obscure.* Here we have clear-cut tales of failure and disaster; we know who gets it in the neck (or wins by a neck); there are no sotto voce intimations of victory-in-defeat, or other paradoxes or reversals, to render the fictional thought susceptible of opposite interpretations. The bitonality reflects, then, a duality in Hardy's feeling about the sources of misfortune; one kind of feeling leads him into a formal theory, the other rests on his artistic intuition. On the one hand he nags, on the other he perceives and records; on the one hand he blames cosmos and society, on the other he apprehends character as fate. Repeatedly he speaks of the Mayor's off-and-on wife Susan and of his daughter Elizabeth-Jane as miserable victims, even while they are surviving difficulties and in time successfully achieving heart's desires; Hardy is inclined to blame Angel Clare and exonerate Tess, even while imaginatively relating their actions to representative complexities in their natures; and he almost regularly treats Jude and Sue as undeserving victims while giving them emotional and psychic constitutions out of which happier lives could hardly have come. Hardy, then, is both an involved protester (with the advantage of knowing that not much can be done about the imperfections complained of) and a detached artist. He wavers between his grudges and his grasp of things. The former leads through plaint and polemic to a tone of despair; the latter through understood actuality to a tragic tone. Here, however, I want to say just enough to introduce the general issue of pervasive doubleness of tone, and so I only skim over points that I address in essays 19–21.

One way of dealing with pervasive bitonality is to assume, in the novelist, some falling short of unity of consciousness (an inevitable human state that in the noncreative appears in day-to-day inconsistencies, "changes of mind," and so on). By "falling short" I do not mean a disastrous shortcoming, because I cannot think of a work that "fails" conspicuously because of an internal incoherence of such origin. On the contrary, the nonachievement of consistency may even help save a writer from himself: if Hardy, for instance, had been able to force his portrayal of life into conformity with his doctrine of hostile forces, he would surely have written lesser novels. Many years ago Kenneth Burke speculated about a division of impulses in the writer, about the co-presence of one belief or commitment which would dictate a formal direction and course, and of another which might give especial vitality to parts of the work at variance with the formal commitment. This can happen when a writer assents, wholeheartedly as far as he knows, to prevailing habits of thought or feeling but also entertains, perhaps unknowingly, sympathies or passions outside the main currents of his time (a pattern often seen in Dickens); or when he registers equally the impulses of a given sensibility or way of life that are actually contradictory or at least seem so as they are sharpened up in the work of art (for example, mariolatry and *amour courtois* in some romances); when unfettered energies lead to accents that we do not reconcile easily with the apparent overall emphases of the work (such as the snobberies, self-defensiveness, and condescensions that get into Charlotte Brontë heroines); or when doctrinal fixity begets one order of assertions, while imaginative flexibility opens the door to fuller and less simplistic fictional statements (as in Hardy). These are possible ways of accounting for the bitonality that appears in *Moll Flanders* and *Pamela*.

iv

Though the coexistence of two tones may a priori seem unlikely in an eighteenth-century work, the problem is attested to by the quarreling over *Moll Flanders* and the fluctuations of attitude to *Pamela*.

In *Moll* the division is between the story of spiritual regeneration (Moll as repentant sinner, and her tale as cautionary guide to error and evil) and the story of worldly success (Moll as pound-and-pence thinker, and finally as rich woman). Interpreters get into trouble when they discover an underlying oneness: at one extreme Moll is said to have convinced us of her goodness, and at the other she is read as a satirized embodiment of bourgeois materialism. Ian Watt has pretty well disposed of such rewritings of the book and has offered a very satisfactory reading: that what appear as inconsistencies to us were not so to the kind of Puritan mind that saw no contradiction between spiritual salvation and material security. My approach differs from his in that I find two tones present in the book and attribute them to Defoe's mixture of talents and convictions (without trying either to derive these from, or to declare them independent of, the historical context).

The two tones have different manifestations. They assume a principal form as early as the fourth and fifth paragraphs of the novel. The fourth ends with Moll's saying that she was "brought into a course of life which was not only scandalous in itself, but which in its ordinary courses tended to the swift destruction both of soul and body." The fifth begins:

"But the case was otherwise here. My mother was convicted of felony for a certain petty theft scarce worth mentioning, viz. having an opportunity of borrowing three pieces of fine holland from a certain draper in Cheapside." The tone in the first is moral earnestness; in the second it is amoral flipness. The tone of moral earnestness recurs throughout the novel—in self-criticism (often with terms of self-abuse such as "whore"), in reproof of others, in much talk about the "reproaches of my own conscience," in expressions of remorse and assertions of repentance, in allegations of moral improvement (the book ends with Moll's promise that she and her husband will "spend the remainder of our years in sincere penitence for the wicked lives we have lived") But another tone is created by the more numerous passages in which Moll records all her monetary losses and "profits"; by her treating gains from sex relationships as manna from heaven to be held on to; by the failure of her conduct to match her protestations (she erupts with verbal horror at her incestuous marriage, but for financial reasons feels compelled to keep the secret— "and thus I lived with the greatest pressure imaginable for three years more"); by her sound worldly observations (careless, imprudent mistresses "are justly cast off with contempt"); by an indifference to children (clashing with occasional violent protestations of maternal feeling); by the ease with which she becomes a thief; and particularly by occasional shrewd observations on herself which undercut her didactic pronouncements, frequent as these are ("But it is none of my talent to preach," "I am not capable of reading lectures of instruction"). In a word, there is on the one hand the naive and uncriticized rhetoric of repentance and instruction; on the other, the shrewd moral realism of a worldly old lady who doesn't kid herself ("sometimes I flattered myself that I had sincerely repented"). The result is the bitonality of the reform story and the hardboiled success story, or, in characterological terms, of the willed innocence and the periodically erupting knowingness that we sometimes see together in the ideology-directed minds of our own day.

I believe that the situation is most successfully described in generic terms and that the basic tones in *Moll* are those of two modes that were to have a considerable play in the rest of the century—the picaresque and the sentimental novel. The former, if I am right, is basic in Defoe. The most zestful scenes, the ones in which he is most spontaneous and buoyant, are those in which Moll is skillfully putting things over on others, outside the law but roguish rather than criminal, doing serious hurt to no one, making a small or maybe large profit and then of necessity hurrying on to the next exploit—most notably in the score or so of thieving episodes that begin at midstory, lively and often gay; but also earlier when Moll helps a woman get a husband by a planned manipulation of style and rumors, on the principle that one must "deceive the deceiver"; when Moll gets herself a husband by the same tricky campaigning ("though he might say afterwards he was cheated, yet he could never say afterwards that I had cheated him") that always has a part in her man-hunting ("it was necessary to play the hypocrite a little more with him"; "I played with this lover as an angler does with a trout"); when rumors of her own wealth lead to her marrying her "Irish" husband, her long-term spouse; when she shifts with such readiness from whore to thief and instinctively masters a new expertise. Others play like games, and we also see Moll as the victim of calculation, experiencing the bad luck that belongs equally to the picaro's diet: picaresque from two perspectives ("double fraud," she calls it in one ironic case). Moll has the complete picaresque spirit, anti-regular in acquisitive action, but wholly orthodox in prejudices and ideas: she is skeptical of Catholics, doesn't think it proper to be married in an inn at night, doesn't paint, will enter liaisons for money but not for "the vice" of it, and of course vociferously supports the conventions and moral codes of her society (a picaro is never a rebel). And it is just a certain excessiveness in this moral line that creates the tone of the sentimental novel. (In not wanting to call *Moll* picaresque, Robert Alter works from the implicit assumption that the novel has to be wholly one thing or another.)

Historically the sentimental novel is several different things. Here I refer to the Puritan version which gratifies a certain consciousness by a happy ending compounded of monetary and moral triumph—a staple of fiction from Richardson to Horatio Alger. It is not necessary to demonstrate how much of this there is in *Moll*. The contrast with *Vanity Fair* is interesting: Thackeray puts the picaresque behind him by turning the rogue's ceremonial comeuppance into substantial punishment, Defoe in the opposite way by having the ceremonial comeuppance (Moll in the jug) superseded by a substantial going up in the world. Was Defoe's climactic crowning of virtue (riches plus verbal self-chastisement for out-of-bounds sex) a penance for his undoubted joy in the picaresque? Defoe was a complex fellow, and even these two dominant tones, as I take them to be, do not altogether exhaust the tendencies one sees in *Moll*. The novel reveals that he was something of the instinctive entrepreneur, of the bookmaker with a very accurate intuition of a public's contradictory yearnings—of its desire, to pick a central case, for clean thoughts and dirty scenes: you can enjoy the illicit lustful embrace when you know that you are only gaining a painful saving knowledge of evils to be shunned. When Moll and a man sleep naked in the same bed for two years, enjoying "all the familiarities" but the ultimate one which would terminate their "innocence," and thus proving that nude loving-kindness need not be naughty, Defoe pulls off a classical piece of pre-free-speech porn. His strong documentary sense is less strip-teasing but still titillating when he gives us three detailed price-schedules for birthing a bastard, and it appears neutrally in his schematic psychology: he is at times not a bad psychologist, but in a logical and theoretical rather than an imaginative way; he has made a tenable paradigm of human responses, but he cannot flesh it out with a convincing imaginative fullness (he knows that man can become habituated to anything, but he so speeds up the process of habituation that we don't believe it).

In *Pamela* there is none of the picaresque (except insofar as there is something delightful in some of Mr. B's bedroom schemes) but much of the sentimental that presents virtue (pertinacious rejection of out-of-bounds sex) as the best policy, with dividends in money, marriage, and status. What the opposing tone is, we have to see. The mingled tonality partly accounts for the clashing receptions of *Pamela* over the years: from glorification to routine laudation to indifference to calumniation. "Changing taste," perhaps, but fluctuations of esteem may come less from optical changes in the beholder than from his focusing, at different times, upon different aspects of the work: *Clarissa* has come back, not because our values have changed again, but because we have learned to recognize, in the novel itself, elements that were always there and that indeed, even though not then consciously perceived, must have accounted for its original sweeping impact. The lack of a similar revival of *Pamela* is due partly, of course, to its lesser range and depth and the greater naiveté of its official "message," but more largely, I think, to the fact that its surface is easier to disparage and its nondidactic or nonsentimental substance is less likely to engage us actively than is the desperate extremism of sexual attitude in *Clarissa*. In our day sex plus evil is more appetizing than sex plus human decency. *Pamela* suffers because *Shamela* tells us the kind of thing we like to hear, and hence we trust it despite our knowing that parodies distort partial truths rather than mirror whole ones.

When someone as unpretentious and shrewd as J. B. Priestley takes a moral heroine of two centuries and declares her a "sly chit"—for us a congenial way of describing one who does not quick give it all away for free—it may seem a rather solemn academic perversity to protest that this will never do. But we cannot dismiss Pamela as a moral cheat just because her creator carelessly betrays his view that virginity is an investment. For that was not the only reading of life made by Richardson's not-so-simple eyes. If it had been, he would have lacked the qualities that enabled him to understand the adverse criticism and to make the readjustments that he did make in *Clarissa*; nor, I wager, would *Pamela* have been capable of making the impact that it did make. For, like Hardy a century and a half later, Richardson had an imagination as well as a doctrine; through it he grasped a different life than that of the profit motive, and along with the sentimental created quite a different tone—that of the mature comedy in which human beings through new understanding and alteration earn a stable relationship (rather than having it given them gratis, as in one of the plots of romantic tone). In this sense Pamela and Mr. B. are a link between Congreve's Mirabell and Millamant and Austen's Elizabeth and Darcy—a slender link, granted, because Richardson's humor and taste cannot quite be relied on, but still a dramatization of the awareness that men and women can learn, make concessions as well as demands, and thus reach satisfying modi vivendi.

As a matter of fact, Richardson imagined Mr. B. not only as a tedious or sinister seducer but as a bright, repeatedly witty, often charmingly ironic man who can challenge Pamela's rather heavy defensive style with amusing logical tours de force. But Mr. B. is a classical comic figure because he has an idée fixe which is at variance with reality: he thinks that as a woman and a servant Pamela is a pushover, and he has to learn that she is an individual. Here Richardson, long before Austen and Meredith, was practicing the best kind of woman's liberation: each woman is to be seen as a person, not as a member of a class. Mr. B.'s task is really harder than Pamela's, for what she has to do is intuit in Mr. B. a latent personality of much greater range than appears in the would-be seducer and rapist. She moves gradually in this direction, responding to a measure of charm that Richardson successfully establishes in Mr. B. (sketching the profound reading of character that he would achieve later in Lovelace). Fairly early in the story, while Pamela in her letters home is formally resolving to flee from the terrors of Mr. B.'s house, she writes more than one P.S. in which she briefly cites reasons for delaying this irrevocable act; in this rather skillful use of the P.S., Richardson suggests the presence in her of an impulse set off from the main body of conscious program, one that she herself does not fully appreciate (letters XVI, XIX, XXIII). This impulse can be interpreted, of course, as sexiness, love of danger, the shrewd sense that Mr. B. is more of a pushover than she, or sheer snobbery. Since there are different tones in the book, I do not deny such possibilities, but it is entirely consistent with other events to see her as drawn by Mr. B.'s general male attractiveness, which has been made quite real. Richardson's gift is to create in both parties a potential charm that is overlaid by their combat stances (these, by the way, we can read, not as passé morality, but as one symbolization of the war of the sexes); the true power to charm has to be actualized in the surrender of the combat role and the risking of the generous act that has no guaranteed outcome. This is the pattern of conduct that Richardson sees as emerging when the mutual charm survives the rigidities of attack and defense: Mr. B. frees Pamela, risking the loss of her, and Pamela returns voluntarily, risking a renewal of the aggressiveness that she has struggled against. But this rapprochement, far from being imposed by the author as deus ex machina, has been prepared with extraordinary thoroughness.

This tone of the high comedy of sex obviously does not displace the sentimental tone of the didactic elements, but the latter has been so much noticed that it needs no further demonstration here. The comic sense, on the other hand, has not been appreciated, and it does need attention. One of its ingredients, it is worth noting, appeared in Molière: a partial distortion of character by hysterical tendencies. Richardson may or may not detect the hysteria as such. In Pamela there is a certain infusion of it which he seems not to identify; I refer to Pamela's intemperateness in, and even something of a clinging to, the fright and anxiety created by Mr. B.'s bedtime maneuvers, but more particularly to the incredible delays resulting from Pamela's nervousness about changing from an engaged girl to a married woman. Richardson is overly bent on establishing that when it comes to being bedded down, a decent woman shows reluctance, and avoids willingness lest it seem impatience; so he lets Pamela's reluctance drift into the neurotic. On the other hand he gives a magnificent, and wholly knowing, picture of the hysterical in Lady Davers's hostility to Pamela as her sister-in-law: Richardson sets out to demonstrate social snobbery and Pamela's conquest of it, but he virtually loses sight of this didactic project in the portrayal of Lady Davers's unchecked emotions, of their sources in her bringing up and in her past relations with her brother, and of her unwillingness to surrender the morbid pleasure of luxuriating in them. This very long episode late in part 1 makes a fine contribution to the mature comic tone which always competes with the sentimental tone for the possession of Richardson's first novel. If we are not aware of it, we miss a genuine source of strength in *Pamela*.

———

Once more: to speak of the two-tone novel is not really to point to a type of failure. Granted, rightly or wrongly one may regret the replacement of an established tone in this novel or that. But more often one may point to a situation in which an insistent tone is challenged by another which is responsible for our sense of quality in the work: the merits of disunity, so to speak. One thinks of bitonality, then, less as a merit or a demerit than as a fact of artistic life which emerges from a fact of all human life: our characteristic nonachievement of total unity, whether in perspective or feeling or values. Unexceptional integration occurs, in novels as in people, only at two levels: at a level of very simple organization where, from the beginning, there is no room for complexer modes of response, and, at the other level, in very special individuals (persons, fictions) in which greater complexities have by extraordinary discipline or special power been brought into a felt and demonstrable unity (the saint, the demonic being; *Don Quixote, The Princess Casamassima, Doktor Faustus*). In between we may expect to find a considerable range of personalities and fictions marked by the coexistence of tones that are not ideally compatible. We may find this troubling, a sign of shortcoming; or we may find it encouraging that a lesser singleness, which might have become dominant, has been opposed by the entry of a more capacious mood, a larger feeling for the *is* and the *ought* that are the borders of reality. For each work in which bitonality appears the problem is to describe it as lucidly as possible and to assess its impact on total quality. In other words, to acknowledge the presence of bitonality is not to give up the critical problem but to redefine or relocate it. It is to give up the quest of the holy grail of organic oneness—a quest which is sometimes quite valid but which, when it is not, may lead to some torturing of the literary countryside in which the critic rides. Lest he find himself whipping dissident elements into a oneness to which they are not disposed—or recklessly gluing masses of shards into the semblance of an encompassing shapely grail—he might first test for evidence that he has a two-tone situation, if not something still more centrifugal, on his hands. He will have to look out for a tendency to resist the evidence, because admitting tonal nonunity can seem an ignominious retreat from the taxing ultimate critical problem. But if he successfully resists his resistance, he will still, as we have seen, have much to do. Reconciling a sense of quality with an aesthetic situation supposed to be adverse to quality is no small task. It will involve him in deriving merit from spontaneities not checked by a rigidity of aim or thought that is one route to uniformity, or unity, or in discovering how counterintentions can collaborate, either to bypass the more restricted effect or somehow to reproduce, in the work itself, the unresolved tensions of the creative consciousness—tensions that, as long as they reflect representative divisions rather than a chaotic disorder out of which creation could not come, create their own kind of vitality.

Innovations in Gothic: Charlotte Brontë

i

IN THAT CHARACTERISTIC FLIGHT from cliché that may plunge him
into the recherché the critic might well start from *The Professor* and
discover in it much more than is implied by the usual dismissal of it as
Charlotte Brontë's poorest work. He might speculate about Charlotte's
singular choice of a male narrator—the value of it, or even the need of it,
for her. For through William Crimsworth she lives in Héger, making love
to herself as Frances Henri: in this there is a kind of ravenousness, in-
turning, splitting, and doubling back of feeling. Through Crimsworth
she experiences a sudden, vivid, often graceless mastery. But these
notes on the possible psychology of the author are critically useful only
as a way into the strange tremors of feeling that are present in a formally
defective story. Pelet identifies "a fathomless spring of sensibility in thy
breast, Crimsworth." If Crimsworth is not a successful character, he is
the channel of emotional surges that splash over a conventional tale of
love: the author's disquieting presence in the character lends a nervous,
off-center vitality. The pathos of liberty is all but excessive (as it is later
in Shirley Keeldar and Lucy Snowe): Crimsworth sneers, "I sprang from
my bed with other slaves," and rejoices, "Liberty I clasped in my arms
. . . her smile and embrace revived my life." The Puritan sentiment (to
be exploited partially in Jane Eyre and heavily in Lucy Snowe) becomes
tense, rhetorical, fiercely censorious; the self-righteousness punitive
and even faintly paranoid. Through the frenetically Protestant Crimsworth and his flair for rebuke Charlotte notes the little sensualities of
girl students ("parting her lips, as full as those of a hot-blooded Maroon")
and the coquettish yet urgent sexuality of Zoraide Reuter perversely
responding to Crimsworth's ostensible yet not total unresponsiveness to
her: "When she stole about me with the soft step of a slave, I felt at once
barbarous and sensual as a pasha."

Charlotte looks beyond familiar surfaces. In Yorke Hunsden she
notes the "incompatibilities of the 'physique' with the 'morale.'" The
explosive Byronic castigator has lineaments "small, and even feminine"
and "now the mien of a morose bull, and anon that of an arch and mis-

chievous girl." In this version of the popular archetype, "rough exterior but heart of gold," Charlotte brilliantly finds a paradoxical union of love and hate; she sees generosity of spirit sometimes appearing directly but most often translated into antithetical terms that also accommodate opposite motives—into godlike self-indulgence in truth-telling; almost Mephistophelian cynicism; sadism and even murderousness in words.

Charlotte's story is conventional; formally she is for "reason" and "real life"; but her characters keep escaping to glorify "feeling" and "Imagination." Feeling is there in the story—evading repression, in author or in character; ranging from nervous excitement to emotional absorption; often tense and peremptory; sexuality, hate, irrational impulse, grasped, given life, not merely named and pigeonholed. This is Charlotte's version of Gothic: in her later novels an extraordinary thing. In that incredibly eccentric history *The Gothic Quest*, Montague Summers asserts that the "Gothic novel of sensibility . . . draws its emotionalism and psychology . . . from the work of Samuel Richardson." When this line of descent continues in the Brontës, the vital feeling moves toward an intensity, a freedom, and even an abandon virtually nonexistent in historical Gothic and rarely approached in Richardson. From Angria on, Charlotte's women vibrate with passions that the fictional conventions only partly constrict or gloss over—in the center an almost violent devotedness that has in it at once a fire of independence, a spiritual energy, a vivid sexual responsiveness, and, along with this, self-righteousness, a sense of power, sometimes self-pity and envious competitiveness. To an extent the heroines are "unheroined," unsweetened. Into them there has come a new sense of the dark side of feeling and personality.

The Professor ventures a little into the psychic darkness on which *Villette* draws heavily. One night Crimsworth, a victim of hypochondria, hears a voice saying, "In the midst of life we are in death," and he feels "a horror of great darkness." In his boyhood this same "sorceress" drew him "to the very brink of a black, sullen river" and managed to "lure me to her vaulted home of horrors." Charlotte draws on sex images that recall the note of sexuality subtly present in other episodes: "I had entertained her at bed and board . . . she lay with me, . . . taking me entirely to her death-cold bosom, and holding me with arms of bone." The climax is: "I repulsed her as one would a dreaded and ghastly concubine coming to embitter a husband's heart toward his young bride." This is Gothic, yet there is an integrity of feeling that greatly deepens the convention.

———

From childhood terrors to all those mysteriously threatening sights, sounds, and injurious acts that reveal the presence of some malevolent force and that anticipate the holocaust at Thornfield, the traditional Gothic in *Jane Eyre* has often been noted, and as often disparaged. It need not be argued that Charlotte Brontë did not reach the heights while using hand-me-down devices, though a tendency to work through the conventions of fictional art was a strong element in her makeup. This is true of all her novels, but it is no more true than her countertendency to modify, most interestingly, these conventions. In both *Villette* and *Jane Eyre* Gothic is used but characteristically is undercut.

Jane Eyre hears a "tragic . . . preternatural . . . laugh," but this is at "high noon" and there is "no circumstance of ghostliness"; Grace Poole, the supposed laugher, is a plain person, than whom no "apparition less romantic or less ghostly could . . . be conceived"; Charlotte apologizes ironically to the "romantic reader" for telling "the plain truth" that Grace generally bears a "pot of porter." Charlotte almost habitually revises "old Gothic," the relatively crude mechanisms of fear, with an infusion of the anti-Gothic. When Mrs. Rochester first tried to destroy Rochester by fire, Jane "baptized" Rochester's bed and heard Rochester "fulminating strange anathemas at finding himself lying in a pool of water." The introduction of comedy as a palliative of straight Gothic occurs on a large scale when almost seventy-five pages are given to the visit of the Ingram-Eshton party to mysterious Thornfield; here Charlotte, as often in her novels, falls into the manner of the Jane Austen whom she despised. When Mrs. Rochester breaks loose again and attacks Mason, the presence of guests lets Charlotte play the nocturnal alarum for at least a touch of comedy: Rochester orders the frantic women not to "pull me down or strangle me"; and "the two dowagers, in vast white wrappers, were bearing down on him like ships in full sail."

The symbolic also modifies the Gothic, for it demands of the reader a more mature and complicated response than the relatively simple thrill or momentary intensity of feeling sought by primitive Gothic. When mad Mrs. Rochester, seen only as "the foul German spectre—the Vampyre," spreads terror at night, that is one thing; when, with the malicious insight that is the paradox of her madness, she tears the wedding veil in two and thus symbolically destroys the planned marriage, that is another thing, far less elementary as art. The midnight blaze that ruins Thornfield becomes more than a shock when it is seen also as the fire of purgation; the grim, almost roadless forest surrounding Ferndean is more than a harrowing stage set when it is also felt as a symbol of Rochester's closed-in life.

The point is that in various ways Charlotte manages to make the patently Gothic more than a stereotype. But more important is that she instinctively finds new ways to achieve the ends served by old Gothic—the discovery and release of new patterns of feeling, the intensification of feeling. Though only partly unconventional, Jane is nevertheless so portrayed as to evoke new feelings rather than merely exercise old ones. As a girl she is lonely, "passionate," "strange," "like nobody there"; she feels superior, rejects poverty, talks back precociously, tells truths bluntly, enjoys "the strangest sense of freedom," tastes "vengeance"; she experiences a nervous shock which is said to have a lifelong effect, and the doctor says "nerves not in a good state"; she can be "reckless and feverish," "bitter and truculent"; at Thornfield she is restless, given to "bright visions," letting "imagination" picture an existence full of "life, fire, feeling." Thus Charlotte leads away from standardized characterization toward new levels of human reality, and hence from stock responses toward a new kind of passionate engagement.

Charlotte moves toward depth in various ways that have an immediate impact like that of Gothic. Jane's strange, fearful symbolic dreams are not mere thrillers but reflect the tensions of the engagement period, the stress of the wedding-day debate with Rochester, and the longing for Rochester after she has left him. The final Thornfield dream, with its vivid image of a hand coming through a cloud in place of the expected moon, is in the surrealistic vein that appears most sharply in the extraordinary pictures that Jane draws at Thornfield: here Charlotte is plumbing the psyche, not inventing a weird decor. Likewise in the telepathy scene, which Charlotte, unlike Defoe in dealing with a similar episode, does her utmost to actualize: "The feeling was not like an electric shock; but it was quite as sharp, as strange, as startling: . . . that inward sensation . . . with all its unspeakable strangeness . . . like an inspiration . . . wondrous shock of feeling." In her flair for the surreal, in her plunging into feeling that is without status in the ordinary world of the novel, Charlotte discovers a new dimension of Gothic.

She does this most thoroughly in her portrayal of characters and of the relations between them. If in Rochester we see only an Angrian-Byronic hero and a Charlotte wish-fulfillment figure (the two identifications that to some readers seem entirely to place him), we miss what is more significant, the exploration of personality that opens up new areas of feeling in intersexual relationships. Beyond the "grim," the "harsh," the eccentric, the almost histrionically cynical that superficially distinguish Rochester from conventional heroes, there is something almost Laurentian: Rochester is "neither tall nor graceful"; his eyes can be "dark, irate, and piercing"; his strong features "took my feelings from my own power and fettered them in his." Without using the vocabulary common to us, Charlotte is presenting maleness and physicality, to which Jane responds directly. She is "assimilated" to him by "something in my brain and heart, in my blood and nerves"; she "must love" and "could not unlove" him; the thought of parting from him is "agony." Rochester's oblique amatory maneuvers become almost punitive in the Walter-to-Griselda style and once reduce her to sobbing "convulsively"; at times the love-game borders on a power-game. Jane, who prefers "rudeness" to "flattery," is an instinctive evoker of passion: she learns "the pleasure of vexing and soothing him by turns" and pursues a "system" of working him up "to considerable irritation" and coolly leaving him; when, as a result, his caresses become grimaces, pinches, and tweaks, she records that, sometimes at least, she "decidedly preferred these fierce favors." She reports, "I crushed his hand . . . red with the passionate pressure"; she "could not . . . see God for his creature," and in her devotion Rochester senses "an earnest, religious energy."

Charlotte's remolding of stock feeling reaches a height when she sympathetically portrays Rochester's efforts to make Jane his mistress; here the stereotyped seducer becomes a kind of lost nobleman of passion, and of specifically physical passion: "Every atom of your flesh is as dear to me as my own." The intensity of the pressure which he puts upon her is matched, not by the fear and revulsion of the popular heroine, but by a responsiveness that she barely masters: "The crisis was perilous; but not without its charm." She is "tortured by a sense of remorse at thus hurting his feelings"; at the moment of decision "a hand of fiery iron grasped my vitals . . . blackness, burning! . . . my intolerable duty"; she leaves in "despair"; after she has left, "I longed to be his; I panted to return"; and for the victory of principle, "I abhorred myself . . . I was hateful in my own eyes." This extraordinary openness to feeling, this escape from the bondage of the trite, continues in the Rivers relationship, which is a structural parallel to the Rochester affair: just as in Rochester the old sex villain is seen in a new perspective, so in Rivers the clerical hero is radically refashioned; and Jane's almost accepting a would-be husband is given the aesthetic status of a regrettable yielding to a seducer. Without a remarkable liberation from conventional feeling Charlotte could not fathom the complexity of Rivers—the earnest and dutiful clergyman distraught by a profound inner turmoil of conflicting "drives": sexuality, restlessness, hardness, pride, ambition ("fever in his vitals," "inexorable as death"); the hypnotic, almost inhuman potency of his influence on Jane, who feels "a freezing spell," "an awful charm," an "iron shroud"; the relentlessness, almost the unscrupulousness, of his wooing, the resultant fierce struggle (like that with Rochester), Jane's brilliantly perceptive accusation, "you almost hate me . . . you would kill me. You are killing me now"; and yet her mysterious near-surrender: "I was tempted to cease struggling with him—to rush down the torrent of his will into the gulf of his existence, and there lose my own."

Aside from partial sterilization of banal Gothic by dry factuality and humor, Charlotte goes on to make a much more important—indeed, a radical—revision of the mode: in *Jane Eyre* and in the other novels, as we shall see, that discovery of passion, that rehabilitation of the extra-rational, which is the historical office of Gothic, is no longer oriented in marvelous circumstance but moves deeply into the lesser-known realities of human life. This change I describe as the change from "old Gothic" to "new Gothic." The kind of appeal is the same; the fictional method is utterly different.

ii

When Charlotte went on from *Jane Eyre* to *Shirley*, she produced a book that for the student of the Gothic theme is interesting precisely because on the face of things it would be expected to be a barren field. It is the result of Charlotte's one deliberate venture from private intensities into public extensities: Orders in Council, the Luddites, technological unemployment in 1811 and 1812, a social portraiture that develops Charlotte's largest cast of characters. Yet Charlotte cannot keep it a social novel. Unlike Robert Penn Warren, who in the somewhat similar *Night Rider* chose to reflect the historical economic crisis in the private crisis of the hero, Brontë loses interest in the public and slides over into the private.

The formal irregularities of *Shirley*—the stop-and-start, zigzag movement, plunging periodically into different perspectives—light up the divergent impulses in Charlotte herself: the desire to make a story from observed outer life, and the inability to escape from inner urgencies that with centrifugal force unwind outward into story almost autonomously. Passion alters plan: the story of industrial crisis is repeatedly swarmed over by the love stories. But the ultimate complication is that Charlotte's duality of impulse is reflected not only in the narrative material but in two different ways of telling each part of the story. On the one hand she tells a rather conventional, open, predictable tale; on the other she lets go with a highly charged private sentiency that may subvert the former or at least surround it with an atmosphere of unfamiliarity or positive strangeness: the Gothic impulse.

For Charlotte it is typically the "pattern" versus the "strange." She describes "two pattern young ladies, in pattern attire, with pattern deportment"—a "respectable society" in which "Shirley had the air of a black swan, or a white crow." When, in singing, Shirley "poured round the passion, force," the young ladies thought this "strange" and concluded: "What was *strange* must be *wrong.*" True, Charlotte's characters live within the established "patterns" of life; but their impulse is to vitalize forms with unpatterned feeling, and Charlotte's to give play to unpatterned feeling in all its forms. She detects the warrior in the Reverend Matthew Helstone; reports that Malone the curate "had energy enough in hate"; describes Shirley weeping without apparent reason; recounts Mrs. Yorke's paranoid "brooding, eternal, immitigable suspicion of all men, things, creeds, and parties"; portrays Hiram Yorke as scornful, stubborn, intolerant of superiors, independent, truculent, benevolent toward inferiors, his virtues surrounding an aggressive *amour propre.*

Shirley is given a vehement, sweeping, uninhibited criticalness of mind; in her highly articulate formulations of incisive thought is released a furious rush of emotional energy. Within the framework of moral principles her ideas and feelings are untrammeled. She vigorously debunks clichés against charity, but against the mob she will defend her property "like a tigress"; to Yorke's face she does a corrosive analysis of his personality; she attacks Milton in a fiery sweeping paean to Eve, the "mother" of "Titans"; in an almost explosive defense of love she attacks ignorant, chilly, refined, embarrassed people who "blaspheme living fire, seraph-brought from a divine altar"; when she insists that she must "*love*" before she marries, her "worldly" Uncle Sympson retorts, "Preposterous stuff!—indecorous—unwomanly!"

Beside the adults who in ways are precocious are the precocious children—the Yorkes who have their parents' free-swinging, uninhibited style of talk; Henry Sympson, having for his older cousin Shirley an attachment that borders on sexual feeling; and most of all Martin Yorke, aged fifteen, to whose excited pursuit of Caroline, almost irrelevant to plot or theme, Charlotte devotes two and a half zestful chapters. Martin is willing to help Caroline see Robert Moore, "her confounded sweetheart," in order to be near her himself, and he plans to claim a reward "displeasing to Moore"; he thinks of her physical beauties. Once he gets between Robert and Caroline at goodbye time; "he half carried Caroline down the stairs," "wrapped her shawl round her," and wanted to claim a kiss. At the same time he feels "power over her," he wants her to coax him, and he would like "to put her in a passion—to make her cry." Charlotte subtly conveys the sexuality of his quest—a rare feat in the nineteenth-century novel.

In Robert Moore, the unpopular mill-owner, Charlotte finds less social rightness or wrongness than his strength, his masculine appeal; her sympathy, so to speak, is for the underside of his personality. It "agreed with Moore's temperament . . . to be generally hated"; "he liked a silent, sombre, unsafe solitude"; against the vandals his "hate is still running in such a strong current" that he has none left for other objects; he shows "a terrible half" of himself in pursuing rioters with "indefatigable, . . . relentless assiduity"; this "excitement" pleases him; sadistically he likes to "force" magistrates to "betray a certain fear." He is the great lover of the story; he almost breaks Caroline's heart before he marries her, and he even has a subtle impact on Shirley, teasingly communicated, though officially denied, by Charlotte. What Caroline yields to is his "secret power," which affects her "like a spell." Here again Charlotte records, as directly as she can, simple sexual attractiveness. From the problem novel she veers off into "new Gothic"; in old Gothic, her hero would have been a villain.

True to convention, the love stories end happily. But special feelings, a new pathos of love, come through. Louis Moore demands in a woman something "to endure, . . . to reprimand"; love must involve "prickly peril," "a sting now and then"; for him the "young lioness or leopardess" is better than the lamb. There is that peculiarly tense vivacity of talk between lovers (the Jane-Rochester style), who discover a heightened, at times stagey, yet highly communicative rhetoric, drawing now on fantasy, now on moral conviction, verging now on titillating revelation, now on battle; a crafty game of love, flirting with an undefined risk, betraying a withheld avowal, savoring the approach to consummation, as if the erotic energy that in another social order might find a physical outlet were forcing itself into an electric language that is decorous but intimately exploratory. Between Louis Moore, who has "a thirst for freedom," and Shirley, to whom finding love is the Quest for the Bridle (for "a *master* [whom it is] impossible not to love, and very possible to fear"), there is an almost disturbingly taut struggle, a fierce intensification of the duel between Mirabell and Millamant, complex feelings translated into wit, sheer debate, abusiveness of manner, and a variety of skirmishings; Louis, the lover, adopting the stance of power and consciously playing to fright; the pursuit of an elusive prey ending in virtual parody of "one calling, Child! / And I replied, My Lord"; over all of this a singular air of strained excitement, of the working of underlying emotional forces that at the climax leads to a new frenetic intensification of style in Louis's notebook:

> "Will you let me breathe, and not bewilder me? You must not smile at present. The world swims and changes round me. The sun is a dizzying scarlet blaze, the sky a violet vortex whirling over me."
> I am a strong man, but I staggered as I spoke. All creation was exaggerated: colour grew more vivid: motion more rapid; life itself more vital. I hardly saw

her for a moment; but I heard her voice—pitilessly sweet. . . . Blent with torment, I experienced rapture.

Nor does Charlotte's flair for "unpatterned feeling" stop here: Shirley, the forceful leader who has already been called "a gentleman" and "captain," languishes under the found bridle of the masterful lover, whom she treats chillily and subjects to "exquisitely provoking" postponements of marriage; he calls her a "pantheress" who "gnaws her chain"; she tells him, "I don't know myself," as if engagement had opened to her eyes a previously undetected facet of her nature. Though "these freaks" continue, she is "fettered" at last; but not before the reader is radically stirred by the felt mysteries of personality. Before Charlotte, no love story tapped such strange depths, no consummation was so like a defeat.

Here Charlotte is probing psychic disturbance and is on the edge of psychosomatic illness. The theme draws her repeatedly. When Caroline thinks Robert doesn't love her, she suffers a long physical decline, described with painful fullness. She "wasted," had a "broken spirit," suffered "intolerable despair," felt the "utter sickness of longing and disappointment," at night found "my mind darker than my hiding-place," had "melancholy dreams," became "what is called nervous," had "fears I never used to have," "an inexpressible weight on my mind," and "strange sufferings," believed at times "that God had turned His face from her" and sank "into the gulf of religious despair." Charlotte divines this: "People never die of love or grief alone; though some die of inherent maladies which the tortures of those passions prematurely force into destructive action." Caroline lingers in illness, has fancies "inscrutable to ordinary attendants," has a hallucination of talking to Robert in the garden. Shirley, having been bitten by a dog that she believes to be mad, becomes seriously ill; psychosomatic illness springs directly from Charlotte's special sensitivity to the neurotic potential in human nature. A complementary awareness, that of the impact of the physical on the psychic, appears when she observes the "terrible depression," the "inexpressible—dark, barren, impotent" state of mind of Robert when he is recovering from a gunshot wound.

To give so much space to a lesser work is justifiable only because some of its contents are of high historico-critical significance. Though *Shirley* is not pulled together formally as well as *Jane Eyre* or even the more sprawling *Villette*, and though the characters are as wholes less fully realized, still it accommodates the widest ranging of an extraordinarily free sensibility. Constantly, in many different directions, it is in flight from the ordinary rational surface of things against which old Gothic was the first rebel in fiction; it abundantly contains and evokes, to adapt

Charlotte's own metaphor, "unpatterned feeling." It turns up unexpected elements in personality: resentfulness, malice, love of power; precocities and perversities of response; the multiple tensions of love between highly individualized lovers; psychic disturbances. And in accepting a dark magnetic energy as a central virtue in personality, Charlotte simply reverses the status of men who were the villains in the sentimental and old Gothic modes.

iii

Of the four novels, *Villette* is most heavily saturated with Gothic—with certain of its traditional manifestations (old Gothic), with the undercutting of these that is for Charlotte no less instinctive than the use of them (anti-Gothic), and with an original, intense exploration of feeling that increases the range and depth of fiction (new Gothic).

As in *Jane Eyre*, Charlotte can be skillful in anti-Gothic. When Madame Beck, pussyfooting in espionage, "materializes" in shocking suddenness, Lucy is made matter-of-fact or indignant rather than thrilled with fright. "No ghost stood beside me" is her characteristic response to a Beck surprise. Once the spy, having "stolen" upon her victims, betrays her unseen presence by a sneeze: Gothic yields to farce. Technically more complex is Charlotte's use of the legend of the nun supposedly buried alive and of the appearances of a visitant taken to be the ghost of the nun: Charlotte coolly distances herself from this by having Lucy dismiss the legend as "romantic rubbish" and by explaining the apparitions as the playful inventions of a giddy lover. True, she keeps the secret long enough to get a few old Gothic thrills from the "ghost," but what she is really up to is using the apparitions in an entirely new way; that is, for responses that lie beyond the simplicities of terror.

First, the apparitions are explained as a product of Lucy's own psychic state, the product, Dr. John suggests, of "long-continued mental conflict." In the history of Gothic this is an important spot, for here we first see the shift from stock explanations and responses to the inner human reality: fiction is slowly discovering the psychic depths known to drama for centuries.

Then, when Lucy next sees the nun, she responds in a way that lies entirely outside fictional convention: "I neither fled nor shrieked . . . I spoke . . . I stretched out my hand, for I meant to touch her." Not that Lucy is not afraid, but she is testing herself—an immense change from the expectable elementary response: the frisson disappears before the complexer action that betokens a maturing of personality.

Finally, Paul and Lucy both see the specter and are thus brought closer together: they have had what they call "impressions," and through sharing the ghost they assume a shared sensibility. Paul says, "I was conscious of rapport between you and myself." The rapport is real, though the proof of it is false; the irony of this is a subtle sophistication of Gothic.

The responsiveness, the sensitivity, is the thing; many passages place "feeling" above "seeing" as an avenue of knowledge. Reason must be respected, for it is "vindictive," but at times imagination must be yielded to, like a sexual passion at once feared and desired. There is the summer night when the sedative given by Madame Beck has a strange effect:

> Imagination was roused from her rest, and she came forth impetuous and venturous. With scorn she looked on Matter, her mate—
>
> "Rise!" she said; "Sluggard! this night I will have *my* will; nor shalt thou prevail."
>
> "Look forth and view the night!" was her cry; and when I lifted the heavy blind from the casement close at hand—with her own royal gesture, she showed me a moon supreme, in an element deep and splendid.
>
> . . . She lured me to leave this den and follow her forth into dew, coolness, and glory.

There follows the most magnificent of all Charlotte's nocturnes: that vision of the "moonlit, midnight park," the brilliance of the fête, the strange charm of places and people, recounted in a rhythmical, enchanted style (the "Kubla Khan" mode) which at first reading gives the air of a dream mistaken for reality to what is in fact reality made like a dream. This is a surrealistic, trancelike episode that makes available to fiction a vast new territory and idiom. The surrealistic is, despite Montague Summers, one of the new phases of Gothic, which in its role of liberator of feeling characteristically explores the nonnaturalistic: to come up, as here, with a profounder nature, or a nature freshly, even disturbingly, seen.

The surrealism of Lucy's evening is possible only to a special sensitivity, and it is really the creation of this sensitivity, in part pathological, that is at the apex of Charlotte's Gothic. In *The Professor* the tensions in the author's contemplation of her own experience come into play; in *Shirley* various undercurrents of personality push up into the social surfaces of life; in *Jane Eyre* moral feeling is subjected to the remolding pressures of a newly vivid consciousness of the diverse impulses of sexuality; and in *Villette* the feeling responses to existence are pursued into sufferings that edge over into disorder. The psychology of rejection and alienation, first applied to Polly, becomes the key to Lucy, who, finding no catharsis for a sense of desolation, generates a serious inner turmoil. She suffers from "a terrible oppression" and then from "anxiety lying in wait on enjoyment, like a tiger crouched in a jungle . . . his fierce heart panted close against mine; . . . I knew he waited only for sun-down to bound ravenous from his ambush." Depression is fed by the conflict between a loveless routine of life and her longings, which she tried to put down like "Jael to Sisera, driving a nail through their temples"; but this only "transiently stunned" them and "at intervals [they] would turn on the nail with a rebellious wrench: then did the temples bleed, and the brain thrill to its core."

These strains prepare us for the high point in Charlotte's new Gothic—the study of Lucy's emotional collapse and near breakdown when vacation comes and she is left alone at the school with "a poor deformed and imbecile pupil." "My heart almost died within me; . . . My spirits had long been gradually sinking; now that the prop of employment was withdrawn, they went down fast." After three weeks, storms bring on "a deadlier paralysis"; and "my nervous system could hardly support" the daily strain. She wanders in the street: "A goad thrust me on, a fever forbade me to rest." She observes a "growing illusion" and says, "My nerves are getting overstretched." She feels that "a malady is growing upon" her mind, and she asks herself, "How shall I keep well?" Then come "a peculiarly agonizing depression"; a nine-days storm; "a strange fever of the nerves and blood"; continuing insomnia, broken only by a terrifying nightmare of alienation. She flees the house and experiences the climactic event of her illness: she goes to a church and despite the intensity of her Protestant spirit enters the confessional to find relief.

From now on, overtly or implicitly, hypochondria and anxiety keep appearing in the story—the enemies from whose grip Lucy must gradually free herself. At a concert she spots the King as a fellow victim of "that strangest spectre, Hypochondria," for on his face she sees its marks, whose meaning, "if I did not *know*, at least I *felt*." When, after her return to Beck's on a rainy night, things are not going well, a letter from Dr. John is "the ransom from my terror," and its loss drives her almost to frenzy. She describes night as "an unkindly time" when she has strange fancies, doubts, the "horror of calamity." She is aware of her "easily-deranged temperament." Beyond this area of her own self-understanding we see conflicts finding dramatic expression in her almost wild acceptance of Rachel's passionate acting of Phèdre ("a spectacle low, horrible, immoral"), which counterbalances her vehement condemnation of a fleshy nude by Rubens (one of the "materialists"). Paul identifies her, in a figure whose innocence for him is betrayed by the deep, if not wholly conscious, understanding that leads Charlotte to write it: "a young she wild creature, new caught, untamed, viewing with a mixture of fire and fear the first entrance of the breaker in."

There is not room to trace Lucy's recovery, especially in the important phase, the love affair with Paul which is related to our theme by compelling, as do the Jane-Rochester and Louis Moore–Shirley relationships in quite different ways, a radical revision of the feelings exacted by stereotyped romance. What is finally noteworthy is that Charlotte, having chosen in Lucy a heroine with the least durable emotional equipment, with the most conspicuous neurotic element in her temperament, goes on through the history of Lucy's emotional maturing to surmount the need for romantic fulfillment and to develop the aesthetic courage for a final disaster—the only one in her four novels.

Some years ago Edmund Wilson complained of writers of Gothic who "fail to lay hold on the terrors that lie deep in the human soul and that cause man to fear himself" and proposed an anthology of horror stories that probe "psychological caverns" and find "disquieting obsessions." This is precisely the direction in which Charlotte Brontë moved, especially in Lucy Snowe and somewhat also in Caroline Helstone and Shirley Keeldar; this was one aspect of her following human emotions where they took her, into many depths and intensities that as yet hardly had a place in the novel. This was the finest achievement of Gothic.

Gothic is variously defined. Leslie Fiedler has implied that Gothic is shoddy mystery-mongering, whereas F. Cudworth Flint has defined the Gothic tradition, which he considers "nearly central in American literature," as "a literary exploration of the avenues to death." For Montague Summers, on the other hand, Gothic was the essence of romanticism, and romanticism was the literary expression of supernaturalism. Both these latter definitions, though they are impractically inclusive, have suggestive value. For originally Gothic was one of a number of aesthetic developments that served to breach the "classical" and "rational" order of life and to make possible a kind of response, and a response to a kind of thing, that among the knowing had long been taboo. In the novel it was the function of Gothic to open horizons beyond social patterns, rational decisions, and institutionally approved emotions; in a word, to enlarge the sense of reality and its impact on the human being. It became then a great liberator of feeling. It acknowledged the nonrational—in the world of things and events, occasionally in the realm of the transcendental, ultimately and most persistently in the depths of the human being. (Richardson might have started this, but his sense of inner forces was usually overlaid by the moralistic; thus his followers all ran after him only when he ran the wrong way.) The first Gothic writers took the easy way: the excitement of mysterious scene and happening, which I call old Gothic. Of this Charlotte Brontë made some direct use, while at the same time tending toward humorous modifications (anti-Gothic); but what really counts is its indirect usefulness to her: it released her from the patterns of the novel of society and therefore permitted the flowering of her real talent—the talent for finding and giving dramatic form to impulses and feelings which, because of their depth or mysteriousness or intensity or ambiguity, or their ignoring or transcending of everyday norms of propriety or reason, increase wonderfully the sense of reality in the novel. To note the emergence of this "new Gothic" in Charlotte Brontë is not, I think, to pursue an old mode into dusty corners but rather to identify historically the distinguishing, and distinguished, element in her work.

4

The Comedy of Conscience:
Trollope's *The Warden*

i

IN CHAPTER 16 of Anthony Trollope's *The Warden*—the sixth from the end—the Reverend Septimus Harding, "verging on sixty years," runs away from the Barchester cathedral to London, plays a nervous hide-and-seek for a day, survives for a nocturnal rendezvous with a lawyer, and is finally put on the carpet by his kindly firm, motherly daughter and his severely paternal son-in-law. These episodes, rambling along with the familiar Trollope unhurriedness, are funny enough. Yet at first contact with them we may sense an invitation to a too-easy response—that of the ancient game against the simple soul. In this game, good sense belongs to the worldlings, and the unworldly are likely to resemble the village idiot. It is a structure that Boccaccio likes; in his version of it, the world of sexual sophistication has the laugh on the ignoramus. The latter is so biologically uninformed that he gratifies the knowing reader, who is free to smirk condescendingly at the simple soul. This is too easy an experience for an adult, unless of course he happens to be hampered by the simple soul within himself.

In his treatment of naïveté, however, the writer need not stop at ridicule. In the kind of Boccaccio tale that I have mentioned, ignorance, though laughable, is curable by education; in the exercises proposed by an ingenious tutor, the ignoramus gets the hang of things and ripens rapidly in the joy of new learning. The reader who laughed from above now grins in fellowship; we are all in the carnality guild together. Conversely, naïveté may be made the carrier of virtue, as in noble-savage fiction. Here the simple soul is the true philosopher; we identify easily with this unsophisticated man, for through him we lay bare the ways of the world and become wiser than sophistication itself.

Trollope neither converts his simple soul to worldliness nor makes him the pat exposer of worldliness; thus he avoids the ancient in-group ploy and the later romantic-outsider ploy. His method is less obvious: he never forgets the laughableness of simplicity, but he discovers its estimableness too. Insofar as he asks sympathy—that is, dramatic identification—with the simple soul, he may encounter a certain unarticulated

55

resistance in us. Though we do not want to be caught in the latent sadism of deriding the unworldly, we also live in an age that shies away from the sensibility of unworldliness and that hardly questions its own bias toward the metropolitan, the knowing, the modish. To be allied with the simple soul may revive all the distress of remembered insufficiency in affairs, deprive us of all our laboriously inlaid sophistication, our finished hardwood at-home-ness in the world.

Any uncertainty in our response to Harding is likely to be increased by what at first glance we may take to be Trollope's own uncertainty about his course. He seems only to happen upon Harding's anxiety now and then as he wanders around in other terrains—accounts of a tea party and of Grantly's children, essays on the Pre-Raphaelites and morning services at Westminster, parodies of contemporaries, and mock-heroic jests. If Harding is in serious trouble, why bother with his petty embarrassments at chophouse and "cigar divan"? And if the Barchester world is an image of reality, why undermine it by using such names as "Haphazard" and "Quiverful"? Or forget it in an elaborate pinking of journalistic complacency? With all these apparent affronts to artistic high seriousness, Trollope succeeds in convincing some readers that he is careless, disorderly, and even trivial.

In the final six chapters of *The Warden*, however, Trollope reveals his ultimate control of the diverse materials that often seemed out of control. In these chapters the form of the book finally becomes evident. For all of his insouciant excursions and camera stops, Trollope does have a destination; the book does have a clearly segmented structure.[1] As we identify it, we see what Trollope has chosen to include, how he has arranged his materials, what pared away, what eventually focused on and, in human meaning, declared central and compelling. We see, too, how he has conceived of his materials and how disposed us toward them. From structure we move naturally to his technique and his management of genre.

ii

Harding's flight to London gives primacy to his conscience, a theme noted first by Henry James and later by other critics. In his appeasement of conscience Harding holds stage throughout the last six chapters; he successfully resists one champion of the world after another; his triumph is to reject triumph in the world's terms. His stands come one after another in an unbroken line; even the last-chapter Victorian survey of other careers hardly disturbs the linear structure.

Despite the hit-or-miss air of the book, Trollope did not just chance upon Harding's conscience after trying other alternatives. In chapter 1,

Harding, hearing of "murmurs" in which "there might be truth," increases the daily "pittance" of the old men, and in chapter 2 he is "becoming uneasy."[2] In chapter 3, John Bold, the reforming physician, calls on Harding; as a result "for many a long, long day" Harding "was neither happy nor at ease." In chapter 5, Harding is embarrassed and pained by Grantly's dressing down of the old men, and, fearful of opprobrium if his position is actually questionable, "he became all but fixed in his resolve that some great step must be taken." When, in chapter 9, Grantly brings him the news that they are safe because of Bold's legal errors, Harding slides still closer to the slough of despond. In chapter 10 his low spirits are so evident that his follower Bunce believes, quite ironically, that Bold has won. Harding dreams of "escape," but he still fears Grantly. "'Give it up!' Oh if he only could." But by chapter 13 an antagonistic editorial in the *Jupiter* drives him toward resignation, though as yet the only step clearly in mind is a trip to London to "have this matter settled some way." On that course he embarks in chapter 16.

On the one hand Trollope makes a conventional preparation for focusing on Harding in the final six chapters. On the other, he has gradually identified, among all the issues he has introduced, the one with greatest artistic potential. This is remarkable, for he did not intend to write a story of conscience. His original purpose, he tells us in the *Autobiography*, was to satirize ecclesiastical graspingness and journalistic excess. Fortunately he was, as he puts it, "not the man," that is, not the partisan satirist, for these "two objects" (the first of which he turned over to characters whom he saw in humorous perspective). Trollope uses other words that contribute to our continuing debate on the role of "intention": *The Warden*, he says, "failed altogether in the purport for which it was intended."[3] It succeeded, we may say, because Trollope did not impose a prior intention on the materials but discovered better formal possibilities latent in them.

Trollope's first discovery is the repercussive quality of a legal action; Bold's suit inaugurates many nonlegal actions. It excites the combative spirit of the church militant in Dr. Grantly, who can move vigorously in different arenas. It puts Bold's sister Mary and his fiancée-to-be, Eleanor Harding, into a conflict of loyalties, and Eleanor in turn imposes a more serious conflict upon Bold. It stirs the Bishop into new exercises of friendship, and various lawyers into considering their profits. It leads some of the bedesmen into dreams of profit, some of them into a conflict of loyalties, and all of them into a microcosmic civil war. It calls into play the reforming spirit of the age, which finds an outlet in editorials, pamphlets, and popular fiction. Above all, of course, it catalyzes Harding's conscience.

It is as if Trollope had a hyperactive associational fancy and let it rip in all directions; as if he were discovering so many relevant issues that they could not be brought together in a unity. But there is a unity, I am convinced, and we can approach it by considering the presence and extent of several different kinds of formal control exercised by novelists. We sometimes claim "thematic" or "tonal" unity when events seem diffuse and yet do not give us a total sense of ungoverned diffuseness. Thematic unity *The Warden* has: the theme of reform is directly or indirectly present in almost every episode. Tonal unity there assuredly is: Trollope rarely departs from the manner of an amiably smiling Olympian, though he may sharpen it a little for satire, or soften it a little with sentiment. A third approach, and a more interesting one in its theoretic implications, is to see *The Warden* as a multiplicity novel, with the parts paralleling or succeeding each other in the manner of variations—say the romantic, familial, institutional, social, publicist, legal, and spiritual versions of a crisis. This will do up to a point. The difficulty is that, whereas in a true multiplicity novel the variations persist in unending separate courses, their nonnegotiable counterclaims rarely admitting of resolution, Trollope judges, cuts off, resolves. The essential multiplicitarian, though he may have preferences among multiple alternatives, cannot deny to any of them the kind of validity which they have by enduring; he has to keep on portraying them because they keep on existing. Trollope judges that one is of less significance than another, and he gets rid of it; he keeps doing this until he has only one alternative left. This is the most important one, and to it he gives the fullest attention—the response of conscience to crisis.

iii

Thus in the act of seeing that *The Warden* does not have a true multiplicity structure we perceive what its structure is: it achieves form by moving from the less essential to the more essential, from the peripheral to the central, from a many-phased situation to a single action. At first Trollope seems to be saying that many perspectives must be kept in mind; at the end, that only one of these can be held to at length. His structure is climactic. What is more, it reveals an underlying sense of proportion: the story divides itself into thirds—really very neatly, but with just enough irregularity so that the neatness is not thrust at us like a parcel but has to be discovered. The twenty-one chapters fall naturally into groups of eight, seven, and six.

In the first eight chapters Trollope initiates action on all fronts—the romantic (in his own ho-hum way), the familial, the ecclesiastical, the societal and political, the editorial and homiletic, the ethical. But at the center is the legal. Bold's suit is the primum mobile without which there would be no unhappy lovers, troubled families, archidiaconal militancy, parliamentary speeches, journalistic fervor. In all ways the novel seems pointed toward a climactic court scene, a full-dress legal duel that will settle all fates. Then suddenly in chapter 8 this likelihood disappears, and the first part ends.

In thus quashing Bold's suit, Trollope says in effect that though it is initiatory, it is not intrinsically important. Yet Trollope also sees that the lines of action inaugurated by the suit are not so easily ended; they have now taken on a momentum of their own. Bold, the scourge of malfeasance ("His passion is the reform of all abuses" [2]), has cracked his whip, and immediately there have come into play, in different quarters, self-interest, self-protection, self-sacrifice, and self-doubt. They do not easily subside. Trollope follows their courses in the second and third parts of the novel; the second part is panoramic, the third has a single focus. Trollope moves, as we have noted, from spread to intensity, from consequences in general to the most significant consequence.

Even in the panoramic second part, Harding is conspicuous enough to foreshadow his eventual primacy. In his self doubt he also doubts Grantly, now a figure of self-interest triumphant. Harding unintentionally misleads his chief supporter in the hospital as well as his daughter. She resolves on self-sacrifice, but in attempting it, she puts so much pressure on John Bold that his self-protection as a lover leads to his self-sacrifice as a reformer. His self-sacrifice exposes him to arrogant abuse by Grantly's self-interest, and her self-sacrificial effort, triumphant though it is, leaves her dissatisfied because her father's self-doubt inhibits the gratitude she expects (the lively scenes of Bold humiliated and Eleanor unappreciated are juxtaposed in an excellent parallelism). In self-interest the *Jupiter* continues to attack clerical misconduct ("the *Jupiter* is never wrong" [14]), and the theme is taken up by Dr. Pessimist Anticant in a pamphlet, *Modern Charity*, and by Mr. Popular Sentiment in a novel, *The Almshouse*—brilliant parodies of Carlyle and Dickens, burlesques that have endured a singular history of puristic and misguided abuse. They are relevant in the panoramic or multiplicity structure, and they make concrete the polemics that Harding has feared. Trollope obviously enjoys his satire of the self-righteousness and self-deception of journalism. (He does wander off course a little in his critique of the Pre-Raphaelites, to whom Tom Towers the journalist is addicted [14].) Chapter 15 ends the broad survey of certain personal, familial, and social responses to and consequences of reformist actions. Among all the echoes of the prime event, only one is vigorously intransigent—the echo in Harding's conscience. It is the subject of the third part of the novel.

In chapters 16–21 either Harding holds the stage alone, or others who share it are seen only in their relationship to him. He runs away from Grantly to London, spends a solitary day waiting to see Sir Abraham Haphazard (16), and then talks with him at 10:00 P.M. (17). Sir Abraham has a counterpoint role: his letter-of-the-law view throws him into astonished incredulity at Harding's resolve to surrender what is "not justly mine." Harding is next seen in contrast with his daughter and son-in-law, the Grantlys: they urge him not to resign, but he is immovable (18–19). He escapes them and returns alone from London to Barchester. For a moment he is offstage, but now he is talked about by Grantly and his lawyers, Cox and Cumming, who duplicate Sir Abraham's amazement at the Warden's "madness." But they push the action ahead by coming up with a new strategy for "saving something out of the fire" (19), namely, getting Harding to exchange posts with Quiverful, the needy father of twelve, who could endure all journalistic attacks. So Harding goes on from resistance against pressures to resistance against temptation—that of the Quiverful pulpit and, in addition, of two offers of succor from his friend the Bishop. Then he moves to smaller quarters, his actions and manner observed by all. The last in the series of contrasts in this third part is that between Harding and the bedesmen, and it is rightly a relatively long scene: his good conscience against their uneasy consciences.

So from a great quantity of materials, which at times seem to follow each other haphazardly, a very orderly tripartite structure emerges. In shorthand: the legal issue, the social issues, the moral issue. To put it thus is to underscore another aspect of structure already mentioned: the climactic arrangement of parts. But with Trollope, climax is a rather tricky affair.

iv

Take part 3 and its conclusion: the most important theme is the final one, and the action ends in the Warden's triumph. Climax. But the climactic triumph is not quite usual; the triumph is that of the whisper over the shout (Grantly "has been somewhat loud" [2]), the triumph of surrender over victory. Harding has won content by settling for a small fragment of the world that he could have held on to in its entirety. His former wards have won discontent by having to settle for a smaller fragment of the world than they had. If this is nemesis for trying to grab more of it than they had, it is less a climactic thunder of justice than a mild ironic ricochet of events. Victory and defeat are both soft-pedaled; the climaxes may be said to have in them something of the anticlimactic. This term, which we usually apply to structure, takes us automatically into an aspect of Trollope's method.

At the end of part 1, as we have noted, Trollope suddenly kills off the legal issue that had seemed to be heading toward a final decisive court clash. The legal issue goes out not with a bang but almost with a yawn; Trollope "throws it away," as it were, in an unaccented conversation in which Chadwick tells Grantly that in Bold's suit there is a technical flaw which in effect sends the reformist attack down the drain. The casual manner contributes to our momentary sense that the center has dropped out of the story. Insofar as the actions under way have led us to anticipate a courtroom climax, the solution by procedural error, dropped without warning into a chapter devoted largely to other matters, is an anticlimax. This, as we shall see, is characteristic of Trollope, for he has a deflationary kind of genius. And yet his anticlimax can have its own ambiguities. It can be an end in itself, it can be a form of comment, or it can be a door to another kind of climactic movement. Here, it is this last: when the apparently central legal operation is deflated, we go on to a more significant kind of action. But then, within this action and at the end of it, as we shall see, there are drop-away devices that help define a Trollope brand of irony.

Trollope has a flair for the ironic letdown, not the pratfall or the reductio ad absurdum or the puncturing of a balloon so much as the lesser blow instead of the expected big punch, and yet the lesser blow that has a double-take effect in at first seeming less than it is. He can do this in style as well as action. Grantly has been trying to persuade Harding not to resign: "The archdeacon's speech had silenced him—stupefied him—annihilated him; anything but satisfied him" (9). The first three verbs are in a rising series; in the fourth there is a palpable dropdown—until, in a split-second redo of our response, we catch, beneath the blunt decrescendo, a definition of a more fundamental, thoroughgoing kind of impact that Grantly, with all his power, has not managed.

The irony that involves an ambiguous diminishment appears in the mock-heroic that Trollope uses intermittently throughout *The Warden*. At the beginning there stalks in Barchester a personified Scandal (1), who echoes the Fama that *crescit eundo*; near the end we have Quiverful, a "wretched clerical Priam," struggling desperately "to feed his poor Hecuba and a dozen of Hectors" (20). The Warden, trying to get people to mix at his tea party, is a "general" trying to "induce a charge," and the eventual social intercourse is described in military terms; at a table of whist the archdeacon triumphs like an epic hero in single combat, crying "as David did Goliath" when "at the fourth assault he pins to the earth a prostrate king" (6).

If these are casual jests at the unepical quality of Barchester doings and doers, something a little more complex is going on when Trollope devotes considerable space to presenting *The Times* as *The Jupiter* (hurling "Thunderbolts" [7]) and its realm as "Mount Olympus" (14), and when he turns Bold into a legendary reformer and Eleanor Harding into a mythic figure of sacrifice. (Compared with those of Joyce, Trollope's classical parallels are less plotted and systematic; the playful amateur precedes the brilliant pedant.) *The Jupiter* gets most of two chapters, and Bold and Eleanor each part of a chapter. Bold has "all the self-assurance of a Danton" (2); his mock-heroic position is more fully developed later when his sister Mary challenges his reformist moves. Note these sentences, occurring one each on successive pages, but connected by their structure: "And Bold began to comfort himself in the warmth of his own virtue." "And Bold consoled himself with the consolation of a Roman." "And the Barchester Brutus went out to fortify his own resolution by meditations on his own virtue" (6). Trollope uses the same device to connect the section on Bold with one on Eleanor: "And then she slept; and then she arose . . . ; and met her father; . . . and then . . . she started on the commencement of her operations." Here, in a chapter entitled "Iphigenia," he chronicles Eleanor's plan to save her father by sacrificing her love for Bold: she will be a substitute victim. She speaks "with a staid and solemn air, quite worthy of Jephthah's daughter or of Iphigenia either" (11).

But this is more than mock-heroic, more than ironic letdown. Trollope is not merely saying that *The Times* is laughable as Jupiter, Bold is laughable as Brutus, Eleanor is laughable as Iphigenia. Not that littleness is not amusingly revealed by the juxtaposition of bigness. But littleness can take on another dimension by self-conscious aspiration or by purging itself. In Bold we can see both—a grasping at the heroic but then, more conspicuously, a relinquishment of role and an acceptance of punishment. Imagine the historical Brutus yielding to a give-it-up Portia, visiting Caesar to withdraw his challenge, and being dreadfully abused at the moment of sacrifice. Even for the pseudo-Brutus to go through these steps is to grow, at least in sympathy. Besides, Bold, who once felt elation at finding the paper a co-partisan (7), finally sees through *The Jupiter*—its love of power and its presentation of its own "private interests" as the pursuit of "public justice" (15). With Bold, the mock-heroic leads on into a recovery of ordinary human status and to the virtue of helping expose *The Times*.

The judgment on *The Times* is not that it is not Olympian but that it has taken itself to be and wants to be. Trollope makes this point brilliantly in his description of Tom Towers, the journalist, as "studiously striving to look a man, but knowing within his breast that he was a god" (14). The man who is amusingly insignificant if compared with God evokes a different response when he wants to be God or takes himself to be; the comic laughter at diminutiveness shifts into the satiric revelation of disingenuousness and vanity. Though the newspaper is Trollope's largest target, his treatment of it is partly echoed in his treatment of Eleanor. It is not that as a sacrificial victim she is a pygmy compared to Iphigenia, but that she manages to obtain the goal of sacrifice without sacrifice; as Trollope sums up, "And so [again the quasi-heroic initial "And"] the altar on the shore of the modern Aulis reeked with no sacrifice" (11). By a sheer instinct for tactics she plays Ann Whitfield to Bold's Jack Tanner: Trollope is inadvertently a pre-Shavian theorist of the Life Force. Eleanor grows from laughable mock-heroic daughter, earns respect, and evokes, if not exactly fear, at least a certain watchfulness.

V

Trollope's quasi-deflationary strategy, with its gradually emerging convolutions that belie the simplicity of demeanor, reaches a height in the treatment of Harding. If his daughter Eleanor is Iphigenia, Harding of course is Agamemnon, and Trollope spells it out: "Was not so good an Agamemnon worthy of an Iphigenia?" (11). Since we have already been told that Harding lacks a general's skill, and since he is already thinking of withdrawing from a throne instead of toppling a rival kingdom, the Agamemnon metaphor seems initially to do no more than remind us again of Harding's nonheroic proportions. But already he has been feeling his way toward the personal action that, running counter to the urgings of everyone around him, betokens a moral quality such as is indeed found in heroes. As Trollope puts it, in another of the epigrams that abound in *The Warden,* "What he could not endure was, that he should be accused by others, and not acquitted by himself" (9). Once more the double take. Our quick first unspoken assumption: an anticlimax, in that we want to be absolved in public as thoroughly as we are in private by the more lenient judge inhabiting the self. But then we flash to the second recognition: that for Harding the tougher judge is actually the one within. Harding continues growing into the hero who acts by the firm inner light rather than by the easier shading of the socially admissible, who is "not so anxious to prove himself right as to be so" (3). He gains the quality that not only justifies but necessitates his holding the stage from chapter 16 on.

Yet again in this last third of the tale, finally and most strikingly, the technique of the mock-heroic or the letdown. For how does Trollope present the hero of conscience? As a runaway, a jittery fugitive from justice, and finally as a fearful and awkward boy. Harding has to "give his son-in-law the slip"; he has a convict's "dread of detection" "on the morning of his escape to London." For one day he feels "safe." He hopes to "throw the archdeacon off the scent." He makes "a most piteous entreaty" to Sir Abraham Haphazard. He thinks repeatedly of "escape," and he "take[s] sanctuary in Westminster Abbey" (16). So far we might feel only that we are to be amused, if sympathetically, by the unheroic diffidence of a foolish person not up to confronting authorities recklessly defied.

Then Trollope goes a mock-heroic step beyond the picture of Harding as a drolly incompetent outlaw. After his 10:00 P.M. interview with Sir Abraham, Harding returns to his hotel "with a palpitating heart," for, though he "almost longed to escape," he anticipates punishment (17). He is right: the Grantlys are there. As the old waiter puts it, they "are waiting up for you" (18). The last deflationary subtlety: the elderly spiritual hero as naughty little boy brought to book by his seniors. Here, of course, Trollope is not extemporizing but is capitalizing on some earlier groundwork. Backing away from a financial discussion with Bold, Harding himself insists, "I'm as ignorant as a child" (3). Grantly tells him, "a child is not more innocent than you are in matters of business" (9). Harding and Eleanor speak together of the archdeacon "as two children might of a stern, unpopular, but still respected schoolmaster" (10). Having planted these hints, Trollope makes the most of them when he calls Harding a "truant" in London (16) and has him, like a disobedient child after staying out too late, brought to the bar of parental justice—"a runaway school-boy, just recaptured by his guardian" (18). "Papa, I thought you were never coming back," his daughter chides him in a perennial maternal idiom. As accusations pile up, the Warden is "standing on the rug, moving uneasily from one foot to another"—literally on the carpet, a child made uneasy by guilt. His daughter refuses to go to bed, however, fearing that "her papa might be bullied if she were away"—the mother, though offended, still protecting son against father. Questioned further, the "warden hung his head, and made no reply"—the very image of a boy caught in misconduct. Grantly wants a "promise" of future good behavior from Harding; he finally puts his request in this climactic form: "Come, . . . promise Susan to give up this idea of resigning the wardenship." This "promise mama" leads into further pressures, and Harding gives another child's response: "A hot tear stood in each of the warden's eyes." The archdeacon closes the scene by directing to his wife a powerful summary of his frustration: "Your father is like a child" (18). Later Grantly makes one more effort, again a failure; he makes "allusions to the follies of youth and the waywardness of age, as though Mr. Harding were afflicted by both" (20).

Childhood or second childhood—in this image deflating the hero's

state, Trollope again anticipates a Shavian kind of irony. The more profound irony that follows, however, is the genuine maturity that the Warden achieves; it appears in the unaffected security of his relations with
all the others, most notably in the mastery of the long final interview
with the bedesmen. It appears in the easy deprecation of his reply when
he is addressed by the title he has relinquished: "No, no, . . . not warden
now, only precentor" (21)—words that felicitously close the book. Since
Harding does have a triumph, it might be argued that the imaging of
him as a child—he first suggests the role, others easily cast him in it, and
he falls in with a sort of unconscious kinetic acquiescence—is too easy an
aesthetic gambit, too obvious an incongruity, a jest that, somewhat like
those of Boccaccio, plays too simply to the self-esteeming reader's knowingness. We will avoid this condescension, however, if we keep in mind the
ambiguity of Trollope's mock-heroics—that the letdown, though it may
be an end in itself, is often a skillfully unexpected entry into a coun-
teraffirmation, possibly a subtle one. This sequence takes place here.
On the one hand, the morally struggling man as a child—this is funny; it
is funny if a man is so like a child that he does not know how the world
goes, and is serious or indifferent at times when grown ups are supposed
not to be. He is unworldly, innocent. Innocence—this is the key, the
crossover term. If in one direction it means naiveté—Harding is repeatedly naive where most people would be knowing—in the other it means
uncorruptedness. It is that uncorruptedness which is Harding's triumph—a triumph not only in itself but also because he finds within
himself the seeds of the worldliness which in some way or other has penetrated all the others, and can do what he has to do to prevent them from
taking root. He snatches innocence, as it were, from the jaws of sophistication. He intuitively seeks the state which Polixenes attributes to
Leontes and himself in their boyhood:

> We were as twinn'd lambs that did frisk i' th' sun,
> And bleat the one at th' other. What we chang'd
> Was innocence for innocence; we knew not
> The doctrine of ill-doing, no, nor dream'd
> That any did.
>
> (*The Winter's Tale*, 1.2.67–71)

Yeats spells out the whole process of recovery: "When we are dead, according to my belief, we live our life backwards for a certain number of
years, treading the paths that we have trodden, growing younger again,
even childish again, till some attain an innocence that is no longer a
mere accident of nature, but the human intellect's crowning achievement."[4] Yeats's words amplify an earlier definition of spiritual alteration:

"Except ye be converted, and become as little children, ye shall not enter into the kingdom of heaven" (Matthew 18:3).

Childhood: innocence. This is the equation that finally dominates *The Warden*. Trollope had several options in the use of this equation. He might have made Harding programmatic, but that would have risked a dangerous self-consciousness. He might have made Harding nostalgic, like Mme. Ranevsky in *The Cherry Orchard*: "My nursery, dear delightful room. . . . I used to sleep here when I was little. . . . And here I am, like a little child. . . . Oh, my childhood, my innocence!" (act 1; Constance Garnett translation). But he simply converts Harding into the boy by metaphor. This imaging of innocence is the climactic part of the mock-heroic; the sound climax is not produced by technical manipulation but flows finally from a sense of reality. In actual life we do not find innocence in symbolic purity; we have to take innocence whole. We get it only with its other side operating too—naiveté, an unknowingness akin to ignorance, incompetence in ordinary affairs. Innocuousness means, among other things, inattentiveness. Trollope's vein is actuality, not allegory. So the child that signifies innocence also introduces childishness. In an adult world, childishness is laughable; Harding is funny. The advantage of having him at once as exemplar and as joke is fullness—a virtue in itself, and a hedge against the solemnity that always threatens the effort to dramatize a virtue.

vi

The laughable, too, is the overt sign of the comic. No one doubts, of course, that *The Warden* is comic, but we may not notice at first that it is remarkable that it is comic. A *comedy* of conscience? Conscience operates in the realm of the tragic. The theme of comedy is the way of the world; the spirit of the world is accommodation, the compromise between the ideal and the possible, between the desired and the achieved. Conscience shuns compromise; Harding makes none. He rejects the way of the world that the others espouse with ease. He rejects the comic view of life; his concern is of the kind found, sooner or later, in tragic heroes. Yet in his rejection of the comic way and his choice of a noncomic style he becomes comic. Trollope has pulled off something rather remarkable.

His trick, really, is to activate conscience in a realm ordinarily ruled by prudence or good sense. The tragic conscience identifies the forbidden that one has lusted after or seized—the grab, the aggression, the deed of hubris; it accepts the burden of guilt, without mitigation by the modern device of redefinition. Harding's conscience acts not by naming a grab that he cannot resist, or by demanding expiation for the grab already carried out, but by forestalling the grab implied by his continuance in a situation that he now for the first time sees as questionable. In tragedy he would try for too much of, or in, the world. In ordinary comedy he would find it legal or expedient to remain as warden, or else withdraw because staying on would not be feasible, that is, would be contrary to prudence or good sense. Harding does have some of this: he cannot stay on because he could not stand journalistic attacks. But his disability is rooted in the judgment of conscience that for him the position is not morally tenable.

By conscience, then, he does not curb or atone for an excess but chooses a deficiency (we have to keep in mind the more comfortable options that he is pressed to accept). It is his mode of adjustment, of that accommodation to the world, which is in the idiom of comedy. Harding adjusts in another way, too: his conscience does not inhibit the worldly virtue of good manners, as it does in many whose rectitude is indistinguishable from humorlessness and self-righteousness. His conscience observes moderation; it does not tyrannize over others, as some consciences must do to be sure of themselves; having insisted on abdication, it takes worldly form in the urbanity which is the highest personal achievement in comedy of manners. As guide to innocence rather than scourge of vice, conscience aids comedy by opening the way to the childhood images which, as we have noted, naturally beget a comic incongruity. But it is important that this comedy of innocence does not drift, as comedy representing a private rather than a social virtue is likely to do, into sentimental comedy. Trollope would risk the sentimental if, glancing at innocence, he understated its difficulty or overstated its value. He does neither. On the one hand, he sees to it that innocence is adequately tested; Harding is never unconscious of inner and outer obstacles. On the other hand, Trollope never underrates his more worldly characters; he understands that when the arena is the world, worldliness is going to appear and is indeed indispensable. He neither excoriates lack of innocence nor deprives the worldly of their own charm.

Trollope likewise protects his comedy against melodrama, which is a real threat because comedy and melodrama are different ways of dealing with the world (the ways, respectively, of compromise and of a strong combative style that must end in victory or defeat). The reform theme could automatically slide into the simplest kind of melodramatic form: good reformer versus evil reformee. Since zealots, demagogues, destroyers, and occasionally even good men want to impose this pattern on life, an artist electing the reform theme must be able to recognize and resist a good deal of pressure. Trollope can and does. He does not envisage sharp triumph or defeat for either side. In the realm of reform he shows that he has only the faith that Orwell attributes to Dickens—faith not in institutional reordering but in the private change of heart. He looks, then, to the springs of action, and as artist he looks, without precommitment, at the motives on both sides. Thus he accomplishes the difficult feat of translating a topical issue, which has been described by many critics, into the permanent terms of art. He turns pamphlet into fiction in a day when the tendency is to turn fiction into pamphlet; in terms of Victorian fashion, he is a radical. When reform is a matter of intense seriousness, he makes it a laughing matter, jesting not only at the times but at human stances which in all times are held with partisan intensity. He turns potential problem play into comedy of manners—a rare metamorphosis. So we see in reformers a spectrum of motives, from the good intentions of the habitual dissenter to the self-interest or self-deception or opportunism of lawyers, politicians, journalists, and homilists; and in reformees we see clever evasive tactics, institutional self-interest, complacency, and its opposite, self-judgment (*The Warden* precedes *Middlemarch* in noting the complexities that quickly crowd in when a reformer goes to work).

Then, in addition to the comic contrast between the moralist who wants others to be good and the moral man who wants to be good, Trollope innovates in his treatment of the third party, the presumptive beneficiaries of reform. Here he introduces, in a most unostentatious way, the great problem of the de jure versus the de facto, the ironic cleavage between the experienced adequacy and the vision of surplus induced by doses of promissory literal-legal stimulus. Clearly Trollope is not denying the just claims of true have-nots; he is not talking about poverty at all. Rather his subject is human insatiability, and he is trying to trap us all by attributing it, not to the oversupplied haves who are the cliché images of it, but to the have-enoughs who want to be have-mores. In the picture of the discontented pensioners the story glances briefly at what the best comedy of manners never shirks—the bitterness that occurs in the world. But the pensioners are not all greedy, and, more important, there is the warden, who, as we have seen, can find content as a haveless. The comic range of the story is epitomized in the final contrast between the most unregenerate of the wards and the regenerate Warden. The former is "poor old Bell," who "had nearly outlived all human feelings." All but one, as Trollope brilliantly perceives: " 'And your reverence,' said he, and then he paused, while his old palsied head shook horribly, and his shrivelled cheeks sank lower within his jaws, and his glazy eye gleamed with a momentary light; 'and your reverence, shall we get the hundred a year, then?' " (20). Here Trollope catches one basic aspect of human nature. But he also catches a quite different aspect of it in

those symbolic lines, already quoted, in which the Warden gently refuses his old title: "'No, no,' he always says when so addressed, 'not warden now, only precentor'" (21). This comedy does, then, what the best
comedy must do as it portrays the variety of human responses to the
world and its perquisites: it shows an equal unangry awareness of the
plaintive, urgent, deathless craving for more and of the unaffected,
graceful making do with less.

■ 5 ■
Tragic Unity in Conrad's *Lord Jim*

LORD JIM was published in 1900. Seventeen years later, while writing rather defensively about the novel, Joseph Conrad could still call it a "free and wandering tale." He was more openly critical of it in his inscription of a copy for his friend Richard Curle. There he called the novel too long, the product of a "resolve to cram as much character and episode into it as it could hold." But on the whole Conrad's artistic instinct was better than his retrospective judgment. Parts of the story that at first glance may seem excrescent turn out to have significant functions.

For instance, the numerous characters that drop in and then disappear as if the author were only momentarily attracted by their stories are a significant part of the drama of Jim: he is given depth, and resonance, both by contrast with others and by his impact on others. The field of meaning of which he is the center is completed by the portraits of a dozen other characters who help register him for us. The rest of the *Patna* officers, Cornelius, and Gentleman Brown are significant not only for what they do in the story, but also for what they feel: their strong dislike of Jim helps place him and measure the range of his potentialities, just as does Marlow's interest in him, in another way. The spectacular DT's of the engineer are a special kind of flight—the flight which, at the time of the hearing, Jim rejects. In Brierly's career we see Jim's secret vision of himself come true, in Brierly's suicide we see the sick spot risen to the surface and found intolerable by its possessor; in this version of the "one of us" theme, Brierly acts out Marlow's theory of the hidden weakness from which "not one of us is safe" (5; all references are to chapters). Against the brilliance of Brierly's record and of Jim's hopes are the solidity and enduringness of Brierly's mate Jones, who, however, pays a price for his virtue. No one gets home free. The French lieutenant embodies not only the sense of duty and honor that keeps a man on a dangerous assignment but, more than that, the courageous realism that permits him to say, "One is always afraid" (13)—the truth that Jim wanted not to face. Chester and Robinson are what Jim might become, and Chester spots him for his own; Marlow's refusal to cooperate with Chester marks his decision that Jim is salvageable (as well as his facing up to the human situation by not "putting out of sight all the reminders of our folly, of our weakness, of our mortality" [15]). Jim's impact on his various employers shows the area of his strength, indeed of his growth. In the story of the ambush of Stein, and of his catching the butterfly—the inclusion of Stein's life might be made to look like "cramming" the story with "episodes"—there is a salient development of the readiness theme that is one of the strands of connective tissue running through all the book. Jim takes Hamlet's "The readiness is all" as one of the cornerstones of his own belief, and we see him moving from unreadiness not only toward readiness but toward a maturer conception of it: readiness to act gloriously is readiness for death.

And so on through the wealth of episodes in the Patusan story: some usefulness of the narrative parts in time comes home to us. Take that strange part of Gentleman Brown's story, his running away with the dying wife of a missionary. Maybe excessive, but still. In it we see a revolt against order, a fury of devotion, a desperateness, a gambling spirit, a frustration of feeling turning into venom—all the forces of personality that make him more than a run-of-the-mill buccaneer and therefore help account for his extraordinary effectiveness in dealing with Jim.

The "free and wandering tale" is sometimes said to break apart in the middle, and it is true that the *Patna* and Patusan are not bound together by a conventional continuity of action such as we see, say, in *Victory* or *The Rescue*. Perhaps it would be impossible to construct a single line of action that could be the working-out of a life so split, as Jim's is, into two phases—defeat and rehabilitation. Nevertheless, the sense of split, as an aesthetic fact, can be overemphasized. A truly damaging split exists only if we are aware of an ending and then of a new beginning. But at midpoint in *Lord Jim* we have no impression of an ending. Jim is in a situation where no writer could stop; we have a sense of progression through the need of Jim's life to go on and achieve whatever new form his growing moral awareness makes possible. Conrad uses various devices to objectify the moral continuity or oneness of Jim's failure and his reconstruction. For one thing he makes use of the nonchronological method that is conspicuous in *Lord Jim*. He has Marlow tell his listeners, before the *Patna* affair is entirely ended, that Jim would be "loved, trusted, admired" (16); the end of his downfall we are thus compelled to see in the light of his other potentialities; we must look ahead even while summing up. Later during the Patusan events, Jim and Marlow both make many remarks that connect present with past, for example, "he, who had been too careful of it once, seemed to bear a charmed life" (29). Repeatedly we are reminded of Jim's leap from the *Patna*; images of jumping—of jumps that are made or that might be made—are regularly threaded into the text, as in Marlow's reference to "the very spot, where Jim took the second desperate leap of his life" (41).

This verbal tying together of the parts by Marlow brings us to Conrad's major method of yoking—and it might even be called identifying—Jim's past and his present: he pointedly gives to the situation and the actions in Patusan a form that makes them a parallel to, or a duplication of, the *Patna* events, as if Jim were finding his salvation not in unrelated opportunities come upon by chance in a distant land, but in a kind of replay of his earlier crisis. The effect is one of a subtle, partly concealed, and yet firm and objective unity—in Jim's life and in his story. In Patusan, as on the *Patna,* he has responsibility for hundreds of people of an alien race, and they have complete faith in him; in both situations he is alone, in "total and utter isolation" (27); both times he has to meet a crisis that is a rigorous test, admitting no evasion or compromise; both times he is subject to painful pressure from members of his own race; both times there is literally waiting a boat on which he can escape. And it is just these insistent resemblances that, in creating the sharp sense of his having a second chance, help dramatize the difference of his conduct in the second test. Through comparison we can see how much more strenuous pressure he must deal with at Patusan—not that of the wretched crew of the *Patna,* but that of Tamb' Itam, his devoted follower, and of Jewel, whom he loves; and, in quite another way, that of the formidable Brown, who, like Iago, knows how to break into the moral world that he despises. In yielding to the *Patna* crew's hypnotic cries of "jump," Jim responded to an inner cry for safety that he did not know was there; but in yielding to Brown's request for safe passage, he chose a course that he had to take because of what he did know about himself. Only out of complete assurance of his own moral position, out of a rejection of all questions, could he have condemned Brown to death. He acts, then, on a new plane—that of self-knowledge. One outcome of his decision, Brown's treachery, shows that Conrad has again put his hero into a diabolically difficult situation, in the way of mature artists who permit neither easy choices nor perfect choices. And the artist has his hero act in fidelity to what has become a growing moral determinant in his life—self-confrontation.

It is the progression toward self-knowledge that is the ultimate source of unity in *Lord Jim,* for there is an almost organic relationship among the phases through which Jim develops. At first he identifies himself so easily with visions of splendor that his failure on the training ship only briefly interrupts his inward cinema of glory savored as though already won. He seems unaware of a certain shrinking during the stormy voyage to the East, or of the implications of his staying in the East and signing on such a boat as the *Patna*—lapses in awareness ever so delicately hinted to the reader. The *Patna* episode seriously damages the fantasy without immediately giving Jim a trustworthy reorientation to actuality; he cannot credit the ugly surprises from within, but must defend and blame, as if he were merely a victim of hostile circumstance. True, he faces the court, as the other *Patna* officers do not, accepting disgrace; yet, as Marlow puts it, "He made so much of his disgrace while it is the guilt alone that matters" (16). His partial flight from reality—it is partial, as we see from his increasing willingness to acknowledge "I did jump"— takes another form when he runs from jobs as soon as the *Patna* story catches up with him; the irony of his being known without knowing it points up the error of his thinking "this thing must be buried" (18) instead of accepting it. Yet he is facing himself in another way, now: not taking the private visions of grandeur for the real thing, but finding the energy and courage, the daily discipline of self, to give them some substance in life—first in the port jobs, and then in the great feats of reconstruction at Patusan. But something else is necessary: like the hero of Robert Penn Warren's *World Enough and Time*, Jim has needed not to flee his guilt but to flee his innocence. He was both different from and similar to the other *Patna* officers, and his error of mind was to claim only his difference; yet his separateness from them could not be made actual and active until he acknowledged also his identity. Brown brings up this issue again, and in his dealing with Brown, Jim tacitly admits the kinship with evil that is the human liability, and that his reveries of self had excluded. This is the new pattern of responsibility, accepted, not with cynicism and despair, but with the deepening of perception that leads on to his final act of responsibility: his rejection of escape and his presenting himself, unarmed, at Doramin's court. In this act of responsibility, knowledge and self-knowledge come together most profoundly: what Jim now knows—knows in the centers whence action comes—is that he who would save his life must lose it.

If Jim's pilgrimage from the *Patna* to Patusan is one journey, our sense of its oneness is strengthened by the interpretation which it is Stein's chief function to make: "A man that is born falls into a dream like a man who falls into the sea. If he tries to climb out into the air as inexperienced people endeavor to do, he drowns—*nicht wahr?* . . . No! I tell you! The way is to the destructive element submit yourself, and with the exertions of your hands and feet in the water make the deep, deep sea keep you up. So if you ask me—how to be? . . . That was the way. To follow the dream, and again to follow the dream—and so—*ewig—usque ad finem*" (20). In view of Jim's earlier tendency to float away—in fact, to stroke energetically away—from the realities of existence, Stein might have used his water image for a different exhortation: seek the shore, and walk steadily on the ground of the real. Now this alternative would be very banal, and hence the usefulness of contemplating it, for it emphasizes the brilliance and profundity of Stein's paradox (which he restates when he calls Jim "romantic" and adds, "And that is very bad—very bad. . . . Very good, too")—the paradox that safety and danger, glory and disgrace, are not polar opposites but are mysteriously allied, sprung from a common source. The sea might kill or sustain; the dream may be the ruinous illusion of grandeur or the image of the ideal that disciplines man. (In his essay on *Nostromo* Robert Penn Warren identifies the dream as man's need to serve the "idea" that "redeems" action—a basic Conrad theme stated formally in "Heart of Darkness.") The fantasy which is a commonplace human experience may be idle egomania or may fashion the goal of aspiration; it may destroy, or man may live in it by the exertion of hands and feet. We are reminded of the aphorism that Yeats, attributing it to "Old Play," prefixed to his volume *Responsibilities:* "In dream begins responsibility." This duality of the dream, as escape or responsibility, is really at the heart, also, of a series of passages in which Marlow comments on the closeness of "truth" and "illusion." The paradox of the "destructive element" states the philosophic unity of Jim's life, and of Conrad's story: the dream led Jim first to illusion, then to truth.

Lord Jim, in all its remarkableness, is hardly explicable as the product of Conrad's literary experience and taste and his forebears. He preferred Turgenev to Dostoyevsky and in fiction in English had some fondness for Cooper and Marryat. A long admiration for Dickens perhaps reflects itself in certain comic elements in *Lord Jim* that have a Dickensian flavor—the affected style of Brierly's successor on the *Ossa* (6), the grotesque comedy of the terrified officers on the *Patna* (9), Sigmund Yucker's dyspepsia, recounted in broken English (19), Stein's ship captain's fancy language (23), the grotesqueness of Jim's muddy state when he escapes to Doramin (25), the description of Doramin (26). In the direct application of philosophical awareness to the materials of fiction he has some rough affiliations with George Eliot, Meredith, and Hardy, but in contrast with at least the latter two Conrad is much less likely to bog down in topicalities—science, the state of society, conventions, the church, and so on. He might be thought of as continuing from Eliot: both are concerned with the underside of the success story, the drift into guilt, the regenerating act; both have that profound consciousness of man's dual potentiality—his ability to damn himself and to save himself—that is essential to the writing of the tragic novel (when the consciousness of man's doubleness is lost, we get, on one side, the literature of despair and disaster and, on the other, that of sentimental optimism).

Part of Conrad's greatness is his very inclusive sense of good and evil. His spectrum of evil includes the bald nastiness of the *Patna* captain, the cringing and whining treacherousness of Cornelius, the soulless scheming of Chester (who, as the man outside the "dream," prescribes, "You must see things as they are" [14]), and above all the merciless virulent destructiveness of Gentleman Brown—the Lucifer type of villain (who after his fall from "high place" becomes the intellectual and moral leader of a predatory mob and whom Conrad, as if fascinated, explores again in Mr. Jones of *Victory*). These human monsters Conrad can imagine wonderfully and yet limit them to a peripheral role in order to save the center of the stage for the conflict of good and evil in Jim. For Jim is that rare creature in English fiction—the tragic hero. He is, as Stein says, certainly "good": "What is it that by inward pain makes him know himself? What is it that for you and me makes him—exist?" The good man must come to terms with what we have called ugly surprises from within—the realm of human danger that Conrad, as tragic writer, is more concerned with than with the deeds of all the men wholly committed to evil. Jim's flaw could lead to disintegration, but Conrad sees him as capable of finding the spiritual salvation which, in the tradition of high tragedy, transcends the catastrophe of events. Jim has to go through the tragic course of knowing himself and thus learning the way to salvation, for, like many a tragic hero, he tries at first to live in a melodrama where what is wrong is in others and in circumstances. "Was ever there any one so shamefully tried!" is his early complaint (9).

Finally there is the range of Jim himself, who is a very inclusive character. In him is the universal skeleton in the closet; not the heroic pride that would leap over all common bounds (Faust, Macbeth), but that defect in the heroic which makes him slip out of common bonds. In him we see generic man as he is endowed with the "romantic" imagination that may open a pit under him or supply him with the grace to earn the heroic; the man whose failure makes all sentient men worry profoundly (Marlow) or despair (Brierly). As we read his story we sense its affiliations with other stories and even with genres of story. Jim may seem at first an unlikely double of Othello, yet their lives have a common pattern: they give up for lost what is not lost, and a sense of self pries them away from faith and obligation. To go even further in finding likeness at the heart of apparent unlikeness: on the one hand, Jim's story is a version of the modern "success story"; on the other, of the ancient myth of Oedipus. Jim is the prototype of the boy who "makes good," but what Conrad does is to explode the popular stereotype by ultimately defining the "good" in qualitative and spiritual instead of quantitative terms. We find, on inspection, that the success story is not entirely alien to the

Oedipus myth. For Oedipus, too, has "ability in the abstract"; he has the talent for saving a distressed community, as Jim has. Jim's "success" comes after he has sought to escape the truth by moving from port to port, just as Oedipus has sought to evade destiny by a change of scene—both versions of the common myth of "leaving town." When at last there is nowhere else to retreat to, they discover their deepest talents; for both the ultimate deed is a paradox, success-in-failure.

Parallels such as these suggest the range of Conrad's achievement.

◼ II ◼
STRUCTURE, SYMBOLS, METHODS

■ 6 ■
E Pluribus Unum:
Parts and Whole in *Pride and Prejudice*

i

PRIDE AND PREJUDICE and *Sense and Sensibility* (and we might as well include *Love and Freindship*) are, as titles of fiction go, of a rare type (the titles of Jane Austen's other four major works are of types that appear much more frequently—two place names, a baptismal name, an abstraction). Not that pairs as such are exceptional; they always flourish. There are basic formats: he and she (*Troilus and Cressida, Paul and Virginia*), he and he (*Gargantua and Pantagruel, Sandford and Merton*, and, plurally, *Fathers and Sons* or, mixed, *Joseph and His Brothers*), two human types (*The Prince and the Pauper, Manservant and Maidservant, Dr. Jekyll and Mr. Hyde*—two-in-one, of course), man and beast (*Of Mice and Men, Androcles and the Lion*), two beasts (*The Owl and the Nightingale*), two scenes (*The Cloister and the Hearth*), two basic conditions (*War and Peace*), two things, concrete or abstract, literal or symbolic (*The Sound and the Fury, The Power and the Glory, The Moon and Sixpence, Bread and Wine, World Enough and Time, The Red and the Black, Decline and Fall, The Web and the Rock*).

What this title search in literary realty does not turn up is a pair of human qualities, attitudes, personality types, responsive patterns. Oddly enough, the nearest analogue to the Austen titles is *Crime and Punishment*—at least in the sense that one might think of crime as a deviation like prejudice, or a way of life like sensibility; the difficulty, of course, is that punishment is a sequel rather than an alternative. For Austen parallels, however, it would seem likelier to turn to the eighteenth century. Yet there the pickings are thin. Such a title as Mrs. Inchbald's *Nature and Art* sounds apropos (and it does name a subject to which Austen turns more than once), but the novel itself is a primitivist tract, than which anything more non-Austen could hardly be imagined.

But stand *Nature and Art* up beside *Sense and Sensibility*: one might expect some resemblance between the novels, for *nature* and *sensibility* are kindred forms of the new radical feeling after about 1760, and to sharers of this feeling a person committed to "sense" might seem equally capable of being ensnared by "art." I refer, of course, to the type of

79

expectation that the titles might create. Yet the difference is that Mrs. Inchbald's dualism is terminal and Austen's is experimental; Inchbald names exclusive modes, Austen, alternatives to be neither wholly rejected nor wholly glorified. Though sense and sensibility may look like absolutes, they are only possibilities that need the test of experience; though the title may suggest an allegorical design, it simply names options to be explored.

If Elinor's "sense" is to be admired, and it is, nevertheless the fact is that it renders her no less vulnerable to the harrowing vicissitudes of experience (her lover inflicts almost as much pain on her as Marianne's does on Marianne) and that it burdens her with additional responsibilities in a family whose other members are more given to emotional self-indulgence. While it is good if people have sense, nevertheless sense is not an omni-efficient value, a warranty against the dangers of life and the misery that others impose. What is more, there is such a thing as too much sense, an excess dramatized in John and Fanny Dashwood, who live by a chill calculation that insulates them not only against emotional disturbance but against legitimate claims on their human responsiveness. Marianne's ex-lover Willoughby is another man of sense: assailed by financial pressure, he denies what he takes to be the dictates of his heart and marries money. When we cross over to sensibility, we see that Marianne's allegiance to it produces more pain than gratification; it seems almost a way of life that might be chosen by a masochist or some other neurotic. Yet Austen does not allegorize this position and make Marianne illustrate a thesis. For Marianne's sensibility, troublesome as it is, is also partly justified in that her intuitive perception of Willoughby's response to her is not a fantasy; she has seen something real, even though Willoughby chooses not to act in terms of it. But Marianne's sensibility is more emphatically justified when she is seen in contrast with the Steele sisters, who have no sensibility at all. Their characteristic insensibility to others makes Marianne's hypersensitivity look good, for, while their vulgarity of feeling is incurable, her hypersensitivity is a modifiable excess of a central warmth and spontaneity of feeling that are humanly indispensable.

Austen, then, has so arranged her characters that they enact a commentary on the values embodied in her title. She "outflanks" the two key positions and thus modifies them instead of holding to them inflexibly. "Sense" is a virtue but is not an absolute; there can be a disastrous excess of it. "Sensibility" can be mistaken for an unqualified virtue by cultists, and it can be, if not actually a vice, at least a troubling disorder; yet it is not so much an essential error as it is an excess of a virtue. In sum, though her title suggests a pair of allegorical opposites, Austen is sturdily anti-allegorical: she finds a duality not between clear-cut virtues and clear-cut vices, but within apparent virtues and apparent vices. An a priori rightness and an a priori wrongness undergo the corrective of experience—linear experience in which unfoldings in time add new perspectives, and analogical experience in which concurrent actions supply panoramic illumination. It is the kind of excellence that keeps *Sense and Sensibility,* despite its shortcomings in detail, alive.

ii

As a title, *Pride and Prejudice* resembles *Sense and Sensibility* and yet differs from it. The obvious likeness is that two habits of personality are designated by abstract terms that make us expect the allegorical method. In *Pride and Prejudice,* however, we seem to have not an opposition of superior and inferior but a pair of shortcomings. *Prejudice* can be read in only one way. To a reader consciously on guard against booby traps, "pride" might immediately mean "self-respect," but the chances are against it. The magnetic field of "prejudice" influences the connotation of "pride," but even without this it would be hard to resist the implication of "vanity," "arrogance," and "hubris," of "pride goeth before a fall" and "pride, the never-failing vice of fools." A title more like *Sense and Sensibility* would be *Pride and Humility,* for, as we shall see, there is a substantial humility theme, and both opposites are dealt with complexly. But the phrase that Fanny Burney used a number of times in *Cecilia* and that presumably caught Austen's eye was "pride and prejudice," not "pride and humility."

"Prejudice" is less on target than "humility" would have been, at least in the sense that prejudice is thematically less evident. It is present, of course, both in Bennets and in Darcys and is modified in the individuals capable of self-modification. Yet it remains relatively subsurface and passive, probably because Austen saw that there isn't really very much to be said about it. It hardly goes beyond banality to inveigh against prejudice. The thematic possibility of prejudice becomes larger only if one approaches it with a strained paradoxicality that might take this line: while prejudice is commonly a prejudgment that remains indifferent to evidence, it may also be the lightning intuition of truth that seems to proceed without evidence but will in time be confirmed by evidence. But lightning intuition of truth is not the form of prejudgment that distinguishes the characters in *Pride and Prejudice:* they become open to truth only after evidence has knocked heavily on the doors of their minds. Austen would not seek the rare virtue in prejudice any more than she would inveigh against the vice of it. Her natural ground is a central one, equidistant from the tortured and the truistic.

This hypothesizing grows out of the fact that, while one of the title words keeps cropping up like a leitmotif, the other appears very little. Though the two family groups are prejudiced, though Elizabeth is prejudiced against Darcy and in favor of Wickham, though Wickham alleges that Darcy is prejudiced against him, though the younger Bennet girls are prejudiced in favor of men in uniform, and though Collins lives by prejudice alone, the concept does not often surface in the verbal specification that would reveal Austen's awareness of it as a principal counter. The concept is charmingly intimated when, in passages separated by only a few pages, Austen playfully puts Elizabeth and Collins into the same emotional boat: Elizabeth fears "To find a man agreeable whom one is determined to hate!" and Collins presents "the determined air of following his own inclination" (18; all references are to chapters). It is just on this occasion that Elizabeth—more playfulness by Austen—suggests to Darcy that he may be "blinded by prejudice." For another hundred pages (and roughly a score of chapters) the word is missing; then it has a little flowering of more than casual meaningfulness. Rejected accusingly by Elizabeth, Darcy writes a long letter explaining the actions that had annoyed her. Elizabeth approaches the letter with "a strong prejudice against everything he might say," but in a little while begins to perceive that "she had been blind, partial, prejudiced, absurd" (36). This comic anagnorisis is at the heart of Elizabeth's personal drama; her self-perceptiveness is a central strength of the book. Despite the genuineness of the pain in Elizabeth's self-understanding, it is right for the tone of the book that a little later she can jest ironically about herself: "And yet I meant to be so uncommonly clever in taking so decided a dislike to him without any reason. It is such a spur to one's genius, such an opening for wit to have a dislike of that kind" (40). Yet the laughter at self does not preclude straightforward self-censure: "But the misfortune of speaking with bitterness is a most natural consequence of the prejudice I have been encouraging." Two paragraphs later Austen makes Elizabeth refer to the "general prejudice against Mr Darcy [which] is so violent that it would be the death of half the good people in Meryton to attempt to place him an amiable light." Though the point is not made overtly, the repetition of *prejudice* lets us infer Elizabeth's recognition that she has been behaving not like a discriminating individual, but like a thoughtless public ever quick to leap to conclusions.

This is virtually the end of prejudice as a publicly identified theme. True, Mr. Gardiner attributes "family prejudice" to Mrs. Reynolds, the housekeeper, when she praises Darcy (43), and Elizabeth explains to Darcy how "all her former prejudices had been removed" (58, 60). True, Mrs. Bennet's shift from con-Darcy to pro-Darcy when she finds that

Elizabeth is to benefit from his "ten thousand a year, and very likely more" (59) suggests an indecently hasty reorientation of prejudice. Austen does not push this; nor does she make the point that prejudgments, which are an inevitable tentative way into experience, become prejudices only when clung to, in the face of modifying evidence, as emotional supports; nor does she go into the distinction between prejudices about individuals and prejudices about classes (fortunately she eliminates the class issue by having virtues and vices easily surmount all social barriers). To make these notations, however, is not to disparage; it is only to say that, as a theme, prejudice never quite takes on the vitality that appears in the treatment of pride. Not that Elizabeth's and Darcy's overcoming of it is not significant, but this conquest, as we shall see, is an auxiliary way of articulating the central drama.

iii

Though I have talked as if Austen's two-part titles provide essential keys to general structure, it is clear by now that this assumption needs qualifications. For one thing, Austen fundamentally modifies the expectations that the titles may be supposed to arouse. Again, a title word such as *prejudice* may not stir her imagination enough to exert a principal influence on the story, but may simply pop into view now and then. Further, a significant theme such as humility may not appear in the title at all, though it may be implied by the presence of *pride*. Obviously there are various totally untitled themes. Of these, a major one is marriage. It is important in the present context because the treatment of it is closely interwoven with the treatment of pride; at certain crucial points, the two are hardly separable. This interdependence, however, is not immediately apparent. Hence it is better to postpone a direct look at the marriage theme until we have laid some groundwork by seeing what Austen does with pride.[1]

Pride comes into play very early and then is dramatically active, or is the formal object of attention, in about half the sixty-one chapters. Austen sees that the word itself stands for a medley of psychological and moral states, rooted in a common human ground but growing out diversely as they are nurtured by, and nurture, different personalities. But this absence of oneness appears only after some time has passed. Initially Austen treats pride as if it were wholly unproblematic, a failing no less clear-cut than prejudice.

Darcy is "discovered to be proud," "above his company and above being pleased"; he is called the "proudest, most disagreeable man in the world," "so high and conceited" (3); likewise the Bingley sisters are "proud and conceited" (4); and Mrs. Bennet records the community opinion: "everyone says that he is ate up with pride" (5). The observers believe that they are seeing a sense of superiority, snobbishness, excessive self-approval; yet very soon we also see that what is called pride includes reserve, an apparent unresponsiveness to overtures, a holding back from conventional intercourse, pleasantries, and small talk. An accusation of pride, then, may be quite justifiable, but it is also a way of disapproving partial noncompliance with neighborhood social ways; in the observer there may be as much strength of feeling as there is sharpness of eye or even more. Both possibilities are present when Austen observes, "Elizabeth saw superciliousness in their treatment of everybody" (6). It gradually becomes evident that one can point to pride perceptively, defensively, aggressively, or even (much later) admiringly.

The faint duality that first hangs over the issue of pride is amplified in a Lucas-Bennet round-table discussion (5). Charlotte Lucas proposes that Darcy "has a *right* to be proud"—the right of character, status, and fortune. Elizabeth, on the other hand, "could forgive *his* pride if he had not mortified *mine*": for the first time pride is less an unarguable vice than an *amour propre* which is a fact of every life. Mary picks this up and articulates it formally in a little essay that she contributes, pedantically but by no means stupidly: "Pride is . . . very common . . . few of us . . . do not cherish a feeling of self-complacency. . . . A person may be proud without being vain. Pride relates more to an opinion of ourselves, vanity to what we would have others think of us." (Austen uses Mary's sage words against her a little later when Mary sings to entertain others: "Vanity had given her application . . . likewise a pedantic and conceited manner" [6]—the first judgment in which we see a virtue and a vice plainly brought together under one name.) When pride is said to be universal and is distinguished from vanity, it is something more than a gross attribute of bad men who because of it can be pointed at by good men. Though the symposium ends anticlimactically with the declaration by "a young Lucas" that if you have enough money pride need not be worried about, the opinions serve a dramatic purpose: all participants view pride not absolutely as a failing but relativistically; it is felt and understood differently as different perspectives are brought into play. Interestingly enough, it is not long before Austen has Darcy himself echo Mary's distinction. This occurs when Elizabeth, confident of her assessment of him, inferentially accuses him of "vanity and pride" (11). Darcy replies that while "vanity is a weakness," "real superiority of mind" will keep pride "always under good regulation"; that is, pride is a neutral quality that becomes undesirable only when it gets out of hand. Elizabeth turns away to "hide a smile," and we smile at her.

It is not long, then, before we are pushed beyond the allegorical singleness of meaning which the title might lead a reader to expect. The theme of pride is constantly subjected to modification by new developments. Austen sees pride as very much in people's minds, either as an unspoken attitude of their own egos or as an easy name for displeasing manners and traits in others. Elizabeth has to "tremble lest her mother should be exposing herself again" (9) and lest all her family "expose themselves as much as they could during the evening" (18). Darcy is "ashamed of his aunt's ill-breeding" (31)—she is the only embodiment of the heavy-handed snobbery that for many of the characters is the primary meaning of pride. Since Elizabeth is the Bennet most sensitive to others' obnoxious pride, it is a delightful irony that Miss Bingley should attribute to her "a mixture of pride and impertinence," a "conceited independence" (8), and "that little something bordering on conceit and impertinence" (10). So it works in both directions. Miss Bingley is an unreliable witness, but then Elizabeth may be too.

iv

These bright turns are peripheral to the more searching account of pride achieved through the introduction of the humility motif. Once we see the world *humble* we might well expect a familiar moralistic antithesis of the proud who will fall and the humble who shall inherit. But again it does not work out that way. Austen not only rejects a cliché view; she further undercuts expectation by straining the humility theme through two sharply contrasting characters, Bingley and Collins. The Bingley episode is brief but lively and meaningful. Amiable Bingley says that his thoughts flow faster than he can write them down; hence his letters often do not make sense. With a tinge of gentle irony Elizabeth praises his "humility." Darcy then leaps in with the sharpest observation that he has yet made: "Nothing is more deceitful than the appearance of humility. It is often only carelessness of opinion, and sometimes an indirect boast." To Bingley he attributes "The indirect boast, for you are really proud of your defects in writing . . . the power of doing anything quickly is often much prized by the possessor" (10). Humility, then, is not set up as a virtue countering the vice of pride; rather we have the paradox that qualities accepted as opposites may coincide. Complacency may garb itself in the humility of self-denigration; a man may be vain of his lack of pretension. No truisms here.

Only a little later we come upon the same issue in a different guise—different enough, perhaps, to obscure the thematic identity. Though paradoxicality is suggested by the "mixture of servility and self-importance" that Mr. Bennet gleefully points out in Collins's letter (13), Collins initially seems no more than a minor Uriah Heep almost four decades ahead of his time. His ceaseless refrain of "humble abode" and "humble parsonage" and his assurance in his "proper humility of behaviour" (18) suggest only an oafish muddy-eyed insensitivity. Here, we do at first appear to have an allegorical character, one who has turned the traditional virtue of humility into a monstrosity and thus must make one long for pride in any form. But what is striking is that Austen is unwilling to let him go as unrelievedly one-dimensional; she tells us directly that he combines "humility of manner" and "the self-conceit of a weak head," that he is a "mixture of pride and obsequiousness, self-importance and humility" (15). Though these are assertions rather than drama, they have the dramatic life inhering in the perception that mutually contradictory elements may coexist—a carrying on of Austen's essential impulse to shun easy moral categories. When both the likable Bingley and the repellent Collins reveal an essential pride beneath a ritual humility, we perceive not only the spread of pride among contrasting human types, but a further complication of meaning in a word that has already been used to denote both a diversity of qualities in men called proud and the animus of those who level the charge. We might well imagine that Austen is going to solve the problem of definition by declaring for a total relativism.

V

To lead us in this direction is an admirable ploy in one who is of course going to do no such thing. It is Wickham, ironically, through whom Austen first pushes us toward the permanent center of meaning. Wickham's entry into the story, as well as his role, is the source of more than one ironic effect. Collins's objectionableness predisposes Elizabeth in favor of the relatively charming and by no means stupid Wickham, as self-conscious as Collins but much more "aware." Elizabeth's antagonism to Darcy, and Wickham's defensiveness against Darcy as the man who has the goods on him (we do not yet know this, of course), bring Elizabeth and Wickham into a rapport that, though its central ground is anti-Darcy feeling, still has a freedom that opens the way toward a more reliable definition of pride than has so far been present in anyone's use of the word. Granted, both use the word in conventional, undefined ways. Elizabeth reports with assurance that "Everybody is disgusted with [Darcy's] pride," and Wickham asserts, "His pride never deserts him" (16). Yet in between these conventional observations both people—as if freed from narrowness by a congeniality that both ironically take to be greater than it is—slip into usages that imply the broadest and most useful definition of pride so far presented to us. They open up the title theme vastly.

Elizabeth "wonder[s] that the very pride of this Mr Darcy has not made him more just to you," that "he should not have been too proud to be dishonest." Wickham replies that, indeed, "almost all his actions may be traced to pride; and pride has often been his best friend. It has connected him nearer with virtue than any other feeling." Here Elizabeth, her emotions rising, slips back into the commonplace: "Can such abominable pride as his have ever done him good?" But Wickham, who strikingly combines occasional clarity of mind with deviousness and crass opportunism, goes on to speak of Darcy's pride in terms that at last take us into the thematic center of the book:

> Yes. It has often led him to be liberal and generous, to give his money freely, to display hospitality, to assist his tenants, to relieve the poor. Family pride, and *filial* pride, for he is very proud of what his father was, have done this. Not to appear to disgrace his family, to degenerate from the popular qualities or lose the influence of the Pemberley house, is a powerful motive. He has also *brotherly* pride, which with *some* brotherly affection makes him a very kind and careful guardian of his sister.

(Long afterward, Wickham is again able to register such a view of Darcy's pride [41].)

At this point we are compelled, whether we think it through or not, to recognize that while "pride" can become a cliché of multiple uses but limited usefulness, behind the cliché there lies a profound human motive that manifests itself in different ways. The neutral center of pride, the single root nurturing several stems, is a universal self-regard or self-esteem, an inevitable fact of life that can take contrary forms. In one direction it can become self-admiration, in another, self-respect; in one direction, complacency and sense of privilege, in the other, sense of obligation; in one, the assertion of assumed quality, in the other, commitment to a quality to be maintained by constant effort; in one, the freedom to look down on the world, in the other, the need to live up to the standards that claim one's loyalty.

Once such a definition has been put into play, the problem is always how pride operates in each individual, and we see a wide range from abrasive superciliousness at one extreme to a light-minded absence of decent pride at the other. The gradual buildup of this structure of attitudes, working in conjunction with the formal definition made possible by Wickham's analysis of Darcy, puts us in a position of increasing detachment with respect to the attributions of pride made in the second half of the story. We relish the jest at the ordinary use of the word when Mrs. Gardiner, on being pushed, "was confident at least that she recollected having heard Mr Fitzwilliam Darcy formerly spoken of as a very proud, ill-natured boy" (25). It is less amusing when Elizabeth passionately reverts to her original anger at Darcy: "his pride and caprice were the cause of all that Jane had suffered," his "pride . . . would receive a deeper wound from the want of importance in [the Bennets] than from their want of sense"; yet even in this context she can be capable of a mild modification and term his motive "This worst kind of pride" (33). Then he does indeed acknowledge just this "pride"—that is, his judgment of her family—when he proposes. Here he exhibits candor rather than grace, but when Elizabeth retorts angrily he is shrewd enough to charge, in reply, that her "pride [has] been hurt by my honest confession of [my] scruples." He is right, but just stuffily defensive enough to render understandable Elizabeth's falling back on an undiscriminating accusation of "pride . . . abominable pride" (34). She wants, needs, to find him guilty of the "worst kind of pride," and yet by now we realize that what she charges him with is not the whole truth.

After the proposal crisis Austen goes back to an earlier game of seeing how easily people use the word *pride*, either as an outcropping of their own emotions or as a loose name for characteristics that they are unable or unwilling to define precisely. When Darcy's housekeeper, Mrs. Reynolds, speaks well of him, Mr. Gardiner attributes this to "pride of attachment." Mrs. Reynolds thinks that when people call Darcy "proud" it is "only because he does not rattle away like other young men" (43). Elizabeth herself sees that though Miss Darcy is called "proud," she is no more than "exceedingly shy" (44); this would make "those who felt themselves inferior" think her "proud and reserved" (45). Hence Elizabeth now understands that Wickham lied to her in calling Georgianna "proud, reserved, disagreeable" (47).

More important, Elizabeth is able to see Darcy in a different light. In wanting to meet the Gardiners, he seems to forsake the "pride" once offended by her family (43). She notes other changes "in a man of so much pride" (44): though she clings to her old word, she is beginning to make excuses for him. The Gardiners take a "so what" attitude to "the pride he probably had" and think that if he didn't have it, "it would certainly be imputed by the inhabitants of a small market town, where the family did not visit" (44): social nonparticipation as pride. While such revaluations are going on, it is only the very silly people who persist in the uncritical usage that was general at the beginning of the book. Kitty still thinks of Darcy only as "that tall, proud man," and Mrs. Bennet hopes to cook adequately for "the appetite and pride" of such a man (53). At the end she insists that he is "a proud, unpleasant sort of man" (59)—a joke to the reader, of course, yet more than that. For Mrs. Bennet is the thoughtless, indefatigable marrying mother who has no pride at all; anything goes. Besides, Austen has said of her that she was in no way "humbled" by her daughter Lydia's misconduct (49). Mrs. Bennet has achieved something in the world of the novel: she is incapable of both pride and humility.

When Mrs. Bennet calls Darcy "proud, unpleasant," Elizabeth replies, "I love him. Indeed he has no improper pride" (59). This completes the principal thematic development in *Pride and Prejudice*. But Elizabeth has come to this point only through a crucial central experience— a peripeteia—which I have so far passed over silently. This peripeteia takes place at a point where the pride theme and the marriage theme are both active and are notably interdependent. To get the full impact of the peripeteia we need to have a clear picture of the marriage theme and how it is established in the overall structure.

vi

In nineteenth-century fiction we take marriage so much for granted as an objective, or way of life, or resolution of uncertainties and tensions, that we may not immediately notice its role in *Pride and Prejudice* as an object of contemplation. Austen presents six marriages—two established ones and four in the process of being put together. Of the two established marriages, that of the Gardiners is too shadowy to have a dramatic role; we are only dimly aware of it as a satisfactory relationship between two apparently like-minded people. The Bennet marriage affords a detached comic view of a working, if unideal, relationship between a featherbrained, humorless, very conventional woman, once very pretty we are told, and a witty but lazy man whose only serious activity is making ironic comments on his family and their associates. Austen is neither satiric nor sorrowful nor protesting; in the imperfections of this match she sees, it appears, less a disaster than a model of ordinary marital relationships which survive some incompatibility in the partners. The portrayal results from a comic acceptance of the way things are.

And that, too, is the tone in which Austen reports on the four marriages that are her central narrative material. These have actional interrelationships: Elizabeth can visit the Collinses and thus be within reach of Darcy, Darcy's interference in the Bingley-Jane affair precipitates Elizabeth's wrathful rejection of Darcy, Collins gloomily condoles on the Lydia-Wickham affair, and his endeavor to interfere with the Elizabeth-Darcy rapprochement is ironically unsuccessful. The Lydia-Wickham elopement convinces Elizabeth that Darcy will never have anything more to do with any Bennet, but everything turns out contrary to her predictions.

Such narrative ties prevent an effect of disjunction, creating a sense of unity among strands of action that could seem quite separate stories. But the more important interconnection among the four new marriages is that of analogy; *Pride and Prejudice* employs a sophisticated analogical structure very early in the history of the novel. We see the marriages in the light of each other; they represent four different kinds of human relationships. Austen is capable of imagining the different styles but, more important, refrains from an adversary role. She is not the angry scourge of imperfect arrangements, but the comic observer of different modes that reflect the qualities of the participants and that may fall short of, or resemble, or improve upon the relationship of the Bennets senior. Each represents a certain principle or justification. The Charlotte-Collins marriage is pure convenience; for each party, better this than nothing. The Lydia-Wickham marriage is society's conventional rescue operation for the sexy runaways (Wickham is Richardson's Lovelace scaled down from the demonic to the small-time seducer). The Jane-Bingley marriage is the automatic union of two gentle, amiable, modest, similar souls. The Elizabeth-Darcy relationship is a more difficult, complex affair: both parties are sharp, critical, strong-minded, and given to firm stands upon initial grounds that need modification. Hence both parties have to work through barriers of unfavorable judgments, misunderstandings, and self-justifying postures.

The novel says, in effect, that these different kinds of marriage all occur, all are inevitable, and all are more or less workable: this is the comic acceptance of the world. Yet it does not simply equate them. It says that each embodies a modus vivendi adequate for the participants, but also it never assumes the human equivalence of the participants. In fact, one of the great things in the book is its subtle combination of acceptance and judgment. No character, and no narrative thrust, really makes a case against Charlotte's marrying Collins and Lydia's being married to Wickham, but Austen does use Elizabeth to voice the conventional romantic objections to the former and to criticize society's conventional approval of the latter. Yet Austen is so detached that she does not grant Elizabeth equal authority in both cases. On Charlotte and Collins, Elizabeth is so incredulous that she hurts Charlotte's feelings (22) and so insistently condemnatory that we feel the hyperbole in her polemic and are ready for the quiet defense of the arrangement made by Jane (24). What is pressed upon us is the comic discrepancy between Elizabeth's unyielding idealist position and the realities of life which introduce the nonideal and render it workable. On the other hand, when no one at all objects to the matrimonial legitimatizing of the Lydia-Wickham sexual adventure, and when some observers, including

Mrs. Bennet, regard it as an objectively desirable and valuable outcome, Elizabeth is "sick of this folly"; as she says, "How strange it is! And for *this* we are to be thankful" (49). This is in the best comic spirit: one accepts society's arrangements, but one is not taken in by them any more than one revolts against them.

Austen sets up against each other the planned prudential marriage (Charlotte "set out to meet [Collins] accidentally in the lane" [22]), the institutionally rectifying (shotgun) marriage, the spontaneous uncomplicated marriage, and finally the slowly developing *earned* relationship of more complex personalities. Though they are all valid for the appropriate personalities, they are not equally significant or interesting. The less interesting they are, the more quickly Austen disposes of them. Charlotte catches Collins in a chapter, and the comment occupies part of several following chapters (22–24). We hear quickly about the Lydia-Wickham elopement after it has happened (46); the aftermath winds on through six chapters (47–52), its interest lying not in the elopers, however, but in the impact of their escapade on others. The mutual attraction between Jane and Bingley begins to creep into visibility very early (3), but then external obstacles intervene, and the engagement takes place only near the end (55). In a sense, then, the story is a long one, but its apparent length is much greater than its bulk. The truly long story is that of Elizabeth and Darcy: Darcy first begins to be aware of Elizabeth fairly early (6), their engagement is the last one to be effected (58), and the adjustments between them continue through another session of postmortems (60). But more important than the duration of the Elizabeth-Darcy story is its fictional magnitude; it is worked out in great detail, and it is at the moral center of the comedy. It *has* to be done fully, since the problems created by independent, assertive, and partly mistaken minds must be worked out with care. For Darcy and Elizabeth this means a greater understanding both of the facts outside the self and of the self. The parties have to learn much to *earn* their accommodation.

vii

We have spoken of the title themes—pride and prejudice—and of the marriage theme. They all come together in the crucial stages of the achievement of reciprocal understanding and confidence by Elizabeth and Darcy, and this makes evident the remarkable structural unity of the novel, or, perhaps better, defines a close coherence that we feel despite the almost lavish multiplicity of procedure. Not only do Elizabeth and Darcy, of all the pairs, have the most serious problem of surmounting barriers of misconception and adverse feeling, but they are the most sensitive—both in susceptibility to injured feelings and in capacity for getting to the center of things—to matters of prejudice and pride. The chief line of action begins to straighten itself out when the two principal characters work out a mutual adjustment in terms of the basic conceptual matters of the book.

The cardinal phase of the clarification begins with Elizabeth's spirited and accusatory rejection of Darcy's proposal, a proposal obviously sincere but burdened with overconfidence and a partial, though by no means total, ineptitude of style. Each has made a note of the other's "pride." Then Darcy writes to Elizabeth. "I write," Austen skillfully makes him say, "without any intention of . . . humbling myself" (35). But in truth he does humble himself, and in the very best sense, not only by writing to her when he might understandably take refuge in offended silence, but by writing at great length and in explaining, fully and in carefully neutral tones, his belief that Jane was not seriously attached to Bingley ("If *you* have not been mistaken here, *I* must have been in an error"), his regret that he "condescended to adopt the measures of art," and, finally, the whole Wickham-Georgianna story which accounted for his treatment of Wickham denounced by Elizabeth in her ignorance of the facts. Elizabeth approaches this letter with a "strong prejudice" against it (as we noted earlier), and with conviction that it is "all pride and insolence" (36). But if Darcy humbles himself by refusing to take refuge in offended dignity and by coming down from a high place to explain, Elizabeth humbles herself by gradually retreating from her initial hostility to the letter, by considering the evidence and the probabilities, by gradually revising her whole attitude, and in the end by seeing her own errors. Neither of the principals gets locked into a defensive-aggressive stance that forbids growth; both move from a tendency to be stiff-necked to a saving flexibility. Chapter 36 is a remarkable tracing of Elizabeth's coming around to a completely changed point of view. And Austen makes her couch her new vision in the central thematic terms of the book. She felt that she had been "blind, partial, prejudiced, absurd. 'How despicably have I acted!' she cried, 'I, who have prided myself on my discernment! I who have . . . gratified my vanity in useless or blamable distrust. How humiliating is this discovery! Yet how just a humiliation! . . . But vanity, not love, has been my folly. . . . Till this moment I never knew myself.'" Thus she reaches the high point that is possible in the comic experience, the anagnorisis, and it is at the center of the thematic progression. She attributes her errors to pride and vanity, which so far have been largely the vices of others. Yet anagnorisis of this kind need not, and does not, lead to somber self-accusation. Elizabeth recurs to the subject readily enough to give dramatic evidence of her sharper sense of truth, but, like the well person she is, she does it playfully or wryly. She thinks of Darcy's proposal and subsequent explanations as matters that "must . . . so highly gratify whatever of her own vanity she had not yet been able to reason away" (38). To Jane she acknowledges that she has cultivated her "prejudices" and has been "weak and vain and nonsensical" (40). Her most painful recognition is of "the reproof contained in [Wickham's] believing" that "her vanity would be gratified" by a renewal of his attentions to her (41).

Equally important with Elizabeth's mastery of a new insight into pride and prejudice is the dramatic definition of pride as the acceptance of responsibility. This indispensably fills out a story that has devoted a good deal of time to the view of pride as an easy and blind self-esteem. The new definition of pride picks up where Wickham had left off in attributing Darcy's virtues in part to his pride (16). It is a pleasant irony that Wickham should then contribute to the definition of pride as a virtue by running off with Lydia—a risky fictional stereotype that Austen handles freshly and originally,[2] making the banal vital. One of Elizabeth's own responses makes a fine contribution to the pride theme. Elizabeth guesses diffidently that Darcy's intervention was "done . . . for her," but she also "felt that even her vanity was insufficient" to let her imagine his going beyond that. Darcy allied to someone allied to Wickham—unthinkable! In Elizabeth's inner words, "Every kind of pride must revolt from the connection" (52). Here Elizabeth accepts pride as a kind of irrefutable judgment of flawed being, an inevitable placement of self with respect to defective quality. So we have a double irony: Elizabeth has reversed herself on pride, and she is wrong about Darcy. The revelation of her error is a major part of the remaining action.

We are prepared for the revelation, however, by Darcy's entry into the seduction imbroglio and his contribution to getting the elopers married. Here we have another Darcy-Bennet tension; this time, however, there is a direct contrast between Darcy and Mr. Bennet. Mr. Bennet has not "done his duty," he welcomes a solution "with so little inconvenience to himself" and "with such trifling exertion," and he quickly returns "to all his former indolence," that is to say, to ironic disengagement (50). Perhaps nowhere else in fiction is there so shrewd a treatment of the ironic commentator: the source of all his delightful wit is a detachment which also means an incapacity for the attachment, that is, the committed action that is plainly called for in the situation of which he is a part. The thematic point of this episode is that Mr. Bennet lacks pride; his failure is not put literally in such terms, but the sense of it is unmistakable. While he has not "done his duty," Darcy defines it as his own "duty to step forward and endeavour to remedy an evil which had been brought on by himself" (52); that is, to him it is "mistaken pride" not to have exposed Wickham publicly and thus to have saved others from his opportunism. Darcy's pride was that "his character was to speak for itself," without annotation by the facts that he could supply. Interestingly enough, it is an understandable pride—a kind of self-confidence based on knowledge of right conduct. It is quite different from the pride that Elizabeth had imputed to him. Yet he is now a sterner critic of himself than she was, for he repudiates a kind of pride for which a case can be made. What comes into play here is a subtler distinction than those utilized by the earlier narrative—the distinction between the pride that rests with assurance upon genuine achievement (the honorable conduct that we know was Darcy's) and the pride that imposes continuing activity lest achievement itself not be effective against the self-seeking ever present in the world. Darcy rejects the former and elects the latter—in his word, "duty." Here the novel reaches the apex in the complex structure of definitions of pride that give both form and life to the story. What looked very simple initially has turned out to contain an exciting and enlightening range of possibilities. Art forces us out of the simple omnibus concept of daily life into the conceptual discrimination on which truth depends.

The drama of definition, we have seen, is not a separable element but is an intimate part of the drama of Elizabeth's and Darcy's earning their relationship. The final accommodation is summed up in three separate but related passages. Before she knows of Darcy's role in getting Lydia and Wickham married, Elizabeth is sure that her family's "alliance" with Wickham will alienate Darcy permanently. "She was humbled," Austen tells us (50). Austen might have said "embarrassed" or "distressed"; but to say "humbled" is not only to tie this event into the thematic structure but to show Elizabeth in that kind of reversal which life imposes upon people in the growing-up process. Austen underscores this in the next paragraph when she makes Elizabeth think, with a new sense of loss, of "the proposals which she had proudly spurned only four months ago." We see her and Darcy both rejecting the kind of pride— the mode of self-esteem—that had actuated them before. Elizabeth is still wrong in another way, however: she is sure that her rejected suitor must be relishing this new contretemps which can only seem to him to have justified all his prejudices. He is "generous," she knows. "But while he was mortal, there must be a triumph."

Then she learns, with a thrill that she firmly holds in check, that he has had a central role in gracing the runaways' weekend amour with marital sanctions. "For herself she was humbled," says Austen (52), using the phrase for a second time, meaningfully: again Elizabeth comes down from a high place, this time through a new perception of stature in the man who she had thought was only walking stiffly on the stilts of status. Austen goes on immediately: "but she was proud of him. Proud that in a cause of compassion and honour he had been able to get the better of himself." Here is a new increment to the ever-expanding significance of *pride*: admiration for the moral quality revealed in the mastery of prejudice. For both, pride as a responsibility to truth leads to humility as an acknowledgment of error.

Yet Austen sees instinctively that the story has not gone quite far enough, that it needs an additional rounding out for the final achievement of form, and she comes up with it in the Elizabeth-Darcy postmortem very near the end. Now it is Darcy's turn to register formally a self-understanding such as has been implicit in his actions and explicit in Elizabeth's various reflections on the course of events. It is remarkable that here indeed Darcy acknowledges the kind of pride that Elizabeth had originally imputed to him. Of his rearing: "I had been given good principles but left to follow them in pride and conceit" (58). He goes on to speak of his habit of looking down on the rest of the world. But then came Elizabeth: "You taught me a lesson, hard indeed at first but most advantageous. By you I was properly humbled"—brought down from high complacency and converted to the more substantial pride of which he had always the capability. Both lovers have gone through self-corrective experiences that can be rendered in the same vocabulary; in being "humbled," both have learned to see themselves in a less exalted perspective.

The repeated juxtaposition of *pride* and *humility* (or *proud* and *humbled*) would, in its exploitation of a traditional tension, be effective without any support. But surely it gains something from our recollection, subliminal though it may be, of Collins, whose self-conscious professions of humility scarcely concealed a pressing, if unrecognized, self-satisfaction. The split between Collins and Darcy-Elizabeth, then, is not between admirable humility and lamentable pride, but rather between much richer possibilities in human character: a union on the one hand of vulgar humility and vulgar pride and, on the other, of right pride and true humility. In different qualitative ranges, opposites coexist.

In the final chapters there is another charming accent by contrast, this one overt. Elizabeth, as we saw, is "proud" of Darcy. Compare Mr. Bennet's praise of his new son-in-law Wickham: "He simpers, and smirks, and makes love to us all. I am prodigiously proud of him" (53). While the daughter pays tribute to quality, the father ironically pays tribute to its absence. It is the ironic man's comeback from a failure rooted in his irony (his irony is not unlike Wickham's charm, a substitute for principle).

viii

The term *multiplicity* which I used earlier applies, it is now clear, both to the pride theme and to the marriage theme: people use the word and manage the institution in many different ways. Comedy examines all options and in effect forgives all (when *all* options are untenable or humanly inadequate, comedy becomes "black"). Here, comedy accepts all versions of semantic and matrimonial practice—in the sense that it knows these diversities to be inevitable and that, unlike satire, it does not inveigh against any of them. Yet "accept" does not imply either a chaotic medley of undifferentiable alternatives or a chaotic formlessness in a story embracing too many options to achieve coherence through an order of values. The novel does not say, "People use *pride* in many ways, and it doesn't really matter how you use it." It says, rather, "Some people use the word more discriminatingly than others," and it makes clear that the more discriminating users, far from being academic precisians, are the better human beings. The novel does not say only, though it does say, "Everybody has some form of pride"; it goes on to say, "There are better and worse forms of pride, and happily for the world and for human quality some people are drawn to the better forms." Again the novel says, but it does not only say, "There are many types of marital relationships, and they all work more or less." It also says, "Some marriages exact more maturing effort from the human being, some bring into play a fuller humanity, and some are more interesting because they entertain a wider and deeper vision of human possibility." Thus the multiple elements do not lie passively side by side, in value equivalent or indistinguishable; rather they shed light or cast shadows on each other, and thus some become brighter and some dimmer; some become larger, and some smaller. The dramatic relationships, entirely unaided by exegetical discourse, gradually erect, if not a hierarchy, at least a scale, of values, and thus the novel, as a narrative embodiment of thought, takes form. To borrow a phrase from a possibly unlikely source, we can indeed say, of *Pride and Prejudice, e pluribus unum*.

The oneness is served not only by the unobtrusive sense of values that orders the main strands with respect to each other but also by an equally unobtrusive sense of proportion. Austen gives primary and amplest attention to the pair who exhibit the values by which, without thinking about it, we judge the stature of all the other men and women. Elizabeth and Darcy are the characters who experience most deeply the problem of pride (and of prejudice, though less extensively than that of pride); they are capable initially of a commonplace pride but eventually of a superior pride and of a proper humility; they come to use these key words with more accuracy and with a keener consciousness of meaning than nearly all of the others do; and they have to reorder their preconceptions of themselves and of each other. We look longest at this pair who exemplify what I have called the "earned" relationship, the one that calls most extensively upon human powers of understanding, of revaluation, of self-recognition, and of self-correction. To undiminished vigor they add good sense and courtesy. Thus they bring most fully into play the qualities that make civilized life possible. They have to be the most significant, and hence the most interesting, couple.

Elizabeth had used a cliché term that was inadequate because it represented a conventional point of view that oversimplified truth; Darcy initially employed a conventional point of view that did not do justice to all the Bennets. Incongruity and discrepancy are a central Austen subject, and its most characteristic form is a disparity between cliché or convention on the one hand and, on the other, the reality for which at first they appear to be a reliable shorthand. This disparity appears repeatedly in her fiction, and it is handled with gradually increasing subtlety. The juvenilia parody various motifs of eighteenth-century popular fiction: the humor turns on the ludicrousness of styles and plots that, losing their lifelines to actuality, have stiffened into clichés and conventions. *Northanger Abbey* increases the complexity of the jest: a literary convention that once seemed to introduce a new reality now cuts off its devotee from an adequate sense of reality. In *Sense and Sensibility* a popular convention of feeling, taken to be intrinsically meritorious, is shown to increase the difficulties of actuality, both for the feeling person and for those affected by what she does; yet here the picture takes on additional dimension, for the conventional feeling, though it leads to unhappy distortions, looks much better than no feeling at all. In *Emma* and *Pride and Prejudice* the situation is markedly richer: complacent individuals, proceeding from stereotyped expectations, try to make circumstances conform to their a priori notions. By a slow revision of preconceptions, as we have seen, Elizabeth and Darcy "earn" the better insight and the rapport that insight makes possible. Emma varies from them by being more managerial, but the range of *Emma* is less: while Emma earns a better sense of fact by dismay and even humiliation, still she is less involved in the misconstrued world, and has a great deal of help from the man whose good sense is a given. In working with a somewhat thinner mixture, *Emma* occupies an intermediate ground between *Pride and Prejudice* and both *Mansfield Park*, written earlier, and *Persuasion*, still to be written. In the latter two what is missing is the earning of a better self and life that is at the dramatic center of *Pride and Prejudice*; Fanny Price and Anne Elliot see things pretty accurately from the start and have little learning, at least about themselves, to do. Their a priori rightness, instead of undergoing correction by, secures affirmation by, experience. We wait, not for the ironic graduation toward rectitude of perception, but for people and circumstances to catch up with a rectitude that is a given. This simpler movement, largely without the exploration of the discrepancy between prejudgment (by cliché, convention, complacency, or willfulness) and reality which is the most characteristic ground of the Austen comic mode, doubtless accounts for the less favorable judgments of *Mansfield Park* and *Persuasion* (which lead in turn to clashes over their merits). To look at these two in these terms, though with a haste that is not quite fair, is to gain an additional perspective on the breadth and depth of *Pride and Prejudice.*

■ 7 ■
Charlotte Brontë, Reason, and the Moon

i

A READER IN SEARCH of handy formulas of placement might under-standably think of Jane Austen as "classical" and Charlotte Brontë as "romantic," or, more precisely, as exemplars, respectively, of "reason" and "imagination." But neither writer is so simply placeable. Austen's diversity we have described. Brontë's use of the imagination, as we have seen, enabled her to give new life to an old convention, the Gothic. Still there is a problem here, indeed a great irony: one of Brontë's major fears, a biographer has said, was fear of the imagination; entry into the imaginative could actually seem to her to be a guilty self-indulgence. This is not untrue, and yet Charlotte was anything but consistent; one minute she was in the mood of the Frenchwoman who cried out en-thusiastically at a party, "J'adore la logique," and then she could turn around and warmly anatomize the defects of reason. The truth is that few artists can have been so beset as she was by the competing claims of the rational and the nonrational upon art and life.

She falls between the counterforces described by Robert Graves in a somewhat teasing postscript[1] to his "controversial" *White Goddess* of 1948. "The avowed purpose of science," says Graves, "is to banish all lunar superstitions and bask in the pure light of solar reason." In one mood, Charlotte Brontë would surely subscribe to this purpose. But Graves takes a dim view of this progress, which he says would be fatal to all true poetry; and he foresees historical developments that will include the emergence of a new goddess of "intuition." There is no doubt that among pre-Gravesian devotees of this religion Charlotte would also have to be counted.

We can learn something about Charlotte Brontë's personality and her art by observing how deeply her novels are penetrated by the counterat-tractions of reason and whatever "superstition" or "intuition" or other impulses arise to oppose it. I want to look first at some expository pas-sages, and this will mean risking the catalog; but the assembling of key statements will make a valuable background against which to see how, at important dramatic crises, the very shape of the action is determined by

Charlotte's consciousness of the duel, in Graves's terms, between Apollo and the White Goddess.

Even in *The Professor* and *Shirley*, where Charlotte is consciously restrained, essaying the social-pictorial, and therefore implicitly "Apollonian," the struggle appears. In *The Professor* she insists on the "plain and homely," scorns "the idealists, the dreamers," earnestly adjures "novelists . . . never . . . to weary of the study of real life." Her aesthetic is rooted in a rationalistic ethic: "the man of regular life and rational mind never despairs." Crimsworth avers, "Reason was my physician; [and] . . . did me good" and rejoices that in Frances "the more dangerous flame burned safely under the eye of reason," which could "reduce the rebel, and humble its blaze to embers"; with almost doctrinaire insistence he theorizes that Reason must secretly justify even those impulses "which control us." Such maxims are meant to determine the development of both character and plot.

Yet, after all of this, the more sentient and disorderly Brontë emerges—even in the domain of theory. Crimsworth, the apostle of reason, refers to "my darling, my cherished-in-secret, Imagination, the tender and the mighty." When this "sweet temptress" pictures for him an evening with Frances Henri, he fears that he may not be able "to address her only in the language of Reason and Affection." This is chronologically the introduction to "Imagination," one of Charlotte's two great terms for the nonrational that pulls her strongly. The other is "feeling," and its spokesman in *The Professor* is Frances Henri. Through her the true Charlotte pathos escapes in revolt against the world of rationality that Charlotte formally proclaims as the domain of her first novel. To Yorke Hunsden, Frances retorts, "Better to be without logic than without feeling," and she amplifies the retort into a firm attack on him for "interfering with your own feelings, and those of other people" because "you imagine" them to be "inconsistent with logic."

In *Shirley* there is less direct talk about reason and its counterforces, yet the tendency of both talk and action is toward the validation of the spontaneous. Social order is the rational theme, but the private intuition is where Charlotte repeatedly comes to rest. Caroline Helstone defends "instinct," "the voice we hear in solitude," as the source of trustworthy knowledge. A "strange, excited feeling in my heart" is a clue to stirring events. In the name of "common sense" Mrs. Yorke makes a violent attack upon Caroline for relying upon "impulse" and "*feelings*," which she says is sentimental and romantic; yet the reader is meant to sympathize with Caroline's earnest credo: "Of course, I should be guided by my feelings: they were given me to that end." Of Shirley, Louis Moore says, "Once I only *saw* her beauty, now I *feel* it." And Charlotte, who constantly wishes to be anti-romantic, clearly intends that we accept Caroline's declaration of faith on Shirley's love affair: "It *is* romantic, but it is also right."

Since it is a historical commonplace that Charlotte was imaginatively most free in her second and fourth novels, we might expect to find little play of the "pure light of solar reason" in *Jane Eyre* and *Villette*. Yet, despite a feeling for the "dark" that is of great aesthetic importance, Charlotte is always plagued by the claims of the light. In the fortune-telling scene in *Jane Eyre*, Rochester interprets what Jane's "forehead declares". "Reason sits firm and holds the reins, and she will not let the feelings burst away and hurry her to wild chasms." When Jane thinks that she has let herself love a Rochester who is really in love with Miss Ingram, she reports that "Reason" has told "how I had rejected the real, and rabidly devoured the ideal." It is on this occasion that she tries to "bring back with a strict hand" such "thoughts and feelings" of the heart as "had been straying through imagination's boundless and trackless waste, into the safe fold of common sense." All this might be the burden of an age-of-reason novel—except that reason is undercut, for imagination's trackless waste turns out to be exactly the route to Jane's well being. On another occasion reason is almost justified by being given the odd role of aide to feelings. When Rochester ruthlessly pressures Jane to be his mistress, she reports that "my very conscience and reason turned traitors against me, and . . . spoke almost as loud as Feeling: and that clamoured wildly. 'Oh, comply!' it said."

At another time Jane sets forth the basic dualism of Charlotte's moral awareness: "Feeling without judgment is a washy draught indeed; but judgment untempered by feeling is too bitter and husky a morsel for human deglutition." On the whole, the washy draught is the lesser of two dangers; Jane's regular impulse is to say "I feel" this or that, to insist, "I know what I feel." When she splits her inheritance with the Riverses, she calls it "as much a matter of feeling as of conscience: I must indulge my feelings; I so seldom have had an opportunity of doing so." Though feeling may not always be reliable, its dependability appears to grow with the intensity of the crisis; Jane trusts utterly that "feeling . . . as sharp, as strange, as startling" as an electric shock that awakens her to Rochester's telepathic cry. "That wondrous shock of feeling had come like the earthquake which shook the foundations of Paul and Silas's prison; it had opened the doors of the soul's cell." It saved Jane. And here, surely, Charlotte is writing poetry under the auspices that Robert Graves approves.

After the insistent justification of feeling in *Shirley* and the triumph of the intuitive in *Jane Eyre* we might expect that by the time she came to *Villette* Charlotte would not have to refight the old battle of values. But no such freedom is hers; Lucy Snowe must live through the same conflict in which Crimsworth and Jane Eyre were caught. In religious dispute, of course, Lucy is content to be on the side of Reason (nearly always capitalized in *Villette*), which she is sure condemns Catholicism. On one distressed occasion she feels a "wild longing," but it is "softened into a wish with which Reason could cope: she put it down." Toward the Brettons, her rescuers, she feels "an importunate gratitude, which I entreated Reason betimes to check"; she approves "these struggles" that help give conduct "that turn which Reason approves, and which Feeling, perhaps, too often opposes." But the rational virtues are much less attractive in Mme. Beck, who, like other characters that Charlotte does not admire, consults only her "judgment" and is not "led an inch by her feelings," and what is more attributes M. Paul's devotion to Lucy to his "unreliable, imaginative temperament."

Yet as artist Charlotte sees clearly the complex facts of life; she makes Lucy observe that we dislike and avoid some people "though reason confesses that they are good people." At times Lucy simply cannot stand the "dry, stinting check of Reason" and thinks that she must yield to the "full, liberal impulse of feeling." In *Villette* as a whole Charlotte takes especial pains to justify feeling, almost as if she had to beat down the principles of a too-rational world. "Before I *saw*, I *felt* that life was in the great room," says Lucy. "Deep into some of Madame's secrets I had entered—I know not how: by an intuition or an inspiration which came to me—I know not whence." When someone whom she assumes to be a workman opens her door, she "felt a little thrill—a curious sensation, too quick and transient to be analyzed"—and the entrant turns out to be Paul. Lucy recognizes a fellow hypochondriac by facial marks whose meaning "if I did not *know*, at least I *felt*." Polly Home shares the trust in feeling as a way of knowing: "how strange it is that people seem so slow to feel the truth—not to see, but *feel!*" In these characteristic passages we find not only "intuition," which for Graves denotes a positive value, but three distinct occasions on which "feeling" (repeatedly italicized) is made prior or superior to "knowing" or "seeing"—an implicit rejection of the "pure light of solar reason."

At the apex of the terms in which Charlotte expresses her conflict in impulses and values stands "Imagination." Naturally Lucy is compelled to pit its claims against those of Reason. But against what Reason? A beautiful, Athena-like figure? No, against "This hag, this Reason," with its "withered hand" and "chill blue lips of eld": "Reason might be right; yet no wonder we are glad at times to defy her, to rush from under her rod and give a truant hour to Imagination—*her* soft, bright foe, *our* sweet Help, our divine Hope." But for this defiance Reason, "vindictive as a devil," exacts a "terrible revenge." All the ambiguity of Charlotte's feelings is concentrated in the word *imagination*; it means to her, in one mood, a snare and a delusion; in another mood she could exclaim with Thomas Mann's Felix Krull, "What a glorious gift is imagination, and what satisfaction it affords," and even crave it as a road to safety. Happily Lucy yields to it, or is ravished by it, one summer night after Mme. Beck has given her a sedative:

> Imagination was roused from her rest, and she came forth impetuous and venturous. With scorn she looked on Matter, her mate—
>
> "Rise!" she said; "Sluggard! this night I will have *my* will; nor shalt thou prevail."
>
> "Look forth and view the night!" was her cry. . . .

This introduces the most wonderful of Charlotte's nocturnes: the surrealistic park scene that opens the English novel to an extraordinary new perceptiveness and style. The essence of the long passage is the casting of a strange and fascinating veil of illusion over familiar things; through the enchanting veil Lucy makes some errors, and then she rebukes herself—how? "Ah! when imagination once runs riot where do we stop?" And twice she spanks her "Fancy" for leading her astray. But if Lucy thus gives voice to the "rational" element in Charlotte, fortunately the artist in Charlotte lets stand, untouched, the thrilling account of all that Lucy felt and fancied when "Imagination was roused from her rest."

ii

The conflict between reason-judgment-common sense and feeling-imagination-intuition, a conflict that lasted through Charlotte's life as an artist, existed not simply as a routine echo of a general human problem but because of the profound attraction that the nonrational had for her. Hence the frequency with which it comes into the words of all her major characters and, more important, into conflicts between and within characters. But still beyond that, what is at stake is the kind of artist Charlotte is to be; and by that I mean the kind of aesthetic excitement that she is to create when her characters are engaged in crucial actions; that is, in actions in which they must be most freely and wholly themselves. The choice that ends the crux may be "reasonable," but the instrument of decision, the persuasive presence, may be nonrational or suprarational. If the movement in Charlotte's novels—the growth of her protagonists—is toward something that we can call "daylight," the field of significant action is often the dark.

Graves's key phrases are *lunar superstition* and *solar reason*. So far we have proceeded as if "superstition" and "reason" encompassed all that is to be inspected, and as if "lunar" and "solar" were not there at all, or were no more than convenient metaphorical tags. But the adjectives are very important to Graves, whose stance is vigorously anti-Apollonian and who attributes "creative power in poetry" to "inspiration," and "inspiration" to "the Lunar Muse." He is almost ostentatious in his salute to the moon, which "moves the tides, influences growth, rules the festal calendar of Judaism, Islam, and Christianity, and possesses other unaccountable magic properties, known to every lover and poet."

Well, if Charlotte Brontë, the anguished devotee of feeling and intuition, had followed Graves in time, it would be difficult not to describe her as under his "influence." Or if a follower of his had set out to establish a lunar cult by fictional propaganda, he could hardly have exploited the moon more fully than she has done. Whether by plan or through an unconscious or semiconscious sense of forces at work in the world, Charlotte tends to make the "White Goddess" a presiding deity, if not over her novels as a whole, at least over moments of crisis.[2]

Even in *The Professor,* that intendedly matter-of-fact tale of plain lovers, Charlotte's attraction to the moon adds a fanciful note. On the night when Crimsworth has a significant interview with disturbing Yorke Hunsden, "there was a crescent curve of moonlight to be seen by the parish church tower." Later, on a "glorious night," when "an unclouded moon poured her light" down into a beechwood glade, "Hunsden held out under her beam an ivory miniature"—a likeness of an old love in whose face Frances Henri sees signs of a "triumphant effort, to wrest some vigorous and valued faculty from insupportable constraint." The mild note of revelation in these passages becomes stronger in the episode in which Crimsworth sees Mlle. Zoraïde Reuter, who has been making eyes at him and getting some response from him, carrying on with his employer Pelet: "above me was the clear-obscure of a cloudless night sky—splendid moonlight subdued the tremulous sparkle of the stars." Later Crimsworth remarks that Pelet was ignorant that "the still hour, a cloudless moon, and an open lattice had revealed to me the secret of his selfish love and false friendship."

In *Shirley* Charlotte presents a much subtler triangular situation, and she does it in a much better realized scene. It is in the "moonlight beauty" of the estate that Caroline Helstone sees Shirley Keeldar and Robert Moore, whom she wrongly supposes to be in love:

> Tree and hall rose peaceful under the night sky and clear full orb; pearly paleness gilded the buildings; mellow brown gloom bosomed it round; shadows of deep green brooded above its oak-wreathed roof. The broad pavement in

front shone pale also; it gleamed as if some spell had transformed the dark granite to glistering Parian: on the silvery space slept two sable shadows, thrown sharply defined from two human figures.

The word *spell* does not beg the question for Charlotte's art, which here begins to make us respond to the special scenic and tonal vividness to which the moon inspires her.

This is in *Shirley*, where Charlotte is most fully committed to the daylight view of experience. It tells us a great deal about her that even here she is repeatedly drawn to the moonlight, to the shiver of the strange which for her it communicates, and which she communicates by stylistic originality. On a night when Caroline is suffering from her emotional illness we are told not that there is a "full moon" and a "blue sky," but that the sky is "gravely blue" and "full of the moon." Caroline meets fifteen-year-old Martin Yorke, whom she fascinates, under a "pearl-white moon" that "smiles through the green trees." Robert Moore meets a "mad Calvinist" on a "clouded" but "very windy night": "the moon was at the full, and Michael was as near crazed as possible." If this has more of the conventional, we find the special Brontë frisson on the night Robert is shot from ambush, when Mr. Yorke says of the moon that it is "rising into the haze, staring at us wi' a strange red glower. . . . What does she mean by leaning her cheek on Rushedge i' that way, and looking at us wi' a scowl and a menace?"

However, Charlotte lets go most excitingly when the lunar contributes to the kind of task she nearly always performs originally—the exploration of personality. At the end of a hallucinatory period in Caroline's psychosomatic illness, "The moon, lately risen, was gazing full and mild upon her: floating in deep blue space, it watched her unclouded." By this personification, which she uses a number of times, Charlotte edges away from the pictorial toward a concept that can be used thrillingly—the idea of a cosmic sensibility observing mortal actions. This implies a sensitive mortal responsiveness, and with Caroline this sensitivity takes the form of a profound anxiety. She observes, "The moon shines clear," and she imagines grimly that "within the church just now that moonlight shines as softly as in my room. It will fall through the east window full on the Helstone monument. When I close my eyes I seem to see poor papa's epitaph in black letters on the white marble. There is plenty of room for other inscriptions underneath." As often, the moonlight leads to a concreteness that creates the life in the scene.

Or the moon may sponsor a romantic fantasy. Shirley's lover, Louis Moore, who calls himself a "rapt, romantic lunatic," picks a stormy moonlight night to savor waking dreams of Shirley: "the great single cloud . . . tossed buoyant before a continued long-sounding, high-rushing moonlight tempest. The Moon reigns glorious, glad of the gale; as glad as if she gave herself to his fierce caress with love." The erotic shiver, which frequently breaks into Charlotte's fiction, is right enough here, for Louis, insisting, "I *do* dream: I *will* dream," eventually has a vision of Shirley as a Juno replaying the Jupiter-Semele story and becoming, when seen directly, "an insufferable glory burning terribly between the pillars" and destroying a rival lover. The White Goddess admits a destructive hatred into sentimental reverie.

Shirley, who, "her eye full of night and lightning," evades her lover Louis in a cold "moon-lit hall," and who walks at night on "the chance of meeting a fairy," also has nocturnal visions: under a "new throned and glorious" moon she feels a "still, deep, inborn delight."

> This joy gives her experience of a genii-life. Buoyant, by green steps, by glad hills, all verdure and light, she reaches a station scarcely lower than that whence angels looked down on the dreamer of Bethel, and her eye seeks, and her soul possesses, the vision of life as she wishes it. No—not as she wishes it; she has not time to wish: the swift glory spreads out, sweeping and kindling, and multiplies its splendours faster than Thought can effect his combinations, faster than Aspiration can utter her longings. Shirley says nothing while the trance is upon her . . .

Here the lunar muse sets free, for its own sake, a kind of vision that fiction had not known since Bunyan.

A virtuoso with the moon, Charlotte uses it to reveal not only "swift glory" but also fascinating horror. Again the vision is Shirley's, and now she tells how a mermaid might appear. Here again the moon is personified, as if it had a mysterious hand in the affair, for Shirley and Caroline are supposedly on the deck of a ship, "watching and being watched by a full harvest moon":

> something is to rise white on the surface of the sea, over which that moon mounts silent, and hangs glorious: the object glitters and sinks. It rises again. I think I hear it cry with an articulate voice: I call you up from the cabin: I show you an image, fair as alabaster, emerging from the dim wave. We both see the long hair, the lifted and foam-white arm, the oval mirror, brilliant as a star. It glides nearer: a human face is plainly visible; a face . . . paleness does not disfigure . . . I see a preternatural lure in its wily glance: it beckons. Were we men we should spring at the sign, the cold billow would be dared for the sake of the colder enchantress; being women, we stand safe, though not dreadless. She comprehends our unmoved gaze; she feels herself powerless; anger crosses her front; she cannot charm, but she will appal us: she rises high, and glides all revealed, on the dark wave-ridge. Temptress-terror! monstrous likeness of ourselves!

Here once more is the surrealistic toward which Charlotte swings when she is creatively most uninhibited. It is wonderful pictorially, but her adventurous imagination goes beyond stage setting to express a stirring new intuition of reality. The moon visions always partake of the revelatory—of human possibility or human actuality, or of the quality of mind of those who have the visions. When Charlotte wants to make a quick plunge into the rare essence of a character, she instinctively demands the presence of the lunar muse.

iii

Though one may not be prepared for the frequent appearances of the moon in *Shirley,* he would indeed expect a Charlotte devoted to the White Goddess to bring her constantly into the kind of book that *Jane Eyre* is. He would be right; in *Jane Eyre* the moon is an aesthetic staple, at times a scenic element inherently charming to the writer, at times almost a character; at its most interesting it reveals an author groping for a cosmic symbolization of reality, or toward a reality beyond the confines of everyday actuality, toward an interplay of private consciousness and mysterious forces in the universe. In a book one of the illustrations that catch Jane's eye is of a "cold and ghastly moon glancing through bars of cloud at a wreck just sinking"; in one of her extraordinary surrealistic paintings, the woman "rising into the sky" bears "on the neck . . . a pale reflection like moonlight; the same faint lustre touched the train of thin clouds from which rose and bowed this vision of the Evening Star"; again, when she is "sketching fancy vignettes . . . [from] the ever-shifting kaleidoscope of imagination," Jane draws "the rising moon, and a ship crossing its disk"; she cannot help imagining how "strange" the antique beds on the third floor at Thornfield would have looked "by the pallid gleam of moonlight." Rochester is moonstruck too. Of a past mistress he became jealous on a "moonlit balcony," and he describes one "fiery West Indian night" when, with "black clouds . . . casting up over" the ocean, he listened to his maniac wife shriek curses: "the moon was setting in the waves, broad and red, like a hot cannon-ball—she threw her last bloody glance over a world quivering with the ferment of tempest." The physical universe is in tune with his private agony.

But this is only a start. In Jane's life every crucial event has its special lunar display. To leave Gateshead, she dresses "by light of a half-moon just setting"; at Lowood she and Helen Burns first visit the friendly Miss Temple's room when the "rising wind" swept "some heavy clouds" away and "left the moon bare; and her light . . . shone full both on us and on . . . Miss Temple"; again, "the light of the unclouded summer moon" aids her on her way to what is to be the death scene of Helen Burns.

Always there is the suggestion of a transcendental force mildly at work; but above all, these lunar nocturnes have an air of mystery. Jane meets Rochester by moonlight and accepts his proposal by moonlight; Mrs. Rochester once raids the lower house by moonlight; the moon has a share in the terrors of the night before the abortive wedding, in Jane's decision to leave Thornfield, and finally in her rejection of Rivers and return to Rochester.

On the night Jane meets Rochester she is constantly aware of the moon, which appears on page after page. "On the hill-top above me sat the rising moon; pale yet as a cloud, but brightening momently: she looked over Hay." Here the moon is detached observer; after Jane meets the fallen rider, "the moon was waxing bright," and she could see him clearly. The moon is protective: "I am not at all afraid of being out late when it is moonlight." They look at Thornfield Hall, "on which the moon cast a hoary gleam"; Jane observes a willow "rising up still and straight to meet the moonbeams." The encounter is exciting, particularly because she has been helpful; in this state of mind she hates to return to dull Thornfield and turns instead to the sky:

> a blue sea absolved from taint of cloud; the moon ascending it in solemn march; her orb seeming to look up as she left the hill tops, from behind which she had come, far and farther below her, and aspired to the zenith, midnight-dark in its fathomless depth and measureless distance. . . .

The lunar being, which can serve as a source of sympathy with an existent mood (here it is a kind of fellow aspirant), can also inspire a fitting mood. One night

> when the moon, which was full and bright . . . , came in her course to that space in the sky opposite my casement, and looked in at me through the unveiled panes, her glorious gaze roused me. Awaking in the dead of night, I opened my eyes on her disk—silver-white and crystal-clear. It was beautiful, but too solemn: I half rose, and stretched my arm to draw the curtain.

At this moment the house is thrown into terror by mad Mrs. Rochester's attack on Mason.

On the night of Rochester's proposal the lunar symbolization of disorder works somewhat differently. At first the garden is charming in the light of the "now-risen moon"; Rochester's shadow is "thrown long over the garden by the moon not yet risen high," and he urges Jane not to go to bed, "while sunset is thus at meeting with moonrise"; when he formally proposes, she commands him to "turn to the moonlight," as if for verification. Then: "But what had befallen the night? The moon was not yet set, and we were all in shadow: I could scarcely see my master's face."

It is, I believe, rather easy to overrate the conventional in the scenic details here; this is more likely to happen if we take the episode alone and fail to see it in relation to the whole pattern of lunar imagery. The symbols of the proposal scene—the moon, and the chestnut tree split by lightning—lose whatever they have of an extemporized, melodramatic air when they are carried on into the stormy pre-wedding-night scene and become direct objects of Jane's anxiety-filled contemplation. As she is addressing the two parts of the split chestnut, "the moon appeared momentarily in that part of the sky which filled their fissure; her disk was blood-red, and half-overcast; she seemed to throw on me one bewildered, dreary glance, and buried herself again instantly in the deep drift of cloud."

Through the moon the outer world becomes consonant with Jane's own misgivings. Since it is "moonlight at intervals," Jane looks for Rochester, who is away on business, but he does not come; finally "the moon shut herself wholly within her chamber, and drew close her curtain of dense cloud. . . . rain came driving fast." Jane gives way to "hypochondriac foreboding," relieved when she finds that "the moon had opened a blue field in the sky, and rode in it watery bright"; she sees Rochester returning. She tells him of a dream of Thornfield Hall in ruins, and herself wandering there "on a moonlight night," looking for him and finally crashing down with a crumbling wall. But he comforts her; the west winds blow the clouds away, and there is a benediction: "The moon shone peacefully."

In *Villette*, as in *Jane Eyre*, the moon comes into its sharpest dramatic role late in the story. But it obsesses Charlotte enough to keep sliding into earlier scenes: Lucy looks at sleeping Polly Home "by the fitful gleam of moonlight," walks on a European street "by a fitful gleam of moonlight," or gazes at "the polar splendour of the new-year moon—an orb white as a world of ice." In this last, the pictorial fact betrays an odd quiver of aesthetic life, as it does, too, when Miss Marchmont tells of her lover's death: "I see the moon of a calm winter night float full, clear, and cold, over the inky mass of shrubbery, and the silvered turf of my grounds"; her lover is thrown from his horse, and she asks, "How could I name that thing in the moonlight before me?"

Gradually we become aware that in some vague way that Charlotte has not defined for herself the moon stands for something. This is how Lucy puts her envy of the gay Ginevra Fanshawe: "I too felt those autumn suns and saw those harvest moons, and I almost wished to be covered in with earth and turf, deep out of their influence; for I could not live in their light, nor make them comrades, nor yield them affection." What is significant here is that the sun (the only time it appears in a serious treatment of feeling) and the moon could be felt as "comrades" by and could exert "influence" on a human being. (Brontë uses the astrological term, but does not think astrologically.) The power to influence is more strongly implied in a later reflection of Lucy's:

> Where, indeed, does the moon not look well? What is the scene, confined or expansive, which her orb does not hallow? Rosy or fiery, she mounted . . . while we watched her flushed ascent, she cleared to gold, and . . . floated up stainless into a now calm sky. Did moonlight soften or sadden Dr. Bretton? Did it touch him with romance?

Such passages prepare us for the series of garden scenes involving the "apparitions" that are important in the story. Lucy's first experience of that frightening event takes place—yes, on a moonlight night.

> A moon was in the sky, not a full moon, but a young crescent. I saw her through a space in the boughs overhead. She and the stars, visible beside her, were no strangers where all else was strange: my childhood knew them. I had seen that golden sign with the dark globe in its curve leaning on azure, beside an old thorn at the top of an old field, in Old England.

Now this scene is linked with a subsequent crucial garden scene not only by the moonlight but also by Lucy's association of one lighted night scene with another (a habit which shows that Charlotte's lunar sensibility was regular and stable, not casual and erratic). In the later scene Lucy's moral growth is dramatized by her burial of some letters from Graham and by her refusal to flee from the apparition. "At seven o'clock the moon rose," Lucy notes in the documentary style that often finely supports her nonnaturalistic episodes.

> The air of the night was very still, but dim with a peculiar mist, which changed the moonlight into a luminous haze. In this air, or this mist, there was some quality—electrical, perhaps—which acted in a strange sort upon me. I felt them as I had felt a year ago in England—on a night when the aurora borealis was streaming and sweeping round heaven, . . . I felt, not happy, far otherwise, but strong with reinforced strength.

The night Lucy refers to was one on which, returning from a visit, she "should have quailed in the absence of moonlight" but for the "moving mystery—the Aurora Borealis": "Some new power it seemed to bring." On that occasion she resolved to go to London, leaving a desolate life behind her, just as now in the garden she is taking steps to leave a life of fear and psychic dependence behind her; each time it is a nocturnal light from the sky that she identifies as the source of the ability to advance: of power and strength.

In the affair with M. Paul that is the major experience in Lucy's life two key scenes are moonlit—one of them in the same old garden. On this night Paul is distressingly cool and detached: "once again he looked at the moon. . . . In a moment he was gone; the moonlit threshold lay pale and shadowless before the closed front-door." Then he gives her a Catholic pamphlet meant to convert her, one of the moves in the sober dramatic treatment of the important religious theme (to be compared, for instance, with Scott's trivializing of it in *Rob Roy*). The moon presides over a still more serious event, this time in another garden: when Paul gives Lucy a school of her own, "Above the poplars, the laurels, the cypresses, and the roses, looked up a moon so lovely and so halcyon, the heart trembled under her smile." Although the passage is ambiguous, Lucy appears to be addressing the moon when she apostrophizes: "White Angel! let thy light linger; leave its reflection on succeeding clouds; bequeath its cheer to that time which needs a ray in retrospect." (Paul's surname is Emanuel, and "the assurance of his sleepless interest . . . broke on me like a light from heaven.") The religious implication of the moon imagery is carried further after Paul's proposal: "We walked back to the Rue Fossette by moonlight—such moonlight as fell on Eden— shining through the shades of the Great Garden, and haply gilding a path glorious for a step divine—a Presence nameless." This is the last use of the moon in Charlotte's last novel, and it is the ultimate reach in her interpretation of the moon—the moon that could hallow a scene, be a comrade, exert an influence, supply strength, echo a great myth, and suggest the presence of the divine. Such a range would not be possible if she were idly summoning and manipulating a cliché.

iv

Nor would a cliché permit such striking passages as the three to which I finally turn—two in *Jane Eyre* and one in *Villette*. In these what is immediately remarkable is the way in which the moon steps vividly out of the decor to penetrate the dramatic action; and because it penetrates the action, we see the relation of these scenes to the theme which we have been considering in Graves's formulation, and to the underlying, never wholly articulated, meaning that the moon has for Charlotte as artist.

In *Jane Eyre*, we remember, Charlotte assiduously gives "reason" and "judgment" their due but keeps leaning toward "feeling" as the truly desirable and dependable quality in humanity. In fact, when Rochester pleads with Jane to stay with him, her reason all but supports her impulse to give in. But despite this double pressure she leaves. Under what aegis, then? All the forces that make for her departure are summed up in a fortifying dream, and it is right after the dream that she leaves. The dream starts by recalling a childhood terror—a mysterious light moving on an inside wall and seeming to be "a herald of some coming vision from another world." The light pauses "tremblingly" in the center of the ceiling.

> I lifted up my head to look: the roof resolved to clouds, high and dim; the gleam was such as the moon imparts to vapours she is about to sever. I watched her come—watched the strangest anticipation; as though some word of doom were to be written on her disk. She broke forth as never moon yet burst from cloud: a hand first penetrated the sable folds and waved them away; then, not a moon, but a white human form shone in the azure, inclining a glorious brow earthward. It gazed and gazed on me. It spoke to my spirit: immeasurably distant was the tone, yet so near, it whispered in my heart—
> "My daughter, flee temptation!"
> "Mother, I will."
> So I answered after I had waked from the trance-like dream.

Jane's almost immediate departure can hardly be said to come from "reason"; in fact, a devotee of reason might well attribute it to what Graves calls "lunar superstition." For the moon is there, the thrilling center of a highly original dramatic expression of another "feeling" that effectively counters the feeling (and the reason) that urges her to live with Rochester. This force is "immeasurably distant" but as "near" as a whisper in the heart: Charlotte's strong sense of the paradoxical alliance between the intimately personal and the universal.

Now let us observe the lunar relationship between this scene and the one in which St. John Rivers almost hypnotizes Jane into marrying him and she is saved by the telepathic summons from Rochester. The structural parallel between the scenes is amazingly close: in each, Jane is being subjected to almost overpowering pressure to accept a man who has some "reason" on his side and whom she only partly resists. Initially we recall that she rejects Rivers not for "good reasons" but because of a "sensation" of "unspeakable strangeness," a "wondrous shock of feeling"; indeed, Rivers is repeatedly described in a way that might make him a sort of figure of reason—for example, by images of cold and ice. By now we can see that Charlotte would inevitably make a night scene of Rivers's climactic effort to win Jane, for only in this way can she find the suitable dramatic form for her notion of how reality becomes known. The long scene starts with Rivers in the garden watching "the rising of the moon," and his turning "quite from the moon" to address Jane; then we move indoors and Rivers reads from the Bible—by a curious propriety from Revelation, for such scenes are always revelatory; and with great irony, since what is to be revealed is quite foreign to Rivers's expectations. During the reading "the May moon [is] shining in through the uncurtained window, and rendering almost unnecessary the light of the candle on the table." We begin to suspect an implied, perhaps not wholly conscious, contrast in the "lights" by which people act, and our suspicion is reinforced by what follows. Jane almost gives in to Rivers, but she struggles to find a decisive clue to the act of choice. As she puts it, "I contended with my inward dimness of vision, before which clouds yet rolled. . . . 'Show me, show me the path!' I entreated of Heaven." Her entreaty to Heaven is followed by this:

> The one candle was dying out: the room was full of moonlight. My heart beat fast and thick: I heard its throb. Suddenly it stood still to an inexpressible feeling that thrilled it through, and passed at once to my head and extremities.

This is the call from Rochester, and what is more, we find later that at this very time, when Rochester himself, having "supplicated God," had uttered the call that Jane heard, he, "by a vague, luminous haze, knew the presence of a moon." For Jane, the moonlight has put out the candlelight within the minister's house: some larger vision (marriage for love) has transcended a narrow call (marriage for "duty"). The moon is no accident; it is present to two people who have "dimness of vision" and who have called on Heaven; it assists in a discovery which the story presents as utterly right. The lunar light has been present at Jane's two rejections of men, and at her subsequent acceptance of an inexplicable call from one of them. For Charlotte it has become an aesthetic objectification of an "inner light," and yet also a means of relating that inner light to a universal illumination. Charlotte might have described the cosmic imperative by such an abstraction as "Divine Law." That she did otherwise shows the working of a fine aesthetic sensibility: for the simple naming of authority she substitutes a symbolic presence—concrete, pictorially exciting, stimulatingly rich in its undefinedness and in its undeniable suggestion of independent animistic forces and indeed of the pagan. And in the symbolization of an interplay between private feeling and cosmic order, as well as between minds physically far apart, there is an unresolved mystery that takes us far beyond any everyday rationale of things and events.

To some extent in all the lunar scenes, and overwhelmingly in the strongest episodes in *Shirley* and *Jane Eyre*, we respond to that strangely compelling effect which we call "surrealistic." In the most original and stirring scene in *Villette* this rejection of everyday realistic surfaces is not a momentary peek into mystery but is so extended that a whole new atmosphere is created and the effect is one of "enchantment." This is the night when Lucy's "Imagination" takes over, scorning "Matter, her mate," and conducts Lucy, who has had a sedative, on a remarkable midnight tour of the city on a fête day. Our problem is with the artistic means by which the scene is made literally "charming" when Imagination takes over.

> "Look forth and view the night!" was her cry; and when I lifted the heavy blind from the casement close at hand—with her own royal gesture, she showed me a moon supreme, in an element deep and splendid.
> To my gasping senses she made the glimmering gloom, the narrow limits, the oppressive heat of the dormitory, intolerable. She lured me to leave this den and follow her forth into dew, coolness, and glory.

Here is the moon again, at this point foremost among the nocturnal beguilements, identified now not with "feeling" as in *Jane Eyre* but with that other challenger of Reason, Imagination. Lucy yearns to enter the "moonlit, midnight park"; she wants to know the hour, and is sure she can read the school clock "by such a moon." Out she glides into the "wanderer-wooing" night: "I see its moon over me; I feel its dew in the air." Continually she pictures herself coming to a huge stone basin filled with water; she "longed to come on that circular mirror of crystal, and surprise the moon glassing therein her pearly front." In the park she reaches one wooded spot "aloof even from the lamps," but "with that full, high moon lamps were scarce needed." But this is an urban fête, and there is a wealth of artificial lighting; in one street, "moonlight and heaven are banished." Or artificial and natural collaborate. Of Madame Walravens's dress: "neither the chasteness of moonlight, nor the distance of the torches, could quite subdue the gorgeous dyes of the drapery." At a moment when a particular assemblage of characters seems to portend a "revelation," the "blaze" of a torch "aided the pale moon in doing justice to the crisis." At this point a very interesting problem comes up: Lucy misinterprets what she sees (she thinks Paul is in love with his goddaughter), and since she is viewing people in a mixed light, it would be easy to read the lunar vision as obscured by manmade lights. But consciously or not, Charlotte does it less simply than that; indeed, Lucy's self-critique is initially puzzling. From a questioning of Imagination itself she goes on to ask, "What winter tree so bare and branchless—what wayside, hedge-munching animal so humble, that Fancy, a passing cloud, and a struggling moonbeam will not clothe it in spirituality, and make of it a phantom?" "Cloud" and "moonbeam" as the source of vital error: it is as if Charlotte is destroying her favorite artistic instruments. And of another occasion when a mere arrangement of clothes had seemed a ghost: "Here again—behold the branchless tree, the unstabled Rosinante; the film of cloud, the flicker of moonshine." But fortunately Charlotte is not declaring for the rational and the literal, and in the end renouncing lunar superstition, on which she has built so many of her best effects. Rather she is restating in lunar imagery the problem with which she was always concerned—the distinction between an imagination that falsified reality by creating specious comfort or needless fear, and imagination that intuited truth. She rejects moonbeam mirages but never the moon. If she is on guard against quixotic mistakes, it seems to me safe to say that she never rejects the quixotic vision.

In fact, returning from the fête, from the "radiant park and well-lit Haute-Ville," Lucy seems relieved to return to "the dim lower quarter." Then she continues:

> Dim I should not say, for the beauty of the moonlight—forgotten in the park—here once more flowed in upon perception. High she rode, and calm and stainlessly she shone. The music and the mirth of the fête, the fire and the bright hues of those lamps had outdone and outshone her for an hour, but now again her glory and her silence triumphed. The rival lamps were dying: she held her course like a white fate. Drum, trumpet, bugle had uttered their clangour, and were forgotten; with pencil-ray she wrote on heaven and on earth records for archives everlasting. She and those stars seemed to me at once the types and witnesses of truth all regnant. The night-sky lit her reign: like its slow-wheeling progress, advanced her victory—that onward movement which has been, and is, and will be from eternity to eternity.

"The rival lamps were dying: she held her course like a white fate." Here is, finally, the antithesis we would expect—the same antithesis that informed the scene in which Rivers's candle was outshone by the moonlight in which Rochester called and was answered. The "white fate" has made itself felt, in Charlotte's four novels, in a score of crucial actions, of revelations and intuitions; in Louis Moore's dreams; in Caroline Helstone's sufferings and Robert Moore's danger; in Shirley's visions of millennial glories and of harsh human realities; in Jane Eyre's movements and perceptions and saving choices that relieve her from almost shattering pressures; in Lucy Snowe's moments of danger and discoveries of strength, and in the transient bliss that she has earned. "White fate" reminds us of Graves's "White Goddess," and this swings us back to a signal aspect of Charlotte's lunar scenes—the fact that, the more fully they are developed, the more their complex harmonies turn on the note of divinity. But we cannot finally assign an explicit symbolic value to Charlotte's moon. We know it is a "witness of truth"; we know that it represents another realm than that of the "Reason" where she at times aspired to dwell; we know that, in her struggle to find an accommodation between the traditional insight and the private vision, the moon had something of the mediatrix; we know that she wanted to abjure hallucination and the self-indulgent dream and to discover transcendent truth, and that in this struggle her ultimate reliance on feeling recurrently brings the lunar symbol into play.

Definition need not go further than that. In his prose ode to the lunar muse, to the lunar inspiration, Graves ultimately hymns the "muse poetry" that gives readers the shivering spine and the crawling scalp, that is "moon-magical enough to walk off the page." "Moon-magical"— that is the quality of Charlotte's best lunar scenes that we must feel, even though we do not precisely pin their meanings: the quality of those nights when the moon watches serenely from the grave blue, or is glad of the gale; of the mermaid rising from the sea, a temptress-terror; of the glorious gaze that is too solemn, a prelude to evil; of the hand that slides through the sable folds of cloud, preceding a form that speaks; of the far-distant call borne by the moonlit air; of dew, coolness, and glory—the moonlit, midnight park. In these the novel felt a tremor of new life.

■ 8 ■
"Stealthy Convergence" in *Middlemarch*

"STEALTHY CONVERGENCE," it need hardly be said, is extracted from a longer phrase in *Middlemarch*: "the stealthy convergence of human lots" (11; all references are to chapters). It is George Eliot's compact description of an ironic development of interconnection among people who do not expect it. It is in effect a restatement of "No man is an island." Yet its emphasis is different: less on the denial of separateness than on the almost imperceptible, or unperceived, process by which apparently independent lots turn out to be related. The primary process takes place, obviously, in the human experience depicted. But there is also a secondary process that is worth attention: it is an important ingredient in Eliot's methods of depiction—her ways of bringing parts into coalescence and ultimate oneness. *Convergence* then not only denotes a conceptual position but is a metaphor for artistic ordering. For Eliot's characters *stealthy* means a near invisibility of the developments that tie their lives together. For Eliot's readers it images the inconspicuous devices by which the artist draws us from area to area—the local transitions as well as the organic fusions.

The oldest and simplest tie that binds is the chronological, the transition effected by the ticking of the clock. A temporal sequence seems to the human mind to have an inherent oneness. *Middlemarch* is chronological in traditional ways. After Dorothea says "yes" to Casaubon, all that happens comes to us as it happens in time. Eliot gives no ground for another essay on how artists two-time time. (One may remark, in passing, that it is time for critics to untime themselves; time-talk must have a stop, for all its early paradoxes have aged into banalities.) Eliot's few variations from time-order are as old as epic practice—flashbacks and inset narratives. One flashback catches our eye because it is very subtly tied in. Eliot climaxes her long initial portrait of Lydgate (15) by recounting an earlier episode in his life. Here she shifts remarkably from her usual full specification to "stealthy convergence," which at this point is a symbolic connection between past and present that remains unstated. As a medical student in Paris, Lydgate had tried to marry an actress who, he was to discover, had coolly murdered her actor-husband during a stage scene in

117

which her stabbing him could seem an accident. Overtly, Eliot says only that his proposal was due to Lydgate's "impetuous folly." What she does not specify is the deeper symbolic tie between Lydgate's youthful proposal and his actual marriage, that is, his virtually suicidal attraction to beautiful, ruthless, even destructive women. Laure would reappear as Rosamond Vincy. (This use of the Laure story remarkably anticipates the Conrad technique of the "pilot episode," just as the interpretation of a medical type remarkably anticipates what Somerset Maugham and Sinclair Lewis would see in doctors whom they portrayed.)

But in a multiplicity novel with as many strands of action as *Middlemarch* has, the problems of relationship are less temporal than spatial. How make ties among parallel strands? Actionally, of course, the parallel lines alter to convergent lines: as characters fall into unexpected relationships, the plots gradually blend in a massive dramatic movement that includes all participants, major and minor—Dorothea and Ladislaw, Lydgate and Rosamond, Vincys, Bulstrodes, Garths, Featherstone, Raffles. Perhaps no other novel so well symbolizes, by its merging streams of narrative, the inevitability of linkages that forge an unanticipated community within, and involving much of, the literal community of Middlemarch.

My subject, however, is not the familiar one of unity from multiplicity, but the bridges between parallel lines, and the techniques of convergence. Cumbersome as she can be at times, Eliot never falls, if my observation is sound, into the old mechanics of grossly derricking the reader from Action A to Action B, as in this old standby: "Let us now leave Esther seated in the park and renew our acquaintance with Coldfield in his cell." Instead of such bald shifts there are various ingenuities of transition. One of these is an innovative employment of a technique that would become, much later, a standard feature of another art. It is significant enough to justify describing one example in some detail.

Dorothea Brooke dominates the first nine and a half chapters as she progresses to the altar with Casaubon; observers' comments on this affair introduce us indirectly to six supporting characters. Then Lydgate dominates the next eight and a half chapters, which also identify people important in his later life. From the Casaubons to Lydgate looks like a big shift in focus. Yet Eliot does not crudely drop the honeymooners, saying, "We will now take a look at the stay-at-homes." Rather she sneaks us across an invisible borderline between the newlyweds and others so smoothly that we hardly notice the process. Chapter 10 describes a big dinner just before the wedding. This is the right occasion for Eliot to use more intensely her method of having friends and neighbors discuss the principals: in doing this, the townspeople portray Dorothea and Casaubon further, introduce and sketch themselves, and reflect community tone. We are given almost a tape recording of random party chatter, but beneath the air of randomness a controlled process directs our attention. Some speakers compare Dorothea with Rosamond Vincy; others, noting Casaubon's unrobust look, talk of illness and thus naturally allude to the town's new physician, Lydgate. Then it is Lydgate who opens chapter 11, and he thinks about a subject continued from the party discussion: the difference between Rosamond and Dorothea. From this Eliot slips easily into portrayals of Rosamond and the other Vincys, including Fred Vincy and hence his girl, Mary Garth; and so on, until we have met Mary, Featherstone and his household, Bulstrode, and the hospital problems that involve Bulstrode, Lydgate, and Farebrother. These details may be tedious, but we need them if we are to see clearly how Eliot, without palpable break or rude leap from one topic to another, has taken us adroitly, imperceptibly, from one love affair to the makings of two different ones and to the supporting casts of some size. We have been gliding along a continuum of segments of a community-in-action, segments as of now independent or loosely connected, but appearing serially for one initial inspection as if they were panels of a polyptych.

This comparison suggests a series of separate but related "stills," to use the photographic term. One goes in a natural, nonspasmodic, arranged route from one display to the contiguous display in a gallery, that is, from fictional object to object. They have been juxtaposed; the curator—in our case the novelist—has skillfully put side by side the actors, commentators, themes so that the observer goes naturally from phase to phase of an ordered exhibit. This description, however, is only partly accurate. We must not rest in a sense of stills and static displays, of elements that we make stops in front of. Instead we must attend to the narrative movement, the movement that I have called gliding and graceful, the artist's moving line of sight that we follow. Of course, there it is: moving pictures. Long before it emerged as a standard device, Eliot was using a cinematic technique. It was "panning," that is, proceeding panoramically from one to another of the neighboring components of groups or scenes. Let me return to chapter 10 to note more precisely a detail of the camera work. We first see the engaged couple enter the drawing room; we move to the observers who talk about the couple, and then from these talkers to other men and women whom they talk about; then we follow those talked about—especially Rosamond and Lydgate, he thinking about her—into their lives beyond the party. No other nineteenth-century novelist, as far as I have observed, has hit upon this polished way of transferring us, if not insensibly at least without our feeling the graceless yank of an author's derrick, from part to part. (The comparison with cinema is purely to define, not to praise. We are too much given to lauding a predecessor for pioneering a style, method, or attitude that we think especially characteristic of our later time. Eliot's virtue is not to have anticipated a modern film technique, but to have hit on an admirable device which we can best identify as like a movie method.) Well, throughout *Middlemarch* Eliot often proceeds by topographic proximity, but I forgo inventory of such transitions to observe some comparable aspects of her art.

Panning depends upon the artist's ability to see as neighbors, or bring together as neighbors, the elements that permit a visual crossover. The invited crossover is also a way of leading into meaning, for Eliot has a strong sense of parallels, analogies, and thematic variations. With or without physical juxtaposition, there is frequent psychological or moral juxtaposition. Eliot's sensibility tends toward next-door or side-by-side relationships, be they parallels with differences, or differences with parallels. She pans, so to speak, among ideas or meanings. Early on we see that Dorothea is a creature of ideals, but then we learn that the tough Rosamond has an ideal too, and that Lydgate seems to embody it (12). Lydgate, in turn, has an ideal of medical practice. Eliot's caption for book 2, "Old and Young," seems commonplace. The theme is indeed an ancient one—egotism, power, and will in conflict with hopes, dreams, and ambitions—but it gains freshness through Eliot's juxtaposition of three variants among which she pans. Dorothea hopes to serve an old husband, but he is too self-enclosed to be open to help. Fred Vincy hopes to be served by a legacy from old Featherstone, who can therefore sadistically push Fred around. Lydgate hopes to serve the community in old Bulstrode's hospital, and so he is pressured by Bulstrode's self-righteousness and rigid evangelicalism.

Now, just when Lydgate caves in to Bulstrode on the hospital chaplaincy (18), Eliot suddenly picks up the Casaubons (19), whom we left as they took off on a honeymoon in Rome (10). At first this shift may look like the rude puppeteering of a novelist falling back on an arbitrary transition. Yet we really have, not a gauche leap, but a juxtaposing of complementary narratives on the same theme—two eager idealists feeling educative blows by unanticipated crude reality, one in professional, the other in domestic, life. Eliot is panning thematically. She does this very ingeniously in a relationship hinted at by the rubric of book 5, "The Dead Hand." This phrase clearly applies to two similar cases but serves most effectively in tying in with them a third action that is superficially dissimilar. There are two literal "dead hands," that is, wills through which dead men seek power over the living. Eliot treats ironically the testamentary ploys of Casaubon and Featherstone, whose plans are not carried out by history. But in Eliot's profoundest irony, their reversals are reversed by the reversal of Bulstrode. Just as the dead hand of the past cannot will the future for others, so one's own present, and hence future, cannot will one's own past dead. As Eliot put it, "a man's past is not simply a dead history." In the subtlest of the "dead hand" variants, Bulstrode wants to rule his own past dead; he can try to kill it by letting Raffles die, but this leads only to new disasters that are, in Eliot's words, the "second life [of] Bulstrode's past" (61). This dead hand does rule on.

Eliot's putting things side by side in literal or metaphorical space—be it a preliminary to or an aspect of the "stealthy convergence" both in human histories and in her rendering of them—reflects a deep strain in her sensibility. It appears, finally, in her modal inclusiveness. *Middlemarch* achieves, as far as my knowledge goes, a fuller convergence of fictional modes than any other work of the century. Two unlike modes that emerge from the eighteenth century—the novel of manners and the Gothic novel—both appear in *Middlemarch*: one in the wit of the author and of Mrs. Cadwallader, in the amusing dialogue and the recording of social styles; the Gothic in the mystery and ominousness of the Raffles episode and the secret history which it encloses. In its persistent play of ideas, the novel is philosophical; yet it also encompasses some wonderful farce, as on the occasion of Brooke's sherry-built campaign speech. It has strong elements of the grotesque: the "expectations" theme, embodied in the hopeful heirs hanging around Featherstone, might be a fresh version of the unseemly Pockets surrounding grotesque Miss Havisham in *Great Expectations*. Then there is Eliot's dominant manner—the realism that we often think of casually as a historical displacement of these other modes. The diversity of modes does not mean incoherence; the modes converge into one unified history of a community, the disparateness of its components represented in part by the tonal variety.

There is an analogous convergence of stylistic modes: the frequent abstractions of Eliot's analytical and meditative passages joining with the richness of diverse sensory images by which she gives a concrete reality to scenes and people. Or she can merge conceptual opposites in the vitality of epigram or paradox. One excellent example is this: "Marriage . . . had not yet freed" Dorothea from her "oppressive liberty" (28). Being "freed" from "liberty," and "liberty" as "oppressive"—a remarkable convergence of apparent contradictions in a very fine insight (one with especial applicability in our own day).

The convergence of modal and stylistic opposites in Eliot's technique is comparable to what happens in the marriages she portrays. Lydgate, the idealistic would-be scientific benefactor of mankind, marries a self-indulgent, whim-of-iron materialist. Fred Vincy, a leaner without much direction, marries sturdy, sensible, well-organized Mary Garth. But the most interesting marriage is that of Dorothea and Ladislaw, which, as Professor Gordon S. Haight observed long ago, is a convergence of the moral and the aesthetic. In this union, which I find much more expectable and probable than some readers do, there may be a faint allegorical touch of cultural history. Romantic as she is in various ways (she even imagines a Pantisocracy or Brook Farm [55]), Dorothea has a strong Victorian cast: her sense of duty, her needing to serve, her wanting to quell selfishness, her accepting the importance of being earnest. Ladislaw, on the other hand, is pure Romantic, whether by formal design or by not quite conscious thrusts of the creative imagination. He is the outsider, the man without ties, the possessor of an acute sense of honor. His mother eloped with a Polish refugee-musician, the son of a political radical (one thinks of the Lensky-Skrebensky presence in Lawrence's *Rainbow*). He says to Dorothea, "You see I come of rebellious blood on both sides" (37). He seems a "kind of Shelley" (37) to Mr. Brooke, who later modifies his view and sees Will, now his editor and political aide, as "a sort of Burke with a leaven of Shelley" (51)—a one-liner convergence of the twain. Meanwhile, Mrs. Cadwallader has called him "a sort of Byronic hero—an amorous conspirator" (38). To describe Dorothea's voice Ladislaw twice uses that famous Romantic image, the "Aeolian harp" (9, 21). Eliot herself gives a romantic picture of Will singing: "he looked like an incarnation of the spring whose spirit filled the air—a bright creature abundant in uncertain promises" (47). This acts as a riposte to lawyer Hawley's unromantic view of the entirely certain promise in the romantic young man: "He'll begin with flourishing about the Rights of Man and end with murdering a wench. That's the style" (37). Rights of Man, Shelley, Byron, Aeolian harp, spring song, a heritage exotic, rebellious, and radical—may not these reveal, in Eliot's imagination, an unarticulated sense of Will as Romantic (with an uppercase R imposed on a lowercase r)? And hence a historical complement, as well as a moral one, for Dorothea as an embodiment of the Zeitgeist felt by the novelist? And further, the author's prescription for herself, whom, with great detachment, she partly embodies in Dorothea?

Such teasing speculations merely sketch a possible addition to the many instances of that convergence which in *Middlemarch* governs both substance and actional design. My business is less interpretation than exploration of the equivalence of the what and the how: what is experienced by the actors (the stealthy convergence of lots) imitated by how the audience experiences the actors in roles that will converge. The actors slide unperceivingly into relations unforeseen; the audience slides unawares from a focus on one apparently independent actor to another close by. This anticipation of cinematic panning requires proximity, but in *Middlemarch* the proximity never seems arbitrary. Rather it is an inconspicuous symbol of a connectedness to be revealed. The person—or theme—nearby turns out to be a moral near relation. Such relatedness is, of course, the index of community, that interactive whole which accommodates, without dissipating it, the infinite variety of beings and existences. Eliot grasped this fusion of disparates as few have done since. She enacted her vision in her art, which molds many into one: actions and scenes, attitudes and meanings of characters, and then even literary modes (manners and Gothic, philosophy and farce, grotesque and realistic) and styles (the abstract and the concrete, the straightforward and the paradoxical). Convergence has many dimensions—in content, in ways of seeing it, in ways of forming it and presenting it.

Nomad, Monads, and the Mystique of the Soma: D. H. Lawrence's Art and Doctrine

i

IT IS MANY DECADES since E. M. Forster called D. H. Lawrence a "bardic" writer "whom it is idle to criticize." But this form of idleness has persisted; it has claimed vast energy and passion; and idleness has begot idleness, as critique has led to refinement, modification, or countercritique—whether in the earlier cycle of personal and biographical judgments in which J. M. Murry had the first word, or in the later round of literary studies in which such expounders as Father William Tiverton, Graham Hough, and F. R. Leavis have been glossing and reglossing the texts, giving some of the innumerable pats and pushes by which history slowly defines the permanent station of genius. Perhaps it is idleness to assume that critical exercises can bridge the gap between revelation and discussable meaning; but presumably it can distinguish the authentic voice, the charged murmur in the cave, from the strident cries of the barker, the program-seller, the revivalist; it can judge the depth and resonance and range of the voice, it can mark its themes and idioms. If it cannot translate, it can identify.

Forster uses the word *prophet* too, and he might have ventured an even stronger metaphor. For the history falls into the ancient phases of esteem: the devotion of the small band of partisans; the official condemnation and punishment; the gradual upsurge of general acceptance; the canonization. It has been so for the two literary saints of our day, Lawrence and Stephen (if the clean parallel justifies the slight onomastic strain): the energetic patience of disciples; then the public torment for heresy and blasphemy (the fire of censorship, and the slings of outraged fortunes); a passing martyrdom, quick revival (the phoenix and the crown), an unusually early identification of miracles, and promotion to the canon. As mortals, the two oddly alike: born only three years apart, maturing under devout mother and bibulous, cumulatively unsuccessful father; teaching, toying with another art, each doing his first major fiction by surveying himself as artist; escaping from the "spiritual" woman, suddenly recognizing the creature of earth, sticking to a single marriage (a compound of love and war); both plagued by a persistent ailment, ruthless in the use of friends, being in some way "outsiders" and choosing alienation; wandering, dying abroad like Romantic poets. Yet they managed to revive a pre-Romantic system of benefactions, while exemplifying an ultra-romantic state of being: rootlessness. The rubric "Nomads and Patrons" could subsume some of the more notable biographical paradoxes. The revolts against Catholicism and Protestantism were paradoxical: both men cutting apron strings with one hand, but clinging to the skirts with the other; defying, making declarations of independence, but never quite escaping from the respective brands of puritanism; feeling restraints, as much from within as from without, and in resistance ostensibly against the latter but intrinsically against the former, having periodically to splurge against pieties and taboos with chalk on wall, a youthfulness never totally overcome. In partial secularization they stuck to inherited patterns: one the logician, catholic, striving to fuse a universe of differences and repetends into a formal, all-inclusive unity; the other proclaiming the Inner Light, protesting, preaching, forming new missions everywhere, surrounded by women's missionary societies. The half-rebels against older orthodoxies tended to impose a rigid conformity upon their bands, the disbelievers assumed messianic roles. Stephen played at anti-Christ (*non serviam*), Lawrence wrote anti-Jesus sermons; both felt crucified by the temple forces whom they challenged.

But whatever their parallels in literal history or in paradox, we see the likenesses eventually dissolve into complementation. In the end they complement each other by paradoxical achievements that reveal something of the styles and quests of our age: the word made flesh, and the flesh made word.

The gifted rejector's cycle: from being rejected to being fully received, from excommunication to beatification. Hagiography is inevitable, either in its pure form, or in that later fusion of the hagiographic and the positive-historical which produces massive recording and documentation: Stephen has his Ellmann, Lawrence has his Moore (not to mention Nehls), both devout, but not uncritical. Documentation itself means a certain distance, and hence a new kind of scrutiny: not now the elders' screams at the enfant terrible insolently brooming the temple and setting up new divinities, but the steady inspection of the new saint—the endeavor, in a word, to estimate at what level of Paradise he will be "manifested."

Eliseo Vivas's book[1] on Lawrence is of this kind. He wants to cut between two extreme positions—the unqualified dismissals by T. S. Eliot and Bertrand Russell, and the "abandoned panegyrics" of F. R. Leavis (which sometimes seem more anti-Eliot than pro-Lawrence). Quite aside from his endowments as critic, Vivas has some special equipment for this task: his book came out of his divided response to Lawrence's work, so that by long habit he was without partisan commitment. He endeavors to deal with this divergency of attitudes, to organize them into a tenable position. He shows enthusiastic admiration as often as he points to bad art or thought. But he is not uncertain or inconsistent; he works from firm principle. He is precise, orderly, penetrating, and detached, and in being so he will not entirely please those for whom Lawrence is either divine or diabolic.

Forster said that one had to ignore the preacher in Lawrence and submit to the bard; Murry sought the troubled individual that was projected into the books; whereas Russell and Eliot thought Lawrence was spiritually dangerous, Aldous Huxley, Father Tiverton, and Leavis have seen him as a bearer of positive values (Leavis, indeed, as a "great tradition" man, a sort of George Eliot in modern dress, or with white coat and prophylactic instruments). Vivas has points of contact with most of these. He develops to its fullest the Forster theme that Lawrence was preeminently the artist, but he also sees that the preaching has to be dealt with. He appreciates the utility of the personal as a key to the flops of the artist. He knows that as spokesman for certain values—in his homilies or in his art—Lawrence must be reckoned with, must, indeed, be examined with the circumspection and alertness required by a man whose highly original talent, powerful feeling, inner discords, and only fitful self-criticalness would naturally lead him into a troubling mixture of the sound, the silly, and the downright pernicious. Vivas tries, in other words, to discern the pros and cons in both attacks on and defenses of Lawrence. But, though he is doing a number of things, his basic task is discriminating between the true prophet and the purveyor of evil, between the artist and the pamphleteer. To it he brings considerably better than average experience in systematic aesthetics and ethics, as well as an acute sense of text; and he makes a very important contribution to Lawrence criticism.

ii

Occasionally, in endeavoring to account for Lawrence's failure as novelist, Vivas speculates about his mind (for instance, his view of art as means to an end) and his personality, especially his essential alienation. Vivas finds Lawrence's alienation manifested in one direction in his utopianism and hence his reformism; in another direction, in his need to dominate, his love of power; in still another, in his misanthropy, his incapacity for love, his rejection of agape, and his attribution of metaphysical value to sensation. His reformism appears in the doctrinal materials that vitiate a great part of the later work, especially *The Plumed Serpent* and *Lady Chatterley*; his love of power obtrudes in the male protagonists in *Kangaroo* and *The Plumed Serpent*; his failure of love results in an incomplete humanity that mars all the later works and diminishes the stature of even aesthetically successful novels like *The Rainbow* and *Women in Love*. Vivas's identification of such artistic deficiencies is sure and final, and his relation of these to the author's life and psyche is in general convincing; the basic theory of alienation is capacious and flexible enough. Some readers might question whether we have an adequate cause for the continuous difficulties after the rather early high point of *Women in Love*; the idea is that rarely after the age of thirty or thirty-one, even in the years when he had Frieda, friends, and growing fame, did the artist Lawrence consistently win out over the needs and obsessions of Lawrence the man. Vivas fixes on Lawrence's traumatic wartime experiences as the key: these so confirmed the inner alienate-reformer that, despite growing skill and venturesomeness, the artist never again regained full freedom.

To make this speculation entirely unanswerable would require, perhaps, a good deal of argument from the data of personal life. Even while making necessary use of it, Vivas tends to disparage the reliance on biographical evidence—in part from the modern reaction against genetic studies that leave critical issues untouched, in part from confidence in the "autobiographical 'feel'" of some of the novels and in the meaning of this. Though the subtlety of such a critic as Vivas protects him, deductions from "feel" are questionable; one thinks with dismay of the "feel" of problematic books to less gifted and less self-critical readers. Nevertheless it is a fact that to an extraordinary degree Lawrence's novels seem entanglements of the artistic object and the writer's psychic urgencies, and automatically—in the spirit of following a trail, not of erecting a proof—one probes back into the confused spirit from which these pages emerged. One is pushed toward the writer, on the one hand, by the obsessive consistencies; on the other, by the almost systematic contradictions. On passion he is almost too passionate; the high-pitched, reiterated insistence begets a doth-protest-too-much air; one cannot help asking what dreams and frustrations are emerging here. (Herbert Read's observation, in the *Sewanee Review* of spring 1959, that *Lady Chatterley* might well be called *The Prude's Revenge*, is more than a quip.) There are the numerous small, dark heroes, the gamekeeper types, who mysteriously have it; sleeping beauties awaiting reveille, as played on one or another Aaron's potent flute; the worldly males, from Skrebensky and Gerald Crich on to Rico and Clifford and lesser characters, who mysteriously don't have it (Vivas shows how Lawrence loads the dice against his destined victims). These appear to come from an unfree imagination, forced into certain channels. On the other hand, one senses the over-free imagination, one that too easily gives rein to competing forces in the personality, when one finds erotic explorations now ecstatic, now shameful; love one time a satisfying annihilation of self, another time compatible only with a fanatic retention of self outside the common enterprise; spirit now condemned, now claimed as the name for alternative virtues; complex character attenuated—as in Gudrun, for the most part—into a succession of unintegrated moods. Ultimately the obsessive consistencies and the almost systematic contradictions tend to merge in the paradoxes of personality. If Lawrence's alienation expressed itself in an incurable antipathy to the men who, intellectually, socially, or industrially, held power in the world, nevertheless, as Vivas has shown, Lawrence himself craved power and at the same time "hated himself because of his lust for power"; we see, then, that the Crich-Clifford stereotype, however much it incarnated a hostility to Mr. Worldly Wiseman, reflected also self-hatred, a self-hatred experienced with a Puritan relentlessness that denies all grace to the sinner. What gets into the picture is the highly ambiguous response of the bohemian to the bourgeois: a singular compound of repulsion and attraction that is evident to any observer of bohemian attitudes. Birkin, we remember, offered love to Gerald. Still another convolution of motive appears when we recall that Lawrence's attacks on power men are paralleled by his ceaseless campaigning against women with wills. However well he may have diagnosed a kind of female power-drive and anticipated momism (that secular, egalitarian, polytheistic mariolatry), the constancy of his tune takes us from the art to the man. He gives us a clue when Birkin talks about the "murderee," who secretly lusts to be murdered and to find his murderer (to come to his unmaker). For Lawrence, or rather a part of him, is the "dominatee," the instinctive discoverer of the dominatrix, the submitter in some way unable to maintain unconsciously his equality; only such a person could cry out so continuously against dominating women and read them lessons in mastering a wholesome subordination. Lawrence would have given a much more satisfactory account of the murderee if besides the will to find the murderer he had also recognized, clashing with it, some will to resist the murderer, just as he presented at least a rudimentary conflict of motives in "The Woman Who Rode Away." For along with his own impulse to become the dominatee there is the quest for power, not to mention the castigation of it: the basis for unresolved tensions in life and art.

Such issues run parallel to critical issues; they belong in the highly speculative area of the relationship between the psychic constitution of the artist and his artistic accomplishments. All formulations tend to be quicksilverish. One may never question that alienation is the principal clue to Lawrence's personality and yet, at the very threshold of inferences, recall that for Dickens a comparable outsiderism was accompanied by a quite different orientation in art. For, despite efforts to make him an all-denying rebel, Dickens was rather what might be called the critical insider, capable of discerning a wide array of falsities and vices and yet treating them as deviations from what was possible rather than as evidence of essential corruption; hence he was not driven to enunciating new redemptive faiths. In other words, if the artist is characterized by some sort of disability, the problem is to see how, if at all, it is related to his art. W. H. Auden has suggested that the function of disability is protective: it keeps the artist from the routines of family or civic life that would distract him from using his talents properly. It is possible that sensitivity may be so heightened by disability that the artist may thus come to extraordinary perceptions not available to even the gifted man better endowed, according to the prevalent standards, with inner order and well-being. But it is also possible that disability may mean a limitation of vision, may restrict the artist to partial insights, however intensely these may be rendered.

When Vivas engages in the personal explorations that he wittily calls "critical spelunking," he is always interesting and generally convincing. But the effectiveness of his book does not depend on the analysis of the man. Primarily he is a student of texts and their implications, and there he seems to me to have finesse and authority.

iii

Vivas devotes the first half of his book to the basic defects of *Aaron's Rod, Kangaroo, The Plumed Serpent, Lady Chatterley's Lover,* and *St. Mawr,* and the second half to the success of *Sons and Lovers, The Rainbow,* and *Women in Love.* In the first half he gives a just and telling picture of characteristic flaws: the incoherent structure, the labored symbolism, the incomplete or partisan characterization, the intrusion of personal and doctrinal matters not artistically assimilated, the philosophic unsatisfactoriness of ingredients that insist on being taken philosophically. My only complaint here is that Vivas did not choose to exercise more fully his talent for the analysis of general form; his method is rather to concentrate on some representative shortcoming, as a diagnostician might point to a patient's deformity instead of making a complete organic analysis. Thus in dealing with *Aaron's Rod,* though there is much else to justify the contention that it is Lawrence's worst book, Vivas restricts himself to analyzing the aesthetic incompleteness of

Aaron: we are supposed to sympathize with Aaron as a fugitive from home fires, but his desertion is never given dramatic justification, so that he seems only irresponsible; besides, the text doesn't clarify Aaron's relationship with Lilly, a troublesome affair. What we really suspect is that Aaron was in flight from his own insufficiencies and blamed his wife for them; but the art does not follow through on what it teases us into thinking. Vivas treats *Kangaroo* as an *olla podrida* of untransfigured biographical reportage and untenable ideas, which he analyzes trenchantly; even without the developed formal analysis that we would like to see, the chapter amply refutes Hough's view that *Kangaroo* has an "underlying unity" reflecting "an authentic process of living growth." The discussion of *The Plumed Serpent* is the longest in the book because, since the work is overtly one of propaganda, Vivas spends a good deal of time evaluating Lawrence's ideas: not so much the obvious nonsense of the revival of pre-Columbian religion (and the bad taste of the ceremonial hocus-pocus), as the faulty conceptions accompanying a religious bent that in itself has positive values for us: the concept of God as "a vast, shimmering impulse waving on toward an indeterminate end"; a rejection of agape which reflects an incapability of loving; the infallibility of feelings; the "blood" as providing confirmation of knowledge; the denial of traditional ethical values. Though he always makes careful qualifications, Vivas offers a powerful indictment of Lawrence's blueprint for a scarcely human world. At the same time he acknowledges the way in which the artist periodically gets ahead of the doctrinaire ideologue, principally in the extraordinary feeling for an evocation of the spirit of place. To this I would also add that in the treatment of Kate alone, a sense of character steadily fights off the allegorical predetermination: until she is finally pushed unceremoniously into accepting the general's passive-partner notions of sexual intercourse and Ramon's lodge-initiation rigmarole, she feels doubts and aversions that reflect a reassuringly healthy consciousness. I agree entirely with Vivas that *St. Mawr* is, except for the spontaneous act of imagination that creates the horse, a dreary morality, with the familiar Lawrence salvation-army troupers giving us the old pitch on barn-and-ranch virtue and manor vice.

The chapter on *Lady Chatterley* is very good; there is much more exploration of the text, in which Vivas is adept. Despite the great admiration which this novel has aroused in some quite mature critics, it has always struck me as tedious and immature, in part because its hygienic crusade, for all the cheers it has evoked, has seemed of doubtful necessity, and artistically much the same as cleanup movements of a different content (some people who don't go for reform art at all are completely bewitched by this particular rustic-renewal project). Immaturity is what

Vivas discovers in the execution: "the book falls apart into two stories whose relationship has been bungled." Lawrence has taken so many potshots at his lifelong target character that the book becomes an "anti-Clifford tract" rather than a novel of character; as Clifford evokes pity, and Mellors and Connie, in their snobbishness and misanthropy, evoke anything but admiring sympathy, the intended effects are simply not subject to mature control. A more careful inspection of the erotic doctrine reveals, in addition to the reassertion of the physiological basis of love (an old truth that Lawrence did not invent), the presence of certain garnishings (postural novelties, one judges) that Lawrence, always a dogmatist, wants to make prescriptive: the immaturity of making a special bias into a general rule. Further, there are two inconsistencies that betoken a failure of mature thought: it is impossible to sacramentalize sex—and Vivas values this as one of the great affirmative contributions of Lawrence's work—and do away with sex taboos, for the sacred and the taboo are inseparable; and it is impossible to deny obscenity and at the same time claim sexual stimulation as a pleasant virtue in art. Finally, to remove the taboo from taboo words is not to eliminate a nastiness masquerading as good taste but to impoverish the language by doing away with the verbal equivalents of ineradicable emotional states; hence "we shall have to invent others to take their place."

Vivas always insists on the points at which these books come closer to success. He alludes constantly to Lawrence's great artistry, as if this were a fact to be periodically reasserted even while showing up his nonartistry. When he comes to *Sons and Lovers, The Rainbow,* and *Women in Love,* Vivas specifies the ingredients in Lawrence's high art: the subordination of ideas to drama; the transformation of autobiographical materials into novelistic form; the relative freedom of the persons from ideological pressures; the superior general structure and, especially in the two later works, such mastery of style that even when the language is strained by Lawrence's demands, it succeeds in conveying the felt quality of experience; a brilliant mastery of creative symbol. In noting a number of problems in *Sons and Lovers,* Vivas calls attention to the unexplained failure of the relationship between Clara and Paul. We have here, I suggest, structural symmetry: Paul does not find what he wants either in the "spiritual" relationship with Miriam or in the sexual one with Clara. We may regard these as data that define Paul, rather than as results intelligible only through a prior analysis of motives in Paul. We might argue that on this rare occasion Lawrence repudiated two extreme positions, or that he "presented" a selfish refusal of all relationships, or perhaps an artist's rejection of personal allegiances (like those of Stephen Dedalus), or even something of all three.

The chapter on *The Rainbow* shrewdly identifies the presentation of affective states, erotic and religious, as the triumph of the novel; detects that in the affective world the relationships are not between full characters or "substantial selves" but between "centers of consciousness"; and argues that in these terms all experience tends to be the same. The theoretical statement is highly revealing, but the substance of the novel seems not to fit comfortably within the theory; I doubt that the erotic experiences in the three generations are undistinguishable, despite the reliance on some of the same image patterns. For the preceding and subsequent behavior of the three couples is sharply varied, the note of frenzy and alienation is cumulatively increased in the two later generations, and the human incompatibility and dissociation from place are made more explicit. In the analysis of religious emotions, too, the complexities of the clash between Anna and Will require fuller analysis, as do the ambiguities in the personality of Ursula; and I would like to see Vivas discuss the more difficult symbolic scenes and their place in the general structure.

In the two chapters on *Women in Love*, which interests him more, Vivas outlines admirably the formal relationships of the whole, establishing the function of many parts that to an uncritical reader might seem irrelevant. He is able to regard the book almost unreservedly as an achieved whole because he believes that the lecturing, which to some readers still seems obtrusive, is for once controlled dramatically through Ursula's rejection of the ranting "Salvator Mundi" in Birkin. Perhaps. Vivas also believes that there is a structural wholeness that derives authentically from the variable development of passional experience. Again, perhaps. The problem turns on how many ebbs and flows can be accommodated without a perceptible slipping from the integral to the diffuse, without a naturalistic recession of art into the amorphousness of existence. There is a key in chapter 22, when Ursula complains of the contradictoriness of Birkin (a candid self-reading by the author, if you will). Lawrence not only dramatizes a host of competing moods, impulses, and quests, but presents each one so immediately and unreservedly that the moment seems authoritative, definitive, ultimate in verity, as if the author were irretrievably caught up in it, bound by it, and, like a tempestuous person flooded by passion, unable to relate it to the rest of being. This makes for terrific scenes, and the terrific scene is Lawrence's forte. But how they join together into a sum is another problem. What kind of whole can emerge when each competing part is so set free, so magnavoxed, so exploded in the foreground that aesthetically it claims autonomy, finality, totality of revelation?

What is dramatized is an existence of discrete emotional episodes, where integrity is fidelity to the immediate passion. It is for this reason that both *Rainbow* and *Women in Love* lack that seal of formal whole-ness, a conclusion; each one less moves to a resolution than simply stops on one of its series of moods, an arbitrary cessation of the endless flux, as in *Finnegans Wake*. (*Sons and Lovers*, on the other hand, has a conclu-sion: what is presented at the end is an intrinsic solitariness of an ego that is the fulfillment of potentialities made evident and explored in the developing drama.) What I am saying here is not, I believe, entirely out of line with Vivas's assessment of *Women in Love*. He accepts the tradi-tional view of the book as formed by the contrasting love affairs, but he breaks with tradition by denying that the Ursula-Birkin affair is wholly successful and therefore normative: in one of his most penetrating argu-ments from the textual evidence he shows that the marriage is for Birkin only a partial solution which leaves various needs and longings of his—of a Krafft-Ebing sort, evidently—unmet. At best, then, this would leave us with an abortive structure of meaning. But Vivas gives unqualified praise to certain symbolic scenes (such as the "marriage" of Gerald and Gudrun by the rabbit, or Birkin throwing rocks at the moon, which has excited comment for thirty years) that contain the essence of the charac-ters in the relationship and the secret, indescribable heart of the rela-tionship itself. In them, indeed, Lawrence the brilliant and original scenemaker is at his best.

iv

The studies of the individual works take Vivas into many subjects, such as the full nature of pre-Columbian religion, the physiology of sexual intercourse, the character of "western orthodoxy," the essence of secu-larization, that is, the differentiation and autonomization of human ac-tivities. This last provides a technical definition of disintegration, and it furnishes an analogical definition of what happens in those novels of Lawrence's in which his episodic sense of life does not bow the neck to his sense of program and its aesthetic consequence, the dictatorial im-position of order. When he is true to his artist's awareness, the move-ment is centrifugal; when the lawgiver takes over, conduct and events are pushed toward a preestablished center. If I am correct in seeing in Lawrence a strong tendency toward a "secular structure" (the differ-entiation and autonomization of the parts), then this is a significant irony for a man who proclaimed himself a "passionately religious man," and whose work is felt by various critics to have a genuinely religious dimension. In Vivas's terms, Lawrence is not a "moralist," that is, an artist whose matter is human relations, but a "cosmologist," concerned with "destiny," with man's relation to the cosmos. He had a direct feeling for mystery in the universe, a "deep piety for the cosmos"; he felt a "desire to approach all of life in a sacramental attitude." This is a central Lawrence value, as Vivas insists, though this will hardly be palatable to the anti-religious among Lawrence's admirers. Yet the impulse to sacramentalize sex, however much must be said for his revolt against the mechanical-toy view of erotic activity, has to contend with severe limitations in the raw material; to achieve it would require the bringing-in of a more inclusive openness to mystery. The mystique of the soma is too slender a generative principle for a nothing-is-sacred age; it is reductive, really; one is trapped and shut in, ultimately, if a beyond may be experienced only by kinesthetic vision, by tactile revelation. Insight by palpation will reduce communion to blindman's bluff, and even a universally available all-body braille will leave many areas of wisdom untouched. All I am trying to get at is the insubstantialness of phallolatry. A sexual life which has "value" involves a constellation of events, kinds of contribution, confluences of attitudes, moods, personal style, and tone; trying to derive all of these from the physiological—and, as Vivas shows, from the physiological faultily conceived—imposes on it an excessive and eventually destructive burden, the kind of unbalance and excessiveness that, by the familiar mechanism of reaction, must lead inevitably to a counterextremism of narrow-gauge faith. This would be a form of asceticism. Orwell has remarked that Lawrence died because he knew that his religion of sex was insufficient. But even in *Women in Love*, the language of which includes many images of transcendence, Lawrence was striving for something metaphallic; Birkin lectures Ursula about it, and on at least one occasion (chapter 23) that skeptical girl seems to have felt it. Yet Ursula's general offishness to Birkin's more rarefied erotic theory, like that of Kate in *The Plumed Serpent*, seems to flow out of doubts in the author himself.

In reserving his main praise for Lawrence the artist and severely restricting the credit of Lawrence the thinker, Vivas cuts the ground from under one kind of Laurentian—the kind that tends to regard him, and indeed all writers, as sources of doctrine, and to dismiss the artist's art. Some admirers of Lawrence are attracted by the anti-Jesus note, without observing either the disastrous loss in the rejection of agape or the opposition to promiscuity that could come from the church itself; without remembering that Lawrence even more fiercely opposes the humanistic commitment that arises as an alternative to traditional religion; without fully grasping his misanthropy or his disposition to vest authority in an elite of infallible sensationalists. Vivas notes that in broadest outlines Lawrence's sex doctrines are now old hat, however much they may once have had to buck Victorian predilections. But the fact is that in some quarters Lawrence still appears as a fine cudgel to wallop Victorians with, though the game is no longer meaningful or respectable, just as damning one's parents is not mature conduct for adults. It is time, indeed, for a new stance toward Victorianism, one that will resign the platitudes of condescension and self-righteousness, and an assumption of deeper wisdom, for an effort to discern the realities, and to understand the fashions that may reflect differences in taste rather than distortions of nature. The old stereotype of Victorianism is kept alive as a target: it is a necessity for a kind of critic who cannot operate as a critic unless, like an army doing war games, he can find or invent an enemy to work out against. He is on the lookout for any regime that seems ancient, and Lawrence looks like an ally because he seems to have put a lot of old fogies in their place. His almost constant fury against other human beings attracts the polemic spirit to his camp. There is irony in the heroic portrait of Lawrence tilting against a joyless, sexless world: it is difficult not to suspect that, aside from attaching a sacramental value to sex, Lawrence campaigned for something always known, always possessed, and always experienced in fact as fully as Lawrence the artist does it in words, perhaps even more "fulfillingly," to adapt a favorite word of his, because entered into with a more complex sensibility than that of the free phallic sect.

Lawrence appears to have been precociously early in spotting the dangers of mechanized life, and I imagine that no one questions the value of his insight. Nor need one expect him, as artist, to have come up with any more helpful alternatives than the flight and nomadism of Birkin and Ursula. But Lawrence has a special appeal to a kind of social critic who won't or can't come up with anything more than a repetition of Lawrence's abuse of society, though the real problem is how to reconcile an indispensable society and an irreversible mechanization with individual needs of an instinctual and emotional order. In journal after journal one can read, often with a bow to Lawrence, complacent jibes at the horrors of our society; it is the old anti-Victorian habit with a new target, as automatic as saluting in the army or crossing oneself in church, a ritualistic claiming of right-heartedness. This cliché upending of Pollyannaism (our fascination having shifted from her honey curls to her unseemly rear), this going up and down in the world announcing what an ugly and dirty place it is, is both sentimental and naive, for it is an intellectually and emotionally easy gamesmanship with a half-truth as whip, in place of the adult difficulty of understanding a complex and self-contradictory actuality, in which the ugly and the dirty are mixed with their opposites in a way that ought to defeat all heartwarming simplicities of attitude. This phenomenon of immaturity helps us understand a Lawrence whose separatist rage feeds the easier quick-profit polemic moods. Compare the maturity of George Eliot, who knew the extent of evil in the world without supposing that only evil existed in the world, and who was sympathetic with assaults on evil without attributing their failure to malign circumambient darkness or finding that failure a justification of vindictive bitterness.

Again, Lawrence has been particularly used by the I-am-for-"life" school. Biolatry, as I have called it elsewhere, may appear in pure form in a youthful resolve to "worship life," or in the somewhat tainted polemic form in which "life," never defined, becomes an unexaminable, ultimate value term. Vivas admirably disposes of this stance by observing that "Life qua life is value-free, is a mere biological process," that even the possession of it in the profoundest sense cannot be supposed to generate values, and that in being "for life" a moralist is actually using "life" as a metaphor for some conception of the "good life." It may be added that such a metaphorical use is inadmissible in serious discourse because it is a device, not for securing a fuller meaning than is possible to a discursive definition of "good life," but for evoking emotional support in place of understanding. In fact, like advertising and propaganda, it aims to gain adherence by preventing examination.

In examining some of the ideas of Lawrence and Laurentians, Vivas brings into play two other important concepts. The first of these is "intention"; he makes the essential distinction between the "intention of the author," which he points out that some admirers of Lawrence always accept as final, and the "intention of the work," that is, the import of the fictional evidence. Thus, despite the intention of the author, *Sons and Lovers* reveals the resentfulness and hardness of Mrs. Morel, and *Women in Love* the inner complexities of Birkin that make his marriage with Ursula somehow wanting. The second is the concept of "aesthetic obscenity"; in this, Vivas widens the popular idea of obscenity by making the term applicable to other materials besides sex, and makes it more precise by defining exactly, in terms of the function of art, the mode of impropriety. The obscene is a mode of interference with aesthetic experience, which centers in "intransitive attention"; the obscene stirs the contemplator to a "transitive" state, a going-across toward action of a noncontemplative sort. (Compare Stephen Dedalus: "The feelings excited by improper art are kinetic, desire and loathing. . . . The aesthetic emotion . . . is therefore static. The mind is arrested and raised above desire and loathing.") If, then, Lawrence's writing is aphrodisiac (and therefore immature), as some readers find it, it is obscene—not that it is "dirty" but that it distracts one from the aesthetic object to other objects. Vivas goes on to argue that Lawrence's great talent for "presenting" experience carried him into "such immediacy" that readers are disturbed rather than intransitively attentive: a quarrel between the Morels in *Sons and Lovers*, for instance, or between Ursula and Birkin in *Women in Love* "becomes a partisan emotional experience." Though I assent to the concept of the obscene and regard it as critically valuable, I question its applicability to the kind of scene adduced; I am not sure that immediacy in the presentment destroys intransitivity, or that intensity of scene necessarily leads to partisanship, or that the "unpleasant" is an objective, workable aesthetic criterion. There may be a legitimate intensity, a legitimate "partisanship." We can distinguish, I believe: (1) the partisanship striven for by the author's will, for example, Lawrence's taking it out on his target character, Clifford Chatterley; (2) "partisanship" resulting from objective differences between fully presented persons (such as Iago and Desdemona); (3) nonpartisan intensity (that is, the central symbolic scenes in *Rainbow* and *Women in Love*, which nearly all critics tend to call "disturbing," and which Vivas regards as the high point of Lawrence's art); (4) the actual obscene, in which the management of the "matter" takes the reader out of the aesthetic act (contemplation) into nonaesthetic action or the desire for it—the aphrodisiac, which stirs sexual activity; the philogenic and especially the misogenic, which stir personal, social, or political action, and so forth; the pathogenic, that which consistently excites revulsion even after the novelty of the matter has worn off and simple misoneism is no longer a danger. (1) is not obscene, because with time it falls short of the aesthetic response, not to mention going beyond it. (2) is not obscene because it is an inevitable part of the contemplation of moral differences, provided that the affective response to these is controlled by "full presentation"; the treatment of Iago would be obscene if it led an auditor to want to murder some actual person of like nature, or to seek reform of promotional rules in the army. (3) may not be judged obscene unless history establishes a persistent intolerableness in the materials that come under the category. The problem here is that the twentieth century, though it has not invented intensity in art, has made a business of it; since this massive exploitation of immediacy coincides with the exploitation of subjects once taboo, we have such a flood of novelty to deal with that we may cry "obscene" prematurely. We will have a time separating the legitimately intense from that which is nonaesthetically exciting. Tentatively we may suppose that new fictional techniques for creating immediacy are analogous to such innovations as stereophonic reproduction, and that once we have accommodated ourselves to a more inward placing in the scene, we may find that its powers to stir do not break up the detachment of esthesis.

Different parts of Lawrence's fiction fall, I believe, into all of these categories. I have been trying, not to deny the presence of obscenity in Lawrence, but to preserve that tenuous and fragile border between the obscene on the one hand and, on the other, the intense and immediate. In effect this is to trust in the paradox that immediacy and distance are compatible. Here I have barely suggested the terms in which the case might be argued.

V

Whereas Herbert Read calls Lawrence a great moralist and an artist so bad that he is "grotesque," Vivas tries to separate the good and the bad in the moralist, and the good and bad in the artist. His course is the sounder one. As for the didactic materials in the novels, they have no programmatic value, though Vivas goes further than I can in conceding their diagnostic value. As for the art: what is authentic and compelling is the rendering of the outer world of nature, the look and feel of it; the feelings of persons, especially in their intensity, variability, and contradictoriness; certain qualities of relationship, especially the perverse sensations and passions that enter; the surrealistic scenes elaborating unique, hardly translatable symbols. One must acknowledge Lawrence's integrity of feeling: he follows his impulse, his intuition, wherever it leads him, into the extraordinary or into the silly. It leads him into a variety of intense affective moments, into a sequence of moods; the sense of inner life is episodic; there is hardly a continuum of dramatic personality to take us from scene to scene; moral identity has been sacrificed to autonomy of impulse. In one sense this is a reaction—an early phase of a reaction that was to become rather widespread—against a rational ordering of personality that in the traditional novel could too easily bury inconsistencies and violations of the expected. This is the key to Lawrence's historic role: he challenges the limitless claims of reason, reveals the nonrational realities, the need of mystery. On the other hand, when he talks as though "mental consciousness" could be repealed, he is out of touch with reality. Again, if his ideas of blood knowledge be taken in any literal or unqualified way, they are silly or worse; V. S. Pritchett pointed that out long ago. But if his attacks on the cerebral or his exaltation of somatic wisdom, indeed if all he writes, be taken as a metaphorical reminder that there are nonrational as well as rational sources of value, and that it is perilous to neglect these, this will amply authenticate his prophetic status.

Whatever kind of emphasis and corrective his works add up to, as art they bring into play a phase of human sensibility and responsiveness that before Lawrence had to act in other ways or remain latent, unbidden. Richardson performed this historic function in the 1740s, Scott after 1815; their long fame, their exalted position among the most intelligent of readers, points to the ironic discrepancy between a timeliness that is overwhelming and an acquired timelessness. Like them, Lawrence contributes to a new kind of emotional freedom; as innovator in feeling he acquires a comparable aura of greatness; the problem is what happens when the historic role is played out. In the end, history is the only critic: for Lawrence it can rule a fade-out after his work is done; or it can discover, beyond his role for his own day, either a durable revelation of truth or the decadent brilliance of a fringe artist. Beyond what is said by the preacher to his own times, and the ambiguous revealer of those times, lies the problem of how much else he reveals, of how much of all times, of how much the historic role is joined by a nonhistoric role. Aesthetic contemplation—intransitive attention—endures, we may hazard, because of wholeness in the object. When the object is incomplete, this incompleteness, though it may long be obscured by the sheer genius of the rendering, will eventually obtrude and deflect or disturb the aesthetic consciousness, or cause it to fade and wander. In one way Lawrence makes a stronger appeal to aesthetic contemplation than some of his predecessors: he pushes the novel toward a greater completeness by his awareness of complex emotional states, of the instinctual, by his embrace of cosmic piety, of the sacramental. He spots a partialness and moves against it. But does he spot it from a perspective of wholeness, or is one part calling another part incomplete? When new elements come into the picture from one side, is the picture enlarged, or are other elements crowded out of it? In the new Lawrence landscape there is a singular absence of tolerance, obligation, mutuality, warmth; in the phallic or metaphallic faith, there is almost never a parental, familial, or social dimension. There is an oppressive restrictedness, which at times approaches pettiness. The key to this lies in Vivas's profound insight that in Lawrence's dramatis personae there is no "substantial self" but only a "center of consciousness"; further, in erotic and religious experience, the persons are "solipsistic"; they are "monads."

It may be argued that this appalling isolation, this failure of community, is forced on the artist by the milieu in which he lives; that if the age suffers from such an incompleteness, the artist is doomed to it also. If this is true, we can understand that in his partialness he will never evoke an intransitive attention that will not be broken into by an awareness of historical damage. But it is also possible that an artist may be faithful to his age without being a slave of it. The measure of his wholeness is that he is able to combine historical with metahistorical fidelity: a sense of actual partialness with a sense of the wholeness slighted by his time. It is always there potentially, waiting to be created. What limits creation is not the ailment in the clay but the ailment in the potter. And though Leavis demands respect, his insistence that Lawrence's work makes for health is baffling; I find it hard to deny a pervading air of illness. Granted, though a sick man's setting up as health commissioner is incongruous, it may not be bad for the patients—provided he doesn't take his own unwell state as a model for imitation. But I find a troubling coming-together of brilliance, integrity, and disorder; ailment issuing a powerful, suave invitation; ill health given a compulsive charm. La belle dame sans merci hath thee in thrall.

If the times are incomplete, the very incompleteness of the artist will lend him some enchantment; what he lacks will seem excrescence, what he gives essence. If he has an extraordinary gift for presenting the idiosyncratic as universal, for offering his maimed self as exemplary, and for doing this in hypnotic symbol, he can but seem great—not only to those similarly ill, and those with like grudges, like antipathies, and like platforms; but to those who respond to the adventurous, to new vistas, to the prophetic personality, to unhesitant conviction, to talent. Maybe the impression of greatness will last. Maybe a new age, differently constituted, will look back with wonderment that such partial talents could have been so impressive. But leaps into the future are not very productive. What they can do, though, is give us a momentary perspective on the present, and permit us to see how our incompleteness may conceal from us the incompleteness of an artist who beguiles us by tendering, often with the most seductive magic, new fragments of wholeness.

I began by noting some coincidences between Lawrence and Joyce, and I will close by noting another. Vivas observes, as we have seen, that Lawrence's world is incompletely human, and refers this to Lawrence's "incapacity to love." Denis Donoghue, in the Sewanee Review of spring 1960, points to Joyce's "gradual abandonment of the finite order, the virtual rejection of the human, the dissolution of time and history" and attributes this to "a defect of love." Lawrence leaves us with separate "centers of consciousness," with "monads"; Joyce leaves us with "nothing . . . but words." But the nomads who fled community and became monadic narcissi had still to make their own desperate lunges for community and transcendence—in the humid mystique of the soma, and in the oppressively convoluted edifice of archetypes and cycles. These are chilly refuges from alienation, all trance and will, cave and labyrinth, all flesh and all word. Genius but. . . .

■ III ■
PAIRS

■ 10 ■
Lemuel Gulliver and Tess Durbeyfield:
Houyhnhnms, Yahoos, and Ambiguities

i

TO THROW GULLIVER, the Yahoos, the Houyhnhnms, Tess Durbeyfield, Angel Clare, and Alec d'Urberville all together for a single critical inspection may seem like a final mad act of yoking together by violence the most heterogeneous persons, subjects, and kinds of fictional art.

But wait. Gulliver, bearing the stain of the Yahoos, falls in love with the Houyhnhnms; they regard the stain as fatal and throw him out, and he is compelled, though nostalgic and desperate, to pick up, *faute de mieux,* life with those he regards as Yahoos. Tess, bearing the secret stain of Alec, who is something of a Yahoo, falls in love with Angel Clare, who is very much of a Houyhnhnm; when he learns of the stain, he considers it fatal and throws her out, and she is eventually compelled, as conditions get more desperate and she gets more sick at heart, to take refuge with Alec.

Granted, this may look too easy; the unparallel elements that damage the scheme will easily suggest themselves. Gulliver, it may be argued, is a kind of hero, Tess a victim. And yet, is Gulliver possibly a victim? Or Tess a heroine? To ask this is not to push for the profits of easy paradox but to suggest comparable ambiguities in both works. Nobody doubts, of course, that book 4 of *Gulliver's Travels* is ambiguous; the problem is how to place and live with an ambiguity that many readers instinctively try to reduce to a simplicity. Perhaps everybody would doubt that *Tess* is ambiguous; the problem is whether we have not unconsciously reduced it to a simplicity that is not altogether accurate. The ambiguity that few would deny in *Gulliver,* and that few may credit to *Tess,* can be traced to similar sources: each writer is working, alternately or even simultaneously, in two modes. On the one hand he is being a topical commentator, a satirist, or allegorist; on the other, a fictionist. On the one hand he is making points; on the other, telling a tale. He uses different kinds of machinery, and these make us respond differently. The doubleness of modes guarantees complexity in the development of the Houyhnhnm-Yahoo theme. In Hardy the allegorical skeleton of the theme is more deeply covered by human flesh and blood, but it is there all right. So we have good grounds for suspecting that the *Travels* and *Tess* can shed some light on each other.

ii

The most convincing interpretation of the Yahoos (it can be found, with different emphases, in several of the numerous criticisms of part 4) is this: they are intended as a rebuke to man's pride, a reminder of many features that he tends to forget when he thinks of himself as a noble being created in the likeness of God—from physical imperfections to spiritual flaws such as pettiness, greed, filthiness, malice, and pervasive animality. The satirist does not weaken his case by introducing the formal qualifications that might occur to the gentleman, the detached explorer of truth, or the wider-gauge artist; the satirist's business is to rub our noses in the mess, without relief. That will vex us, as Swift said he intended to do. But he can vex us still more if he can make us see a happier alternative, let us think that this is what we have coming, and then rudely throw us out as unworthy. Hence the Houyhnhnms. Swift kicks our pride from two sides at once: you aren't as rational as you think you are, he insists, and in fact you couldn't even qualify for a truly rational community; and you have no idea how truly bestial you are. All this is an admirable foil for the human complacency that takes the contemporary as the apex of history, takes for granted our benevolence and perfectibility (if not perfectedness), and believes that various kinds of sentimental and scientific utopias are near at hand.

Well, as we know, that isn't quite the way part 4 has been read over the years. It isn't the dominant reading even now, when, simply from having been at exegesis so long, we are likely to protect ourselves against the rasher explications. The Houyhnhnms have seemed less a reminder that we could be more reasonable than we are, less a standard for emphasizing the shortcomings of the Yahoos, than a total definition of what man ought to be. Their kicking out of Gulliver has seemed a final repudiation of mankind. The Yahoos have seemed less a daring jest on man's moral shortcomings and his ancient and persistent animality than a declaration that mankind is nothing but a foul unregenerate beast. Swift has seemed to present a diptych of "Man as he ought to be (but never can be)" and "Man as he is (and always will be)." Hence offended man's outcries against the writer, perhaps the most remarkable series ever lavished on a traditional thinker: Misanthrope! (Of course Swift helped this one along, just as Hardy did the "Pessimist" that protesters hurled at him.) Madman! Sick man! Life-hater! Perhaps it is safe to say that now we are past this sort of ad hominem indignation. But it has taken us mountains of interpretation to give us a better view, and still we see different landscapes in book 4.

Another type of reader, knowing something of Swift the man and of his other writings, thought that Swift couldn't possibly so view mankind, sought a way out, and moved toward opposite conclusions. As in "A Modest Proposal," Swift only pretended to praise; he had to be aware of the limitations of reason, and Gulliver is a naive victim of the Houyhnhnms' self-esteem. This simplicity, demanding an awareness of irony, affords a more sophisticated pleasure: one has seen what ne'er was seen before. Nor is this seeing entirely delusive; rather it is also a way of evading the problem of ambiguity.

Swift, as Irvin Ehrenpreis has noted, was passionately fond of hoaxes; he pushed them as far as they would go, and in executing them (as in the Partridge affair), he could introduce remarkable convolutions and manage a deluding series of masks. A hoax could become a work of art; but a work of art could also extend into a hoax. Swift wants to tell man not to forget the beast in himself, and then pushes it so far that he seems to be saying that man is only a beast. There is more deliberate complication at the end of chapter 12, when Gulliver makes a climactic attack on human pride: Gulliver is the voice of the author's satire. But the pride attacked is nowhere more evident than in Gulliver himself, though he accuses all others, dramatically the pride belongs to him alone. So Gulliver becomes the object of satire; he is the victim of his own words. This traditional irony makes the situation fictional rather than one-directionally satirical: we see a drama created by a personality instead of a homily delivered by a mouthpiece. But we try to file the fictional down into the satirical if we read Gulliver as only the voice of satire, or only its object.

Swift's art in this final scene is what it has been in most of book 4—that of the satirist constantly under pressure by that of the fictionist. There is no doubt that as satirist Swift uses the Houyhnhnms as critics of human failures; they are sharp about many things, and they sharpen up Gulliver's perceptions. They call people Yahoos, and Gulliver believes them; the old hoaxer in Swift may be at work here, like a politician damning an adversary while an admiring throng cries, "Pour it on 'em, Jack." Gamesmanship, however, is not the only begetter of doubleness. Saeva indignatio itself may assert that people are Yahoos, but it is imagination that interferes and qualifies. Satire naturally asserts that people are Yahoos, for it can register only what can be condemned and scorned; but fiction, which cannot help seeing a wider truth, records what else people are besides Yahoos. Satirical indignation confers total rectitude on the Houyhnhnms; the fictional imagination reveals the limits of their authority. In satire the narrative is the agent of intentions outside itself; in fiction the narrative gains autonomy. (Insofar as something is being asserted, the move from satire to fiction is from "There is no doubt about it" to "Yes, but.")

Throughout the *Travels*, Swift's narrative is constantly taking off on its own. In part 1 some tales of the little people, and in part 2 of the giants, are wholly free of satire; they are pleasurable in themselves; bigness and littleness are then dramatic counters, not symbols. On occasion part 3 moves into science fiction, from the mechanics of the Flying Island to computer composition. With such instances in mind, we can see a leap into a profounder kind of fiction in part 4—a quite spontaneous leap when the central character, apparently bound to a rather narrow purpose, takes on imaginative life and makes us respond to him as a full person. It is fine for satire when Gulliver worships the Houyhnhnms: human aspiration contrasts with human grossness, emphasizes it. But Gulliver, equipped with feelings and personality, is imagined as well as used; he is a person as well as a voice; and as a person he himself is engaged in the eternal human attempt to reduce life to a simplicity it cannot have. In this he is a little pathetic and a little silly. We see that the Houyhnhnms are not really up to his admiration; he is a fanatic pupil, and they are complacent professors, with real acuity, but without the total mastery of truth that he and they think they have. As the voice of satire, Gulliver can scorn human irrationality by walking and talking like a horse; as a human being, he can go equine only at the cost of seeming ludicrous and even neurotic. As the voice of satire, he can proclaim his great happiness and serenity among the Houyhnhnms; as a human being, he seems both improbable and priggish. As the voice of satire, he can humbly accept the judgment of the Houyhnhnms against him; as a human being, he seems a little like treason-trial victims pleading guilty to all crimes. As the voice of satire, he can think of his family as Yahoos, faint at their smell, and retreat to the barn for a restorative whiff of the horse stalls—a brilliant jest at the malodorousness which a sensitive person can find in man's nature and conduct; as a human being he can carry on in this way only at the cost of being priggish and pathological. (I have elsewhere termed his illness the "intellectualist neurosis"—that secure conviction of being intellectually "saved" by which a rigid mind can condescend unceasingly to the differing thoughts and tastes of other men.) For a good many years I have watched the responses of students to part 4: almost invariably their spontaneous view of Gulliver is that he has gone off his rocker. Though this view is too simple, it does establish that Gulliver comes through as a human being; that is, he is a product of fictional art as well as of satirical technique. The same fictional art has created the ordinary decent humanity of the Portuguese sea captain and of Gulliver's tolerant family; were satire the only mode present in the work, they too would be Yahooish and would make Gulliver's responses to them seem inevitable rather than disordered.

Wayne Booth's view that Swift's standards have been lost to us is a rather attractive way of accounting for that elusiveness in the *Travels* which leads to variant interpretations and to disputes about meaning. We might extrapolate from this and theorize that disparate standards in our own day (for instance, inconsistent evaluations of the Houyhnhnm and Yahoo roles in life generally) inevitably make the work ambiguous for us, and that later cultural clarifications might enable us to see it in as single a light as that of Thackeray a century ago. But against this possibility of a unitary accounting for the *Travels*, I accept the ambiguity as inherent, and posit the necessity of living with conflicting perspectives—that of the satirical animus and that of the fictional imagination. We can take this back to Swift's personality if we will, and say that he was a divided person—both a jaundiced observer of vice and a sympathetic observer of man in all his manifestations. We can say that as a satirist he naturally overstates his case but then instinctively protects himself against being caught with only a hyperbole in hand. I like to think of Swift in the *Travels* as the indignant and disgusted man betrayed, finally, by the whole man; the determined literal flogger of vice partly superseded by the ironic contemplator of a wider human scene; the literal satirist, who might be of only limited historic significance, overcome by the imaginative fictionist who alone could do a work that still retains universal interest. We cannot make Swift into a limited monochromatic writer. For in the end the *Travels* seems to us more complex than satire can be; it embodies a fiction far more exacting, for both writer and reader, than are the rather obvious bursts of misanthropy. If satire asserts that we are only Yahoos, fiction presents them as undeniably our kin, but not sole kin; if satire presents Gulliver as right in embracing reason and rejecting the irrational, fiction shows both that he has come across a good thing and has got an overdose of it; if satire makes the Houyhnhnms the infallible voice of rational excellence, fiction shows them as sometimes funny, sometimes pompous, sometimes narrow. This is simply to spell out the duality that must result when the satirical paradigm is imaginatively expanded into the human tale, when the agent of satire also becomes a free agent. Without this ambiguity—a new perspective added, but the first not surrendered—the *Travels* would be a lesser work than it is.

A final word on the Houyhnhnms. The reader for whom they have undiluted authority looks too exclusively at Gulliver's laudatory terms for them, and not enough at the total drama of their tepid existence and their disruptive effect on Gulliver. He ignores, among other things, Gulliver's own criticism of their expulsion: "I thought it might consist with reason to have been less rigorous." This implies that a truly rational program of existence would be inclusivist rather than exclusivist. The Houyhnhnms are exclusivist, and hence they exert a secret charm wholly unrelated to the virtues publicly assigned to them: they offer the temptation of simplicity, of a monistic ordering of experience. Like many readers, Gulliver is hypnotized by the simplistic view even though he is finally victimized by it; after he gets back to England, it is what he has to recover from. It boils down to an unwillingness to come to terms with individuals and their inconsistencies and contradictions; it is easier to judge the individual by the class to which he belongs and about which we have already made up our minds. The Houyhnhnms have found Gulliver perfectly satisfactory as an individual, but they kick him out because they are sure he belongs to the Yahoo class. Reason, in other words, is making lump judgments and refusing individual discriminations—a pattern of conduct familiar in human practice that does not even pretend to be rational. The Houyhnhnms are much more inflexible than the Europeans who have said to many an American, "Americans are awful, of course, but you are different." The pattern is even clearer within one country, our own. We know the Houyhnhnm line: "What do you expect of him? He is a black. He is a Jew. He is a Catholic. He is a Republican. He is a Wasp." I heard recently the story of a black who was made literally hysterical by the impact of some evidence that a white man might be a good man. Among all social temptations, judgment by class is the hardest for men and women to resist, for it draws upon one of our deepest yearnings, the perennial source of disappointment or disaster—the passion for simple rules. Insofar as they secretly offer this temptation, the Houyhnhnms subtly encourage us to forget the shortcomings of their virtues.

iii

Whatever may have been his private conviction about their meaning, Swift in the Houyhnhnms and Yahoos effected a splitting of humanity that was prophetic. One could construct a fairly substantial segment of English literary history, and perhaps social history, on the basic theory that for a time Houyhnhnmism became an ideal, and Yahooism was ignored, shoved under the rug, ghetto-ized. The rational, the orderly, the sensible, the controlled were taken for granted as achievable and beneficent; this meant a shying away from, a distrust of, irrationality, passion, instinctual drive, "animality." Richardson, however, continued Swift in a different key, discarding the allegorical and satirical, and intensifying and deepening the fictional into the tragic: in *Clarissa*, as Ian Watt has shown, the catastrophe results from intransigence in both Clarissa and Lovelace as each insists on a single value. Houyhnhnm Clarissa denies the Yahoo in her nature, and Yahoo Lovelace the Houyhnhnm in his; both are destructively and self-destructively rigid. In Smollett the Yahoo element frequently erupts in indecent, aggressive, nastily retaliatory conduct in "good" characters. But my impression is that, for roughly a hundred years from the late eighteenth century on, Yahooism tended to be forgotten, ignored, or segregated in bad guys (Cenci, Fagin).

In our own day, of course, the Yahoos have come back with a bang, and the Houyhnhnms are left with hardly a whinny. Neo-Yahooism takes two forms. One, as I have remarked elsewhere, is in the doctrine of D. H. Lawrence: in this, the instinctivism that in the original Yahoos is base and gross becomes the source of human values, and Houyhnhnm rationality is arid, sterile, and even destructive. (Compare the opposition of "instinct" and "the system" in Meredith's *Ordeal.*) Then there is the post-Lawrence development: Lawrence's moralized Yahooism is super-seded by a nonmoral characterology in which a Swiftian Yahooism appears to dominate human nature. I refer, of course, to the sense of man as dominantly aggressive, violent, indecent, irrational, and malicious that appears in so much midcentury fiction and drama. The Houyhnhnm element seems hardly to exist. In this reversal of the nineteenth-century situation, Gulliver seems justified at last. people are Yahoos.

There appear, then, to have been two antithetical movements lasting about a century each: total denial of the Yahoos as a mirror of human reality, and then total acceptance of them. Thackeray's denunciation of Swift will serve as a high-water mark of the first, and our own condescension to Thackeray symbolizes the second. As far as major fiction is concerned, Hardy initiated the turn away from Thackeray to the "modern" that we now know. In fact, we can place Hardy a little more accurately if we can see him in an intermediate position between Jane Austen[1] and D. H. Lawrence. In Austen, values are defined by the social norm, and outbreaks of the natural (instinctive, passional) tend to be deviant and disapproved; Hardy is troubled by the contradictions between the "law of nature" and "social laws," between what is instinctive in natural man and what is acceptable to social man intent on order; and Lawrence, as we know, would resolve the conflict by making the passional the basis of order.

It is rather as if, toward the end of his career, Hardy decided that the Yahoos had not had a fair shake and decided to do something about it. In *Jude the Obscure* he chose to press home the point that sex is not a questionable subject best committed to silence but a fundamental urgency to be accepted and dealt with openly. Jude's sexual urges are an open problem that the reader is asked to sympathize with (too much of an assignment for some readers then), and he and Sue are said, after their relationship has become overtly sexual, to have experienced a joyful paganism. Here Hardy plunges further into an argumentativeness that grows upon him in his last three great novels—*The Mayor of Caster-bridge* (1886), *Tess of the D'Urbervilles* (1891), and *Jude the Obscure* (1895). In *The Mayor* there is at least pressure of ideas, and the characters have the greatest magnitude; Tess, of course, is a very ample character, but without the role in public life that gives Michael Henchard a traditional tragic dimension, and Alec and Angel are at least tinged by restricting allegoricalness; Jude and Sue have a much larger function as mouth-pieces, and their querulous tone is one index of their being much weak-er characters, with a pitiable inadequacy finally symbolized by tuber-culosis in one and neurosis in the other. The *Tess* characters, then, occupy a middle ground between the forceful ones who would rule the world (in *The Mayor*) and fragile ones who lie helpless before adversities in their own makeup or in the cosmos (in *Jude*). A sense of attenuation in *Jude* is traceable to a splitting up of the rich dual nature of Tess into two lesser figures in the later novel. Tess is on the one hand a natural, sensu-ous, earth-mother kind of figure, on the other a woman of taste, thought-fulness, and imagination. Her physical being, notably her full figure, is made more obvious and coarsened in Arabella; and her qualities of mind and spirit are thinned out and made more tense and self-conscious in the delicate, intellectual, self-centered Sue. The allegorical inclination in *Tess* becomes more emphatic in *Jude*. Tess is sought out by two lovers, whom we can call Sensual Man (Alec) and Ascetic Man (Angel Clare); Jude is in the identical situation, suspended between two women who represent the Sensual (Arabella) and the Spiritual (Sue).

In each paradigmatic trio the character in the middle is a full-natured everyman caught between incomplete options, that is, personalities dominated by a single human potential. Now, to look back: Gulliver is also the full-natured man in the middle, flanked by the Houyhnhnms and Yahoos that carry different potentialities of his to logical extremes—a close enough parallel to Tess flanked by Angel and Alec, and to Jude flanked by Arabella and Sue. At the end of his career as novelist Hardy twice picked up the Swift theme. Even with some obvious differences, the basic sense of a split in human nature is the same, and the ambigu-ities in presentation are comparable. In Swift, as we have seen, a fic-tional perspective is superimposed upon a satirical perspective without really superseding it; we are forced into a more complex view without being entirely able to discard the simpler one. Something very similar to this happens in Hardy.

Since *Tess* is our main fare, let us look briefly at *Jude* first. Hardy adopts an argumentative position like that implied in Swift: he will com-pel people to recognize the strength of one aspect of Yahooism—irra-tional, unselective sex. So Arabella is something less than lovely; though her weapons are guile and calculation, she is not unlike the Yahoo girl who would like to rape Gulliver. Hardy is a little squeamish about her. Yet his fictional imagination modifies her allegorical role: along with all her limitations she acquires heartiness and a folkish, feet-on-the-ground sense of actuality that is not contemptible. Hardy gives every sign of approval of Sue as a special, delicate, charming, independent creature of mind and spirit—a Houyhnhnm even in her sense of superiority to the Yahoo world; but as the complete artist takes over, Hardy reveals her also as finicky, selfish, willful, and, in a Houyhnhnm-like way, unable to tolerate the mixed, unideal fare of ordinary life. Jude's final strictures on society are as pointed as those of Gulliver, but neither is a final authoritative voice; Gulliver has become laughable, Jude pitiable. Jude and Sue inherit from Tess and Angel an anti-traditional rationalism that Hardy seems certainly to approve; but in his presentation it never affords a basis for adequate living.

There is something announced and schematic about *Jude*, so that such ambiguities come as a needed, and yet almost surprising, relief. *Tess* is a subtler enterprise, but since on the surface it looks less subtle than it is, we have been slower to grasp its ambiguity. The Gulliver-figure, Tess, is overtly injured by both her Yahoo and her Houyhnhnm lovers, and to many readers she has been only a victim, the treatment of her, as Joseph Warren Beach once put it, a triumph of pathos. Hardy contributes to this view of her by his admiration and sympathy, his snappish cracks at and images of a church that is cold and formalistic, and his indignation at people and events that contribute to her suffering. But while he is working at this level of editorialist and attorney for the defense, his fictional imagination is also at work. It makes Tess more of a person and less of a helpless victim, more of an agent and less a passive recipient of the actions of others. This newer sense of her has been fairly widespread in recent criticism. Evelyn Hardy and Desmond Hawkins have detected something of the masochist in Tess; though this seems mechanical to me, it is one way of defining her invitation to her fate. In his enthusiastic account of Tess as woman, Irving Howe pauses briefly to note in her a certain responsiveness to Alec. Hawkins is good on this subject—the strength of her involvement with Alec. In this view Tess is no longer a single-natured plaything of fate, but is herself drawn in different directions. My own view is that in various ways she is a divided character and makes her own choices—very clearly, for instance, in her dealings with Angel before they are married. Roy Morrell goes further than anybody in making Tess responsible for her own downfall, and he spells out in detail what he sees as her weakness and lack of will.

We can dispose of ambiguity in *Tess* by declaring it the product of a transitional period in which we are moving from one kind of reading to another. But I believe that, as in *Gulliver,* the ambiguity is intrinsic rather than extrinsic. It is not wholly wrong to think of Tess as a victim; Hardy himself pushes that view by means of all the external incidents—weather, coincidence, and so on—that appear to conspire against her. He shows Alec and Angel both acting selfishly, and Tess as suffering from their selfishness. In that sense he writes melodrama. But now we see that Hardy is also aware of her own actions as a source of her suffering. Thus he moves toward tragedy. The late Hardy is characteristically of two minds: he has a powerful sense of the pressures and misfortunes that make men wretched, but he also remembers men's own contributions to their downfall. He tends to talk melodrama but imagine tragedy. That is another way of defining his ambiguity.

iv

Hardy also sees Alec and Angel from more than one perspective, but, if I am right, this fact has not received the critical recognition gradually accorded to the complex treatment of Tess.

In the critical accounts of Alec there are two traditions, one deflationary and one inflationary. In the first, Alec is simply a stereotyped villain of melodrama, and occasionally he is still called that. Some of his attributes account for this—his cigar, moustache, reckless driving, plotting, and stage-worn vocative "My beauty." In the other reading, this standard figure of unregenerate worldliness is enlarged into a satanic being; he is promoted from a vulgar myth to a myth that exalts him, at least into respectability, and perhaps on toward grandeur. Hardy, of course, gives some verbal leads that encourage the satanizing of Alec, who jests openly on the subject (50; all references are to chapters)—his quips about Paradise buttress Edenic-Miltonic readings of the novel; and since Alec has his day as a parson, something can be made of the devil quoting Scripture. Doubtless in Alec there are hints of a world-flesh-devil allegory, and we should not ignore them; but the opposite error is to give final authority to such an allegorical reading. It is too simple; it makes Tess an even more helpless victim; it ignores the fact that devils do not get murdered in bed. To symbolize or mythicize evil as demonic is suitable, indeed, only when it has a metaphysical quality or that ultimate viciousness created by the union of calculation, energy, and malice, as in Iago. Alec is rather the ordinary sensual man who is willful and therefore given to stratagems of procurement, who wants his own way and is sulky and resentful when balked. For him the diabolical is hardly more than a Halloween mask.

If recent critics are right, as I believe they are, in seeing Tess as more strongly attracted to Alec than she may know, then the attraction needs to be accounted for. We could of course see her as perversely turning to evil, but that Dostoyevskian or modern reading is not supported by the evidence. She is simply drawn to Alec as a man. Here we come back to the central subject of ambiguousness. Hardy may well have started by thinking of Alec as a villain-seducer, an image of forces that victimize innocence, a figure to be deplored and reprehended, a subject for sermons; many people have read Alec only in this light. But Hardy's fictional imagination was also at work, and thus he also sees in this man, defective in restraint and scruple and in visualizing and understanding another's desires and hopes, qualities that make him more than a figure of disgust. The potential Yahoo becomes a more inclusive human being. D. H. Lawrence was probably the first critic to proclaim the masculine attractiveness of Alec, a judgment that still puzzles some readers. Lawrence may have been pushing his own dogma, but what he says is not out of line with the Alec dramatically presented in the story.

In the earlier scenes Alec has a certain jesting playfulness; he has an ironic humor; he is the amiable instructor in whistling. This diversity of manner helps explain the "singular force" that Tess sees in his face (5). When Tess leaves him he shows concern rather than the relief of one who is flinging a used article aside; there are odd touches of devotion in his manner; he offers help now and in the future (12). If his conversion is delusive, a temporary allotropic manifestation of passional energy ("sensuousness" as "devotional passion" [45]; a "new sensation" influenced by his mother's death [46]), still it reveals an imaginativeness that gives Alec some variety and makes him more than a single-track schemer. Alec is candid, he sees himself rather objectively, he quietly accepts Tess's criticism of his later life, he blames himself for her predicament (whether from policy or from conviction), and above all he proposes marriage to her (45, 46). Hardy ingeniously reverses the popular cliché: it is not Tess who pleads, "Make me an honest woman," but Alec who wants her to "make me a self-respecting man." He is shrewd enough to perceive Tess's situation as a deserted wife, to understand the loss of his new evangelical faith, and to see that Angel Clare's doctrines, as transmitted to him by Tess, ironically eliminate the sanctions that would be a barrier between himself and Tess. If his continued returns and pressures have an air of persecution, still they are caused by a powerful attraction; Alec's angry rebuke to Farmer Groby is spontaneous. The point is that, if an unwelcome lover, he is still, within his limits, a lover rather than an egoistic schemer who wants to conquer her out of vanity. His growing self-assurance seems to come less out of self-esteem than out of his estimate of Tess, including a partly reliable sense of a certain responsiveness in her.

He is not without charm as he shows up at Tess's workfield in a comic outfit, jests about himself as the serpent in the Garden of Eden, professes concern about her hardships, and is angry about her betrayal of him as an imitation d'Urberville (50). All this is not to say that Alec is an admirable, desirable, or innocent man, but that Hardy's art has taken a conventional villain and made him into a plausible complex figure—casually self-indulgent and yet capable of obsessed singleness, crass yet not stupid, cynical yet vaguely drawn toward commitments of an order-creating sort, insensitive in crucial ways yet able to understand some kinds of needs, tenaciously self-serving yet with some deftness and charm, seeking what he cannot have yet settling for what he can get—in a word, within a limited range human enough to make his sudden death seem a shock rather than an anticipated or hoped-for execution of justice. In sum, the Yahoo, who would be a subject for satirist, homilist, or allegorist, becomes a human personality, the field of the fictional imagination. Hardy had in him something of the extra-artistic pleader, but he rarely failed to come under the control of the artist's imagination.

v

We see this even more fully in his treatment of the rationalistic, moralistic, nonearthy—that is, Houyhnhnmistic—Angel Clare. But here the situation is still more complex. Readers so much tend to focus on Angel's harsh wedding-night treatment of Tess that they forget what precedes it—the long dramatic demonstration of his genuine virtues. A freethinker, he is candid to his clerical family but sympathetic rather than quarrelsome; he independently and uncomplainingly takes on a new mode of life; though "genteel" he is a good companion to the dairy folk; he is kind and decent enough so that four different girls fall in love with him; with Tess he is considerate and scrupulous, and he knows that her strong response to him gives him an especial responsibility. Decent but distant, kindly but superior, Angel becomes "godlike in [Tess's] eyes" (29). He is the Houyhnhnm "master" to her Gulliver. Then he discovers the Yahoo taint and throws her out—an expulsion quite comparable to that of Gulliver. Our standard responses to the two similar events are apparently opposite: the Houyhnhnms have reason, Angel is intolerably irrational. But beneath our apparent going along in one case, and our strong resistance in the other, we are, I believe, responding identically: we are taking the satirical thrust of the episode as its essence. We accept Swift's satire of humanity as more Yahoo than it would like to admit, Hardy's of the critic as not tolerant enough of humanity with its Yahoo strain. At the moment of rejection, Swift seems to have justified Houyhnhnm exclusiveness, Hardy to have undermined it.

We have already seen, however, the ambiguity in Swift which pushes us beyond approval of the rejection into another response. We have yet to see how Hardy pushes us beyond disapproval of the rejection into another response. In general, Swift leads us from understanding of the motives to judgment of the action, Hardy from judgment of the action to understanding of the motives.

We should not, of course, minimize Hardy's satirical animus. For into his portrayal of Angel's severity against Tess there enters, if David De Laura is right, Hardy's strong disapproval of the general intellectual position embraced by Angel—the "neo-Christianity" that, "modern" and "advanced," endeavored to compromise with scientific naturalism by rejecting Christian belief and dogma while retaining Christian feeling for moral guidance, solace, and so forth.[2] But however wrong Hardy thought Angel, still he so managed Angel's rejection of Tess that it embodies, for anyone who will look closely enough, not only the leap of satirical energy but also the steady flow of fictional imagination. We have tended to look superficially, to miss the total, complex Angel, and—in this way Houyhnhnms all!—to settle for the easier, simpler solution: rejecting Angel for rejecting Tess. We call him "prig." This handy dismissal would seem to belong to an earlier day, but Irving Howe picked it up as late as 1967. When a gifted interpreter of fiction can so dispose of Angel, we still need some work on the text. In the Houyhnhnms (and even in Gulliver himself) we have to detect the underlying prig; we do this when we feel them as characters and not only as satiric voices. In Angel we have to detect the underlying humanity (that is, the representativeness); we do this when we feel him as a complete character and not only as the mediator of a satirical intention.

One other preliminary note: dismissing Angel as a prig has unfortunate critical consequences. It minimizes the novel, makes it fall short of a sensed magnitude. If Angel is only a moral nincompoop (an Alec of another hue), the story shrinks: it offers only the heavy irony of an extraordinary woman injured by an unworthy man. More serious, calling Angel a prig separates the reader from him, puts the reader into the easy role of condemnation, and spares him the more difficult and profound experiences of imaginative participation in Angel's conduct. It is too simple just to despise Alec and Angel and feel indignant on Tess's account; anyone can take that safe and complacent course. To shift to other terms: the more prig Angel, the lesser the tragic potential of the novel. The priggish and the tragic are at odds: the tragic character is caught between incompatible values, the prig is wholly secure in a single value.

Hardy had several options in his treatment of Angel's response to

Tess's disclosure, and if we look at these, we can see that Hardy finally chose the most complex treatment. In a story bound by social convention Angel, as if victimized by Tess, might simply cast her off and end everything. In the opposite kind of story, one of pure satire, Angel might simply be excoriated for his inhumanity. In a sentimental tale he might be quick to understand, to sympathize, and to forgive. There are two possible romantic treatments of the theme. In one, Angel might be a bold spurner of taboos and actually welcome Tess's past as an enhancement of her value beyond the conventional. In the other, Angel might, like R. P. Warren's Jerry Beaumont, undertake to avenge Tess's honor, and indeed it is in this spirit that Angel does knock down a man who speaks an "insult" to her (33). This survey of alternatives makes clear that Hardy is interpreting much more deeply: his treatment is tragic, if not in ultimate development, at least in basic form. For Angel is a divided man incapable of a peace-producing singleness: he acts cruelly out of one side of his nature, but he is bitterly unhappy because of the other side of himself—his love for Tess, and a repressed intuition of her that is far keener than his formal judgment. He is a potential Othello.

To say that Angel is tragic is to say that we do, or ought to, understand and sympathize with his conflicting motives (the word is *sympathize*, not *approve*). Though some critics such as Richard Carpenter have grasped the complexity of Angel, in general we find it too easy to repudiate him. In part we are the victims, I suspect, of twentieth-century parochialism: we do not place a high value on virginity, therefore Angel's aversion to his wife's maculate state is simply odious or incredible. Hence we miss the fact that Hardy goes beyond satire to treat Angel sympathetically— that is, not as a man who is doing the right thing, but as a man who is acting understandably; not as a man who does the wrong thing through an egregious folly that demands only contempt, but as a man whose failure reveals a recognizable pattern of human conduct; not as a man clinging to outmoded ideas, but as a man erring through basic impulses that endure through changes of ideas. In Angel's view, Tess had concealed from him a fact of such fundamental importance that she had in effect misrepresented her nature and her character to him. If we think the fact concealed, and therefore the act of concealment, no longer significant, we relegate *Tess* to the low rank of novels dealing with topical issues outdated by the passage of time. However, *Tess* has a strong air of truth and relevance that could not be created by a work agitating problems no longer alive for later generations. We have to conclude that Angel was presented with a serious issue, and that Tess's not revealing that she had been a mistress and mother, though literally it may not seem momentous, does carry a great symbolic weight. Perhaps we can best appreciate this by substituting concealments likely to have a strong impact in our own day—say the concealment of a past history of syphilis, of drug addiction, or of time served in jail. The always-living issue is the extent to which one's past history is integral to present personality, particularly when that history seems to involve moral choices about which reasonable men may differ. Hardy has introduced an issue to which there are not easy answers (though his technique of dramatizing so extensively the virtues of Tess may make a solution appear easier than it is); one's past may or may not be essential in defining one's present being, and the individual who has to make a judgment on this will have to call on all his powers of discrimination. We cannot suppose that Angel stupidly missed a point that almost any other man in the same circumstances would see clearly.

Hardy makes Angel not romantic or obnoxious or wise, but a rather representative man who, despite his special endowments of sensitivity and intellectual independence, is driven by an utterly unforeseen crisis into familiar human patterns of feeling and behavior. These patterns need definition. In making his definitions Hardy again acts on two levels—that of satirical animus and that of fictional imagination, tending to make Angel on the one hand more shallow and, on the other, more deeply representative. It is Hardy the satirist who makes Angel a creature of "convention," that is, the contemporary modernist who has gone only partly modern. Angel adopts the role of the husband who expects obedience, anticipates what people will say to his and Tess's children (36), and then thinks of Brazil as free from "conventions" that oppose his union with Tess in England (39). Hardy directly calls Angel a "slave to custom and conventionality" (39) and makes Tess think of him as unable to "despise opinion" (42) and lament his "conventional standard of judgment [that] had caused her all these latter sorrows" (44). There is a minor irony in that Angel, who believes himself heterodox in thought, shares conventionality with "Sir John" Durbeyfield, who is worried only about the social repercussions of his son-in-law's flight (38), and Alec d'Urberville, who refers to his and Tess's "unconventional business" in the past (46).

Yet much of the talk about the conventional in Angel seems like editorializing that springs from historical annoyance rather than insight into character. Only once does a reference to convention become dramatic by pointing ironically to something deeper. When Angel impulsively invites Izz Huett to go with him to Brazil, he thinks of this step as a revenge on society and "convention" (40), as if convention were a force wholly outside himself, like a law of man or nature. By so viewing convention he can be free of responsibility for Tess's fate and hence can the more easily hold on to self-esteem. Here Hardy is not scoring hits against a contemporary habit of mind, but offering a more fundamental insight into Angel's representativeness, and portraying it not topically but time-lessly.

For the characteristic human experience that Angel undergoes is really the suffering of a wounded ego. His dominant self-concern is evi-dent throughout the scene in which he and Tess exchange confessions. He rejects Tess's proposed suicide not out of feeling for her but because "I don't wish to add murder to my other follies" (35). Later, thinking for a moment of taking Izz Huett to Brazil with him, he forces her into re-peated statements of how much she loves him (40); he needs this reas-surance for self-esteem. It is as though he himself is diminished when he learns that his knowledge of Tess is smaller than he thought because she had not told him everything. When we deplore deceit, we profess to uphold the moral supports of life; but it is also true, when we ourselves are deluded, that deceit makes us feel lessened, treated as if we could be put off with part-truths or managed by lies. Feeling injured begets sar-casm: Angel snaps at the "want of harmony between your present mood of self-sacrifice and your past mood of self-preservation." He regards her as "a species of impostor"; she twice mentions "deceit" (once to deny it), and he assents (35, 37). Hardy accurately defines Angel's harshness as "the cruelty of fooled honesty" (35) and makes Angel think of himself as "a dupe and a failure" (39).

Angel has a rather subtle and yet not rare form of injured ego. When Tess says, "It is in your own mind what you are angry at . . . ," she points in the right direction. His confident mind has framed a truth (his origi-nal evaluation of Tess), and now it turns out to be inaccurate. He has been so sure of this truth that he has made it difficult for Tess when she has tried to amend it (30); he acknowledges this (35), but the fact does not assuage the wound. She became "a visionary essence of woman" (20); now he is "swayed by the antipathetic wave which warps direct souls . . . when once their vision finds itself mocked by appearances" (36). "Mocked" is the right word; it expresses his sense of being ridiculed, deflated. Hardy sees that we identify with our ideas and are wounded if they are shaken; he is very shrewd in making Angel say, "the woman I have been loving is not you," and hence declare forgiveness irrelevant; we forgive an error that lets us hold on to our preconceptions, but not a metamorphosis or "prestidigitation" that makes nonsense of them. (This is one of various subtleties in the forgiveness theme.) Hardy sees how intensely we would like to hold on to them. "He looked at her imploring-ly, as if he would willingly have taken a lie from her lips." But she will give him no help. She is solidly there, in her truth contradicting and denying him. For him, whose "love was doubtless ethereal to a fault, imaginative to impracticability," she might have been more appealing in absence, since absence creates "an ideal presence that conveniently drops the defects of the real" (36).

Though Hardy remarks that Angel is wrongly named, it is difficult not to seize on his name and view him as an embodiment of "angelism," which, as Allen Tate puts it, denies "man's commitment to the physical world," "tries to disintegrate or circumvent the image in the illusory pursuit of essence," and involves loss of "the gift for concrete experience." (The words, we see immediately, are applicable not only to Angel but also to the Houyhnhnms and their pupil Gulliver.) Referring to Poe, Tate goes a step further and notes a "consequence" of "intellectual liberation from the sensible world," namely, "the exhaustion of force."[3] "Exhaustion" is a stronger term than we need, but it does suggest a paleness of quality in Angel and the Houyhnhnms and even in Gulliver before he has begun his slow reentry into the "physical world." The relevance of angelism here is that it establishes another tie between the two works we are examining and provides a useful category for the phenomenon dramatized. The danger, of course, is that it may seem to take Angel away from the representativeness that I am claiming for him. Not so. Angelism is the philosophical version of a most human situation. Angel represents man in his addiction to ideas, visions, ideals, and his conviction that life should conform to these, and thus not deceive him.

When man's prior conceptions rigidify into propositions that he holds to fixedly, he becomes doctrinaire. Angel undergoes this development of personality too: if doctrine and actuality do not mesh, so much the worse for actuality. Angel has his theory of the value of new stock, and of the exhaustion of old family lines (19), and by it he explains Tess's "want of firmness." "Decrepit families imply decrepit wills, decrepit conduct"; the portraits of the d'Urberville women seem to him to reveal "sinister design" and a "concentrated purpose of revenge on the other sex," and he is sure that Tess looks like them (35). "Hidden in his constitution" is "a hard logical deposit" which "blocked his acceptance of the church" and then "blocked his acceptance of Tess." The question, he assures her, is "one of principle!" He holds to his "consistency," though it makes him "cruel." He wrestles with theoretical formulations—Alec is really Tess's "husband in nature"—until "thinking" has made him "ill," "eaten out," "withered." Tess perceives his fear that he may "change [his] plans in opposition to [his] reason," and she is "appalled by the determination revealed in the depths of this gentle being" (36). After he has left her, he even criticizes himself for not having acted on his doctrine earlier: "When he found that Tess came of that exhausted ancient line, and was not of the new tribes from below, as he had fondly dreamed, why had he not stoically abandoned her, in fidelity to his principles? This was what he had got by apostasy, and his punishment was deserved" (39). Just before leaving for Brazil, he reviews the case again, and again he is doctrinaire: "the facts had not changed. If he was right at first, he was right now" (40).

In Angel, then, Hardy has caught a doctrinaire rigidity that is a widespread human trait, widespread both among the learned who are conscious of doctrine and the unlearned who hold to it unconsciously. But Hardy has also caught the more subtle point that consistency is a source of self-esteem, principle a buttress of the self-image. Like his first mentor Meredith, Hardy has perceived how man's *amour propre* attaches to his ideas. Sir Austin Feverel's ego gets so implicated in his "system" that he cannot give the system up even when it is no longer relevant; in the name of the system he tries to impose his ego on his son's history. Angel fears that flexibility may be only flabby self-indulgence, that a wavering in thought may be a moral backsliding; his ego is at stake. It is in the light of such basic patterns of feeling and action that we have to say, not "There goes that prig," but "There go I." Granted, a rigid doctrinaire figure could be inhumanly narrow. He might be the political or social fanatic who could exist only as the object of satirical exposure. He might be the inflexible one-idea man who is often a butt in comedy. But if Hardy's satirical impulse and his topical concerns urge him partially in such directions, his fictional imagination so rounds Angel out that he is neither sinister nor funny but, in Conrad's phrase, "one of us."

On the one hand, his principal misdeed is humanly not eccentric but characteristic. On the other, his flaw is not all we have to judge him by. He has substantial virtues: he is constantly self-critical, he means to be considerate, he is in love without knowing it, he lies to his family to protect Tess, and he suffers constantly. Above all, his rigidity is a prop, not an irreplaceable structural element in his personality. He becomes flexible and inconsistent; he reverses himself and criticizes himself, and he feels "remorse." Finally, he makes a self-judgment in precisely the terms suitable to his conduct: his fault was "allowing himself to be influenced by general principles to the disregard of the particular instance" (49). He knows that he has been doctrinaire in judging Tess only by two criteria: by a past event, and by her family descent. Thus he has exemplified one of the oldest and most enduring and most widespread forms of injustice—seeing and judging other human beings not as individuals but as members of classes (races, nations, religions). He has been a true Houyhnhnm. In this he can stand easily for the twentieth-century white man, bearing at last the penalty for ages of judgments by class, and gradually awakening to the moral role in which he has been implicated. Whether his awakening is as full as Angel's remains to be seen. Angel comes to accept Tess's charge of "injustice"; he accuses himself of "a love 'which alters when it alteration finds'" (53); when Tess, now with Alec, tells Angel to "go away," he says, "Ah—it is my fault!" (55); he prepares to protect her, "whatever you may have done or not have done!" (57). Whatever she has done, he now only loves: he has ceased to apply rules and to judge.

Angel has tortured his wife and inaugurated the train of disasters that drove her to murder; he has made himself wretched by depriving himself of Tess, first for a time and then forever; most of all, he has to bear the burden of guilt. He comes to painful self knowledge, and he accepts it. The experiences that he undergoes, then, are tragic. But at the end he is mainly an observer, and there is at least a hint of a happy relationship with 'Liza-Lu, Tess's beautiful sister. The grief of the survivors, looking back from a hilltop, is lyric, and all the somberness does not wholly close out the romantic. In the final chapters Angel has not quite the deep anguish, and certainly not the centrality, of the tragic hero. He has a supporting role.

Yet it is important that Hardy has treated the supporting role completely. If Angel were as uncomplicated as he has often been read—and this goes for Alec too—*Tess* would be much less of a novel than it has been taken to be. Fictional greatness does not come from the dragging down of a single great character by midgets. We have judged Angel and Alec to be lesser figures than they are because we have overstressed their more conspicuous features, those created by Hardy's satirical sense and his topical interests. We have not been sufficiently aware that Hardy is ambiguous, no doubt basically in his sympathies, as De Laura suggests, but also in his narrative form: there the fictional-imaginative is added to the satirical without wholly replacing it. In this aesthetic situation lies the resemblance to *Gulliver's Travels* that makes these works, for all their differences, mutually illuminating. Both mingle the satirical (or precast) and the imaginative (or free) modes. What is more remarkable is that the shared modal ambiguity is combined with a strong thematic resemblance between the works: in both we have the whole or potentially whole character caught between partial beings to whom Swift gave the classic names—Houyhnhnms and Yahoos.

The Lure of the Demonic:
James and Dürrenmatt

IT MAY NOT BE POSSIBLE to resolve in our time the "ambiguity" that makes Henry James's *The Turn of the Screw* present quite different meanings to different readers. For this ambiguity may turn out to be a product, not of absolute textual conditions, but of the conflicting, and indeed competing, senses of reality that characterize a period of philosophical transition. One can imagine a composition of these, an alteration in the philosophic (moral, epistemological) landscape, that may lead to a surer, more generally agreed upon, reading of the text. But it is also imaginable that philosophic differences will persist, and with them the critical dissension that will make possible new collections of essays that disagree with each other.

On the face of it the story is concerned with the governess's battle against an objective evil that is infecting the character of the children, Miles and Flora. Some readers' acceptance of the literal text is hampered by several assumptions of romantic origin and hue: the essential innocence of children; the corruptness of authority, whether political or educational; the untrustworthiness of traditionalist attitudes toward wrongdoing—the last reinforced by a more recent tendency to suppose that concern with "saving" others is a gross imposition unless it is material salvation that is offered. Interlaced with these is the habit of separating the evil and the innocent into different classes (a secularized Calvinism), and of identifying evil with concrete persons, bodies, and institutions that can be blamed, punished, or eliminated. It is almost impossible for a reader of such a philosophical disposition to accept the symbolization of evil by the ghosts, who cannot be blamed, punished, or eliminated; in this symbolization evil is presented as ubiquitous, mysterious, and, though of limited scope, eternal. Evil as an active force in the personalities of intelligent, charming, and well-bred children (not just dead-end kids, who have become a cliché symbol) is equally intolerable, for this implies a universal vulnerability that denies the quarantine, segregationist, or preventive-vaccine view of evil that is fairly popular today. However, evil continues to be "manageable" if it can be conceived as a projection of a private illness (or as an emanation from a special class) for which there are "known" remedies.

Finally, the evocation of the ghosts is done with such technical skill that it is extraordinarily difficult not to sense them as actual and to experience the old dread of such apparitions. But this is a rational age; ghosts do not exist, and we shrink from finding within ourselves a strong residual capacity for so frank a response. Hence the double usefulness of the "discovery of the unconscious" (that is, the coming to consciousness of the unconscious knowledge of the unconscious that had been possessed for many ages). On the one hand, it would provide the final bit of technical assistance needed to isolate the evil in *The Turn of the Screw* in a special ward which our sensibility would find the most comfortable place for it. And on the other, it would free us from recognizing an unpalatable responsiveness to phenomena that belong to less rational ages.

But, apart from severe problems of accommodation to the text, the "depth" approach suffers from some difficulties in the application of the principle. As elsewhere, it appears to do incomplete justice to the total Freudian view by making the unconscious in author or character the whole thing, the invariable, unconditioned truth in all cases. The use of Freudian observations of illness as if they were automatic, universally applicable measures of all truth is, of course, understandable in an age given to mechanical solutions of all kinds of problems: the temper of the times influences literary analysis too. But the rote application of formulas to *The Turn of the Screw* involves, as critics have pointed out, an ignoring of such objective facts as Miles's wrongdoing at school and the governess's obvious good health after the events of the story. Again, the new knowledge that sexuality influences many nonsexual activities is applied eagerly to the governess but not at all to Miles and Flora. Though James wisely leaves undefined what the children are doing under the tutelage of the ghosts, it would be plausible to suppose that sex is involved and to conclude that, despite his shift of emphasis from the clinical to the moral, James had "anticipated" the Freudian discoveries of preadolescent sexuality.

In making these comments I am not arguing against the readings which assume that the governess is having a fantasy or is in other ways doing something different from what she supposes, but suggesting the philosophic habits (attitudes or positions implied or formally held) that encourage such readings. The points of view in themselves may provide valuable formulations of experience, but they may or may not lead to sound literary interpretations; in the case of *The Turn of the Screw* they lend assistance to a reading which I believe conforms to too small a number of the data provided by the fiction and relies on too many assumptions for which there is little or no evidence. However, the points of view and their critical consequences are here, and this creates a familiar problem. One kind of critic may be content to dismiss the problem as simply one more insoluble question of relativities; another may be content to await a new historical orientation of ideas that will provide ground for surer interpretation; another may be willing to drop the matter or simply to insist. A more useful procedure, I suggest, is the presentation of new evidence. New direct evidence—testimony as to the author's purpose, and so on—is not likely to show up, and the text itself has been pretty well combed. But there is a kind of literary evidence that is worth exploring—the evidence of literary works that are concerned with similar themes and that present a comparable sense of human reality. A kindred literary work may cast a light that will throw into relief certain things that James is doing and strengthen their influence upon the reader's sense of the whole. Hence I want to present some evidence that I think tends to confirm that *The Turn of the Screw* is doing what it purports to be doing, and makes it a little harder to maintain that unconscious intentions in author and heroine are the real determinants of what the book is.

The book that I believe to be useful for the interpretation of *The Turn of the Screw* is *The Pledge* (1958) by Friedrich Dürrenmatt, the Swiss expressionist best known in America as the author of *The Visit*, successfully presented in 1958 by the Lunts. *The Pledge*, a novelette a little shorter than *The Turn of the Screw*, has to do with children who are victims of a mysterious evil figure; and in elaborating this theme it has some close resemblances to *The Turn of the Screw*. In tracing these resemblances I am not concerned with sources or parallels interesting for their own sake, but with Dürrenmatt's sense of human reality and its corroboration of a central James insight.

Dürrenmatt's imagination is narrower than James's; he is at once more given to making points (the allegorist) and to pulling off surprises (the showman) so that his art is slicker, shallower, more transparent. But, though he cannot resist "overplanning" his general effect and cuting things up with gimmicks here and there, his work has comparative value on two counts. A lesser work can always provide perspective on a greater one, as the long tradition of source and analogue study shows; and, at his untricky best, Dürrenmatt sees sharply beneath the surface of human nature.

The Turn of the Screw has several interlocking themes, as may be expected in a fiction that has to do both with beings in need of salvation and with an agent trying to effect that salvation. But if we look at the work for the moment in terms of only one of its themes, we see that it belongs to a family of works in which there comes into play an extraordinary influencing of children by adults, works in which some kind of seduction goes on. If we put this in very general terms, it is possible to see how Lewis Carroll's Alice books and Nabokov's *Lolita*, as well as *The Turn of the Screw* and *The Pledge*, come into the picture. The Alice books, it is true, have only slight illustrative value, for the situation that piques us there is a real-life relationship of author and children. In this case the adult acted through the agency of art, and cannot legitimately be compared with figures that exist only in art. Yet there is one parallel: both in real life and in art, an adult makes certain gestures toward children, and we can observe their responses. Whatever kind of private gesture may have lain within Carroll's public gesture of storytelling, or within certain of his narrative details whose secondary meanings have been widely explored, there is no evidence that the total act was received in any other way than that demanded by the public storytelling. It pleased. There was simple responsiveness to the open intention; for us, this situation is not unlike that in a work of art in which we can see the irony of a child's accepting pleasure in which we recognize, whether it becomes actual or not, a latent harm or even destructiveness. It is a matter of speculation whether the Alice stories might in themselves afford an "innocent" reader an entirely unrecognized "forbidden" pleasure— securing an effect comparable to that made upon a television viewer by a word flashed on a screen too rapidly to be formally identified and yet becoming a "presence" in the mind of the viewer.

In *Lolita*, *The Turn of the Screw*, and *The Pledge* there are adults practicing the seduction of children—in the first, sexually; in the second, in ways not defined; in the third, by securing a confidence that evidently obscures or transcends what we take to be the loathsomeness of the adult; and in both the second and third creating a kind of fidelity to the destroyer that seems to cut off an incipient sense of wrongness in the situation. What all these authors have observed is an element of consent in the victim—not so much ignorance, though this cannot entirely be excluded, as a subtle knowingness or readiness for the proffered moves, a minute failure of an initial capacity to reject that might have saved the children in both the James and Dürrenmatt stories. Lolita does come to reject the corrupt and corrupting elder, and, in saying that, one points to the ultimate divergence of the stories. All that I am concerned with here is the significance for the James story of the fact that three authors of different nationalities, in looking at children, have discerned a capacity for "wrong" action that many readers apparently want, or even need, to reject as not credible. The lure of the demonic is not the most palatable dish on the sideboard of human potentialities.

What the James and Dürrenmatt tales have in common is not only the child victim but the dedicated savior, and in each case the story of the latter is done with more than a little complexity. The story of the governess is so well known that it need not be rehearsed here. In *The Pledge* a fifty-year-old police inspector of the Zurich canton, Matthäi, makes a full-time quest of tracking down a psychopathic murderer of young girls; though known as "Matt the Automat," he has been greatly moved by the last killing; the title alludes to his pledge to the girl's parents that he will find the criminal. Dürrenmatt's major concern is with the psychic and moral development of Matthäi. At one level Dürrenmatt is making game of detective fiction because it shows life as yielding to ratiocination (his German subtitle is *Requiem auf den Kriminalroman*). Matthäi makes a brilliant theoretic solution of the case, but eventually breaks down because he expects all subsequent events to conform to his rational plan for them. He has identified the killer in human type and in type of movement and conduct, and has prepared a trap into which the individual killer must fall. However, the killer is killed in an automobile accident, and Matthäi goes to pieces, eternally waiting for his victim to drive into his trap. So much for Dürrenmatt's foreground story, which is almost allegorical and somewhat artificial; the writer, in debunking the forced pattern of detective fiction, has forced a pattern of conduct upon his character. He illustrates only too well his perfectly sound dictum, "Reality can only partially be attacked by logic."

Dürrenmatt is a far more effective artist in dealing with other aspects of Matthäi's obsessive scheme to make the psychopath reveal himself and thus to save other young girls who are the victims he needs. Matthäi starts running a gas station on a road which he is sure that the criminal must use; then, in a climax of detective machination, he brings in to live with him a streetwalker who has a young daughter. He dresses the girl like the previous victim, and with her as "bait" waits for the "big fish" to come by and be caught. This is a fascinating narrative version of the problem of ends and means. Further, the question of means is a way of revealing the complications of personality in a dedicated person with a mission—the possibility of corruption in the pursuit of a meritorious goal. The relation to James is that both writers sense the subtle interplay of devotion and egoism in the rescuer of others; many things go under in the determination to master the problem. Intensity of obligation may weaken judgment and create rigidity. Here the alluring demonic is the triumph of the self. In refusing to call upon the godlike uncle the governess falls into a go-it-alone hubris which, we cannot doubt, reduces the effectiveness that added help might have given her battle. Thinking she has defeated the ghost Quint in his efforts to get at Miles, the governess glories in "my personal triumph"; but she adds, "I was infatuated—I was blind with victory" (pp. 130, 132; references are to the Modern Library edition). Both authors present the signs of strain in the character with a mission. The governess faces the fact that she may be mad (p. 72), and Matthäi knows that he is regarded as insane; near the climax he "sensed" that his "insane expectations" would be fulfilled (p. 95; references are to the Signet edition [1960] of the Richard and Clara Winston translation [Knopf, 1959] of the original Swiss edition [1958]). Indeed, he eventually loses his grip; and the governess develops a tense, almost hysterical manner that has helped mislead some readers. In *The Turn of the Screw* there is a greater problem because James has chosen to use the governess's point of view. Dürrenmatt employs another narrator to give us a firm perspective on Matthäi, whereas James's dependence on a solitary, taut, strained observer increases the difficulty of placing the character in the total fictional landscape. But the point here is that similarities in the authors' management of the savior characters strengthen our sense that a self-consciously heroic quality, a certain excessiveness, a vehement, at times frantic style, self-will, and tension in the governess are signs not of disorder but of a normal, imperfect human being's response to the pressure of enormous difficulties. What ultimately destroys Matthäi—and this is the difference between him and the governess—is a Houyhnhnm-like rigidity of mind that wants not only to discover the truth but to dictate the circumstance of its emergence.

Dürrenmatt and James are even alike in their imagination of the evil enemy. Matthäi's adversary, of course, is a psychopath, but he is given motives and a "character"; he hates women and he seeks revenge against them. "Perhaps his wife was rich and he poor. Perhaps she held a higher social position than he" (p. 74). In fact he was a "chauffeur and gardener" (p. 118) whose marriage to his much older and well-to-do employer was not quite a Mellors-and-Connie affair. Quint was a valet, a "base menial" (p. 54), who had seduced the previous governess, Miss Jessel, "a lady" (p. 48); both were "infamous" (p. 48); they want to "get hold of" the children (p. 47) and make them share their own infernal "torments" (p. 72). (Not until the 1950s would it have been interesting that on one occasion Quint and Miss Jessel are referred to as "the others, the outsiders" [p. 80].) The psychopath won the confidence of little girls with chocolate candy; Quint used to "spoil" Miles (p. 39). These are their demonic lures—the pleasing façade of the revengefulness that both writers detect as central in the evil beings and that both see as creating a need to destroy: in one case physical life, in the other, spiritual life. In *The Turn of the Screw*, indeed, the appearance of the ghosts is regularly described with images of death. Though there is a multitude of differences between the psychopath and the ghosts, the central similarities are marked enough to have critical value; they make it more difficult to suppose that James's ghosts are simply creations of the governess's mind, and they strengthen the view that the ghosts are objective embodiments of moral forces referable to basic human qualities and behavior.

But Dürrenmatt's most marked corroboration of the view that James's apparent story of evil spirits is the true story comes in the treatment of Annemarie, the "bait" through whom Matthäi seeks to entrap the killer. Here the central point is that movement of personality which I have called "consent," though the term has to be used suggestively rather than absolutely. The child is, in a general sense, "seduced"; but the flat tale of the victim, the melodrama of pity, is greatly complicated by the presence of a vulnerability that, going beyond mere pathetic defenselessness, subtly implies a half-willing participation in the suspect terms of the destructive relationship. Not that the girl is a precocious instance of the "murderee" that Lawrence theorizes about. But the young mind, though the questionable, the forbidden, are not concealed from it, is drawn in, or drawn *by*, these and works up an ironic faithfulness to the agent who is outside the pale. In Dürrenmatt the case is simpler than in James, but there is still evidence of a child's subtly sensing illegitimacy in the enterprise and yet having a virtually unbreakable commitment to it. What is very effective in both tales is the picture of an almost adult acceptance of adult beings to whom the more usual childish response, we suppose, would be fear.

Yet, in two of the four children presented by the stories, there is a faint falling short of total acceptance that adds a strange vibrancy to the character; in presenting this, both authors manage a contrast and yet urge it so little that one may scarcely feel it the first time around. Both Flora and Annemarie are, as far as the overt evidence goes, most unreservedly attracted to their secret associates; in them we observe no sense of duplicity in the situation, no counterimpulse to hesitate, doubt, or withdraw. But in Miles the governess detects signs of a despair that indicates unusual awareness of the nature of his engagement; and she feels in him some willingness to come toward her as a helper, some incompleteness in the fidelity to Quint, some faint symptom of resistance to the lure of the demonic. In *The Pledge* the killer has extraordinary success in getting the cooperation of his victims, in securing their maintenance of a secrecy without which the preparatory rendezvous could not continue. But Gritli Moser, the victim whose death is the starting point of the novelette, had, even while continuing to meet the killer, evaded his injunction of secrecy by telling a close friend a "fairy tale" about meeting a "giant" and by drawing a symbolic picture that revealed some important aspects of the killer's identity. As with Miles, the impulse to independent action, the minimal blind man's feeling toward safety, falls far short of establishing protection against the danger behind the proffered and desired sweets. But what is important for us is that two writers, in dealing with such a situation, distinguish between the child who succumbs wholly to the lure of the demonic and the one whose yielding to temptation is ever so subtly qualified by the faint stirrings of an imperfect desire to make possible a rescue. In making the distinction James further strengthens our sense that he is observing human responses in actual beings in an objective situation.

There are some interesting similarities in peripheral circumstance. In *The Turn of the Screw* the climactic scene for Flora takes place in the out-of-doors—"at a distance" (p. 102) from the house. The climactic scene with Annemarie takes place at a clearing in woods along the road from the village to Matthäi's country place. Flora is found along the shores of a pond more than a half-mile from the house (p. 104); Annemarie is found sitting "on the bank of the small, silvery stream" that runs through the clearing (p. 94). But most interesting of all is the general resemblance in symbolic decor: both authors have chosen a scene where fertility images are dominant and have introduced into it images of death or decay—the demonic intrusion into the garden. In *The Pledge*, the clearing in the woods is also the town's refuse dump, and in *The Turn of the Screw*, more subtly, Flora plucks and holds on to an "ugly spray of withered fern" (p. 106).

Each scene is the moment of triumph for the "savior" character, but the triumph is ironically undercut by the course of events. The governess is sure that Flora has been consorting with the ghost of Miss Jessel; Flora is found exactly where the governess conjectures, and then, to complete the victory, Miss Jessel materializes across the pond. But Mrs. Grose cannot see the apparition, comforts the child, and doubts the governess almost to the point of turning entirely against her. In *The Pledge* Matthäi has a number of police with him to surround the clearing where Annemarie goes to meet "the wizard," as she calls the killer; Matthäi is utterly certain that the killer, whom he has long awaited, will now arrive and be captured; but the killer never shows up, and eventually the officers all turn against Matthäi, treating him as if he were the victim of a hallucination. In each story there is a "seer" who has caught sight of an evil being but who, when this being does not become the palpable presence required by ordinary eyes, is rejected by those who go only on immediate sensory evidence.

Although Annemarie is the parallel to Flora, her conduct, as imagined by Dürrenmatt, has some singular resemblances to that of both children at Bly. Once Annemarie has met "the wizard," she begins to disappear without warning; she is believed to be in school when it turns out that the school is not in session; and, when she has supposedly gone to school, it transpires that she is not there. This parallels exactly the way in which the children escape from the governess's vigilance at Bly, though James complicates the picture by having one child absorb the governess's attention to cover the disappearance of the other. Skill increases as scruples decrease. The governess has a sense of the children's retreating into another world, though no word is ever spoken of it. Likewise Annemarie appears, in her trysts with the wizard, to have entered into another consciousness that she will keep closed to the others; when Matthäi finds that she has in her possession some unexplained chocolate candy (the bait regularly used by the wizard) and questions her about it, she either refuses to talk or lies. (When Matthäi finds the chocolate about which she lies, he is "overcome by a tremendous feeling of joy" [p. 97]; compare the governess on Miles: "his lies made up my truth" [p. 127].) Even in the relatively few pages that he has for this part of the story, Dürrenmatt skillfully suggests Annemarie's separation from the ordinary life of others, a separation that the governess has felt in her charges for months; as she puts it, "They haven't been good—they've only been absent" (p. 73). Annemarie waits for the wizard, "full of . . . keyed-up expectation" (p. 99), just as Miles was "under some influence operating . . . as a tremendous incitement" (p. 58). Annemarie waits for the wizard with incredible patience, day after day, just as the children at Bly have always been patient with the governess, diverting her with a possibly "studied" charm (p. 56) as they arrange their secret rendezvous. In entertaining her they sing and play a good deal, for they have a lively "musical sense" (p. 58); in holding her attention on the day of Flora's final escape, Miles plays the piano "as he had never played before" (p. 101). From the time that she first sees the wizard, Annemarie begins singing "Maria sat upon a stone" (p. 95) regularly, and it is a steady accompaniment of her actions to the end of the episode. Open song is the sign of the secret pleasure.

The song might be coincidence, as might the fact that in both books the climactic scenes take place in autumn. What is unmistakably meaningful is the way both girls disappear to the rendezvous scene and conduct themselves there. For a whole week Matthäi and the helping police watch the clearing where Annemarie sits and sings, waiting for the wizard. She would sit "motionless in the same spot . . . with incomprehensible patience" (p. 100), singing, "persistent, bemused, incomprehensible" (p. 101). In a few pages Dürrenmatt records the same withdrawnness, the same patience, the same taking on of certain adult qualities that Flora manifests over a longer period. Annemarie's extraordinary fixation and endurance are psychologically of a piece with the almost super-human feat of Flora in using a large, flat-bottomed boat to get to her wooded assignation place. The girls remain imperturbable, in contrast with their elders, who crack under the strain of dealing with adversaries mysteriously not present, and break out into antagonism against the one to be protected. When Flora, caught up with, simply smiles and remains silent, the governess is goaded into challenging her: "Where, my pet, is Miss Jessel?" (p. 107). Matthäi and his fellow watchers finally leap out of hiding and demand of Annemarie, "Whom are you waiting for, answer me, do you hear, you damned brat!" (p. 103). Annemarie is frightened, as Flora obviously is not; indeed, a reader inclined to think that Flora acts in the manner of an innocent terrified by a madwoman could make an instructive comparison between the relative calculatedness of Flora's responses and the more spontaneous responses of Annemarie. In Flora it is the "quick, smitten glare" (p. 108), "an expression of hard, still gravity," "a countenance of deeper and deeper, of indeed suddenly quite fixed reprobation" (p. 109), and a little later, of course, a flood of verbal "horrors" and "appalling language" that convince even the unseeing Mrs. Grose (pp. 116–17). In Annemarie it is at first simply "eyes welling with tears" (p. 103). But it is this very difference that adds great significance to Annemarie's tendency to move toward the Flora kind of response—first to be silent and then to attack those who threaten the secret idyll. In the style of a "vulgarly pert little girl in the street" Flora denies that she has seen or sees anything and concludes, "I think you're cruel. I don't like you" (pp. 110–11). When the nature and intent of the wizard are explained to her, Annemarie comes back with "You're lying . . . You're lying"; and, even when in their frustration the men outrageously beat her, she fights back, "shrieking," in a voice "uncanny" and "inhuman," "You're lying, lying, lying" (pp. 103–4).

What Dürrenmatt has caught here is the kind of faith that, despite a sneaky, irregular style that might be expected to arouse fear and repulsion, an agent of evil can evoke—an allegiance that makes those who oppose it seem, to the victim himself, inimical, false, and cruel, and that renders the victim capable of remarkable feats in the pursuit and preservation of the new ends to which he has been converted. It is in the perception of these responses in a child that Dürrenmatt has corroborated James's vision and has strengthened the interpretation that what happens to Miles and Flora, and what they do, are to be taken as objective facts brilliantly perceived and reliably reported by the governess.

What is more, we find that, in the ideational matrix of his story, Dürrenmatt has made what is in effect an attack on some of the habits of mind to which I have attributed the disinclination of some readers to accept the James story at face value. His moral, as we have seen, is "Reality can only partially be attacked by logic." If by "logic" we mean the tenets that rationalism admits at any given time, it is clear that the denial of the ghostly corruption of the children is, as Philip Rahv put it a long time ago, a "fallacy of rationalism," or, in Dürrenmatt's terms, an endeavor to control too much of reality by logic. Since Dürrenmatt is in part spoofing detective fiction, his emphasis shifts away from the kind of moral vulnerability that is at the center of *The Turn of the Screw*. But even with this shift of emphasis Dürrenmatt perhaps turns an additional small light on the James achievement. For, writing seventy years earlier, James by implication also delivered a sort of "Requiem auf den Kriminalroman": like his successor, he distinguished between diagnosing an illness and winning the battle against it—the double triumph that is at the center of popular detective fiction. Both writers record the history of a "pledge." James would hardly have been likely to assent to Dürrenmatt's "Chance, the incalculable, the incommunicable, plays too great a part" (p. 13), for this posits an ultimate disorder of things that minimizes the role of character. But James does imagine an ordered evil that creates a disorder which a given character, for all of a Cassandra's insight, cannot cope with, and against which a well-intentioned woman's pride prevents her calling on all the resources that are available.

What I have called the lure of the demonic is related to the charm of the con man; each finds some responsiveness in the intended victim. To that extent such tales as *The Turn of the Screw* and *The Pledge* are related to picaresque fiction. But the two forms illuminate each other by their differences: the picaresque hero means only to outwit, the ghosts and the killer to destroy. The picaro is related to a particular kind of criminal—not to the criminal who destroys by simple violence, but to the criminal who works by means of a seduction that leads to annihilation. Eliminate the deep passional need to destroy, and leave only the game of seducing and tricking, and you have the picaro. Both the picaro and the criminal type of which he is an attenuation proceed, of course, by evoking faith. They are, in a sense, fake divinities. What is interesting about fake divinities is their extraordinary grasp of one aspect of human nature.

■ 12 ■
Lampedusa and Bulwer:
Sic Transit in Different Keys

ONE MAY READ TOPICALLY or aesthetically, as a partisan or a contemplator, as an explorer of novelty or as a creature of habit. One may even read geographically, that is, with a besetting sense of "Where?" I know one or two people who cannot read a novel without using an atlas, and who all but ink in the lines of action on printed maps. If it's Wessex or Yoknapatawpha, they usually turn to the end papers and find the job done for them. Or instead of going from novel to map, one may go from actual scene to novel. Everywhere in Sicily one hears of Giuseppe di Lampedusa: here he was born, here he lived, here he was honored, here he found materials. So one reads *The Leopard* (1958), which, if the publisher's jacket is reliable, L. P. Hartley calls "Perhaps the greatest novel of the century," and William Golding and Louis Aragon and E. M. Forster praise with almost equal unreserve. At Pompeii one does not hear Edward Bulwer-Lytton so trumpeted, though one can buy *The Last Days* in various tongues. But one goes from site to novel, probably with two kinds of curiosity: what could fiction do with such a site, which shouts its *sic transit* theme so resonantly as to leave, one thinks, nothing to be said? Even more, what kind of fiction could so stir imaginations that a hundred visitors clamber over Pompeii to ten for Herculaneum and one for Paestum?

The Leopard and *The Last Days of Pompeii*, for all of their differences, have a common theme, the death of a community: the contemporary novel, the nineteenth-century sunset of a regional feudalism before the rise of the new Italian state under the baton of Garibaldi; the nineteenth-century novel, the death of a gay suburban town, eighteen hundred years earlier, under an eruption of Vesuvius. Neither mistakes death itself for tragedy, and neither tries to find a tragic experience in the death which he surveys. Lampedusa is retelling, in a new setting, the myth of nature: the superannuation and exhaustion of the old order, and the inrush of the new. Bulwer-Lytton retells what we might call the oldest and most primitive myth of nature, the one that we religiously struggle to push into a past where its only life will be that of aesthetic memory for self-confident modernity—the irrational and destructive

173

outbreaks of the physical world against conquering man. Insofar as both novelists are dealing with mortalities that are not related to human choices, they are working in the realm of melodrama, and the problem is one of how far they can move from the stereotypes toward a history of the soul.

It may be possible to argue that the old order represented by Lampedusa's Prince of Salina might have found a less parasitic, less ingrown, way of life, and that its failure to do so had in it something of the tragic flaw. But it is a little bit like arguing that ignorance could make a choice of wisdom, or that the physical being could choose not to age. Are we saying, then, that Lampedusa had no real choice himself, that he was committed to a case history—or at most a panorama—of foolish senility? By no means. Lampedusa was no more limited in his field than was Chekhov in *The Cherry Orchard*, that fine dramatic version of the myth of nature (or than was Tennessee Williams in *Streetcar Named Desire*, a ruder and diminished *Cherry Orchard*). Each secures that wider reality which comes from the knowledge that both death and life, far from being the simple opposites that they are often reduced to in the more naive contemporary criticism (as in the cliché "on the side of life"), are mixed matters. The dying order has charm and grace and breeding and sensitivity—virtues that are essential to life; yet elegance and the power of subsistence have slowly, imperceptibly parted company. Chekhov's Firs, the old faithful retainer, says the family have forgotten how to use the cherries; the Prince of Salina knows that he has lost the economic sense, the sheer ability to manage property. Lopakhin does know what to do with the cherry orchard; Don Calogero, Lampedusa's new man, does know how to manage property and make the money roll in. Yet the men with their feet on the ground, those who are taking over, are gross or rude or calculating—qualities that can lead to death. It is the ironic sense of mingled strength and weakness, or perhaps better, of quality and deficiency, that saves such works from the limited role of lamenting the old or cheering the new.

Chekhov insisted that he wrote comedy, and that is what Lampedusa is essentially doing (we might apply to his work James W. Hall's term *painful comedy*). The heart of comedy is the sense of the world and its ways: the Prince of Salina seeks that compromise which is civility in public action. He knows the difference between what one wills and what will be; he has the comic self-knowledge, that is, a knowledge of one's relation to and place in the world; he can concede without selling out, lament without giving up, and endeavor to buy a small share in the future without assuming that the future is simply for sale. Lampedusa ironically and reflectively observes the Prince ironically and reflectively observing himself and the world; when the Prince dies, the largeness of which the old order was capable is gone. In the Prince's daughters, whom we see finally in virginal old age in 1910, aristocratic independence and self-will have slipped through eccentricity into an absurd and self-defeating isolation; becoming, with their private chapel, more Catholic than the Catholics, they have fallen—how fittingly—into the hands of a relics-broker, and have to be rescued, really through a disciplinary procedure, by the Church itself.

Lampedusa's story is loosely organized in terms of action and character; what holds it together is tone and perspective. With the dominance of the comic view, with the keen sense of the way of the world, with the rejection of illusion, the "wisdom" that has been attributed to it might easily slide into a facile cynicism. It does not do so; the reason is that Lampedusa is not hampered by a shallow sense of personality and human possibility; he has his share in that wisdom which consists in knowing not only what man is up to but also what he is capable of rising to. He can define snobbery as "the opposite of envy," self-deception as the "essential requisite for anyone wanting to guide others," and blaming one's own unhappiness on others as "a solace which is the last protective device of the desperate." He can also say of a character that "she had too much pride and too much ambition to be capable of that annihilation, however temporary, of one's own personality without which there is no love" and speak of days "when many beds had been offered and refused, when the sensual urge, because restrained, had for one second been sublimated in renunciation, that is into real love" (quotations from Archibald Colquhoun's translation). It is the wisdom of facing facts without losing sight of norms, or, alternatively, of a moral realism that does not simplify man into psychological mechanisms.

Perhaps, after sharing in the admiration for Lampedusa, one may seem to have no option but quickly to toss Bulwer's *Last Days*—that obituary of a much smaller piece of Italy—back into the mass grave of popular classics barely mentioned in English courses and perhaps not even read elsewhere, and declare it not even of archaeological interest. A priori, there is good reason to expect prompt reburial. Lampedusa's myth of nature had at least to do with human personality, with the precarious interplay of gift and defect, of tradition and challenge, that is the stuff of crises; Bulwer's, on the contrary, is outside of character, a tale of indiscriminate catastrophe that hardly favors distinctions in quality of being. Another savage handicap to his art is that he chose an obsolete business: now we view man as bending nature and not bending before it. If there are cataclysms, we make them rather than suffer them. What, then, can Bulwer offer us but worn corn? But courage and cowardice, much horror and a little luck, the usual medley of uncomplicated experiences and responses in the face of total and irrational adversity? What can he do but write a novel of disaster, the simplest form of melodrama, saving a chosen few, perhaps, but consigning the multitude to dust and ashes? These are indeed his problems, and he compounds them by fabricating a dialogue style that we might call Archaic Forum: "Could she reveal her true self to the people, Calenus, now incenseless would be those altars!" In addition, he has a scheming, malignant, and all-but-successful villain out of popular melodrama and, to boot, a witch who brews evil potions.

Yet Bulwer brings it off—in the sense, at least, that he has managed an authentic minor classic. It is possible to regard the style, not as an irredeemable monstrosity, but as an outworn convention, and to translate it into a happier idiom as one goes; no doubt one who continues with the book does this to some extent. Yet even a style alien to us may bring something home to us; out of Bulwer's, I suspect, come a little weight and dignity to help head off the supercinematic always latent in the materials. In this respect style may collaborate obscurely with scholarship; Bulwer made a great point of being both archaeologist and cultural historian, and his intentness on full and accurate documentation suggests rather reliability than pedantry. If one forgets aesthetic rules— for example, that art is not history and should not pretend to be—and simply submits to the reconstruction of Pompeiian life, the novel comes through almost as a work of art in itself, with a substance and originality that distinguish it from the popular confection. The historical actuality contributes to the portrayal of the villain Arbaces, an Egyptian priest who not only runs a successful religious racket but almost triumphs in an elaborate plot of rape and murder; he seems less a stereotype in exotic dress than a believable part of a valid reconstruction.

Be that as it may, Arbaces pushes us into the old problem of the evil man and the villain; we say "villain" when we do not believe and "evil man" when we do. In art, the evil man of actuality, whose realness we do not question, may be saved from dismissable villainship by the artist's ability to individualize the type or by the general impressiveness of the human context in which he appears. Individualization is not Bulwer's strong point, but he so well perceives two types of motive that he carries Arbaces a good way toward actualization. For one thing, Arbaces tends to think of himself as superior, and therefore privileged, because he belongs to an older civilization; compared with the Egyptians, the Italians are historical upstarts who deserve whatever he can do to them. Whether he really believes it, or like Iago is seeking justifications, the touch is a good one, for Bulwer has caught that quest for self-esteem which drives the individual to self-flattering generic identifications. Even more important, perhaps, is that Arbaces has developed, to an unusual degree, what we may call the cynicism of office. We have, of course, to allow for an older tendency of one faith to consider another faith and its representatives willfully fraudulent, and for the aesthetic temptation to score easily by exposing darkness within the very sanctuary of light. But even with these possibilities in mind, we can recognize in Arbaces Bulwer's imagining of that process of attrition by which the official personality, even if ecclesiastical, comes to see, in the stream of persons passing through his hands, not individuals to be recognized, but indistinguishable elements to be dealt with; by which "dealing with" becomes processing, processing becomes using, and using the effecting of one's own ends; by which the faith of the many comes to seem credulity, credulity an invitation, and the invitation a promise of profit. Arbaces is perhaps too cool; he might be a little more to our taste if he were a self-deluding fanatic, so bent on ends with a coloring of the ideal as to take his own crookery for justifiable means. But he is identifiable.

Besides, he gains something from belonging to a created world in which the general sense of character is not trivial. Not that character is profoundly conceived, according to modern lights, but that the author's grasp of human experience is not ruled by clichés or partisanship. Bulwer's sense of how things go—of human behavior and of the behavior of events outside choice—is not contemptible. His fickle public are in the tradition of Shakespeare and Fielding. His rich parvenu and the parvenu's money-will-buy-anything daughter have a vitality beyond that of stereotypes. He treats the witch of Vesuvius not as a weird, shocking monster, but as an old woman whose only too human malevolence is at least partly the ego's revenge for a wounded heart. In Apaecides he catches the man desperately in need of belief, but drifting from one allegiance to another as his expectation of perfection in forms and practices is inevitably disappointed; he loses the Roman faith, tries the new fashionable Isis cult, and eventually becomes a Christian. Bulwer notes the way in which all sects and parties interpret the eruption of Vesuvius according to their own lights and ends. He notes the indiscriminateness of fate in apportioning sufferings; merit does not fend off catastrophe. Brutal gladiators are killed in the arena; so is the one fighter with full human sensibility. Volcanic dust, burning rocks, and flowing lava do not pick and choose victims or act as agents of justice. Some lucky people escape, of course, as some lucky people always do; and modern frowns are likely for the hero and heroine who both make it to Greece, unsinged. But Bulwer carefully defines their luck: it is the blind girl Nidia's love for Glaucus, and her blind person's sense of direction, that works when those with sight are confused by the havoc, or simply panic. Nidia's pathfinding we can take, for it has a psychological basis, but the love that makes her a savior—surely this is too much for an age that believes in neither renunciation nor agape. What is fascinating here is that Bulwer, as if writing for the middle of the next century, takes full account of such skepticism. For Nidia as salvatrix is not pure love incarnate: she acts almost automatically, and her rescue of the lovers is virtually a chance disinterestedness between periods of the hostility and despair to which she is driven by her unrequited love. Indeed, it would be more accurate to say that, in guiding Glaucus and Ione out of Pompeii, she is doing penance for an earlier act of spite against Glaucus that contributed to his near disaster at the hands of Arbaces. And after she has engineered the escape from Vesuvius, she cannot stand her own unhappiness and jumps into the sea.

In the context of this trustworthy observation of human fate—that of character and that of event—Arbaces moves plausibly from the pole of pure villain toward the pole of the evil man. Hence, the aesthetic effectiveness of his scheming and his machinations, on which half the book hangs. But the plot of the evil man and his victims yields, finally, to an ironic sense. Destructive Vesuvius actually rescues Arbaces' victims; then the blind girl has to rescue them from Vesuvius; and for her there is no rescue. No, we cannot dismiss as Victorian melodrama this version of the *sic transit* theme; in the end it moves into the realm of somber comedy that, for all of its spectacle, has some kinship with the Chekhovian. So pairing Bulwer with Lampedusa is not altogether an artifice to impose order on a tourist chance. Lampedusa catches the ironic self-observation with which the old order accommodates to the new, Bulwer the irony of circumstances that save a few from a world-destroying holocaust.

■ 13 ■
Versions of Renunciation: Hardy and Waugh

PRECISELY FIFTY YEARS separate Thomas Hardy's Sue Bridehead (*Jude the Obscure*, 1895) and Evelyn Waugh's Julia Flyte (*Brideshead Revisited*, 1945). What first makes one associate the two novels is of course a stimulus so obvious that one almost wants to conceal it—the phonetic echo of *Bridehead* and *Brideshead*. But that singular tie of sound is an accident that leads one on to something essential—a surprising tie of sense. The later novel reuses the human scene of the earlier one; it has the same inner and outer furnishings. The inner identity is the symbolic split, the clash of codes, in the central character. As for the narrative arrangements: Sue and Julia are both unorthodox (Sue is "Voltairean," Jude says), both marry the wrong man, both accept as lover the "right" man, both wish to marry him, and both, in a renunciation which is a final thematic statement, reject him under a religious imperative (Julia says "I need God"; Sue is found lying under a cross at St. Silas's). Each right man is unsatisfactorily married to a woman whose original attraction was mainly or wholly sexual, and each opposes the religious conviction that leads to his mistress's final withdrawal. And no sooner have we summarized these singular parallels than we recognize a surprising parallel between the novelists: each writes from a sense of the inadequacy of the rules or practices dominating the societies in which the principals must make vital decisions. Hardy has doubts about the Christian view of life that still had a strong hold in Jude and Sue's time, and Waugh challenges the secularism that, allowing multiple choices, was becoming stronger in his day. Both authors paid something of a price for running against different public tides. Attacked for writing "Jude the Obscene," Hardy gave up novel-writing. Waugh's Catholicism, which determined Julia's choice, was, it seems safe to say, regarded at best as an unfortunate eccentricity in a witty satirist. Finally, beyond all notations of parallels, lies the problem of art: which of the artists, each employing a "minority view" in looking at a problem underlying remarkably similar plots, does a better job of creating a durable story? That will be my final topic.

First, however, the resemblances and the divergences. Sue and Julia both come to renunciations—to Hardy, a disaster, to Waugh salvation—

through the experience of a deep, enveloping intimacy, both bitter and sustaining, with the renounced. While Hardy disapproved of an old code, and Waugh of a very modern way of life, Hardy went deeper by seeing the conflict between old and new as a bitter one. In living through this conflict personally, Sue was also experiencing a historical crisis, one that was not yet there to impinge upon several of her forebears in English fiction. Half a century before Sue there was Jane Eyre (1847), who also loved a married man but who, though she met the issue with reflective intensity rather than a purely mechanical response, identified firm rules by which to decide against the union. A little later there was Louisa Bounderby in *Hard Times* (1854), a potentially excellent character not much noted in Dickens criticism. Married, Louisa is made love to by James Harthouse; she is clearly moved by him, and Dickens seems for once about to deal with adult passion. But the conflict is dodged after all; Louisa jumps back in fright. She seems a puppet controlled by the rules which in the late 1890s could still damn *Jude* as immoral even while Hardy was perceiving the decline of their authority. Because of that decline, which in time would become loss, Jane and Louisa became Sue and Julia, with skeptical minds that led them into the fiery furnace where they could assay by private desire or conviction. But unsuspected impulses intervene, and both women, so to speak, go back to the rules.

Hardy registered, almost prematurely, the decline of a long-lasting religious force; Waugh asserted the vitality of a faith in its ancient form and centrality. The decline that Hardy sensed had by Waugh's time gone far enough to stir various energies into activities of restoration or replacement, into different centripetal quests. These could be philosophic or popular; the latter could appear in fantastic mass-movement evangelisms. (Hardy's Clym Yeobright might well be a wealthy Bible-waving "personality" in our day.) Ecclesiastical restorations in the Waugh mode do less well on the popularity front. The twentieth century is more comfortable with easy soul-saving excitements than with traditional disciplines. Insofar as it reads, our age finds Waugh the jester and mocker much more congenial than Waugh the Catholic. Hence its reversal of the public attitudes of Hardy's day and its approval of Hardy's regret at Sue's return to a Christian sense of things that she had long, she thought, put behind her. Indeed, Hardy defends the relationship between Jude and Sue in terms that anticipate those of our own day; he calls it "Nature's own marriage." Thus he arrives very early at a naturalistic view much more characteristic of the century after his own.

And yet, despite all these differences, there is in one respect a vast ironic similarity between Hardy and Waugh. At one point their diagnoses are virtually identical. For when Hardy starts thinking instead of storytelling, he simply is not consistent. On the one hand he is all modernist: he stigmatizes the "medievalism" of Oxford, the inflexibility of marriage (a "clumsy contract"), and the distance and peremptoriness of the church. But on the other, forgetting all these implicit demands for "progress," he attacks "the modern vice of unrest." Waugh would surely approve of that complaint about the times.

But whatever the dissimilarities, or the occasional similarity, of thought, the ultimate problem in the novels is, as I have said, the quality of the art. Hardy, who once said that it is the business of the novelist to ask questions rather than to answer them, is the better novelist. Sue is a more profoundly presented character than Julia Flyte. In one sense, I know, it is not quite fair to compare them, since Waugh employs a multiple focus that diminishes the role of each individual; yet the final effect, centered in the Ryder-Julia relationship, depends upon whether Julia "works." But she does not "work" nearly as well as Sue does. For one thing, Hardy presents fully Sue's suffering in her decision to renounce Jude. We see her repulsion at her chosen symbolic act of having intercourse with her husband Phillotson. She hears Jude attack her "enslavement to forms" and her being "creed drunk" and assert that "the letter killeth." Jude's own relapse into alcoholism is part of the dramatic judgment upon her. In Julia Flyte, on the other hand, we see, not anguish or renunciation or horror at a compulsive choice, but the calm of one who, after groping in the murk, has come at last to the light and feels secure. Her lover, though comprehending, registers bereavement; but he is a rather flat figure beside Jude, and we do not much care about him.

Still more important is the artistic problem of dramatizing the existence, beneath the level of overt conduct, of a force of belief-and-feeling with which the overt conduct is at variance, even though the character experiencing this conflict may hardly be aware of it. Almost from the beginning Hardy conveys, with quite unusual subtlety, a sense of a profound inner split in Sue (a split that I describe in detail, as it deserves, later on; see essay 19). But in Julia there is almost no dramatic evidence of clash and struggle. Once she hits Ryder, and several times she is crabby. The split is not realized; it is almost as though her decision were made in advance, and Waugh were only filling in the pages. Even her tone has falsities. Compare the passionate speeches of Sue throughout book 6 with Julia's slightly literary farewell just before the epilogue. Earlier Waugh gives Julia a line as Lady-Windermerish as "Yes, Rex . . . Charles and I are going into the moonlight." The systematic duality of her impulses makes logical Sue's final move, but with Julia we are merely told that everything is not right, and we are not convinced of a private force that, at odds with her public behavior, must eventually dictate her moves. Is it that Hardy the asker of questions fights through Sue's battle, and that Waugh the answerer logically thinks through Julia's, writing it—not all parts of the book—with his head? In the lovers there is the same disparity: Jude's anguished, pleading, incredulous, half-denunciatory expostulations with Sue, his mad, agonized struggle to regain her—he seems a secular Faust beside himself in his effort to seize an earthly salvation—and his saturnine relapse give him complete reality; Ryder senses ominous possibilities, talks petulantly a few times, and asks the naive questions of the straight man building up the lead's punch lines. It is not enough. Hardy is both Sue and Jude; Waugh is Julia restored to the church, and he has to think out the rest.

Thus a return to Sue Bridehead not only lets us consider the aesthetic distance between two versions of the forces that qualify our options but also reintroduces an old inquiry: what are the conditions of artistic creation? Edmund Wilson has written of the utility, to the artist, of being suspended between two cultures rather than being identified wholly with either; W. H. Auden, of the incapacitation—psychic, physical, or of whatever type it may be—for "normal" domestic or social or institutional activities that may serve, not as the source or explanation of the artistic impulse, but as guarantee that the energies required by the artistic vocation will not be otherwise dissipated. What both hypotheses assume is the persistence of certain tensions, important for creation, that might be resolved by the artist's becoming wholly identified with an age or a culture or a society or an institution (state, party, region, church) or a combination of these as the ordinary human being is. The question here, then, is whether identification with a religious institution brings about a total adjustment that dims the novelist's imagination of kinds of experience upon which, nevertheless, he must as novelist draw. Hardy, an outsider and a solitary, could fathom and richly reproduce kinds of experience that Waugh, an insider, fails to give body to; the outsider could imaginatively *be* the insider, with her need and her pain, but the insider has difficulties both with the outsider and with the insider whose entry means rejection as well as acceptance. Waugh is excellent on Rex Mottram because Rex's essence is simply a surface that reflects light ("He wasn't a complete human being at all"), and Waugh is a dead shot with his candid camera. But when Waugh, as the artist who would affirm must, tries more than trick shots, his effects are largely cut-and-dried. Huxley grows the mystic and deteriorates as novelist. It is not that dogma and mysticism are incompatible with creation; with them, and through them, may come fine poetry. Indeed, art is a way of defining allegiances; without them the creator is at loose ends. But when does allegiance threaten to atrophy the artist in fiction? Apparently when the allegiance is so fulfilling, so integrative that the writer can no longer satisfactorily imagine the conflict through which the allegiance is won; his personality is so thoroughly fused, and his being so firmly oriented, that he cannot become, even in creative play, anyone less thoroughly formed and organized than he. Only one truth is now important to him, but it is beyond the stage of imaginable conflict; he has lost the means by which his truth may be dramatically earned, and as fabulist he is thrown back, evidently feeling no monitory jolt, upon assertion. His gift, his talent, his genius, no longer protected for their role in creation, revert to the general fund of energies that purchase salvation. They may be channeled, fittingly, into hymns, even intense and moving hymns, or bubble over, surpluses from the central realities that are complete and undemonstrable, into peripheral gaieties—the adventures of Father Brown, perhaps.

But historically men of deep religious experiences and loyalties have used their genius to create more than adulations and interludes. Must we not assume for them, then, unresolved tensions that can persist on into, or even arise within, the life that has found its unifying principle? Tensions, of illuminatingly different sorts, are obviously at work in Dante and George Herbert. Such irritants we must find elsewhere if we want to understand the condition of creation. That condition is hardly the peace that passeth understanding, but rather the not wholly achieved allegiance, the felt resistances that extend comprehension, the dissonances and intractabilities—at home and abroad—that intrude upon quieting finalities. The subversive streak in utopia and the anguish of orthodoxy, as well as the impulse to discover authority, were entirely accessible to the first portrayer, searching and troubled, of a modern personage, Sue Bridehead.

IV
STYLES

■14■
Greene's Euphuism and Some Congeneric Styles

i

ROBERT GREENE'S *Card of Fancy* (1584) provides excellent prime materials for an inspection of euphuism and hence of some later developments of euphuistic style. There are two reasons for its especial utility. The first is that Greene's work, as a romance, permits us to see the impact of a given style upon a given type of fictional material; thus we have a good perspective for glancing at several later novels that have a partly comparable duality. The second reason for the usefulness of *The Card of Fancy* is Greene's indefatigable application, in almost every sentence, of the various procedures that we know as euphuism. He provides copious data for the description of what we might call fundamentalist euphuism, from which we can then see an evolution to a more centrist practice of the style.

The character of this fiction as a "romance"[1] is apparent enough to eliminate the need for full-scale demonstration. English readers, of course, would feel the romance of the exotic: the action begins in Metelyne (Mytilene), continues in Barutta (Beirut), and has its main body in Alexandria. There is the old identity problem: Gwydonius succeeds as courtier and lover at Alexandria, where it is not known that his father is the hostile duke of Metelyne. There is a love triangle at Alexandria: Valericus becomes vindictively jealous when Castania, the duke's daughter, prefers Gwydonius to him. Then war breaks out between the dukes of Metelyne and Alexandria, and their sons and daughters suffer the conflict between love and political loyalty. But all problems are solved happily in the end: the two dukedoms are united in peace through the marriage of Gwydonius and Castania. We need no further evidence of the generic status of Greene's work.

As for Greene's euphuism, the first task is to describe it fully, both its central schemata and all the variations of these. We should have more than an impressionistic sense of it and hence a better base for observing the modifications in the works of certain epigones. Since a complete record of stylistic practices would be very extensive, I shall restrict discussion to dictional and syntactic matters, which are the main survivors in later uses of the euphuistic manner. (Hence I omit the "unnatural natural history," the classical references and quotations, the proverbs, and the echoes of fable and myth frequent in sixteenth-century euphuism.)

Once the style has been analyzed, I can proceed to two other topics—the relation of euphuism to romance, and the relation of original euphuism to later stylistic developments. Euphuism and romance: the singular marriage of an old generic type and a young stylistic mode. What we find, I think, is this: the overall management of the romantic plot is influenced by the euphuism that Greene relentlessly practices; the structuring of the narrative units shows the impact of euphuistic procedures that had, as it were, taken possession of the author's mind, whether or not he was wholly conscious of this. In brief, certain syntactic principles, and their tonal impact, helped determine the general narrative configuration.

Euphuism and later styles: this coordination may seem a bit odd. Since sixteenth-century euphuism carried "everything to excess" (as A. C. Hamilton says of *The Card of Fancy*), it may well seem incapable of survival. Yet we can argue that it did not die by the time of *Love's Labor's Lost*. For under the blazing features and the ornamental devices that make us speak of "excess" there is a much simpler essence: a persistent quest for order that would continue, or recur, in comparable ways. To anticipate briefly my later argument: the quest appears, in less spectacular form, in various manifestations of neoclassical style, which are most visible in Samuel Johnson's prose. The Johnsonian style had many practitioners in the eighteenth century; then it influenced Scott and, even less probably, Charlotte Brontë. In both of these writers, too, there is much of the Latinate diction that appeared in the original euphuists and, most famously of course, in Johnson; it is picked up by later autodidacts such as Hardy, and hits bottom in the modern style we call "bureaucratese." Since the elements common to these various styles appeared first in euphuism, it seems permissible to use the original term for them.

ii

The main constituents of Greene's euphuism are alliteration, parallelism, balanced elements, and antithesis. He uses alliteration in virtually every sentence, and with all possible variations. There are pairs of connotatively related nouns (counsel/comfort, pleasure/profit, ruth/ruin, wealth/weal), adjectives (sad/sorrowful, cruel/coy), adverbs (charily/chastely), and combinations of several parts of speech (flattering mates/fawning merchants) (173).[2] Since alliteration and meaning do not coincide as often as the euphuist might wish, such pairs are used again and again. Still more frequent, however, are the pairs of words with contrasted or opposing meanings: treasure/trash, vice/virtue, nature/nurture, woe/weal, bale/bliss, sweet/sour, cherish/chastise, loathe/like. The opposed elements may be phrases: "young years"/"hoary hairs" (168) and "merry devices"/"mournful dumps" (209), pairs that illustrate two alliterative patterns often used by Greene: *aabb* and *abab*. Such combinations are almost uncountably frequent. Perhaps less frequent, but still persistent, are triads: "favored and fostered up by fortune" (165) and "inflamed with friendly affection" (177), in the second of which Greene uses a frequent device, alliteration both by vowels and by internal consonants.[3] Greene sometimes uses a pair, or even sets of pairs, to follow up a triad: "her beauty bred his bane, her looks, his loss, her sight, his sorrow, her exquisite perfection his extreme passions" (178), where the overall pattern is *bbb, ll, ss, epep*. Now and then he manages a foursome— "doleful days in dumps and dolors" (166)—or a quartet of phrases—"more care than commodity, more pain than profit, more cost than comfort, more grief than good" (179). He often goes into combinations, such as a triad plus a pair, or a pair plus a triad. Here is a foursome plus a pair: "salve thy sores with sweet syrups, not with cutting corrasives" (217). Of course he can pile up still larger numbers of phrases and even clauses, too space-consuming to record here. The best case of multiplicity that I have noted has some twenty adjectives, distributed through five consecutive sentences, preceded by *so* (166).

In the struggle to combine alliteration and meaning in every sentence, Greene may fall back on phonetic echoes without orthographic identity ("cease from thy suit" [190]), or the converse, the orthographic without the phonetic ("woe and wretchedness" [256]). In relating more than two words, he regularly uses certain patterns, such as the *abab* type already mentioned ("smelled the fetch, and smiled at the folly" [199]). But he always strives for what variety the system permits. Occasionally with a foursome he uses a chiasmic form, *abba*: "hearty love, with loathing hate" (216), which, to a reader well-nigh overcome by routine alliteration, seems a shade less mechanical, as does an occasional interwoven effect such as "his merciless cruelty in correcting his faults, and his moodless rigor in rebuking his folly" (230), in which the alliterative pattern is *abbc, addc*. Greene may struggle against the obvious by avoiding close contiguity of key phrases, as in "the su*gar*ed *p*oison of your divine beauty, as through the extremity of *p*inching *gr*ief" (218), with separation, chiasmus, and use of an internal sound (*gar*) in the alliterating group. In "sleepeth without repentance" (200) both key sounds are internal. "Privy friend . . . open foe" (216) uses a familiar *abab* pattern but varies it in two ways: in the *pfpf* series, all the consonants are labials, illustrating the alliteration by consonantal class that Greene uses occasionally; and in the closing pair there is the assonance that often appears (compare "lawless liberty"/"slavish captivity" [194]). Occasionally a repeated metaphor may substitute for a repeated sound but be combined with a repeated sound: "so *snared* with thy *beauty*, and so *entangled* in the *trap* of thy *bounty*" (227). There is a fairly regular use of rhyme: "not imbrued with vice, but endued with virtue" (205) and "rid us from blame, and reward him with shame" (247). Both examples combine rhyme and alliteration, as does one sentence that I rearrange typographically to emphasize its devices:

> What desire, what lust,
> what hope, what trust,
> what care,
> what despair,
> what fear, what fury?
> (207)

Still another connective is the pun. Castania writes Valericus that "thy doggish letters favor of *Diogenes* doctrine, for in truth thou art such a cynical kind of dunce" (192). Greene's "doggish"/"cynical" is not an accident.

Let us look, finally, at euphuistic management of longer units—clauses and sentences. I shall present most of these in typographic arrangements that will make overall design unmistakable. Here is a triad of verb phrases which, containing a clause and three alliterated words each, achieve a more elaborate effect than we have so far seen:

> Shall I grudge when the gods are agreed,
> or defer it, when the destinies drive it:
> or frown at it, sith fortune frames it?
> (223)

A quartet of parallel predications containing *if* clauses and conclusions produces a more clipped and perhaps more sophisticated effect through the omission of verbs. The passage is about love, which

> if it be lawless, it is lewd:
> if without limits, lascivious:
> if contained within no bounds, beastly:
> if observed with no order, odious.
> (202)

Another series of four parallel *if* clauses is managed differently: the first three (all parts of a quite long sentence) contain respectively 13, 16, and

15 words, and then the fourth, which replaces the *if* with inversion, is as follows: "be she virtuous, be she chaste, be she courteous, be she constant, be she rich, be she renowned, be she honest, be she honorable" (179), the eight brief elements giving a touch of speed in a leisurely sentence that then goes on for another 140 words, with various euphuistic schemes throughout. Finally, a group of four verbal phrases, while using repetition, also aspires to some differentiation:

> for an inch of joy, to reap an ell of annoy,
> for a moment of mirth, a month of misery:
> for a dram of pleasure, a whole pound of pain,
> and by procuring mine own delight,
>   to purchase my father's death and destruction.
>   (237)

In the four statements of indulgence-cum-nemesis, Greene uses four different metaphors—linear measurement, temporal measurement, weight measurement, and purchasing; the fourth is longer than the others, and the first uses both vocalic alliteration and rhyme.

To conclude this sampling of sentence patterns, I will quote two passages with slightly longer units: these should give some feeling of more massive euphuized effects and more complex applications of the system. The first is this:

> how pinching a pain is it to be perplexed with diverse passions,
> what a noisome care it is to be cumbered with sundry cogitations,
> what a   woe it is to hang between desire and despair,
> what a   hell it is to hover between fear and hope.
>   (254)

The almost identical arrangement of words in the four predications is modified by the omission of adjectives in the third and fourth units, and this is compensated for by the use of two objects in the closing prepositional phrases; "perplexed" and "cumbered," parallel passives, are parallel in meaning, as are "diverse" and "sundry" and of course the alliterated "hang" and "hover"; "cumbered" and "sundry" are assonant, and there is some interweaving in the alliteration. My final example is briefer, and it leads in a somewhat different direction:

> Did my Father promote thee to this thou art, from the state of a
>   beggar, and
> wilt thou now presume   to be my better?
>   (213)

Here the antithetical clauses are so different in length as hardly to seem balanced at all, the two pairs of alliterated words (unusually few) are far enough apart to suggest a delicate accent rather than a pressing insistence, and the assonance of *beggar* and *better,* in a context only mildly euphuized, might elude the ear.

So much for the basics of Greene's euphuism, and for the considerable spread of devices by which he seeks to vary and multiply the patterns of alliteration and repeated, balanced, or opposed syntactic elements. Within the school of euphuistic stylists there must have been strong competition in devising variations and refinements of the standard procedures and, among the consumers, a vast admiration for agility in modification and innovation. It is well to see how much invention could be practiced, and how much apparent novelty encompassed, within an essentially closed style. On the other hand, of course, the presence of variables within a system that would seem to exclude them cannot much modify our sense of a monotony that closes off the almost infinite varieties of prose rhythm to which writers of succeeding centuries have accustomed us. Whatever euphuists and their cousins marinists, gongorists, and *les précieuses* might have intended, or even in some cases accomplished, by way of countering a lack of structure, a bumbling inelegance they perceived in general prose practice, their prescriptions for reform—applied with a rigorous mechanical invariability that seemed compulsory—led to a fairly rapid exhaustion of the possibilities.

iii

These truisms are useful mainly as a way into another issue—the relationship of style to narrative design in *The Card of Fancy.* In brief, the habit of mind which appears in euphuistic style appears also in the structure of relationships and events. In verbal and syntactical patterns, whether the semantic direction is toward repetition, elaboration, and reinforcement or toward contrast and opposition, the essential quality evident through many variations is symmetry. Symmetry also appears in the main plot lines. There are two rival rulers, the dukes of Metelyne and of Alexandria. Each has a son and a daughter. The children of Clerophontes of Metelyne are Leucippa and Gwydonius; the children of Orlanio of Alexandria are Castania and Thersandro. In the families there is just one asymmetry, which we can see is analogous to a break in an alliterative pattern: three of the children are conspicuously virtuous, whereas Gwydonius is initially a ne'er-do-well and has to reform, as he does in Barutta and Alexandria. Indeed, his sharp turnaround from the disobedient, dissolute, and rowdy son of the ruling duke to knightly lover, man of principle, and military and political hero has a euphuistic character: it is the narrative form of the syntactic antithesis (which also appears in the total contrast between all-bad Gwydonius and his all-virtuous sister Leucippa). Gwydonius falls in love with Castania, and Thersandro with Leucippa. Each brother has a rival lover. But after many vicissitudes, including a large war between Clerophontes and Orlanio, the Montague-Capulet situation comes to a happy ending in two brother-to-enemy's-sister marriages that unite two dukedoms. Symmetry leads to total unity.

But this euphuistic conception of situation and development is perhaps less striking than the local means by which the plot is advanced. Here, I think, we not only see a parallel between sentence management and plot management but can reasonably assume an impact of stylistic habit upon narrative method. The euphuistic manner—alliteration, series, balance, opposition—is obviously not the natural style of spontaneous, undisciplined, or explosive feeling, for it is planned, controlled, regularized, formalized. It is the method of the disciplined speaker, who is not driven toward incoherence by the pressure of thoughts and emotions but is always aware of the stylistic medium. It is the rhetoric of conscious address, not of strong and unruly expression; of public rather than private life. It is planned and calculated rather than free-swinging and unpredictable. It suggests less the domestic scene than the public platform, less the private room than the stage. A few stage directions punctuate the dialogue. But the dialogue is euphuistic; it has little of informal briskness, snap, and freewheeling give-and-take. Greene's people speak as at a lectern, like debaters with set speeches; brevity, overall or in the parts, is rarely a goal. Their speeches somewhat remind us of the *tirades* in French classical drama and English heroic drama, but there is little or no infusion of the stichomythia that gives variety, for instance, in Racine. Greene's dialogue is usually an exchange of monologues, an antithesis of paragraphs rather than a rush of short, sharp statements. Euphuistic style determines these ordered exchanges, and they provide plenty of opportunity and space for the exercise of that style. Letters do too, and hence parts of *The Card of Fancy* anticipate the epistolary novel that would become a vogue a century and a half later.

We can detect the impact of the euphuistic consciousness in Greene's distribution of space, which can best be represented in number of lines occupied by this or that narrative element (in the text I am using, there are 43 lines to the printed page). Greene's opening narrative, describing Clerophontes, duke of Metelyne, his beautiful and virtuous daughter Leucippa, and his handsome reprobate son Gwydonius, occupies 62 lines of text. Then Greene shifts to Clerophontes' reflections on his son's misbehavior, and this section goes on for 55 lines. The passage is in effect an internal monologue, a form which Greene uses again and

again. But while the modern internal monologue proceeds by asso-
ciative connections that ignore or deny rational order, Clerophontes'
internal monologue is euphuistic, that is, a highly organized product of
a mind making points as it goes. His longest sentence occupies 17 lines,
his shortest 4. To show the euphuistic composition of the words supposed to denote inner turmoil, we may diagram his longest sentence as
follows:

Now (quoth he) I prove by experience,
the saying of *Sophocles* to be true,
that the man which hath many children shall never live without some mirth,
                                                  nor die without some sorrow:
for if they be virtuous, he shall have cause whereof to rejoice,
        if   vicious,   wherefore to be sad,
which saying I try performed in myself,
            for as I have one child   which delights me with her virtue,
            so I have another   that despites me with his vanity,
as the one by duty   brings my joy,
so the other by disobedience breeds me annoy:
yea, as the one is a comfort to my mind,
        so the other is a fretting corrasive to my heart:
        for what grief is there more griping,
            what pain more pinching,
            what cross more cumbersome,
            what plague more pernicious,
        yea, what trouble can torment me worse,
            than to see my son,
                        mine heir,
        the inheritor of my Dukedom,
    which should be the pillar of my parentage,
            to consume his time in roisting and riot,
                        in spending and spoiling,
                        in swearing and swashing, and
                        in following willfully the fury
                                    of his own frantic
                                        fancy.
                                            (166–67)

This is a characteristic Greene sentence. It suggests declamation rather
than a spontaneous surfacing of painful emotions; the rhetoric of inner
disturbance is, to say the least, different from Hamlet's. However, the
point is not to disparage the method but to see how it determines the
nature of both internal and external monologue. Brevity, disordered
syntax, and the rat-a-tat of normal dramatic dialogue were not compatible with the stylistic preconceptions of the euphuist.

Clerophontes' internal monologue is followed by 17 lines of authorial narrative about the duke's verbal attack on his son. Gwydonius replies in a hostile monologue of 24 lines divided into only three sentences (168)— the first spoken lines in the tale. He'll go abroad, he says. Greene uses 10 lines to report that this idea pleases Clerophontes and then turns the lectern over to Clerophontes for a massive pre-Polonius Polonial address to his son—actually 108 lines or over two pages (169–71). The remaining space in the first section is allotted as follows: action (Gwydonius travels to Barutta, continues his dissolute ways, and is jailed), 35 lines; Gwydonius's internal monologue (self-blame and resolve to reform), 50 lines; action (he travels to Alexandria), 18 lines (171–74). Greene has now devoted 142 lines to authorial narrative, and 237 lines to four massive monologues the form of "action" toward which the euphuistic manner regularly drives him.

Greene describes the ducal household in Alexandria, which balances that in Metelyne, rather quickly (174–78). In one respect he proceeds antithetically: in Metelyne the central situation involved father and son, whereas now it is father and daughter. Duke Orlanio employs Melytta as "companion and counsellor" to his fourteen-year-old daughter Castania, enabling Greene to balance, against Clerophontes' Polonial advice to his departing son, Orlanio's instructions to Melytta—a 55-line monologue followed by her 22-line speech of acceptance (175–77). Gwydonius shows up with an assumed but noble identity, makes a 20-line speech of application for a job, and is promptly appointed companion to Duke Orlanio's son Thersandro (177–78). In this short second "chapter" Greene has so much external action going on that he has to devote 78 lines to it, with only a few more—92—to the set speeches. Hence these occupy only 54 percent of the text, as against 62 percent in the opening section.

Then Greene is relieved, one imagines, to put situation-building behind him and shift to a central theme much more amenable to euphuistic expression—love affairs, which occupy fifty-two of his total of ninety-six pages and loom large in a final thirty pages in which war and politics are nominally the central issues. In a love story, little connective tissue is required, and people can talk or write at length in euphuistic manifestos. Greene provides two suitors for Castania—Valericus, who fails (fifteen pages), and Gwydonius, who succeeds (thirty-seven pages). The Valericus-Castania affair goes on for 598 lines, the author assigning only 122, or about 20 percent, to connective tissue, and 476, or roughly 80 percent, to the characters—the highest proportion yet for euphuistic discourse. In Greene's handling of Valericus's failure to win from Castania anything more than a temporary jesting interest in the game, three matters are interesting. One is the apparent apportioning of lines according to intensity of feeling: Valericus has 266 lines of internal and external monologue (in five passages), and Castania has only 39 lines (in one passage). The second is that Greene hits upon letters as excellent carriers of euphuistic formalism: Valericus writes two (60 lines), and Castania a balancing two (40 lines). Third, at one point Greene even makes an approach to "normal" dialogue. Valericus, Castania, Melytta (and the author) split up a 79-line exchange as follows: C, 13; author, 6; V, 17; M, 10; V, 11; C, 7; V, 3; C, 2; V, 3; M, 7. Only three speeches, however, approach brevity, and these are less heavily euphuized. True euphuism led to length.

In the thirty-seven pages required for Gwydonius and Castania to arrive at a mutual acknowledgment of love, the author's connective tissue occupies 251 lines, Gwydonius's monologues, internal and external, 352 lines, Castania's 301, and Valericus's 51 (his anger against them). For these passages the overall percentages are: third-person narrative, 26 percent; characters' speeches, 74 percent. These figures change somewhat when we take into account Greene's introduction of some variations analogous to those he employed in the earlier Valericus-Castania section. Again there is an exchange of letters, two by each lover: Gwydonius, 89 lines; Castania, 91 lines; with 41 descriptive lines by the narrator. Whereas in the Valericus-Castania story there was one approach to dialogue with shorter speeches, in the Gwydonius-Castania story there are three such shifts. In the most complex of these there are four speakers—the two lovers, Castania's brother Thersandro, and her tutor Melytta. The subject is love, and the discussion starts off a little like a Castiglione round table, with four initial papers on a program as it were: Thersandro, 8 lines; Gwydonius, 21; Melytta, 48; and Castania, 41. But then it gets a little looser, more informal, almost enough to suggest dialogue in a Restoration comedy; the numbers of lines in the series of speeches are 9-6-22-7-2-10-3-4-5-4-5-7-6, and the narrator stays out of it entirely. In a second alteration, though less marked than the first, Castania and Melytta have an exchange in which the parts somewhat reduce the usual euphuistic amplitude: M, 31; C, 15; M, 13; C, 16, and M, 8, with the narrator having only 5. In the third such exchange the speeches are cut down a shade more: Castania, 29; Gwydonius, 7; C, 5; G, 5; C, 4.

But though one should notice this occasional thinning down of speeches, they are all essentially in the euphuistic mode, so that they can be included in the overall account of the distribution of space. From beginning to end the Gwydonius-Castania story includes 295 lines of narrative and 1,225 lines of dialogue composed mostly of monologue, 19 and 81 percent; the latter percentage is the highest of all the five sections.

In the final thirty pages, where a war and two three-cornered love affairs are brought to a happy ending, there is so much going on that Greene is driven to a more extensive use of third-person narrative—46 percent of the space, leaving a relatively low 54 percent for monologues.[4] Thus the total spatial design of the book can be seen in the accompanying table.[5]

Narrative material	Pages	Third-person narrative	Monologues
Metelyne and Barutta:			
Gwydonius leaves both	9	38%	62%
Alexandria: Gwydonius arrives	5	46%	54%
Valericus-Castania affair	15	20%	80%
Gwydonius-Castania affair	37	19%	81%
War, love, honor, peace	30	46%	54%

Greene unmistakably prefers the one-on-one situation, which is most conducive to long speeches and internal monologues and hence to the highly euphuistic prose style of which he makes less use in the passages of connective tissue.

iv

Despite the larger presence of authorial narrative, the long final section still has what we might call a euphuistic rhythm. The principle of antithesis controls the actual patterns. The dominant element is the war between Clerophontes and Orlanio. Within this central opposition, other opposing elements are carefully balanced. Clerophontes' son Gwydonius loves Orlanio's daughter Castania, and she him. Orlanio's son Thersandro loves Clerophontes' daughter Leucippa, and she him. Thus all four lovers have similar divided feelings. Valericus wants to break up the Gwydonius-Castania affair; for balance, Greene dredges up at the last moment, as if he had just remembered his narrative design and cared more about it than about any probability at all, a Lucianus to whom Clerophontes wants to marry Leucippa. Topping off this system of balanced antitheses is a duel between Clerophontes and his son Gwydonius, a complement to the early quarrel that inaugurated the situation now being resolved. Gwydonius is disguised, so that we have the Sohrab-and-Rustum situation, but with a difference: the son nominally wins the duel, not hurting his father but displaying an apologetic and magnanimous style that permits the resolution of all antithetical elements into an embracing harmony.

A modern reference book lists *The Card of Fancy* among Greene's "romances of pure adventure and entertainment." This description ignores the vast euphuism in the tale and its impact on the tone and hence on the generic character of the book. Granted, the exotic scene, love affairs, war, love-and-honor motif, and happy ending are the traditional stuff of romance. But the severe discipline of euphuistic style and organization changes the romantic cast. Exotic scenes lose their distance and become almost domestic classrooms. When adventure is patterned, it becomes illustrative rather than unpredictable; it obeys design rather than gives the illusion of spontaneity. If romance connotes escape from the patterns of ordinary life, euphuism imposes rigorous patterns that assert an inescapable modeling of life. This does not mean that the presentation of human nature is always coerced by artifice. Some motives are plausible enough: the jealousy of Valericus and, in Castania, a certain gamesomeness and a certain unsureness about Gwydonius's devotion that faintly anticipate the style of Congreve's Millamant. Still, hanging over everything is a predetermined orderedness that inhibits the sense of freedom requisite for romantic tone.

Compare *The Tempest,* in which the mingling of love and politics and the ultimate resolution of the conflicts between the two and within each are not unlike Greene's basic plot. But there is only one love affair, and hence an absence of imposed parallelism. More important, Shakespeare creates a sense of a gradual evolution, both emotional and moral, toward a workable solution—a free will of the plot, as it were, against a predestination executed by the ever-present hand of Greene. It would be frivolous, no doubt, to propose that blank verse is a less tyrannical mode than the quasi poetry of euphuism, but the metaphor does have some suggestive value.

If romance embodies a dash toward the wonderful and the libertine, euphuism goes along to insist on the inevitable presence of likenesses, relationships, parallels, repetitions, and contrasts that constrain free-floating adventure, novelty, strangeness, and the attractions of disorder. It would be too radical to assert that euphuism turns romance into something else. It is better to reintroduce the shaggy beast that has slouched through much modern criticism, namely, tension, and to say that in euphuistic romance there is always a pulling-apart between opposing ways of managing narrative art, a struggle for different modes of response in the reader (a struggle not present, for instance, in such a combination of euphuism and didacticism as we find in Lyly's *Euphues*). Furthermore, this tension exists not only between a narrative mode and a stylistic vogue but also between larger forces—the romantic and classical impulses that emerge from human nature into cultural manifestations. Though such categories have inspired some revisionist paradoxes, we can use them for their convenience and beg the question of their metaphysical status. Romanticism is so large a subject that here we need do no more than note its inclusion of the world of romances, which Greene somewhat modified. We can go a little further with classical style, or what is better called neoclassical style, for euphuism, as I noted at the very beginning, is the matrix of one distinct neoclassical style and of related stylistic methods traceable in subsequent writing. The practices of later centuries evidence the residual force of the basic euphuistic idea, which appears in a specialized and exaggerated form in the sixteenth-century vogue. The idea embodies the neoclassical aspiration to rational ordering and control.

V

"Specialization and exaggeration": these words immediately suggest what we usually call decadence, the phase of a style that occurs when, as a result of overfamiliarity and hence weakening impact, the consumers require, and the producers supply, ever stronger and more bizarre versions of the stimuli characteristic of the mode. In euphuism we then have a remarkable historical anomaly in that decadence, or at least what looks very much like it, precedes what we might call "normal" practice. If we move ahead almost two centuries to Samuel Johnson's didactic romance *Rasselas* (1759), we find a euphuism that is, as it were, purged of all the tyrannical thoroughness of Elizabethan euphuism. Johnson omits virtually all the learning, literal or fantastic, that decorates Greene's fiction, all the spectacular comparisons, the citations of myth and fable, the exclamations and the rhetorical questions so visible in Greene. What he retains is something of the conceptual euphuism and a considerable amount of the stylistic euphuism that we have described.

By "conceptual euphuism" I mean, of course, the overall patterning of the narrative materials. Johnson's central design is antithetical: the opposition between the more or less ideal but restricted life of the "happy valley" in Abyssinia, and the more mixed, complex life of different individuals in the outside world, that is, Egypt. Rasselas, his tutor Imlac, and his sister Nekayah escape from their safe haven and explore Egypt (of which they see a great deal more than Greene's characters see of Alexandria). The antithetical principle largely governs the narrative pattern: the explorers meet different types and strata of people, believe them to possess and exemplify a "happy" life, and then on closer inspection find that these prospective models also suffer from the dissatisfactions, worries, and troubles natural to humanity generally. Or they contrast different modes of life, such as marriage and celibacy, secular and monastic living; Johnson writes balanced paragraphs of opposing views. Things are not balanced up as neatly as they are in Greene, however; there are intelligent freewheeling discussions that can end indecisively. Indeed, at the end the explorers retain different views of a desirable mode of life even when, rather mechanically, they opt for a return to native Abyssinia. There is enough play of thought and feeling to vary considerably the antithetical sense of things that determines the narrative design.

In style Johnson is remarkably euphuistic—a fact that will be more or less striking in accordance with a reader's expectations or prior reading. If one comes to him from such Augustans as Addison and Steele and Swift, Johnson seems overabundantly euphuistic; if one comes to him from Greene, Johnson seems relatively easy flowing. That is to say that a freedom from dominating euphuistic habits marks enough of his sentences to give an overall sense of a much less constrained rhythm than one finds in Greene. But still the euphuistic tendency is always there; one can find few paragraphs without balance, parallelism, or antithesis. The frequency of Johnson's euphuistic sentence designs can be inferred from the fact that all my illustrations are from the first few pages of the novel and that I am being highly selective in quoting from these pages.

Johnson often comes up with a rather short antithetical sentence such as is fairly rare in Greene: "His wish still continued, but his hope grew less" (617).[6] He frequently uses a more extensive balance to govern part of a sentence: "to forget those lectures which pleased only while they were new, and to become new again must be forgotten" (612). There Johnson uses a chiasmus of meaning (forget-new-new-forgotten) which he relies on more frequently than Greene does. Here is a somewhat more complex example: "He that can swim needs not despair to fly: to swim is to fly in a grosser fluid, and to fly is to swim in a subtler" (618). Johnson often writes a series of three parallel elements, for instance, "to make seclusion pleasant, to fill up the vacancies of attention, and lessen the tediousness of time" (608). Such parallels may prevail in more extended predications—"he neglected their officiousness, / repulsed their invitations, / and spent day after day on the banks of rivulets sheltered with trees, where he sometimes listened to the birds in the branches, / sometimes observed the fish playing in the stream, / and anon cast his eyes upon the pastures and mountains" (610)—where the extra long third element in the first triad of verb phrases creates some variation in the overall pattern of successive triads.

Finally, alliteration. There is some of it in the passages just quoted, but it is incidental rather than enveloping, as it is in Greene. On the

other hand, it is a regular tool of Johnson's; he uses it more frequently—
no page is without it—than later writers would, though less than pure
euphuists did. It appears pretty frequently in phrases and clauses: "the
ignorance of infancy, or imbecility of age" (615), "*neither labor to be
endured nor danger to be dreaded*" (613; note also the run of medial and
final *r*s); "*no power of perception which is not glutted with its proper
pleasure*" (611). It may add emphasis to a balanced sentence: "They wan-
dered in *gardens of fragrance,* and slept in the *fortresses of security*"
(610). Since Johnson manages a moderate infusion of short, neat sentences, as several of the preceding quotations show, his euphuistic effects are much less massive and relentless than those of Greene. But he
is capable of longer and more highly organized sentences that combine
clear structural patterns with alliteration. Here is one of these, typographically arranged to emphasize the internal relationships:

> On one *p*art were *f*locks and herds *feeding* in the *p*astures,
> on another all the *b*easts of chase *frisking* in the lawns;
> the *s*prightly kid was *bounding* on the rocks,
> the *s*ubtle monkey *frolicking* in the trees, and
> the *s*olemn elephant repos*ing* in the shade.
>
> *(608)*

And of course *beasts, bounding, frolicking,* and *reposing* are held together by dominant labials, three of them initial; three of them are participles; and the three animal names—*kid, monkey, elephant*—are arranged
according to increasing number of syllables. Finally, here is a whole
paragraph made up of one euphuistic sentence:

> His chief amusement was to *p*icture to himself that world which he
>   had never seen;
>   to *p*lace himself in various conditions;
>   to be *e*ntangled in *i*maginary difficulties, and
>   to be *e*ngaged   in wild *a*dventures:
> but his benevolence always terminated his *p*rojects in
>   the *re*lief of *di*stress,
>   the *de*tection of *f*raud,
>   the *def*eat of *op*pression, and
>   the *dif*fusion of ha*pp*iness.
>
> *(614)*

Still, the balances emphasized by alliteration are rather less monumental
than those which Greene constructed on nearly every page.

The eighteenth-century revival, with modifications, of a style highly
fashionable for a decade or two in the sixteenth century argues for a
certain enduring utility and even attractiveness in the central devices of

that style. One might argue (1) that it is a linguistic way of representing a perceived or sensed reality in the objective world, or (2) that it is a gratifying way of ordering phenomena whose objective nature is not known, or (3) that it is a natural emanation of the structure of the mind as it comes into contact with an objective world. But while I acknowledge these epistemological problems, I will not pursue them, for my interest is simply in the durability of a mode which, in its first historical manifestations, came to seem fantastically improbable. It is important to see how it sobers up in "classicism," shedding a singular initial excess, a merciless hyperbole, an all but loony paradise of dainty devices of ordering and ornamental intent, but retaining its essential modi operandi and thus embodying the orderliness and rational control that we take to be objectives of the neoclassical mind-set.

vi

Johnson's classicism or neoclassicism of prose style had somewhat of a run in Frances Burney and Maria Edgeworth, though with some thinning out of the dominant equationism and oppositionism. These continued to undergo further purification, or perhaps we should say subordination to other syntactic practices. Not that they should or could disappear entirely but that they began to be reserved for special functions rather than freely indulged on every page. Here are a number of sentences from the last page of the fourth chapter of *Pride and Prejudice*. Austen is characterizing two men who later would marry two of the Bennet sisters (the sentence numbers are of course my additions):

> [1] Bingley was endeared to Darcy by the easiness, openness, ductility of his temper, though no disposition could offer a greater contrast to his own and though with his own he never appeared dissatisfied. [2] On the strength of Darcy's regard Bingley had the firmest reliance, and of his judgment the highest opinion. . . . [3] Bingley was by no means deficient, but Darcy was clever. [4] He was at the same time haughty, reserved, and fastidious, and his manners, though well bred, were not inviting. . . . [5] Bingley was sure of being liked wherever he appeared, Darcy was continually giving offence. . . . [6] Darcy, on the contrary, had seen a collection of people [the Bennets and friends] in whom there was little beauty and no fashion, for none of whom he had felt the smallest interest and from none received either attention or pleasure.

In characterizing Darcy and Bingley entirely by contrast, Austen chooses not to do separate vignettes of a paragraph each but to portray them simultaneously, with alternating specifications. Hence it seems natural for her to rely on syntactic devices that we have seen in both Greene and

Johnson. These are, in the sentences as numbered: (1) a main clause, with a three-word series, opposed by two parallel *though* clauses, and with the only traces of alliteration, and these hardly detectable, in the whole paragraph; (2) two balanced pairs of interlocking prepositional phrases, an initial group balanced against a final group; (3) antithetical clauses; (4) symmetrical clauses, one with a series, the other with an antithesis; (5) antithetical clauses; (6) three parallel subordinate clauses.

Though my series of compact annotations may suggest a euphuistic density of devices, no reader is likely to feel that the passage suffers from oppressive formalism. It is not heavily Latinate, and the devices seem to serve the meaning rather than the author's determination to achieve a certain ring. The relative lightness of the passage would be even more marked if I had included several sentences that have no euphuistic devices at all. Further, this passage does not seem the product of a compulsive pattern: Austen writes pages and even chapters in which there is no euphuism or only a light touch of it. In her hands the classical or euphuistic manner is purged of excess and hence reserved largely for local functions to which it is especially adapted.

vii

If in Austen the style was cut back to what, in contemporary argot, we might call minimalist status, one might predict its ultimate disappearance, especially in such a time as our own, when logicalist perception, if we may so call it, is not a widespread gift among fictionists. A history from then to now would be an interesting one. My own guess is that it would not be, indeed could not be, a history of a declining and finally lost form, detectable only in fossil state. But what one would certainly not expect would be a new development away from the bare-bones Austen condition, a restoration of full-fleshed euphuism resembling the earlier grandiose manifestations. Yet oddly enough such a recovery of an earlier rich panoply of stylistic accoutrements does occur at least once and, still more surprisingly, in a romantic writer in whom it would a priori seem wholly improbable—Charlotte Brontë. Her *Villette* has a rather remarkable infusion of euphuistic practices. Brontë's style is so varied and innovative—it even contains elements of what we can only call the surrealistic—that we can easily lose sight of her resemblances to Austen and even Johnson. Balanced structure, series, and antitheses are everywhere in a long novel. Brontë can use series to comic effect, serialize antithetic pairs, use alliterative effects both obvious and subtle, and a Latinate vocabulary even more marked than that of the sixteenth century. But she can employ such devices to create disturbing emotion rather than impose rational control, and she can infuse highly ordered sentences with intense metaphorical life. She may use euphuistic style in traditional ways—for order and ornament, epigram and wit—but she also adapts them to the powerful expression of the contradictions and pressures of the world and of the psyche.

Brontë's singular employment and adaptation of an old style, as well as her almost unique combining of it with other stylistic modes, I discuss in detail in the next essay. Here I am simply making the historical note that she surprisingly used euphuism with a regularity and fullness that probably surpassed Johnson's and vastly surpassed Austen's. The style was consistent in Johnson with the attitude he wished to instill, the rational control of longings and illusions; and in Austen with an instinctive clearheadedness and good sense in observing an imperfect world. What Greene and Brontë shared was the combination of an apparently rationalistic style with a romantic substance. But the combinations differed because the romantic substance differed. Greene's romance derived from a traditional conception of a world of mainly outer action in which the participants had standard roles and only minimal subjective reality on their way to success or failure; they are subordinate to a hyper-euphuistic style in which relentless formalism competes against the romantic spirit of love, adventure, conflict, the exotic, and so on. On the other hand, Brontë's romantic substance is the passion of the individual soul, more or less "privileged," as we say nowadays, in its conflicts with a larger world that often seemed indifferent, difficult, or downright hostile. And she has so managed her version of an old style—ordinarily used for and, as it seems, inherently committed to a logical, rational mediation of reality—as to make it an unexpected but nonetheless impressive vehicle of the disturbances and tensions in the personality and in the life that impinges on the personality.

■ 15 ■
Tulip-hood, Streaks, and Other Strange
Bedfellows: Style in *Villette*

i

IT IS NOT EXACTLY NEWS that a Charlotte Brontë novel is rather a different thing from a Jane Austen novel. It is perhaps less obvious that
Brontë, despite her rejection of Austen, does have an Austen side. One
need not pursue notoriety by treating that side as if it were primary, yet
to see that Brontë does some things that Austen might do, or does them
as Austen might do them, is one way to get a sense of Brontë's unusual
gifts. In style Brontë has a wider range than any preceding novelist, and
in the command of stylistic tools she is surpassed, if indeed she is surpassed, only by George Eliot and Meredith. On the one hand, she can
choose and arrange words in an eighteenth-century way represented in
the ordered, generalizing, and analytic prose of Burney, Edgeworth, and
Austen; on the other hand, she has a large vocabulary of the specific and
the concrete, an instinct for sensory images, a spontaneous feeling for
particulars—in brief an eye for the streaks of the tulip that Imlac proscribed while he prescribed the abstract conceptual truth of The Tulip.
If Brontë dips into the romantic treasure chest even more easily than
into the neoclassical safe-deposit box, she has a talent for still other verbal and symbolic practices that in their individuality smack of even older
styles as well as of one not yet born. She practices at least four identifiable modes of style. Though this diversity may be found in all her novels,
it is especially evident in *Villette*.

A new reader who came to *Villette* supplied with mental pictures of
Haworth hilltop, moors, wuthering, Angria, troubled personalities, and
Brontë mortality statistics might be surprised at the continual presence
of the Austen mode (which I use as a convenient term for a comedy of
manners or neoclassical way of doing things). The extensive dialogue,
though its more frequent concerns may be distress, disturbance, or even
turbulence of feeling, is often crisp, sprightly, commonsensical, and
witty, especially when Mrs. Bretton is a speaker. With her dry, understated, often ironic style she might be an Austen character. She and her
son Graham (Dr. John) fall naturally into easy banter, at times almost
Shavian, and this tone frequently enters Graham's dialogues with Polly,

205

whom he marries, and Lucy Snowe, who not quite consciously would like to marry him. The exchanges between Lucy and Ginevra Fanshawe can become sharp debates, but often they are skirmishes with verbal tilting, ironic playfulness, and wit. Though Lucy likes to think of Ginevra as trivial and shallow, Brontë makes Ginevra more than a butt. Her lively, flippant, offhand worldliness, coupled with her apparent affection for the censorious Lucy, gives her some charm. A sign of Brontë's range: Ginevra can come up with what we now call "sick humor." Apropos of the theater fire in which Polly was slightly hurt, Ginevra says, "It seems Mademoiselle was nearly crushed to a jelly in a hubbub at the theatre" (24; all references are to chapters).

Single remarks may be jocular or even epigrammatic. Lucy can pun that Ginevra "lay fuming in the vapors" (24); Ginevra jokes that one cannot say *au diable* in English but that "it sounds quite right in French" (6); Mrs. Bretton reports ironically that her son Graham "is so elastic that there is no such thing as vexing him thoroughly. When I think that I have at last driven him to the sullens, he turns on me with jokes for retaliation" (24). Even in her darker days Lucy is often the sharp observer: she calls a waiter "parsonic-looking," and she detects in his fraternity a still familiar style, "a doubtful state between patronage and politeness" (5); all servants sensed her lack of status and cash and "estimated me at about the same fractional value" (7). She can hit off a man's frailty— Paul "hated" sewing implements "mortally, considering sewing a source of distraction from the attention due to himself" (21)—and joke about an institutional regulation: Dr. John has some freedom in a school in which men may not appear, since "there was about him a manly, responsible look, that redeemed his youth, and half-expiated his beauty" (14). Lucy can shuck off a customary solemnity about herself. When Mme. Beck, an administrator who relies on "surveillance," goes through Lucy's chest of drawers and then replaces things neatly, Lucy, instead of raging at the violation of privacy, jokes insouciantly: "Had she creased one solitary article, I own I should have felt much greater difficulty in forgiving her" (13). Lucy can comment wittily on moralistic fiction. Austen herself might have said, when Ginevra eloped, "the reader will no doubt expect to hear that she came finally to a bitter expiation of her youthful levities. Of course, a large share of suffering lies in reserve for her future" (40)—a conventional nemesis promptly aborted by an account of her patterned married life. But Brontë swings away from the Austen manner when she lets a Lucy epigram be tainted with something like self-pity, as in "there is, in lovers, a certain infatuation of egotism; they will have a witness of their happiness, cost that witness what it may" (37). Three-quarters of this is a bright notation of lovers' habits, but at "cost"

Lucy slips into it as the victim that she easily becomes. Lucy's narcis-sistic streak, whether sense of injury or sense of merit, is captured by M. Paul in one of the best epigrams in the novel: "Faithful women err in this, that they think themselves the sole faithful of God's creatures" (41).[1]

Other traits of eighteenth-century style that may or may not appear in Austen persist in *Villette*. Brontë has an immense storehouse of ab-stract words that break out in three ways—in personifications, in general-izations that create an unsought vagueness, and in Johnsonesque polysyl-labic thickets. Her pallid personification by capital letters could supply several volumes of poot Popean verse; few novels are so laden with ab-stractions presumably made flesh in uppercase personhood.[2] Still, two features of her practice suggest either artistic luck or a conscious optimi-zation of a slender possibility—the distribution of the capitalized terms, and certain efforts at fuller personification. Though these nouns appear in about three out of four chapters, they are more frequent at times of crisis—the tensions before, during, and after Lucy's "breakdown" (14, 15, 16); the concert where John breaks with Ginevra, Lucy's return from the Bretton home to the school, and the theater evening that ends in fire, panic, and the rescue of Polly (20, 21, 23); and the penultimate ten-sions of the religious conflict and Lucy's strange evening walk (36, 38, 39). Perhaps, then, the Brontë leaps into uppercase may be less an au-tomatism of elevation than a spontaneous accompaniment of height-ened emotions. When Lucy, rescued from psychic disaster by Dr. John, and questioned by John's mother, speaks of her "single-handed conflict with Life, with Death, with Grief, with Fate" (16), it may seem a facile grandeur if we forget that she is not yet out of a severe emotional crisis. In anxiety and depression she saw Ginevra as the object of "True Love," which she herself despairs of; she would "rise in the night" and "beseech [sleep] earnestly to return," but "Sleep never came!"; as she became more desperate, "Death challenged me to engage his unknown terrors," and she became convinced that "Fate was of stone, and Hope a false idol" (15). If the abstractions are not solidly personified, they are not wholly pallid either; they assist in a generally well-imaged account of a suicidal state.

Again, some personifications appear regularly enough to become al-most minor characters (Fate, Destiny, Hope, Reason, and Imagination); and of these, some gain a faint personality. Reason, which for Lucy means not logical processes but the conviction of disappointment, is a "hag";[3] she has a "withered hand"; she "Frostily touch[ed] my ear with the chill blue lips of eld"; she comes up "stealthily" and whispers "se-dately." She is "vindictive as a devil" and "envenomed as a step-mother";

often she turns Lucy "out by night, in mid-winter, in cold snow, flinging for sustenance the gnawed bones dogs had forsaken." This demonic creature assures Lucy that Graham will never write letters as he has promised (on her return from the Bretton sanctuary to school), and that her life will be empty. So Lucy calls on a "sweet Help," a "divine Hope," a "spirit, softer and better than Human Reason," who brings "a sphere of air borrowed of eternal summer," "perfume of flowers which cannot fade—fragrance of trees whose fruit is life," "food, sweet and strange, gathered amongst gleaming angels, garnering their dew-white harvest in the first fresh hour of a heavenly day," and assuages "the insufferable tears which weep life itself away" (21). This "bright foe" of Reason is Imagination, which here signifies the enjoyment of gratifying images, or fantasizing; the opposing depths and elevation mean that the personifications dramatize depressive and manic tendencies. Though the polar terms (one pole also represented by Intellect and Common Sense, and the other also by Feeling and Fancy) remain conceptual, still the personifications gain some vitality as figures of a thematic conflict (a severe "reality principle" versus releasing daydreams).

A second aspect of Brontë's use of abstractions: they can lead to what Brontë might call "insubstantiality." The shirking of specifics, which may proceed from imaginative inertia or from the aesthetic credo which begot poetic diction, can put us off with hollowness where body should be. Though most of the action in *Villette* takes place in a school, hardly any books are identified. At one time Polly uses a geography that has actual contents; once Lucy reads "a Corneille," and the pair translates Schiller's ballads. That is it. Graham likes to read, "nor was his selection of books wholly indiscriminate" (3), but no titles validate his discrimination; in London Lucy "bought a little book" (6); once she takes from the bookcase "a volume whose title promised some interest" (14); studying German, she works on "the driest and thickest books in the library" (24); Paul brightens the minds of the girls with a "glimpse of the current literature of the day" (28); and so on.[4] Insofar as these passages concern Lucy, they perhaps inadvertently underscore her acknowledgment that she was "Intellectually imperfect" and "could read little" (33)—a brief pause in her rather bluestocking complacency.

The frustrating vagueness is not restricted to intellectual matters. Out of an older art come Lucy's "tiny articles of raiment" (1); her making "the necessary applications" to mitigate the pain of Miss Marchmont (4); Polly's father's undertaking "the management of some affair which required attention" (32); and Lucy's doing vast research on a subject about which we learn only that it was "classical" (35). Finally, it would be hard to suppose that Brontë knew anything of a theater fire and panic or could imagine its true nature. A cry of "Fire!" in a theater instantly produced "panic, rushing, crushing—a blind, selfish, cruel chaos." Good enough as a generality, but Brontë can create no actual "cruel chaos" for Lucy in the exit-rush jam: "Resolute, . . . I penetrated the living barrier, creeping under where I could not get between or over." No problem at all. Then Lucy gives first aid to injured Polly: "seeing what the faint and sinking girl wished to have done, I did it for her" (23). Reality, the chosen matter, is simply absent.

The last infirmity of habitual generality is Latinism and mounds of syllables: the Johnsonism that bypasses Austen, gains a heavy foothold in Scott (Brontë joins him in using the Greek "hebdomadal" [22]), is picked up by Hardy in his intermittent addiction to learned cumbersomeness, and then in our age degenerates into the tumidities of bureaucratic argot and academic cryptese. Brontë is strongly attracted to such words as *ablution, condiment, disapprobation, egress, nutriment,* and *vicinage,* and once she uses *mutism* to mean silence (27). Facing combinations of such words, one can hardly help translating. Examples: "brought us an accession of animation" by "made us lively," "appliances for occupation" by "sewing equipment," and a doll's "possession of sentient and somnolent faculties" by "could feel and sleep" (3); "apostrophized with vehemence" (14) by "spoke sharply to"; "provocative of laughter" (20) by "that made us laugh"; "there can be no oblivion of inferiority" (21) by "you cannot ignore your shortcomings"; "provoked contumacity" by "made me rebellious," and "any imputation the Parisienne might choose to insinuate" by "any charge the Parisienne might imply" (29); "terminated with so concise an abridgment" (32) by "cut the story so short"; and "The spring of junction seemed suddenly to have become palpable" (34) by "The connecting link suddenly became clear."

Yet in such passages the pedantic may be mingled with the effectively individual. Except for the initial wordiness, "the importance of the case was by no means such as to tempt curiosity to infringe on discretion" (16) might appear in Austen. "Tempt curiosity to infringe on discretion" nicely denotes a border and has just a touch of the humor that also hovers about "I restrained deprecation" (34) and "I must expiate my culpable vehemence" (18), both translatable, but neither quite insisting on translation. Brontë perhaps uses the Latinate for humor when Lucy complains of Ginevra's maternal boasts: "extravagant amplifications upon miracles of precocity, mixed with vehement objurgations [another Scott favorite] against the phlegmatic incredulity with which I received them" (40). By combining the accuracy of the Latinate with a conspicuous syntactic ordering she can manage an air of unusual control. When someone plans a situation without your knowing of the plans, "the whole arrangement seems to your crude apprehension the ordinance of chance, or the sequel of exigency" (34). The next step is apothegm, as in this paradigm of lovers' developing intimacy: "out of association grows adhesion, and out of adhesion amalgamation" (25). Overweight yes, but rather charming in the discrepancy, not unconscious, one hopes, between the spontaneity of experience and the schoolmasterish formulation. Brontë's awareness of the stylistic medium is at least implied when Lucy sums up Paul's description of

> How I behaved to him! With what pungent vivacities—what an impetus of mutiny—what a "fougue" of injustice!
> Here I could not avoid opening my eyes somewhat wide, and even slipping in a slight interjectional observation [Brontëese for "interjecting"!]—
> "Vivacities? Impetus? Fougue? . . ." (28)

There is a bit of mockery in her echo of his words and of his series. Still, it is not clear how far Brontë can move from an instinctive, uncriticized Johnsonese to a humorous semiawareness of its tone, from a tic to an acknowledged mannerism enacted with a smile. One remembers the film actress some years ago who managed Jane Eyre's Latinisms with a merry ebullience, as if Jane were combining nature and a game, being herself but also playing herself half-jestingly, with a fringe of parody preempting a possible response by listeners.

Brontë's syntax consistently tends toward the neoclassical logical patterns that are frequent in Austen—balanced and antithetical constructions, parallelism and the series: means of giving form to meaning by symmetry, sequence, and opposition. (More distantly, of course, Brontë's use of these devices is related to the sixteenth-century predecessor of neoclassicism—euphuism and its fanatical mechanizations of order.) Brontë has a flair for apt and lucid pairings: students' "undisciplined disaffection and wanton indocility," "the stirring of worthy emulation, or the quickening of honest shame" (9); an address might be "half dogmatism to the [students], half flattery to the princes" (27); a French dressmaker can "unite the utterly unpretending with the perfectly becoming" (33). Still more frequent are the series of three or more: in her "surveillance" Mme. Beck was "watching and spying everywhere, peering through every keyhole, listening behind every door" (8); a teacher would "take . . . back" an assignment "rejected" by students and "at once, without hesitation, contest, or expostulation—proceed . . . to smooth every difficulty, to reduce it to the level of their understandings, return it to them modified, or lay on the lash of sarcasm . . . [to hold] well up to them . . . their incapacity, ignorance, and sloth" (9); "The school gossiped, the kitchen whispered, the town caught the rumor, parents wrote letters" (11); Mme. Beck would talk to Lucy about a colleague with "an odd mixture of discrimination, indifference, and antipathy" (14).

Brontë can line up balanced nouns in a series: "Her service was my duty—her pain, my suffering—her relief, my hope—her anger, my punishment—her regard, my reward" (4). The antithetical orderings of thought may be neat, sharp, or suggestive. The helpful man, not yet identified as Graham Bretton, "looked high but not arrogant, manly but not overbearing" (7); Mme. Beck's features "pleased in moderation, but with constancy" (11); "Though portly, [Mrs. Bretton] was alert, and though serene, she was at times impetuous" (16); when Lucy lacked appropriate words, others "covered my deficiency by their redundancy" (27); Polly's presence makes a room seem "not inhabited, but haunted" (2). Of Mme. Beck's spoiled child, who regularly simulates illness in power plays: she "overflowed . . . with unmerited health and evil spirits" (10). Lucy's complacent Anglicanism looks down equally on "some Catholic or Methodist enthusiast—some precocious fanatic or untimely saint" (2). The juxtaposition of contraries is especially good when it registers a perceived duality in character; thus it becomes almost a hallmark of Lucy's accounts of Paul—"Never . . . a better little man, in some points . . . never, in others, a more waspish little despot" (26); "quick to originate, hasty to lead, but slow to persuade, and hard to bend" (35). Elsewhere she says, "if I blamed his over-eagerness, I liked his naivete" (27), and "How often . . . has this man . . . seemed to me to lack all magnanimity in trifles, yet how great he is in great things!" (34). Such perceptions belong mostly to the later stages of their relationship; it takes time to grasp and accept the contradictions of personality.

ii

The elements of Brontë style that can be loosely termed "eighteenth century" or "Austen-like"—lively dialogue, with wit and occasional epigram; abstractions that lead into personifications, vagueness, or a Latinistic word-hoard heavy, or laughable, or perhaps laughing a little at times; orderly and ordering forms that imply a rational mastery of the experience depicted (ultimately the euphuistic mode, as I noted in the preceding essay)—are frequent enough to have a share in the total effect produced. Not to be aware of them would be to miss the Brontë range. Yet they are not primary; other stylistic means are closer to the thinking and feeling essence of her art. Even in doing these "neoclassical things" she can make them serve nonclassical ends. Above all, she can do various things that are not neoclassical at all.

We could say that the verbal art of *Villette* is influenced by both Reynolds and Blake—the Academy president who espoused the pursuit of "general . . . ideas," and his rebellious annotator who glossed, "To generalize is to be an idiot." Regularly as Brontë uses abstractions, she has an excellent eye for a concrete world, and words for it—words that mostly lie outside the Austen realm. Of Graham Bretton as a guide to "places of interest" in Brussels, Lucy says, "It was not his way to treat subjects coldly and vaguely; he rarely generalized, never prosed. He seemed to like nice details almost as much as I liked them myself" (19). Though in this scene Brontë is vague herself—no "places" identified, no "nice details" given—she need not be; in London, for instance, she does a good mini-Michelin (6). In describing an exterior she may mingle the polite and the direct: the "turf was verdant" could be Austen, but not what follows—"the gravelled walks were white; sunbright nasturtiums clustered beautiful about the roots of the doddered orchard giants. There was . . . the shade of an acacia . . . vines which ran all along a high and grey wall, and . . . hung their clusters in loving profusion about the favoured spot where jasmine and ivy met and married them" (12), where the detail softens up in a figure edging the sentimental. With "a spade or watering-pot" Paul "looked to the orange trees, the geraniums, the gorgeous cactuses," while his "lips . . . sustained his precious cigar" (36). Brontë's eye is very keen when it is focused on interiors, such as that of the "parlour" in the house secured by Paul for Lucy: "Its delicate walls were tinged like a blush; its floor was waxed; a square of brilliant carpet covered its centre; its small round table shone like the mirror over its hearth; there was a little couch, a little chiffoniere the half-open crimson-silk door of which showed porcelain on the shelves; there was a French clock, a lamp," "biscuit china," "a green stand bearing three green flower-pots," "a gueridon with a marble top, and upon it a work-box and a glass filled with violets in water" (41).

Not only settings but actions may benefit from this solid realization. Lucy weeps: "I wet the pillow, my arms, and my hair with rushing tears" (5). Supposedly asleep, Lucy watches Mme. Beck do a strange nighttime inspection of her clothes: "In my dress was a pocket; she fairly turned it inside out: she counted the money in my purse; she opened a little memorandum-book, coolly perused its contents, and took from between the leaves a small plaited lock of Miss Marchmont's grey hair" (8). Graham remembers how Polly, aged six, "would set a footstool beside him, and climb by its aid to his knee" (he was sixteen). He "could recall the sensation of her little hands smoothing his cheek, or burying themselves in his thick mane . . . the touch of her small forefinger, placed half tremblingly, half curiously, in the cleft in his chin, the lisp, the look" (37). A portrait may mix the seen and the interpreted: Mme. Beck was "a motherly, dumpy little woman, in a large shawl, a wrapping-gown, and a clean, trim night-cap" (7). Her hair was "auburn, unmixed with grey." Though "rather short and stout," she had a "grace resulting from proportion of parts." Her eyes were "blue and serene." In addition to a general "harmony," her face "offered contrast," for along with a "complexion of . . . blended freshness and repose," the general "outline was stern: her forehead was high but narrow; it expressed capacity and some benevolence, but no expanse; . . . Her mouth was hard; it could be a little grim; her lips were thin." She could be a "Minos[5] in petticoats" (8). Finally, Brontë can so equip a personification with physical traits as to make us almost see a person: "Human Justice" was a "red, random beldame with arms akimbo" living in a "den of confusion," indifferent to requests and cries from servants, beggars, and children. "She had a warm seat of her own by the fire, . . . a short black pipe, and a bottle of . . . soothing syrup; she smoked and she sipped and she enjoyed her paradise." When cries for help became too audible, she seized "the poker or hearth-brush" and "effectually settled" the weak; she "only menaced" the strong, "then plunged her hand into her deep pouch, and flung a liberal shower of sugarplums" (35).

Thus Brontë departs from the neoclassical to bring the seeable into the importance that we still attach to it. Further, her eye for colors is almost as keen as George Eliot's. Graham's hair may be "red" (Polly), "auburn" or "golden" (Mrs. Bretton), "tawny" (Graham himself), or "leonine" (Lucy) (2). A theater crowd is "all rose, and blue, and half translucent white" against a background of a "solemn green curtain" (14). Ginevra's "deep crimson" dress goes nicely with her "light curls" and "rose-like bloom," Polly's "white" with the "brown shadow and bounteous flow of her hair" (27). In the Dickensian grotesque[6] Brontë uses color very fully. The dwarf-hunchback Mme. Walravens leaned on the "gold knob" of her "ivory staff"; she had "thick grey brows," and a "silver beard bristled her chin"; she wore a brocade gown of "bright blue, full tinted as the gentianella flower, and covered with satin foliage," a shawl with a "many-coloured fringe," "long, clear earrings," and "rings on her skeleton hands, with thick gold hoops and stones—purple, green, and blood-red" (34). The colors add a sheen or brilliance that nicely sets off the basic ugliness and weirdness.

Though the visual are the most frequent, other sensory images are also sources of vitality. Lucy has a shipwreck nightmare: "the rush and saltness of briny waves in my throat, and their icy pressure on my lungs" (4); she endures the "honey-gall" of hearing Graham talk about Ginevra (18); she has a dreamlike auditory experience: "I heard a gale. . . . I heard it drawn and withdrawn far, far off, like a tide retiring from the shore of the upper world" (17)—an anticipation of a sound effect in "Dover

Beach." The image may be the life of a brief phrase: "the dubious cloud-tracery of hope" (8), the "slippery oil" of "Apology" (42). It may be the soul of wit: Mrs. Bretton "preferred all sentimental demonstrations in bas-relief" (16). It may revivify an old standby: "I knew I was catching at straws; but . . . I would have caught at cobwebs" (7), and "the gambols of this unlicked wolf-cub muffled in the fleece, and mimicking the bleat of a guileless lamb" (36). It may convey a subtle essence: Polly's charm lay "in a subdued glow from the soul outward"[7] (24), or spell out a quality both visual and tonal, as with the "full display of [Zélie's] upper and under rows of teeth—that strange smile which passes from ear to ear, and is marked only by a sharp thin curve, which fails to spread over the countenance, and neither dimples the cheek nor lights the eye" (28). It may capture a stunning vividness: the theater curtain "shrivelled to the ceiling" (14); the evening sky was "a mass of black-blue metal, heated at the rim, and inflaming slowly to a heavy red," and "the forked, slant bolts [of lightning] pierced athwart vertical torrents; red zig-zags inter-laced a descent blanched as white metal"; and, with perhaps a touch of humor, "A yellow electric light from the sky gilded [the] bald head" of a priest sitting in a "shade—deep and purple" (34). The same idiom for an emotional experience: when Lucy hears that Paul must travel to "Basse-terre in Guadaloupe," these words "seemed pronounced over my pillow, or ran athwart the darkness round and before me, in zig-zag characters of red or violet light" (38). This is a long way from the Austen realm of sensible or light-headed social interchange.

Brontë's metaphors are more evident; there are more of them, and some are extended. They may be very compact: Paul's response to a rebuke—"he took the dose quietly" (27); in Graham's "goodly mansion, his heart" there was "one little place under the skylight" for Lucy (38); Lucy's rejection of the hopes kept alive by letters from Graham—"I closed the eyes of my dead, covered its face, and composed its limbs with great calm" (26); "a scene of feeling too brimful" was the worse "because the cup did not foam up high or furiously overflow" (2); an unidentified presence in the garden—"the eyes of the flowers had gained vision, and the knots in the tree-boles listened like secret ears" (13). Or Brontë may extend the metaphor into an elaboration of the thought. Anxiety lies in wait for Lucy "like a tiger crouched in a jungle"; she always heard "the breathing of that beast of prey" and felt "his fierce heart [as it] panted close against mine" (7). Again, she had to "knock on the head" all her longings, like "Jael to Sisera, driving a nail through their temples"; but they were only "transiently stunned, and at intervals would turn on the nail with a rebellious wrench: then did the temples bleed, and the brain thrill to its core" (12)—a brilliant rendering of desires struggling against efforts to repress them. River and sea recur in metaphor as in simile. An exemplary passage has to do with the "goodly river" of hope—letters from Graham to Lucy—"on whose banks I had sojourned"; "I loved my Rhine, my Nile; I had almost worshipped my Ganges, and I grieved" that it "should vanish like a false mirage" (26).

Clearly Brontë often uses a metaphor not only as an identifying image but as an instrument for the exploration of event or meaning. Between Graham and herself Lucy always feels an "invisible, but a cold something, very slight, very transparent, but very chill: a sort of screen of ice" that "glazed the medium" of exchange between them; ironically enough a few words, "warm with anger, breathed on that frail frost-work of reserve" and in effect dissolved it (18). Paul accuses Lucy. she "would snatch at a draught of sweet poison, and spurn wholesome bitters with disgust," and both of them then use this figure to analyze her personality more fully (21). Lucy scorns Graham's prescription that she "cultivate happiness," since it "is not a potato, to be planted in mould, and tilled with manure," but "a glory shining far down upon us out of Heaven . . . a divine dew which the soul . . . feels dropping upon it from the amaranth bloom and golden fruitage of Paradise" (22). Potato versus glory: an especially striking metaphorical contrast.

Brontë's most remarkable extended metaphor governs all of chapter 30—the metaphor of Paul as Napoleon. "He would have exiled fifty Madame de Staels, if they had annoyed, offended, outrivalled, or opposed him." He had "love of power" and "an eager grasp of supremacy," and his "absolutism verged on tyranny." Relations with him had to take the form of "conflict," though he "made his peace somehow" with victims. Lucy could always dream of "one cold, cruel, overwhelming triumph" over him. They "did battle more than once—strong battle, with confused noise of demand and rejection, exaction and repulse." This is one of the frequent military figures that, as they carry on the Napoleon analogy, reveal that it is indeed functional. Paul, physically a short dark man, has an instinctive love of command that Lucy must resist for her own good. It is not that she herself is combative or that she makes a principle of independence, or that, on the other hand, she must resist a temptation to an easy submission and a will-less life (like Jane Eyre when she is proposed to by St. John Rivers). It is rather that she is struggling, not for rights or privileges, or other abstractions that would become petrified in slogans in the next century, but for a certain quality of life, for liberation from a naturally dominating personality. To make Paul a Napoleon is to image the problem with dramatic concreteness and sharpness.

The same figure would do for the Elizabeth-Darcy conflict. But it is impossible to imagine Jane Austen's using it. That is one clue to the distance between the Austen with whom Brontë shares some stylistic traits, and the Brontë who is still more strongly committed to another mode, the literal and figurative concreteness which approaches reality through the streaks of the tulip.

iii

In syntax as in vocabulary Brontë uses two different tracks; or perhaps better, she uses one track in two different ways. Take the devices of balance and parallelism, the pair and the series, and the related antithesis, which, as in the old euphuism where they were given such extensive play, suggest, or even announce, a logical ordering or control of the material. When Lucy says of herself, "Left alone, I was passive; repulsed, I withdrew; forgotten—my lips would not utter, nor my eyes dart a reminder" (36), the rational organization stands out, but "lips" and "eyes" suggest the pressure of feeling upon descriptive history. There is more pressure in two sets of pairs arranged in semichiasmic form: "I saw the horse; I heard it stamp—I saw at least a mass; I heard a clamor." Here the symmetry embodies not the wit of the couplet but the breathless tension of apparently disastrous events. Brontë moves on directly from the two-part balance to the standard three-part series: the horse "stood trembling, panting, snorting" (4)—again not the orderly itemization of events, but the pounding of ominous actions. There is fierce antagonism in Lucy's view of a Catholic legend, "with all its dreadful viciousness, sickening tyranny, and black impiety," and of all such "tales that were nightmares of oppression, privation, and agony" (13). Opposite theme: when Lucy voices religious faith, the intense tripartite pattern embraces several sentences: "Proof of a life to come must be given. In fire and blood, if needful, must that proof be written. In fire and blood do we trace the record throughout nature. In fire and blood does it cross our own experience" (38)—with verbal as well as formal repetition. But the triad, passion-bearing as it may be, often seems too limited to embody the pressure felt by the narrator. This pressure, as it were, demands more than three words. Lucy almost screams as she keeps rephrasing the needed stimuli to action—"I must be goaded, driven, stung, forced to energy"—and the ominous tone of a storm: "a gasping, sobbing, tormented, long-lamenting east wind" (4).

It is obvious how far such trains of words have come from the cool mind's organization of experience by a conventional triad. The Brontë extended series is the outward form of desires, needs, and fears surging up as if out of control. Yet occasionally the piling-up of words can work differently: not denying intensity, but revealing mental energy in the juxtaposing of partly contradictory words. Thus when Lucy calls Polly "the vexed, triumphant, pretty, naughty being" whose "countenance" manifests "utmost innocence . . . combined with some transient perverseness and petulance" (26), the words embody not only some annoyance but also an effort to record not wholly compatible elements. Thus Lucy's thumbnail sketch of Paul—"Magnificent-minded, grand-hearted, dear, faulty little man" (41)—and of Mme. Beck: "Without beauty of figure, or elegance of form, she pleased. Without youth and its graces, she cheered" (11). Such observations push toward paradox, which Brontë can manage very well (with or without a series). She describes the startling atmosphere of a room usually unoccupied: "Vacuum lacked, Solitude was not at home" (13); that is, emptiness was emptied out, absence absented itself. Brontë adds the moral to the psychological in a brilliant statement of Paul's kindness to unkind relatives: "He took on their insolent pride the revenge of the purest charity" (34). Up through "revenge," even through "purest," the words make us expect a retaliatory, punitive act: then, suddenly, the revealing shock of "charity."

iv

A sentence describing Mme. Beck contains balanced and antithetical constructions in which appears another kind of tie that binds: "there was measure and sense in her hottest pursuit of self-interest, calm and considerateness in her closest clutch of gain," and she preferred "such associates as must cultivate and elevate, rather than those who might deteriorate and depress" (26). In "cultivate and elevate" there is an internal sound echo; there is an initial sound echo in "calm and considerateness," "closest clutch," and "deteriorate and depress." Brontë is as addicted to various alliterative junctures as if she were an associate of the original sixteenth-century euphuists. She uses the expectable pairs: "drooping draperies," "prodigal and profligate," "flaw or falsity"; there are threesomes: "perfect in fashion, fit, and freshness," "pain, privation, penury," "adventurous, indocile, and audacious"; there are mixed or split threesomes, a shade more subtle and less pressing than three-in-a-row: "his supple symmetry, his smile frequent," "disciplined by destiny, I demanded," "wind wailing at the windows," "the dancing fairy and delicate dame." Brontë may alter the mixture by alliterating two out of four words in a series, as in "Hard, loud, vain, and vulgar," or enrich it by juxtaposing two pairs: "mute and motionless she kept that post and position," "flattery and fiction . . . in a manner lighter and livelier," "a pair of cold-blooded fops and pedants, sceptics and scoffers." She can tie four words together, the uniformity slightly amended by interruption or separation: "Paul's anger . . . was artless, earnest, quite unreasonable"; Lucy's was "dead blank, dark doubt, and drear suspense"; and, less overtly, a teacher's seeking Mme. Beck's "alliance in any crisis of insubordination was equivalent to securing her own expulsion." She can arrange pairs in a sequence: "all that was animated and amiable vanished from her face: she looked stony and stern, almost mortified and morose," and "the utmost innocence in her countenance—combined with some transient perverseness and petulance."[8] She can contrive an alternating or over-lapping alliteration in a brisk antithesis—"lapsing from the passionate pain of change to the palsy of custom" (21); in a balance of units—in Paul's expression "there were meanings composite and contrasted—reproach melting into remorse" (36); and in a longer predication—"must I again assay that corroding pain of long attent—that rude agony of rup-ture at the close, that mute, mortal wrench . . . ?" (41).

If the effect can be pressingly public, it can also be muted: auditory enhancements may be or seem partly underground. Take this sentence recording happiness: "Once haply in life one golden gift falls prone in the lap—one boon full and bright, perfect from Fruition's mint" (41). One promptly spots "golden gift" and "boon . . . bright," but they are only a small part of the sonic effects contributing to an air of eupeptic coherence. There are *falls* and *full*, tying in with the distant *Fruition* and with various liquid consonants: the *l*'s in *golden* and *lap*, the *r*'s in *prone, bright, perfect*, and *Fruition*; the *m*'s and *n*'s in *golden, prone, boon*, and "from Fruition's mint," and the almost musical vocalic variety through-out. Quiet additions to the junction by sound are made by the internal *f*'s in *gift* and *perfect*, and by the eight initials that are labials—falls, prone, boon, full, bright, perfect, from, Fruition—and the fact that four of them are followed by *r*.

Brontë ranges, then, from insistent alliteration to subtle patterns of repetitive sound. The latter appear in two sentences that use but go beyond simple alliteration:

> a composite feeling of blended strength and pain wound itself wirily round my heart. (21)
>
> —too terribly glorious, the spectacle of clouds, split and pierced by white and blinding bolts. (12)

Although we notice *wound-wirily, spectacle-split*, and *blinding-bolts*, more interesting are the quasi-alliterative effects of a series of labials. In the first, *wound* and *wirily* are quietly tied in with *feeling, blended*, and *pain*, and these in turn with the *p* in *composite*; and then there are the labial-liquid combinations of *f-l, bl*, and *lf*, all in a rather rich phonetic inter-weaving. In the second there is also a run of labials, initial and internal, and an even more remarkable series of liquids in combination—in order, *bl, gl, cl, cl, spl, bl*, and *b-l* (as well as the internal *r*'s in three words).

The more obvious echo of *wound* and *round* leads to another point: while her alliterative patterns do serve emphasis and coherence, Brontë undoubtedly enjoys sound effects in themselves—assonance, consonance, onomatopoeia, and even rhyme. Sounds do support sense when Lucy mentions her students' problems with English, with "the lisping and hissing dentals of the isles" (15). But we cannot so argue for the *p*'s and the accumulating liquids in "a pair of glacial prodigies, cold, proud, and preternatural" (26), and the emphatic final *d*'s in *cold* and *proud*; or, in "there falls a stilly pause, a wordless silence, a long blank of oblivion" (24), for the host of sibilants and the closing line of liquids, and, in *falls* and *pause*, a strong assonance bordering on rhyme. In "weeks of inward winter" (24), "inward" and "winter" produce an anagrammatic echo. The assonance is not pushy in "subdued and unobtrusive" (27) and "trumpets rang an untimely summons" (38), but Brontë does not draw back from even outright rhymes: "panic, rushing, crushing" (23), "the flat and fat soil of Labassecour" (27), "I had been taught and sought" (38), and even a dactylic rhyme: "He watched tearlessly ordeals that he exacted should be passed through fearlessly" (30).

The fact is that the Lucy who so volubly asserts her plainness of person and soul—no pink dress for her, no painting more vital than a small still life, no music more rich than a simple Scotch ballad—has a taste for fancy things; she has her own paradise of decorative devices. Actually, she moves in two directions from the subdued plain being that she takes herself to be: toward a pressing, pounding urgency, and toward a sensory and architectonic elaborateness; toward passionate revivalism, and toward aesthetic vivacity. She may push or relish, drive or decorate, emphasize or ornamentalize; and the two may come together in ways that this polarized description does not do justice to. By now we can see that Brontë regularly practices an old mode that I have mentioned several times in passing—her version of Elizabethan euphuism. Her new euphuism, if we may so call it, is more varied than its ancestor, and its ornateness is less nagging and relentless, but the old patterns are there. We can see them in the Johnsonian effects (Johnsonism is euphuism partly purified), the Latinate and epigrammatic; in the parallel and antithetical structures, especially when these are joined with the pervasive alliteration and related sound effects; in the personifications and the figurative language, especially the similes; and in the mythological references and other allusions. Granted, there are no basilisks, halcyons, and unicorns, but snakes enter metaphorically, as does a boa constrictor, and as does poison; rats and beetles frighten, and nature behaves ominously: storms threaten and oppress, shrubbery and trees seem to misbehave, and moonlight hints the dark and unexplained. Brontë has at least a touch of unnatural natural history.

She has a noticeable infusion of the rhetorical and the exclamatory that are instruments of euphuism. When Lucy is feeling desperately low in London, she combines the parallel and the interrogatory: "What should I do on the morrow? What prospects had I in life? What friends had I on earth? Whence did I come? Whither should I go? What should I do?" (5). She rejoices that suffering stirs rather than disables her: "How I pity those whom mental pain stuns instead of rousing! . . . How quickly I dressed in the cold of the raw dawn! How deeply I drank of the ice-cold water in my carafe!" (21). She can use the exclamatory for contempt, as in a run of sneers at Ginevra's boyfriend de Hamal: "What a figure, so trim and natty! What womanish hands and feet! How daintily he held a glass to one of his optics! . . . Oh, the man of sense! Oh, the refined gentleman of superior taste and tact!" (19). Or for grief over the apparent loss of Graham's letter: "Cruel, cruel doom! To have my bit of comfort preternaturally snatched from me ere I had well tasted its virtue!" (22). Or she can pare down the outburst to a paradoxical ejaculation, as when she receives Graham's letter—"Strange, sweet insanity!" (21).

Brontë frequently uses apostrophe. In her hands it is not the mock-heroic instrument of Fielding, or the sly or sentimental trick of Sterne; it can serve in a Carlyle-like summons to hear or fear, to know or bow. She can address the absent in praise ("Brava! once more, Madame Beck . . . you fought a good fight and you overcame!" [11]) or in a near-censure ("Ah, Graham . . . your estimate of Lucy Snowe: was it always kind or just? [Had she had wealth or position,] would your manner to her, your value for her, have been quite what they actually were? And yet by these questions I would not seriously infer blame" [27]). She can sharply categorize readers: "Religious reader, you will preach to me a long sermon . . . and so will you, moralist; and you, stern sage; you, stoic, will frown; you, cynic, sneer; you, epicure, laugh. Well, each and all, take it your own way" (15). In a pulpiteering tone she directs every man to take his inner life "to your Maker—show Him the Secrets of the spirit He gave—ask Him how you are to bear the pains He has appointed—Kneel in His presence, and pray with faith." Having assured mankind that "the healing herald will descend," she flashes into prayer, "Herald, come quickly!" (17). When she invokes Imagination, she is more tireless and intense: "Divine, compassionate, succourable influence! When I bend the knee to other than God, it shall be at thy white and winged feet, beautiful on mountain or on plain. Temples have been reared to the Sun—altars dedicated to the Moon. Oh, greater glory!" The apostrophe of well over a hundred words ends, "Sovereign complete! thou hadst, for endurance, thy great army of martyrs; for achievement, thy chosen band of worthies. Deity unquestioned, thine essence foils decay!" (21).

The last ingredient in Brontë's new euphuism is inversion, which she uses as frequently as she does alliteration. Sometimes it goes with humor, as in Lucy's joke about Ginevra's claims of maternal suffering ("never woman was so put upon by calamity; never human being stood in such need of sympathy. . . . Five times was [her son] 'in articulo mortis,' and five times did he miraculously revive" [40]). More often it signals seriousness or importance. Sometimes it seems to be a slight gesture toward formality or dignity: "I know not," "well I like," "variety there was not" (1). It may be a mode of emphasis: "Prodigious was the amount of life I lived" (6); "Suitor or admirer my very thoughts had not conceived" (12); "Irritable he was" (14). It may underline approval ("Very good sense she often showed; very sound opinions she often broached" [8]) or disapproval ("Hard, loud, vain and vulgar, her mind and body alike seemed brazen and imperishable" [6]). Lucy may take especial pleasure in character analysis ("Wicked, perhaps, she is, but also she is strong" [23], with the chiasmic arrangement that occasionally appears in her alliterative patterns); in natural scenes ("divine the delight I drew from the heaving Channel waves" [6]; "pleasant was it then to stray down the peaceful alleys" [12]); in acceptance of a mysteriously achieved knowledge ("Deep into some of Madame's secrets I had entered—I know not how" [38]). On the other hand inversion may exactly register the self-pity that Lucy easily falls into: "Me she had forgotten" (5), and "Little knew they the rack of pain which had driven Lucy [that almost juvenile third person!] almost into fever" (38). But on the scores of occasions when Brontë uses inversions, the most frequent note is tension, anxiety, or depression: "Black was the river" (6); "galled was my inmost spirit with an unutterable sense of despair. . . . Motive there was none why I should try to recover . . . and yet quite unendurable was the pitiless and haughty voice in which Death challenged me" (15); "Dark through the wilderness of this world stretches the way for most of us" (38).

v

One aspect of Brontë's astonishing variety of style does not fit into any of the categories that are a convenient means of describing her talent. This is her diversity in rhythm and sentence length. Rhythm has too many ramifications to present more than cursorily here, but one kind of variation can be noticed quickly. Brontë's ordinary rhythm is brisk, pounding, or feverish; the flow of sound and thought reflects intense nervous energy, not relaxed acquiescence in the ways of the world. Against a habitual air of hurry or urgency an occasional sentence stands out by virtue of a gentle or easy rhythm even if physical action is going on. When Lucy is on a two-mile nightwalk, her heart "beat light and not feebly. Not feebly, I am sure, or I should have trembled in that lonely walk, which lay through still fields, and passed neither village nor farmhouse nor cottage; I should have quailed still more in the unwonted presence of that which tonight shone in the north, a moving mystery—the Aurora Borealis" (5). Though she names possible causes of fear, the absence of a hammering series and the multiplying of connectives and unaccented syllables give a fluid psalmist movement that not only avoids abruptness or shock but suggests a walker half charmed by the scene. Brontë does this kind of thing repeatedly in the account of Lucy's drug-induced nocturnal walk. One example: "Amid the glare, and hurry, and throng, and noise, I still secretly and chiefly longed to come on that circular mirror of crystal, and surprise the moon glassing therein her pearly front" (38). Though the initial words name a cacophonous scrambling crowd, the *ands* and the liquid consonants create an almost lilting euphony that fits the pleasing-dream air of the episode. Finally, in the last pages of the novel, Brontë tells of storms, shipwrecks, and losses in a remarkably subdued, even flat rhythm, suitable to a personality with a new strength to endure disaster, to abjure the rhetoric of anguished protest and self-commiseration. In the midst of a held-in grief Lucy adjures herself to leave "hope" to "sunny imaginations." "Let it be theirs," she ordains, "to conceive the delight of joy born again fresh out of great terror, the rapture of rescue from peril, the wondrous reprieve from dread, the fruition of return" (42). The series does not press and pound; it is deliberate, almost mechanical.

Brontë ordinarily tends toward longish, well-organized sentences. A partial exception appears in the plentiful dialogue, where lengthy predications are infrequent. Brevity there may be, but no dialect or slang; the colloquial is often vivacious, but it is usually shaped like written prose, as in this statement by Polly: "Graham, who papa is beginning to discover is a savant too—skilled, they say, in more than one branch of science—is among the number" (26). Dialogue aside, Brontë normally writes sentences of thirty to fifty words; sometimes she goes on, in a thoroughly controlled manner, to a hundred or even two hundred and fifty words. In this context her mastery of the brief and blunt is striking—another type of variety. Sticking to few words may connote a lack or repression of emotion by Lucy. When all others are moved by a departure, "I, Lucy Snowe, was calm." When little Polly is cold, Lucy says, "I took her in. She was chill; I warmed her in my arms" (3), where concision is a hedge against sentimentality. Compactness may mean dry irony. When Catholics hoping to convert Lucy draw her attention to the charm of "Papal ritual and ceremonial," she says only, "I looked at it" (36). Tension may produce short sentences, as during the period when Lucy fears she may not see Paul before he leaves for America: "Morning wasted. Afternoon came, and I thought all was over. My heart trembled in its place." Then she sees him in a group: "He was come." He lets her know that he will try to see her alone. "Could my Greatheart overcome? Could my guide reach me? Who might tell? . . . I awaited my champion" (38). But perhaps the most effective of all the short lines is Lucy's dismissal of Ginevra with a surprising breeziness. "Come, sheer off, Ginevra. I really don't want your company" (21). Such words give a quick refreshing dip into a crisp but not taut world.

vi

Now I move on from the extraordinary variety of Brontë's style to certain excellences that are served by the different devices, or that tend to dim our awareness of the devices manifestly employed, or that are achieved in other ways than through the devices. Brontë makes Miss Marchmont say of her "calamities": "Soft, amiable natures they would have refined to saintliness; of strong, evil spirits they would have made demons; as for me, I have been only a woe-struck and selfish woman" (4). Here she uses inversion, parallelism, antithetical relationships, a faint tinge of alliteration, and a climactic order in which the final element, or bang, is a surprising record of a whimper. The syntactic devices combine to shape a very keen analysis of three types, the third the weakest, but its weakness converted, by a moral self-judgment, into a significance suitable for climax. A little later Lucy makes a somewhat comparable analysis of Mme. Beck, whose talents would enable her to be both "a first minister and a superintendent of police": "Wise, firm, faithless; secret, crafty, passionless; watchful and inscrutable; acute and insensate— withal perfectly decorous—what more could be desired?" This portrait depends on its basic parallelism, with each paralleled group comprising a series or balanced pair, the sequence climaxed by a rhetorical question. The irony of the parallels, enhanced by the omission of connectives ("Wise, firm, but faithless"), makes a superb compact definition of a complicated being. Thus Brontë may combine syntactic tools to form remarkable passages; on the other hand, the tools may almost disappear from sight when some quality of the thing said preempts our attention. Take this observation: "There are people from whom we secretly shrink, whom we would personally avoid, though reason confesses that they are good people; there are others, with faults of temper, etc., evident enough, beside whom we live content, as if the air about them did us good" (17). We hardly feel the marked antithetical structure (between and within the major clauses), I suggest, because of a perceptiveness which denies ordinary expectation. Likewise a sense of the form yields to a sense of careful discrimination when Brontë says of Mrs. Bretton's manner, "not over-sympathetic, yet not too uncongenial, sensible; and even with a touch of the motherly" (3); and a balance of contrasts is an easily passed over means of defining exactly M. Paul's "tone that somehow made amends . . . for many a sharp snap and savage snarl: not a jocund, good-fellow tone, still less an unctuous priestly accent, but a voice he had belonging to himself—a voice used when his heart passed the words to his lips" (29). When Brontë reports that the young Polly's "fixed and heavy gaze swam, trembled, then glittered in fire" (2), the verbs come through less as a series than as acute indicators of overlapping movements in an ongoing transformation. And when Lucy says of Paul, "Really that little man was dreadful: a mere sprite of caprice and ubiquity; one never knew either his whim or his whereabout" (21), what catches our eye is not the pairing as such but the novel combination, "caprice and ubiquity," and the repetition of them in "whim" and "whereabout," with an alliteration that serves not as euphuistic ornament but as a final gesture of playful good spirits.

Finally, without any use of the structurings that are often important, Brontë may simply achieve, in a predication or phrase, a happy rightness of accurate brevity or imaginative light. Lucy can come up with keen phrases about herself: "a perverse mood of the mind which is rather soothed than irritated by misconstruction" (10), and "the degree of moral paralysis—the total default of self-assertion—with which, in a crisis, I could be struck" (38). She neatly sketches others: Polly "fingered nothing, or rather soiled nothing she fingered" (3); Paul was a "mixture of the touching and the absurd" (28); he had a "bridegroom mood," and Mme. Beck's eye was "grazing me with its hard ray like a steel stylet" (41). Lucy "achieved a neat frosty falsehood" for Paul after withholding a warm response to a conciliatory gesture of his; she would not "meet his contrition with a crude premature oblivion" (27). Here the Latinate produces an ironic tone: it seems to confer dignity upon a stubborn persistence in feeling offended; and "crude" not only contrasts nicely with the Latinate but stigmatizes as bad taste the virtue of forgiving by forgetting (as does "premature"). Paul can be witty too, witness his brief depiction of Lucy's provincial and supercilious side, "your high insular presence" (31). Finally, Brontë can doff all rhetorical formulas and figures and make a felicitous plain statement: "I think I never felt jealousy till now."[9]

vii

There remains one stylistic achievement that deserves separate notice— Brontë's techniques of selecting and joining words that account for the tone of the extraordinary nocturne experienced by Lucy when a seda-

tive, far from putting her to sleep, releases a very special enhancing perceptiveness—perhaps, in more recent terminology, a "heightened consciousness" that produces a "good trip" (it is literally a midnight walk in
city and park that seems charmed). Brontë herself uses the word "dreamlike" (all quotations in this section are from 38) but fortunately not until
a dream-feeling has been established by dramatic language that, rather
than naming effects, enacts or incarnates them. She may use devices
such as inversion: "Safe I passed down the avenues—safe I mixed with
the crowd where it was deepest" and "Voices were there, it seemed to
me, unnumbered," where the word order is assisted by the unexpected
words "deepest" and "unnumbered" in maintaining the effect of altered
reality. This occurs in a scene begun strangely with an old standby, personification: "Imagination was roused from her rest. . . . With scorn she
looked on Matter, her mate—'Rise! . . . Sluggard!' . . . 'Look forth and
view the night!'" All we need to do here is see the verbal departure from
a "standard" phrasing, "Look outside and see the night sky." Obviously
"forth," "view," and "night"—which is hardly a visible entity—create a
special effect by evading ordinary reality. Imagination, "with her own
royal gesture"—personification elaborated—"showed me a moon su-
preme, in an element deep and splendid." Again the contrast with the
ordinary—"a beautiful moon in a magnificent sky"—reveals how style
creates a sense of strangeness: the adjectives after the nouns; the adjectives that, though commonplace in themselves, are unusual in this context; and the unexpected "element," as if it were a chemical unknown.
Imagination swiftly changes from a commander to a temptress-guide:
"She lured me to leave this den and follow her forth into dew, coolness,
and glory," the familiar Brontë series creating the unfamiliar by juxtaposing incompatibles—a physical substance, a sensory condition, and
a transcendent state. Lucy longs for the "moonlit, midnight park," the
alliteration accenting the surprising coordination. In a sleep-world absence of sound and almost of motion Lucy glides from her room through
passageways to the main vestibule. Then the heard enhances the not-
quite-real: a distant "sound like bells or like a band—a sound where
sweetness, where victory, where mourning blend," in which mystery
springs from familiarity; the sound is in an indeterminate mode between two familiar ones, and it unites well-known meanings "named" by
abstractions that alone would be trite but combined are almost weird.
"Let me go—oh, let me go! What hinders, what does not aid freedom?"—
where Brontë gives reality to the mysterious kinesthetic inhibition often
encountered in dreams. But the "portal seems almost spontaneously to
unclose," and Lucy moves, magically as it were, for she has "scarce made
an effort." The auditory again: there is a new "sound like a strong tide, a

great flow, deepening as I proceeded." Then with "the suddenness of magic" she is "plunged amid a gay, living, joyous crowd" ("living" is the key word here), and this in "a land of enchantment, a garden most gorgeous, a plain sprinkled with coloured meteors, a forest with sparks of purple and ruby and golden fire gemming the foliage; a region ... of altar and temple, of pyramid, obelisk, and sphinx." New readers often take all of this for a wish-fulfillment dream, and it is easy to see why. In the last passage the mysterious stasis and motion and distant sound are suddenly replaced by a scene of vast unbelievable gaiety; Brontë uses the abstract "enchantment" but makes it good in the details, where her frequent tools—inversion, series, alliteration—work with images of wild color and exotic shapes, with improbably juxtaposed scenes (garden, plain, forest), with an odd mixture of light effects (meteors, sparks), and with the unusual word "gemming" to create a sort of Arabian Nights unreality.

No need to describe further the stylistic means of creating a special experience that continues through a dozen or more pages. There is a constant stream of fresh images and happy phrases: "every movement floating, every voice echo-like—half-mocking, half-uncertain"; "elastic night air," "dubious light"; "storm of harmonies," "instruments varied and countless," "the effect was as a sea breaking into song with all its waves." For such effects there was no model in earlier fiction. Brontë boldly let her imagination go and created a new way of using words. She practiced a mode of surrealism half a century or more before it became a concept and acquired a name.

viii

Though Brontë style may, at virtually any point of inspection, embody a mingling of different vocabularies and orderings of words, we can, for the sake of description or analysis, speak of "a style" as if it were isolatable. In that sense we can say that "the style" of *Villette* has four component "styles," not to mention other qualities that lie outside these categories. I have identified them by a hasty quartet of terms that are suggestive rather than rigorously glossarial: the neoclassical, the romantic-realistic, the neo-euphuistic, and the surrealistic. These are general directional signs rather than tight-fitting designations of precise areas, for the areas have fuzzy borders.

As a rough area-indicator, *neoclassical* is one of several compatible terms that partly overlap. The others are *eighteenth century* and *Johnsonian*, and I have used the unmechanical, elegant Austen version of this mode as a mirror for aspects of Brontë style. One aspect is the plentiful dialogue, generally spirited, sometimes witty, ironic, and even epigrammatic. Another aspect of it is the abstract, analytical, Latinate vocabulary, which may appear in extensive personification, in generalized diction (sometimes vague when we crave specification), and occasionally in an accumulation of polysyllables that seem bookish or even laughable. Here is a touch of the Johnsonian, as there is in the highly ordered syntax that Brontë uses even more frequently than Austen does—series, parallelism, and balanced structure, especially when materials can be shaped antithetically. Yet to some elements of this mode Brontë can give an unexpected turn. Her personifications can move from a pallid presence of disembodied universals, sonorous and decorous, into an embodiment of feelings and moods in tense situations; capitals may reveal passion rather than announce vast polite conceptions; and convention may give way to thematic drama, as when Reason is made a "hag" and Imagination a firm but friendly liberator. Again in her use of a highly organized syntax she is generally less intent upon systematic ordering than she is spontaneously finding an outer form for urgent and pressing emotions that express themselves in repeated blows. Her instinctive end is not logical control but direct realization, not distance but immediacy.

But even while moving ahead, as it were, from the mode I have called the neoclassical, Brontë also makes considerable use of the pre-neoclassical, the Renaissance euphuism which, purged of its worst excesses, would reappear in the Johnsonian. Of Brontë's surprising neo-euphuism, the most visible sign is a device that she uses more frequently than any fictionist since Lyly and Lodge—alliteration. In her hands it may be overly conspicuous or subtle enough to elude casual inspection. It combines with the Latinate vocabulary, the constant parallelism in sentence structure, the less realistic similes, and some drawing on the animal world to produce a Lylyism purified of its original remorseless insistence. The proto-euphuists' aims, order and ornament, have become in Brontë force and spectacle, pressure and special effects (as they say in cinema); that is, a denial of the casual, the expected, the unemphatic. Hence the rhetorical and exclamatory, apostrophe and invocation, occasional archaism, and very frequent inversion.

While in using older mechanisms Brontë characteristically gave them a new role and new life, she innovated in a still more striking way: she moved into, and was remarkably at home in, a quite different style which I have called the *realistic-romantic*. The rationale of this joint term is that both components, incompatible though they may seem, depart from neoclassical habits. By *realistic* I mean achieving, through specifics, the solid palpable presence of things; by *romantic* I mean a language of confidence in the subjective (the emotional and the intuitive) rather than a language pursuing a theoretical "reason" and "nature" (what Imlac called, in voicing an age's commitment to them, "general properties and large appearances"). Brontë's verbal tools include the conceptual vocabulary of tulip-hood, but they are subordinate to all the devices that "number"— that is, observe, present—the streaks of the tulip, which may be the physical reality of persons and things, or the concretely communicable movements of heart and psyche. Brontë has excellent sensory tools for a realization of particularities that is anything but Augustan; she has a good auditory and tactile sensitivity, and an excellent eye for colors and lines and their tonal qualities, for details that create exteriors, interiors, and persons. Scenes range from the ordinary presented in a utilitarian way to the extraordinary bordering on the visionary, persons from every-day types to more complex individuals in whom she detects discords and even paradox, and to the outright grotesque. Similes and metaphors abound; she can use the latter as instruments of thought, notably in the Napoleon chapter which develops an extended metaphor with a unique fullness.

The *surrealistic*—the remarkable fourth of the identifiable styles—is the use of realistic means (essentially sensory specifics) for the realizing of events and scenes so perceived as to make us uncertain of their objective reality. The streaks are all there, albeit unusually arranged and combined, and some of them strange in themselves, so that we may not be sure whether the object is a tulip, an unknown species, or an illusion. In such passages the writer resembles the "possessed artist" that we see in Malcolm Lowry.

I have summarized the ingredients of the Brontë style partly for convenience but mostly to provide a final compact picture of a rare achievement. The most conspicuous qualities are range and variety. As for the substyles that she unites, she may use the traditional ones in a standard way, but she characteristically pushes toward the best possibilities of each, and toward an innovative employment of them. She fluctuates between different poles that one hardly expects to find in the same stylistic world: between the sometimes pedantic and the poetic, between the carefully pictorial and the frenetic, between an impulse for organization and an enthusiasm (in the older and larger sense that made the quality seem a dangerous aberration to an age-of-reason sensibility) that implies a rupture of and with the usual ordering of things. Though she can use certain devices regularly enough to make them seem like habits or mannerisms, there is little, if any, monotony; there is always individuality, but not tedious idiosyncrasy. Though her basic polytonal manner is a dominant virtue, there are moments of especial stylistic effectiveness when combinations of disparate methods brilliantly complete a portrait or present a theme or event. Finally there are passages where the excellence eludes identification by the methods I have used here. We are simply aware of an exact, fitting, highly evocative language, in phrases or complete predications, that is exciting and satisfying.

Insofar as the style is the man, and hence the writer, in this rich style we can see a writer of greater magnitude than one easily imagines derived from life in Haworth (and an interlude in Brussels). Clearly nineteenth-century life in a distant village was not so stifling as some of our contemporaries need to think.

■ 16 ■
Silas Marner: The Explicit Style

i

I FIRST READ *Silas Marner* in high school—I believe about 1921. In the intervening years I have read nearly all the rest of George Eliot's fiction, and I share the common belief that she is one of the great English novelists, the novelist, above all, in whom liveliness of sensibility and steadiness of imagination are accompanied by exceptional vigor of mind. Yet as the adult reads, studies, perhaps teaches *Adam Bede, Mill on the Floss, Romola, Middlemarch, Daniel Deronda,* and even *Felix Holt,* he acts a little as if *Silas Marner* did not exist. He may tell a class that after *The Mill on the Floss* (1860) Eliot "relaxed with *Silas Marner* (1861), which you have all read in high school," and exchange a little smile with the knowing. It is as if, like masques, or didactic couplets, or the fiction of Henry Mackenzie, *Silas Marner* had passed from serious memory on some irrefutable turning of the wheel of history. Why? Doubtless it seems so surely to belong to a past world—the world of the *Idylls, Marmion, Ivanhoe,* and *The Vicar of Wakefield*—that we know it can have no meaning for grown-ups now. We have put off childish things. And even to look back inquiringly may betray a touch of that nostalgia that the alert middle-ager knows is a danger.

Before returning to *Silas Marner* in 1956, I found myself puzzling as to what the book would now appear to be. A high-school text, morally commendable, but without literary merit? Ethically top-heavy? The embodiment of a worldview no longer tenable, enshrined (or petrified) in the curriculum by a dated taste? The children's book that somehow drew upon only a fraction of the artist's powers? The slipup or the soft spot or the tired year from which no great writer is safe? Or perhaps a kind of classic grown stale through custom and compulsion? Or, even, an unappreciated piece of Gulliver-art with two faces: the obverse that is the candid fable for children and all readers of simplicity; and the reverse, as complex as *Middlemarch,* somehow undetected? It seemed hardly likely. But with these possibilities in mind I came to the text. I finished that text with a double sense: with a sense, first, of the obvious appropriateness of *Silas Marner* in the canon of secondary school read-

230

ings; second, and more interestingly, with a sense of a deeper, less apparent appropriateness. In fact, if I wanted to push the latter point into its most provoking form, I should say that, despite my full advance marshaling of possible responses to my return to Raveloe, I was still unprepared to find a book in many ways so mature in the curriculum at all. I wondered if a cultural historian might find that at some time in the past our society was better prepared for such a choice than it would be now. Not that *Silas Marner* is of the stature of Eliot's major works; in estimating it we must also note the artistic choices that withhold something from its potential greatness.

We need not spend much time on the evident reasons *Silas Marner* should go well with younger readers certain traits of "popular literature" which, in making for "good reading," may garnish greatness or junk. Relatively short, it does not make too long a claim on the attention; the variety of characters and actions helps forestall boredom; there is a certain melodramatic accessibility about the villains William Dane and Dunstan Cass, though Dunstan is a more seriously examined piece of humanity; the mystery easily raises the suspense needed by all narrative, and this is aided by some adroit shifts in point of view; for all of the somber sense of human destiny (for example, Eliot's observation on the ways of "men and women who reach middle age without the clear perception that life never *can* be thoroughly joyous," chapter 17), the view of Raveloe life has much of the idyllic, the justice is "poetic," and the ending "happy." And finally, words and actions advance in an atmosphere of easy clarity. The symbolism—for the story does not lack symbols—is not esoteric: golden hair is the clue to the Eppie-gold equation which enables a reader, even a young one, I believe, to sense Silas's miserliness as a perverted love, and his love as a new human currency growing out of the older material one.

ii

Eliot overtly points to meanings of this kind (14; all references are to chapters). She is one of the most regular practitioners of the Explicit Style. And to use such a term as *Explicit Style* is to suggest how far removed we are from the ornamentalism of euphuistic style and the rich minglings of style (neoclassical, neo-euphuistic, romantic-realistic, and surrealistic) that appear in Charlotte Brontë's work. The very term *Explicit Style,* aside from denoting a practice different from various literary traditions, inevitably raises an interesting literary question, indeed the same question implied in a comparable critical term, *poetry of statement.* The question concerns the level or range of literary achievement possible to the Explicit Style. While I do not challenge a principal assumption of critical practice, that the implicit, the indirect, the oblique, the understated, and the half-revealed are the clues to stylistic artistry, nevertheless it is possible for us, in our understandable shrinking from the banalities of sentimental and commercial stereotypes that press in from all sides, to undervalue the Explicit Style, which, as a historical fact, did not frighten writers nearly so much before the development of mass communications since 1920. The Explicit may be an element of strength, a kind of structural framework for the stylistic design, granted, of course, that it is not the only recourse of a writer. The mastery of implication, the ability to take off figuratively, the freedom to force every individuality into style—all these must be there in the first place; the more conspicuous they are, as for instance in Meredith, the more valuable the support of the Explicit. Not that the Explicit, even in Eliot, is always a virtue. It can shrink into gratuitous restatement, the affixing of labels and price tags, and ethical kibitzing, and can thus become a secondary text, a heavy-pointed braille for those who have eyes and see not.

Let us see precisely what Eliot does with style. Her Explicit may decline into a familiar rhetoric of ethical exposition: "[Godfrey] had let himself be dragged back into mud and slime" (3); or into a mildly superior editorializing: "And Dunstan's mind was as dull as the mind of a possible felon usually is" (4); or into a somewhat platitudinous aphorism: "Just and self-reproving thoughts do not come to us too thickly" (12) and "no disposition is a security from evil wishes to a man whose happiness hangs on duplicity" (13); or into an avoidable specification that overextends the distance between reader and subject: "these rural forefathers, whom we are apt to think very prosaic figures" (3); or into a figure that labors a little more than it illumines: "For joy is the best of wine, and Silas's guineas were a golden wine of that sort" (5; compare, as a possible alternative: "Silas got drunk on his guineas"). Or the psychological observation may be so fraught with a kind of magisterial insistence that a whole passage, for instance the concluding paragraph on the religion of Chance (9), becomes virtually a sermonette. Other readers will find other places where the word is too unrelentingly fixed on the thing instead of glancing at it freshly and catching it in a quick glimpse.

Yet despite such flaws, Eliot's Explicit makes generally for the strength of *Silas Marner*. When her analysis shades into comment, as it often does, the style is likely to lead to a sharper sense of reality. She is strongly inclined to the generalizing observation that draws the reader into the experience and hence potentially into a deeper self-knowledge. "I suppose one reason why we are seldom able to comfort our neighbors with our words is that our goodwill gets adulterated, in spite of ourselves, before it can pass our lips" (10). "It is seldom that the miserable can help regarding their misery as a wrong inflicted by those who are less miserable" (12). She spots the power-motive that infects conscious good deeds: Godfrey "was not prepared to enter with lively appreciation into other people's feelings counteracting his virtuous resolves" (19); and the exhilaration of evil intentions: Eppie's mother, tired and ailing, was buoyed up for a while by "the animation of a vindictive purpose" (12). To the old idea of work as a narcotic she gives a new specification: it tends, for every man, "to bridge over the loveless chasms of his life" (2). In the portrait of Godfrey (3) the perceptions are often phrased in language of special vitality: he was "equally disinclined to dig and to beg," with its balance of both sound and sense, on the brink of a grim certainty, "he fell back on suspense and vacillation with a sense of repose," with its skillful play upon verbal discords; he had vices "that were no pleasures but only a feverish way of annulling vacancy."

All those passages are Explicit but not trite or flat or obvious; rather they are in a strong, forthright, and yet tempered language, the compelling instrument of a vigorous mind that sees general human truths without falling into truism and that sees originally without striving for novelty. It is almost without mannerism, and yet it does not surrender the difficult conception; it is precise and direct without being blunt, for the acute vision comes with an easy if studious formality that establishes an air of a courteous, sympathetic mingling of detachment and devotion. It reaches distinction through the common. It is a rare style, and if one regards it only for educational purposes, the least he can say is that it is almost ideal to help train young minds. It flies equally from the hackneyed, the precious, the mechanical, the labored, the mawkish, the coy—from the travesties of human communication that have become the conventions of journalism and of radio and television art for the millions.

What can be said of the style has some application to the book as a whole. In a way the actions and characters all belong to the well-lighted realm of the Explicit. Silas, a victim of injustice, becomes a miser but grows into a better and happier man when his love of gold is replaced by his love of Eppie. Ill deeds meet their nemesis: Dunstan is drowned, and Godfrey must suffer a major disappointment in life. Murder will out: Dunstan's theft is discovered, and Godfrey must eventually tell Nancy about his past. Eppie, nurtured on tolerant love, grows up to make the right choice of life and love.

But that is not all; however Explicit the story is, it is never a lesson; though it is open to young minds, it is not limited to the range of young minds, but draws the reader into a mature vision of experience. Hoarding is not pictured simply as a vice; instead, Silas's gold-worship is a dramatic symbolization of the religion of work and materialism that can be recognized also in our own day. Again, *Silas Marner* can be thought of as a love story, but what animates it is a doctrine of love that draws much more deeply, and hence deepeningly, upon the resources of the responding consciousness than does a routine happy ending or even a romantic unhappy outcome. True, there is the rosy marriage at the end; but Eppie is not a Cinderella, capturing a Prince Charming or a plutocrat from the other side of the tracks; she has chosen a working man, and love is identified not with unexpected profits and wish-fulfillment fantasies but with recognition and acceptance of immediate actuality; what begins, as we see from the house symbolism, is not so much a new life, a breakaway, and a shift of loyalties, as it is an enlarging of the old life and love.

It is a view of love not very familiar in our popular art. There is an inconspicuous but real contrast between this "happy marriage" and that of Godfrey and Nancy. Eppie and Aaron merge the past and the present, whereas Godfrey, aided by some extraordinary chances, endeavors to blot out the past and live in an entirely new and clean present; and it is just this cutting off of the past that cuts him off from a future that he might have—that of the living parenthood of Eppie. In Eppie's marriage there is the rejection of certain rewards dangled before her by Godfrey; in Godfrey's marriage, the privation of certain hoped-for satisfactions. At first Godfrey's marriage looks alarmingly like the stereotyped happy outcome; then in a first twist it becomes the image of inevitable human imperfections; finally in a second twist it becomes the kind of "happy marriage" that is possible, with the acceptance of "the lot that's been given us" and Godfrey's discovery that he can give love without dictating its terms: "I must do what I can to make her happy in her own way" (20).

All this is done so plainly and unostentatiously that we may forget how much is being exacted of readers trained in patterns of crooning love-success or sweetly sad losses. But beyond the dramas of love and marriage is the still more demanding treatment of another love that is presented also in two different relationships: Priscilla Lammeter's love for her father, Silas's for his "daughter." In Priscilla the conventional figure of the spinster is sharply altered, for Priscilla contents herself with a devotion that gives character to her life; yet she is not given a sentimental, limited consciousness, for, as we see in one quick glimpse, she is aware of a gap: if her sister Nancy had a daughter like Eppie, says Priscilla, "I should ha' had something young to think of then, besides the lambs and calves" (Conclusion). In Silas's discovery of Eppie there is an ironic echo of literary conventions: the "girl" appears suddenly, and what follows is "love at first sight." But how different is the rest: love arising in a personality that had rejected all affections, the hard cult of things becoming the tender devotion to the human being, and yet a devotion without the specifically sexual element that would be the easiest and most obvious way of bringing about a fuller life; not that Silas's new life is without return to him, but that the nonsexual gratification opens up for the reader a less familiar range of human potential, at the end of which lies the ultimate achievement of *caritas.* For Silas, love is not simply excitement, glamor, the expectable surprise that we count our common due, but something subtler, namely, a transformer of personality; his experience is like rebirth or conversion. This is one treatment of a problem that attracts Eliot in nearly every book—the problem of opening up, thawing out, unhardening the self-walled, the blockaded personality.

iii

Beneath the Explicit surface various undercurrents amplify theme and complicate structure. There is a regular though quiet movement of contrasts and resemblances. Silas and Godfrey are formally contrasted: the miser and the prodigal; the frantic worker and the loose idler; both outside the normal community, one in a too "closed" life, one in a too "open" life; yet both needing love, one to open his life, the other to give it some order. The coldly malicious William Dane and the "spiteful, jeering" Dunstan are similar embodiments of evil, both with resemblances to Iago; yet one flourishes in conventional dissoluteness, the other in stringent piousness; the ill-disposed man works through whatever forms of life his immediate society offers. Besides the poles of chapel and tavern there are poles of rationality and superstition, which appear in standard opposition in the conflicting theories about the robbery of Silas (10), but which, ironically, can move in the same way: the rational Dane accuses Silas of commerce with the devil, and the superstitious in Raveloe suspect him of the same unholy dealings. In Dane, of course, we see the man of calculation archetypally exploiting the superstition of others. He can do it because of a habit of mind that Eliot suggests is almost universal. The parishioners in Lantern Yard cast lots to determine truth; Nancy Lammeter, of far less restricted background, is equally sure that she knows the "will of Providence" (17) and governs her marriage accordingly.

In the plain story of village life Eliot characteristically finds the universal. In Silas's hoarding she finds a relationship that is in the language itself—the relationship between *misery* and *miserliness.* Wretchedness makes the miser; he suffers less from a vice than from a disease, and the disease is the result of an injury ("a trauma," as we now say). Furthermore, we are forced to see the disease as representative rather than unique. Silas is compared with prisoners who fall into a kind of compulsive doodling, with researchers and theorists whose work has become an end in itself (2). And while hoarding goes with Silas's "hard isolation," it is really a substitute for the activities upon which the community rests. The guineas provide Silas's "revelry" (2, 5); he "loved them all," the coins of all sizes; guineas yet to be earned were like "unborn children" (2); his piety was the "worship of gold" (5). Here were his play, love, parenthood, religion.

These sharp images are characteristic of the style in the chapters on Silas, where Eliot writes most suggestively and allusively, often figuratively, sometimes symbolically; it is Silas who most stirs her imagination and calls forth a language that keeps our sense of the secondary constantly active. When she describes Silas's class of "pallid undersized men," her words also give us a picture of a pale, restricted life without growth. When Silas, robbed, is compared to "a man falling into dark waters" (5), it is as if a movie camera were switching us for a split second to the literal dark waters into which Dunstan is falling. When she tells us that Silas's "face and figure shrank and bent themselves into a constant mechanical relation to the objects of his life" (2), she introduces the theme of the mechanical life which she then develops by various images, for instance, of Silas "deafened and blinded more and more to all things except the monotony of his loom and the repetition of his web" (14). He is variously compared to a spider, to an ant, to an insect, to a "gnome or brownie," as if, though alive, he were less than human. His life is imaged in terms of space: he is shut "close up with his narrow grief," his heart "as a locked casket" (10); he had "shrunk continually into narrow isolation," into "close-locked solitude," thinking in an "ever-repeated circle," his soul "stupefied in a cold, narrow prison" (14). Silas's life is dark as well as cramped, and the first image of restrictedness is nicely joined with a light image: "The little light he possessed spread its beams so narrowly, that frustrated belief was a curtain broad enough to create for him the blackness of night" (2). The "light of his faith" was "put out" (5). His gold was "hidden away from the daylight" (14); there was a "dark shadow over the days of his best years" (16).

These constant figures build up a picture of Silas's gold-period as deficient in variety, vitality, spaciousness, illumination. These examples of Eliot's more packed, suggestive style are matched by other imaginative resources—the inconspicuous parallels in the action, the ways of presenting Silas's aloofness, the changes in Silas's eyes and sight, the concepts of "mystery" and "dream" that she draws on repeatedly, and the important theme of the hidden life. There is, of course, least indirection and most of the full frontal attack in the chapters on Raveloe life (5, 7, 8, 10, 11). Despite dashes of a fine Austen-like humor that laces these scenes, they are likely to become overextended, and we to dismiss them as the product of a dated unthrifty craftsmanship. Yet this dismissal would be partly wrong, for the village-life chapters have a function: they portray the nature of the community from which Silas has been cut off and which he rejoins. Though Eliot interprets this return as a spiritual gain, she will not idealize or sentimentalize community life; so she characterizes it very carefully, at times too carefully.

It is in the last third of the story that Eliot goes farthest beyond the literal Explicit and moves toward intricacy and even richness. As Eppie's life "unfolded," Eliot writes, "his soul, . . . was unfolding, too, and trembling gradually into full consciousness" (14). "Unfolding"—the escape from the closed-in narrowness of which there are many images. "Trembling"—responding, vibrating; the opposite of the monotonous movements of his mechanical life. "Full consciousness"—complete use of the powers of perception, knowing, and feeling. In the first place, opening one's heart to a person rather than a material object. At the same time, acknowledging and taking part in the life of other human beings: reentering the community. Beyond this, full consciousness means his reentry into religious faith, which is the final way of defining the community. He is no longer "cut off from faith and love" (2); Dolly leads him to the doctrine of "trustening" (16); he learns that to make a judgment of God and flee to harsh solitude is not the best way to deal with evil in the world. Community, love, faith: these are different phases of a unitary experience.

Finally, full consciousness has a temporal aspect: Silas, once cut off from past, present, and future, begins to "blend" his "old faith" and his "new impressions, till he recovered a consciousness of unity between his past and present" (16). So he sets out with Eppie to probe the past in terms of the new life, to seek some accord between them; but even though he is now reexperiencing an old habit of feeling, and hence a valuable continuity in life, the old order to which the feeling was attached remains in some ways inaccessible. Chapter 21, the story of Silas's quest, is filled with types of images which we have already seen are important in the story, and which now resolve certain themes. Silas wants to see his old pastor, "a man with a deal o' light," and Dolly encourages his search for "any light to be got up the yard." But the enlightenment that might be the conventional outcome of the story does not take place: Silas finds the old events still "dark" and likely to be "dark to the last." Mysteries that have to do with the nature of evil are not easily solved, and they must be lived with. Eliot chooses Dolly to complete the meaning in terms of the dark-light pattern: some things are dark, she says, some are not; Silas cannot know the "rights" of the evil acts against him; "but that doesn't hinder there *being* a rights, Master Marner, for all it's dark to you and me." Having sought a light that could not be found, Silas now sees formally what the answer is: since "I've come to love" Eppie, "I've had light enough to trusten by." Love and faith: the light that can be set against the dark of evil.

Again Eliot uses her established imagery to comment on Silas's old religion. The place ironically called "Lantern Yard" was near Prison Street, and it is the "grim walls of the jail" that "cheered" Silas with a sense of being at home; Eppie calls the neighborhood a "dark, ugly place"; they come to a "narrow alley," and Eppie feels "like I was stifled." Having thus suggested the darkness and narrowness of the old faith, Eliot unostentatiously pulls her masterstroke: where the chapel once was, a factory stands. Behind the shock we feel a continuity: the chapel religion, from which Silas fled to a fanatic industriousness, was itself more like grinding toil than a freeing of the spirit. Though it once did give Silas a "life of belief and love" (2), his very separation from it prepared the way for what Eliot makes clear is a better meeting of human needs.

Suddenly in the latter part of the book images of a new kind shine out to tell us something more about Silas's new life. In the presence of a child's calm, Eliot says, troubled adults "feel a certain awe . . . such as we feel before some quiet majesty or beauty in the earth or sky—before a steady glowing planet, or a full-flowered eglantine, or the bending trees over a silent pathway" (13). This passage introduces the images from nature that Eliot henceforth regularly calls on to help define the Eppie-world; in chapters 14 and 16 and the Conclusion there is much of the fresh beauty of flowers and of the joy of gardening. The gentle and yet strong note of new life in the Conclusion comes right after the Lantern Yard chapter, with its dominant note of stifling urban gloom—a contrast of the kind that D. H. Lawrence was to use more than once. Yet there is another contrast borne by the nature imagery itself. For Silas has been described as "withered and yellow" (2), as "feeling the withering desolation of . . . bereavement" and having a "withered and shrunken . . . life," and as having, in his isolation from the "fountains of . . . love," a "soul [which] was still the shrunken rivulet" (10). Yet even "in this stage of withering . . . the sap of affection was not all gone" (2), even though there must be "many circulations of the sap before we detect the smallest sign of the bud" (7). When, then, Silas yearns for Eppie and she finally chooses him by pulling at his "withered cheek" (13), we see the end of a spiritual drought and the beginning of fertile spiritual life.

Silas's return to full consciousness, to full human nature, includes an at-homeness in the world of nature. His conversion takes place in Raveloe, "aloof from the currents of industrial energy and Puritan earnestness" (3), its "orchards looking lazy with neglected plenty" (2). Another writer might have brought Silas to rest simply in a physically comfortable humanism or an all-solacing naturalism without problem or question. But Eliot is unwilling to reduce life to naturalistic certitudes, to such explanations and finalities as are provided by society and the natural world. Much mystery remains. Evil is not accounted for, or theorized away; in the end, faith is exacted. And if the wrongdoing against Silas remains always somewhat outside rational explanation, so does the blessing of his life; Eppie's coming is a mystery to Silas, and it always remains so. His catalepsy, too, is a little more than an ailment to be accounted for by the rules of pathology; it remains mysterious, and becomes something of a symbol of his openness to special experience—his vulnerability to harm and his receptiveness to a new good. The good comes on New Year's Eve: the old order changeth. We are told early in the book (2), and often reminded, that the "great change" in Silas's life took place in the Christmas season: a little child came to bring love into his world. Delicately, and yet compellingly, Eliot brings in the suggestion of an ancient mystery. So the story makes a quiet addition to the naturalism which partly fixes its direction, picturing a life that rests both upon an accommodation to nature and upon a metaphysical faith.

iv

I do not wish to overcomplicate a "simple story," in which, in both word and action, there is so much openness and transparency, so much of what I call the Explicit; but it is important for the appreciation of it to recognize the presence of elements that, because of the author's technical unostentatiousness and her easy articulation of the parts, may elude us. Eliot at once gives a sense of life and writes a quiet philosophic novel. To what extent the qualities I find in it could be made available to a high-school audience, if one still exists, I do not know. But I will say two things about the *Silas Marner* that I have pictured. One: it is a work for which teachers could have high respect. Two: the book would be a good one for students to experience, by way of what it does for training their imagination, giving them a mature, untouched-up view of experience. Something of this must rub off on them, must mold their taste a little. To sense its value I have only to think of the professional writers of "juveniles" who "know what the kids want" and who can spice it up with pungent mixtures of topical terrors (The Bomb) to bitter-coat the do-good-ism or get-on-ism.

Silas Marner is not a great book; yet it is a classic. It is not great because it is not, to use Aristotle's words, of sufficient magnitude; Eliot almost writes in shorthand; Silas is sketched rather than done in depth like the leads in *Mill on the Floss* and *Middlemarch*. Take for an example the significant episode of the breaking of the brown water pitcher near the end of chapter 2, reported quickly in a single paragraph of less than a hundred words rather than fully dramatized. There is a certain promptness about Dunstan's disasters, Godfrey's wife's death; a certain lack of difficulty in Eppie's choice between two fathers. Yet virtually all the episodes have what we must call authenticity. William Dane may verge on the melodrama villain, Godfrey and Nancy's childlessness on the pat, yet there is a basic rightness in the vignette of unscrupulous calculation and in the fable of retribution. Eliot gets the essence of the thing, not in a measured series of camera angles, but in one brief, even blunt, shot. And that is why we may call her work classic. She goes to the heart, discarding the fictional completeness of structure through which the artist rises to grandeur. There is an allegoric foreshortening as in *Pilgrim's Progress*. Perhaps today we underrate the allegorical—the abstracting impulse which always, even in the doctrinaire naturalists, modifies the full representation of experience; which may at worst thin out reality into schematic patterns; but which may seize boldly on the vital centers and draw them quickly into the life of art. This last is what happens, I suggest, in *Silas Marner*.

The Muddled and the Masterful:
Style in *The Mayor of Casterbridge*

i

SIGHING ABOUT HARDY'S STYLE is a fairly old game among critics of the novel, and one could make quite an anthology of despairing and witty observations about Hardy's ways with words. One could make an early start with Lascelles Abercrombie and Arthur Symons and come on through George Moore to Pierre d'Exideuil and Katherine Anne Porter and Albert Guérard, who once made an informal collection of head-shaking regrets over the way Hardy wrote. Instead of being simply con-demnatory, however, most critics tend to note the contradiction between the general air of quality in Hardy's work and the frequent ineptitude of the style. There is a prevailing sense of such doubleness in Hardy, of the problematic failure of his work to be all of a piece. Morton Zabel entitles his *Southern Review* essay "The Aesthetics of Incongruity"; Guérard entitles a chapter "Conflicting Impulses" and speaks of "radical uneven-ness"; Virginia Woolf observes the discrepancy between "lumpishness" and "vision" in Hardy. She approaches the Hardy duality in another way when she remarks that "at his greatest, he gives us impressions; at his weakest, arguments." Likewise, D. H. Lawrence insists that as a meta-physician Hardy makes "a poor show" and adds, "His feeling, his in-stinct, his sensuous understanding is, however, apart from his meta-physics, very great and deep."

The general subject that we touch on is the singular Hardian dis-cord—be it the discord between *penseur* and artist, between superiority of achievement and only too obvious flaws in the instruments used, be-tween different artistic tools, between inconsistent uses of such a tool as style. In perspective and workmanship Hardy is highly variable. He can shift without warning from selfless narrator to obtrusive lecturer-dem-onstrator, from skillful manager of a tight and tense story to apparently inattentive chaperon of a lethargic and wandering tale, from hands-off presenter of narrative effects to oversolicitous explainer of what is going on, from stage manager of shilling-shocker surprises and improbabilities to tediously inclusive recorder of the ordinary. An understanding of Hardy's art means a constant awareness of such diversities. This habitual incongruity of methods appears in his style, which, sometimes with-in a single paragraph, can waver between the fluent and the cumber-some, the limber and the muscle-bound. Hardy is all of a piece by being, in so many different ways, not all of a piece. By the criterion of style, he is several men.

Hence Virginia Woolf's remark is understandable: "No style in liter-ature, save Scott's, is so difficult to analyze." The comparison with Scott is a happy one, for Scott and Hardy, different as they are in sense of reality, do a number of things alike. Compare "who remained convulsed on the carpet in the paroxysms of an epileptic seizure" and "quivering with the last convulsions of muscular motion." These might have been written by the same man: the ponderousness, alliteration, and redun-dancy are identical. The former is from *The Mayor of Casterbridge* (39; all references are to chapters), the latter from *The Bride of Lammer-moor*. But Hardy and Scott resemble each other not only in the qualities revealed in these passages; they resemble each other still more notably in the divergencies within their stylistic practices. Since these divergen-cies can be described, the style of neither is so "difficult to analyze" as Mrs. Woolf supposed. Sometimes Scott writes in a direct, pictorial, im-agistic fashion that leads to great concreteness of effect; at other times he is verbose, polysyllabically abstract, and periphrastic in a way that comes close to parodying the academic. In Hardy there is a comparable split, but there are additional complications. For if Hardy can at times write like a pedant, he can also write like an ignoramus or an illiterate, like a mature ironic observer, like an inventory clerk, like a man of great original imagination, like a reader of inferior literature, like a man with no ear, like a man of very fine ear, and, in Woolf's phrase, like a man of vision.

The Mayor of Casterbridge is a copious anthology of Hardy's stylistic variations, and a sketch of these can provide concrete evidence for critics' impressions of Hardy's singular mixture of weaknesses and strengths. I find it useful to employ a familiar handbook terminology, which pro-vides precise technical descriptions of what Hardy does. For instance, subordination—a tool of discrimination somewhat endangered when imitators of Hemingway on the one hand and journalists on the other have symbolically declared the equal value of all things by absolutizing the simple sentence (to which Faulkner's tours de force of subordination by infinite series might be read as an immense jesting reply). But to this way of indicating the complexity of things Hardy comes with an odd simplicity of innocence. In earnestly seeking exactitude or complete-ness he can keep adding modifiers until he has an almost impassable thicket of intertwining phrases or clauses: "While life's middle summer had set its hardening mark on the mother's face, her former spring-like specialities were transferred so dexterously by Time to the second figure, her child, that the absence of certain facts within her mother's knowledge from the girl's mind would have seemed for the moment, to one reflecting on those facts, to be a curious imperfection in Nature's powers of continuity" (3). The reader must study this actively to discover that it means only that since the girl now looks as her mother once did, it is surprising that she is ignorant of some things her mother knows. Aside from finding a remarkably strained way of denoting the resemblance between the two women, Hardy makes up his final clause as follows: three prepositional phrases, a verb, three more prepositional phrases, and then an infinitive right after a *to* phrase.

Hardy has several ways of making a relative clause a painful experience to a reader. The following few words contain a double relative, the second dependent on the first, and a separation of pronoun and antecedent: ". . . into a ravine, where a cottage revealed itself, which he entered" (45). Precisely in the manner of the untutored, he will have an antecedent denote an individual, and the relative the class to which the individual belongs: "The hay-trusser, which he obviously was" (1); "the courtship—which it evidently now was" (43). He has antecedents in the genitive: "nobody filled the Mayor's glass, who still drank . . . water" (5); "It was Henchard's, who stood . . ." (26). He may have an unexpressed antecedent, and impede the meaning by letting some other substantive stand in the place where the antecedent would be expected: ". . . agreed to prepare him some breakfast for a trifling payment, which was done" (2). Hardy continually puts his subordinate thought, especially one with the function of temporal modifier, into a main clause, and his principal thought into a *when* clause: "One day Elizabeth-Jane was passing the King's Arms, when she saw some people bustling in and out more than usual when there was no market" (31), with a second *when* clause to compound the discomfort. Or, in a sentence that should be compound, he may use a *when* clause that runs counter to all expectation: "The creditors . . . looked at the watch, and at the money, and into the street; when Farmer James Everdene of Weatherbury spoke" (31). It is constructions of this kind that elementary lessons in composition try to eliminate.

Hardy subordinates so regularly by means of participles and gerunds that at best there is a simple excess of *-ing* words. Aside from the tediousness, the sheer unprofessionalness, of this, Hardy rarely manages a nonfinite verb phrase without some identifiable clumsiness. In "While they were sitting, the door of the Council Chamber standing open, they heard . . ." (37), the awkward juxtaposition of *sitting* and *standing* is a matter that he characteristically does not notice.

He uses absolute constructions frequently, but not often smoothly. In ". . . the muff, such an article being by no means small at that time" (29), he combines the absolute with the periphrasis and the denial of the affirmative that are habitual with him. As the substantive in the absolute construction he often uses *it*, which seems a slight vessel for the freight it is asked to carry: "it being that motionless hour of rustic daily life" (2); "It being now what the people called the 'pinking in' of the day" (29); "it never occurring to him that" (36).

Though at times he uses a genitive with a gerund, often he does not: "At Elizabeth-Jane mentioning how greatly Lucetta . . ." (29); "a convenience in Lucetta arriving first" (30). His experience in putting asunder grammatical elements that long usage has joined together enables him to effect a remarkable separation of elements within an absolute construction: "In this cottage he occupied a couple of rooms, Jopp, whom Henchard had employed, abused, cajoled, and dismissed by turns, being the householder" (31). Not only is "Jopp . . . being the householder" a clumsy way of denoting ownership, the remarkable isolation of *Jopp* must make all readers, on first seeing the sentence, suspect a typo of major proportions. In his description of the Three Mariners as "somewhat difficult to reach on account of there being but this narrow way" (6), the awkwardness is due to the "there being," the heavy compound preposition, and the alliteration. Finally, we can note Hardy's account of a tense moment in the Henchard-Farfrae wrestling match: "Then Farfrae tried to get hold of the other side of Henchard's collar, which was resisted by the larger man exerting all his force in a wrenching movement" (38). In the relative clause we have not only the ambiguous reference of *which*, the use of the nominative with the gerund, and the awkward repetition of -*ing* words, but, most notably, a passive voice that runs counter to the activeness required by the subject matter. These sentences, then, lead us on from problems of gerunds to other sources of maladroitness—passive voice, cacophony, the management of prepositions. Later we will document these a little more amply.

First, however, a final note on Hardy's use of nonfinite verbs. He says that Elizabeth "could not herself account for it [her attraction to the sea] fully, not knowing the secret possibly to be that, in addition to early marine associations, her blood was a sailor's" (42). Here the awkwardness centers in the heavy prediction based on an infinitive that belongs to Latin rather than English idiom. But at least the participle *knowing* is clearly related to the substantive it modifies, whereas in Hardy dangling participles (and other modifiers) are so frequent that he might be suspected of believing them elegantly insouciant. Some sentences contain somewhere the noun modified, as in "Two farmers met . . . and being quite near the window their remarks could be heard" (23), but Hardy is capable of putting a participle into solitary confinement, with no possible affiliate present in the sentence (or even a neighboring sentence): "Standing in the middle of the arena at that time there by degrees became apparent its real vastness" (11). Or the noun may be in one sentence, and the modifying participle in the next: after noting that Henchard was stopped from talking to Lucetta when she closed her door, Hardy continues in the next sentence, "While pausing the old constable came up" (27). Though such wrenches of structure do not always produce such wrenches of meaning, elliptical clauses with *while* nearly always betray Hardy into dangling constructions (there are actually three of these in chapter 38: "while pausing," "while doing," "while leaning"). There are dangling constructions with perfect participles ("having . . . lost," 31; "embittered," 43), with gerunds ("On hearing," 22; "in doing," 35), with prepositional phrases ("Like all people . . . lightheartedness seemed," 14), and with a plain adjective: "Rigid in this position, more and more words fell successively upon her ear" (35).

Hardy's ungainly handling of subordination appears even in prepositional phrases. He anticipates Dreiser in hitting on cumbersome prepositions. Of the "mask" on Lucetta's house Hardy says that it "suggested one thing above all others as appertaining to the mansion's past history" (21). Equally laborious is his way of saying that only one barn door is open: "The barn . . . was closed save as to one of the usual pair of doors facing them" (29). He may fail to keep prepositional phrases parallel: "this state of things was not so much owing to . . . the landlord's neglect, as from the lack of a painter" (6); or may make parallel a prepositional and a verbal phrase: "either through shyness, or not to disturb his mercantile mood, he avoided . . ." (24).

In such ways Hardy impedes normal forward movement. His roadblock effects may be caused by the passives that take over periodically: "and from any point a view was obtained of the country round" (16). Here the passive causes the separation of elements that, we have seen, is often troublesome. A more remarkable separation is this: "He, in the meantime, festering with indignation at some erroneous intelligence of Farfrae's opposition to the scheme for installing him in the little seedshop, was greeted" (34). An inversion, though it does not cloud the meaning, may hold things up simply by its conspicuousness: "the green door opened, and through came, first Farfrae, and at his heels Lucetta" (33); "Grower nearly ate the end of his quill-pen off, so gnawed he it during the silence" (37). Hardy is careless about the position of modifiers. In "Henchard did not care to ride any further with his chattering companions after hearing this sound" (44), we observe not only the sepa-

ration of verb ("did care") and modifier ("after hearing this sound"), but
the placement, at the very end of the sentence, of the action that came
first. Here is a worse example: "she had replied that she would not hear
him say that many times more before it happened, in the resigned tones
of a fatalist" (2). The reader has virtually to go through a process of discarding various intervening verbs before he is sure that *replied* is the one
modified by the final *in* phrase. Hardy makes us pause by ambiguous
reference of pronouns. He spends several sentences telling about dogs
at Weydon Fair and the one that barked at Henchard and watched his
departure: "He was the only positive spectator of the hay-trusser's exit
from the Weydon Fair-field. [New paragraph.] This seemed to accord
with his desire" (2). We read "dog's desire"—until we stop and realize
that this won't do.

One final quotation will sum up this section on Hardy's less happy
ways of arranging words: "She did not divine the ample explanation of
his manner, without personal vanity, that was afforded by the fact of
Donald being the depositary of Henchard's confidence in respect of his
past treatment of the pale, chastened mother who walked by her side"
(14). Though not a long sentence, this almost needs translation, for it
includes an unusually large number of the practices that we have been
observing independently: ambiguously placed modifier, separation of
antecedent and relative, long succession of phrases (including five *of*
phrases), a second relative clause depending on a first, nominative modifier of gerund, ungainly preposition ("in respect of"). If this section has
been a long one, it is simply that on virtually every page Hardy falls into
one or more of the bumbling practices that drive readers to use such
words as *awkward* and *gauche*. It would of course be pedantic to insist
that any such practice to which we can give a name (say, *dangling modifier*) is always fatal or always bad; the point is rather that the combination
and frequency of these practices are the source of the discomfort that
many readers have felt. Or again, the difficulty lies in Hardy's own style
of departure from the norms of style. When he separates elements that
ordinarily we expect to find together, it is not the separation which any
knowing writer may make for precision, emphasis, or variety; rather he
seems to have fallen into discontinuity through sheer inability (or unwillingness) to arrange effectively the various qualifications of meaning
that a given narrative point stirs up in his mind. It is as though he were
riding a by no means dashing, but extremely perverse and willful, horse,
which he has little control over, but which at its own irrationally changing pace, with its slovenly or stiff-jointed gait, and by its own circuitous
route eventually takes him into the general neighborhood of his destination.

ii

There is of course another side to the story. Insofar as style has to do with arrangement of words, Hardy can also be direct, fluent, unembarrassed. This is how he tells of Henchard's first trip to Casterbridge: "Then he said he would search no longer, and that he would go and settle in the district which he had had for some time in his mind. Next day he started, journeying south-westward, and did not pause, except for nights' lodging, till he reached the town of Casterbridge, in a far distant part of Wessex" (2). Here he has control of the plain, lucid manner that comes down from Bunyan and Swift; there are subordinated and interpolated elements, but they are not obtrusive. He can combine description with narration in an ordered series: "The man stretched his elbows forward on the table, leant his face upon his arms, and soon began to snore" (1). After an initial predication he can add a characteristic descending train of modifiers without letting them collapse into a muddled heap: "He cursed himself like a less scrupulous Job, as a vehement man will do when he loses self-respect, the last mental prop under poverty" (40). Indeed he can occasionally develop this kind of sentence at greater length and still maintain *lucidus ordo*, with no word "feeling" out of place as his words often do: "The Scotchman seemed hardly the same Farfrae who had danced with her and walked with her in a delicate poise between love and friendship—that period in the history of a love when alone it can be said to be unalloyed with pain" (25).

He can combine a series of modifiers and an inverted word order without confusion or loss of force: "Melancholy, impressive, lonely, yet accessible from every part of the town, the historic circle was the frequent spot for appointments of a furtive kind" (11). He can place before his grammatical subject a series of appositives and their modifiers, one of them fairly elaborate, without at all losing track of relationships or direction: "A street of farmers' homesteads—a street ruled by a mayor and corporation, yet echoing with the thump of the flail, the flutter of the winnowing-fan, and the purr of the milk into the pails—a street which had nothing urban in it whatever—this was the Durnover end of Casterbridge" (14). Though Hardy tends to be more at ease with sensory materials, as in his account of the Durnover street, he can also keep under control a fairly ample analytical statement: "But she seemed so transubstantiated by her change of position, and held out her hand to him in such cool friendship, that he became deferential, and sat down with a perceptible loss of power" (25). Finally, one sentence in which parallel main clauses strongly build up the desired effect: "The hams at the top of the poles dripped watered smoke in the form of a brown liquor, the pig shivered in the wind, the grain of the deal tables showed through the sticking tablecloths, for the awning allowed the rain to drift under at its will, and to enclose the sides at this hour seemed a useless undertaking" (16). Yet here an admirably ordered sentence falls off at the end when Hardy's arrangement lets the second infinitive seem, though it is not, parallel with the first: we tend to read, "allowed rain to drift . . . and to enclose. . . ."

It might be possible to quote as many examples of successful sentences as of clumsy and troublesome ones. But a statistical solution, if possible, is not appropriate. In the end it is difficult to escape from the taste and judgment of the critic, and my impression, for what it is worth, is that in Hardy the cumbersome, at least in its impact, somewhat outweighs the fluent and well ordered. If this is correct, it justifies the more ample representation of the former. But the more extensive demonstration of the unsatisfactory is due primarily to my desire to classify some habitual Hardy procedures. There is no call for a similar classification of the ways in which Hardy has not run counter to the effective ways of organizing sentences.

iii

In choice of words Hardy's practices are even more divergent than they are in his syntactical arrangements.

First, however, one matter that does not belong strictly to either vocabulary or syntax, but rather to something intermediate, juxtaposition of words. Hardy often writes cacophonously, either in individual phrases— "mortal commercial combat," "nearing evening"—or even in a whole sentence: "Such was the state of things when the current affairs of Casterbridge were interrupted by an event of such magnitude that its influence reached to the lowest social stratum there, stirring the depths of its society simultaneously with the preparations for the skimmington" (37). Aside from the two suchs, the numerous s sounds, the occasional echo of other sounds, there are t and th sounds in twenty-seven of the forty-three words. Sometimes Hardy's careless "ear" appears in meaning as well as sound. When he says that Lucetta "even proceeded to impair the natural presentation" (35), we have to stop and study to find that he means "tried to make herself less good-looking than she was." When he says that "a cursory view from the summit at noon-day was apt to obscure" the "real vastness" of the Roman Ring (11), we pull up short: a "noon-day" view "obscure"? In time we realize that "apt to obscure" is only a rough approximation of "apt not to reveal."

In "He wished to consider his course in a case so serious" (39), Hardy joins cacophony and what Arthur Quiller-Couch called "jargon." Hardy often lapses into this verbal woolliness: "the sanguinary nature of the games" (11), "she fell back in a fainting state" (27). Akin to jargon are his negative periphrases: "No other than such relationship" (1), "two persons not unconnected with that family" (3). Akin to jargon, also, is a habitual use of "seem" as in "seemed to die" (41), the locution by which amateur writers shirk commitment. Even more regularly Hardy uses "could be seen" or "might have been seen" (or "found" or "observed"), jargon substitutes for "was," "stood," "walked" or other direct and active statements. Related to these passives is a kind of phrasing that we think of as "business English," "legalese," or "officialese": "the aforesaid total absence of conversation" (1), "guarantees for the same" (14), "the by-road aforesaid" (40)—among dozens of examples. Other references to earlier events or statements are made in stereotyped phrases that belong to printed forms, inventories, or audits: "of which mention has been made" (1, 38); "the previously recorded episode" (3); and especially "the day which closed as in the last chapter" (45), with its odd merging of book and cosmos.

The common element in these quotations is something indirect, roundabout, formulaic, sometimes verbose, often vague. It is the language of offices and business rather than of art. To contrast it with a quite different Hardy vocabulary, which we will examine later, we may call it "abstract." Hardy has a considerable penchant toward abstraction. It appears in the Latinate words that often steal stage in the text: "refluent," "gibbous," "flexuous," "reviviscent," "laconism." For a dancer's enthusiasm he writes "saltatory intenseness" (44); for a slum, "the *pis aller* of Casterbridge domiciliation" (26). In these at least the meaning is clear. But when Hardy reports that Lucetta "talked up at Elizabeth-Jane invertedly" (22), we must stop to translate "invertedly" by study; we find that Elizabeth is sitting near or behind the head of the sofa on which Lucetta is lying, so that Lucetta's line of sight is "inverted" rather than direct. Hardy is addicted to polysyllables that thicken the air instead of providing a sharper light of precision: "penuriousness of the exhibition" (instead of "poverty of the display"), "peculiarities of reverberation" (instead of "peculiar sounds"), "concatenations of phenomena," "contrarious inconsistencies," which is redundant as well as polysyllabic. The Latinate appears more in idiom than in vocabulary when Hardy says that the interior of the Amphitheater is "emphatic of the absence of every living thing" (35).

In using abstract language Hardy often names or describes a situation instead of solidly presenting it and thrusting us into it as a palpable reality. There is an absence of specification that may be due to carelessness or even to lack of imaginative commitment, as though practice were betraying intention. When Hardy says only that Elizabeth carried to Farfrae his "tray of supper viands," and to her and her mother's room "their simple provisions" (7), he falls short of the effective concreteness that he is capable of. In some of its aspects his presentation of Elizabeth is too abstract to be convincing. He asserts that she "sought further into things than other girls" (4) but presents no dramatic evidence for this. He wants us to believe that she is beautiful and much admired, but in making this claim he can present nothing more plausible than this phrase, "After an unprecedented success one day" (15). Trying to call on the embittered Henchard she "was advised not to intrude that day" (31); the passive, the generality, the absence of an agent make the episode ineffectual. When she does get to see her father and help him out, Hardy says that she "made the room more comfortable, gave directions to the people below" (32)—words that give no clear picture of anything. When Hardy wants to present Elizabeth as a woman of growing cultivation, he can find nothing more definite to say than that her room contained "books, sketches, maps, and little arrangements for tasteful effects" (21). Repeatedly he tells us that she reads, but he never names a book. He usually writes something like this: she "was netting with great industry between the hours which she devoted to studying such books as she could get hold of" (32). Hence the picture of her as a bluestocking fails. Though it is particularly Elizabeth who attracts Hardy into this disembodied style, he can be equally impalpable on other subjects. Henchard and Farfrae hold parties "in celebration of a national event" (16); Farfrae goes to Weatherbury "about some business which he was conducting there" (39).

When he writes like this, Hardy uses a style not much in evidence after Jane Austen and Scott (who, like Hardy, combined it with other modes). Though it is a style that can be made aesthetically effective by consistency and by full exploitation of its potentialities, Hardy rarely makes it so. It seems simply not to cohere with his own best style, but to be present as an anachronism. Hardy looks backward in the use of hyper-Latinism that suggests "the schools" and the discourse of learned clerks. He falls into a parodic or decayed classicism, centering in an awareness of original root meanings that leads to unfamiliar or polysyllabic words. The resultant note is one of abstraction, of separation from tangible actuality; this appears also in the reliance on generalization once considered elegant.

The irony of it is that Hardy is doubly anachronistic: the abstracting habit of mind is not only regressive but also anticipatory. The tendency to submerge the specific in the generic appears not only in Latinism and generality, but also in colorless, cut-and-dried, mechanical, unindividuated phrases and locutions—*ease, nature, state, not unconnected with, seems, could be seen, aforesaid,* and *the same.* Here we have not only "jargon" but an approach to "gobbledygook": language habits that, though not all original with us, have come into great prominence in our day. (Consider the safe, faceless passives of scientific and bureaucratic style.) Hence to call Hardy doubly anachronistic—"in phase" both with obsolete fashions and with fashions hardly born—is not to suggest an odd co-presence of quite divergent mannerisms. What I am getting at, on the contrary, is that there is an underlying unity, with Hardy as connecting link between different manifestations of a single style. That is the abstract, often Latinate, indirect, nonspecific style which leads, with one emphasis, to "Johnsonese" and, with another, to "officialese." It aspires to general propriety; it is reflected in the exorbitant decencies of poetic diction; and in "gobbledygook" itself we may detect, along with self-protectiveness, a debased and insipid quest of decorum. This long-lived mode can, at extreme moments, burst into a kind of pedantic flamboyance. But its normal aspiration is the innocuous: the draping of naked fact and opinion in colorless and undiaphanous syllables. We may call it the quasi-classical, and perhaps remember its far distant ancestry, at least collaterally, in that early fancy flight from the plain and ordinary, the euphuistic.

iv

But, as with virtually every aspect of Hardy's style, what seems ineffective or outright bothersome is only half the story. For a transition from the vagueness of the quasi-classical to something different, let us look at three passages:

> He found the concoction, thus strongly laced, much more to his satisfaction than it had been in its natural state. (1)

> He was bound also to evolve other Terpsichorean figures in respect of door-steps, scrapers, cellar-hatches, church buttresses, and the over-hanging angles of walls which, originally unobtrusive, had become bow-legged and knock-kneed. (9)

> Vice ran freely in and out certain of the doors of the neighborhood; recklessness dwelt under the roof with the crooked chimney; shame in some bow-windows; theft (in times of privation) in the thatched and mud-walled houses by the sallows. (36)

If we translate the first sentence into "When the furmity was strongly laced, he liked it better," we can see how roundabout and wishy-washy most of the sentence is. What stands out in contrast is the direct and vivid phrase "strongly laced." In the second sentence Hardy starts with cumbersome terms and preposition, and his meaning is hardly clear; compare, "He had to invent dance steps to get around door-steps, etc." But once Hardy has got over the heavy-jocose part, he goes into a fine concreteness and ends the sentence with lively images. The third passage is successful throughout. It is true that the key words are all abstractions, but this archaism is counterbalanced in two ways. One is that, by a carefully managed parallel structure, Hardy achieves cumulative force. The other is that the abstractions are carefully matched with concrete specifications—doors, roof with crooked chimney, bow windows, thatched and mud-walled houses. He sets a definite scene, so that words like *vice* seem less like an evasion of a task than an intended generalization of meaning.

These passages, then, introduce the other Hardy style—the concrete style. He is a master of the set description—of the Fair scenes (1, 2), of Casterbridge in different aspects (3, 9, 14), of the two bridges and the people who frequented them (32), of Mixen Lane and its populace (36). Here he exhibits an extraordinary capacity to be conscious of many kinds of details and to find the specific terms that will render them visible, audible, or tangible and thus evoke a lively response from the reader's imagination. When he starts with known things and beings he is most likely to make them concrete; when he starts with ideas, conceptions, and interpretations, the things and beings to which they are applied are likely to remain vague, indefinite, abstract. However, we are less concerned here with such distinctions than with a particular kind of vocabulary. Hardy can give vitality to a scene by a careful image of one minute detail: "They watched individual drops of rain creeping down the thatch of the opposite rick—straw after straw—till they reached the bottom" (14). He can be plain, direct, and exact, as when he describes the remains of a Roman soldier, "found lying on his side, in an oval scoop in the chalk, like a chicken in its shell" (11). He can envisage the moving as well as the stationary; his large movements across landscapes are well known, but less has been said about his images for the movements of body and even face. Lucetta speaks "with a curious mixture of pout and laugh on her face," but Farfrae "did not laugh half a wrinkle" (23). Again, "the mirth-wrinkles left the listeners' faces, and they waited with parting lips" (1). Hardy can be concrete in a fairly conventional way, as in "She went down on her knees, shovel in hand, when the cat overturned the coal-scuttle" (20), or more strikingly, as in "Elizabeth-Jane's bonnet and shawl were pitchforked on in a moment" (24). In a fine original image he imputes motion to a stationary object: the espaliers "had grown so stout, and cramped, and gnarled that they had pulled their stakes out of the ground and stood distorted and writhing in vegetable agony, like leafy Laocoons" (12).

Here the visual is amplified by the kinesthetic. At times it is joined by the auditory: "tawny and yellow leaves skimmed along the pavement, and stole through people's doorways into their passages with a hesitating scratch on the floor, like the skirts of timid visitors" (9). Hardy presents the auditory with considerable variety. Once he follows through the analogies between river sounds and musical sounds: "At a hole in a rotten weir they [the waters] executed a recitative; where a tributary brook fell over a stone breastwork they trilled cheerily; under an arch they performed a metallic cymballing; and at Durnover Hole they hissed" (41). He can get as much detail and variety without using analogy: "there were long spaces of taciturnity, when all exterior circumstance was subdued to the touch of spoons and china, the click of a heel on the pavement under the window, the passing of a wheelbarrow or cart, the whistling of the carter, the gush of water into the householders' buckets at the town-pump opposite; the exchange of greetings among their neighbors, and the rattle of the yokes by which they carried off their evening supply" (26). Though Hardy uses tactile images less frequently, he can present the feel of a thing skillfully: of an atmosphere presaging storms he says that it "felt as if cress would grow in it" and that it "rubbed people's cheeks like damp flannel" (27).

Characteristically, Hardy's imagery is utilitarian, but at times it can kindle into brilliance of an almost surrealist sort. Thus he sets the scene for a twilight interview in the Amphitheater: "The sun was resting on the hill like a drop of blood on an eyelid" (35). Jopp looks at the top of a burning candle that "had formed itself into a head like a red-hot cauliflower" (36). Often Hardy uses imagery to present an idea or feeling energetically: Henchard's past might have been regarded, if the public had long known of it, as a "rather tall wild oat" (31); Henchard's diplomacy was "as wrongheaded as a buffalo's" (17); he feared that he would "sink to the position of second fiddle, and only scrape harmonies to his manager's talents" (16); "a tone of disappointment, so strong as to make itself felt like a damp atmosphere" (7). As several of these passages show, Hardy has humor outside the genre passages where he is mainly credited with it; thus he comments gaily on Elizabeth's elation "at discovering herself akin to a coach" (5). He has, finally, an original suggestiveness, as in "under-handsomeness" and "handsome in the bone" (4),[1] which he hits upon to describe the potential beauty of Elizabeth.

In sum, Hardy's vocabulary ranges widely between two extremes more distant than may be found in most novelists. On the one hand he can describe Elizabeth as "construed by not a single contiguous being" (20); on the other he can call furmity "antiquated slop" (1) or give a fine, unencumbered image of a man in the street talking to a man in a second-story window: "said Henchard upwards" (9). On the one hand there is the quasi-classical; on the other, the direct and the concrete, sometimes managed with almost a folktale artlessness. At his best moments, perhaps, we find him writing in an intermediate style that draws something from both extremes. Here he goes beyond the pictorial, where he is always likely to be sure, and into the analytical, where his hazard is always a plethora of syllables, but where he finds an accuracy and precision that make the style perfectly accommodated to the thought. In sending Elizabeth to interview Henchard, Susan acts with "a half-hearted willingness, a smothered reluctance" (9). Toward Susan, Henchard conducts himself with a "strict mechanical rightness" (13). Henchard and Lucetta can maintain a long silence, for there is "no pressure of half acquaintance to drive them into speech" (25). On Elizabeth's face there is an expression "of nervous pleasure rather than of gaiety" (44). The event that saves Henchard from drowning affects him like an "appalling miracle" (41). In such passages Hardy is not the heavy-footed don, the cautious official, the genre painter, or the folktale narrator. Instead he is a knowing, flexible, accurate, imaginative writer.

Among his excellences—for they nearly always are excellences—are the innumerable allusions, biblical and classical, that extend the relevance of the episodes and the story generally. While these are not always managed with complete effortlessness, they are not characteristically laborious. Indeed, they are unobtrusive enough so that only recently have they been used seriously in explicative criticism. And they are imaginatively accurate enough so that, once spotted as keys to implications, they open up new perspectives on the patterning of the stories—thus, in recent years, the interpretation of *The Mayor* in terms of its analogies with the Saul-and-David and the Cain-and-Abel stories.

v

Hardy's characteristic inconsistency appears, finally, in his style at two opposite poles of the novelist's work. At one he is the omniscient commentator, emphatically present; at the other he disappears as the characters take over in dialogue.

As formal interpreter, Hardy may be obtrusive or unobtrusive (just as he may be awkward or fluent). This is basically a matter of *what* he chooses to say, but sometimes his judgment of relevance appears to fluctuate with his stylistic tact. When he says that Henchard's chairs "were of the kind which, since that day, has cast lustre upon the names of Chippendale and Sheraton, though, in point of fact, their patterns may have been such as those illustrious carpenters never saw or heard of" (10), the cumbersomeness of the statement and the irrelevance of the petulant remark are exactly matched. At other times, however, syntactic orderliness may not prevent a comment from seeming intrusive. Compare these two editorial interjections, both in parallel structure:

> To keep in the rear of opportunity in matters of indulgence is as valuable a habit as to keep abreast of opportunity in matters of enterprise. (14)

> But nothing is more insidious than the evolution of wishes from mere fancies, and of wants from mere wishes. (15)

The former is homiletic and is therefore aesthetically superfluous; the latter is psychological notation, and is therefore a legitimate extension of the narrative proper. Hence the former, neatly ordered though it is, seems official and pompous, while the latter, balanced though it is, is hardly distinguishable from the texture of pure narrative.

Hardy's editorial assertions may be nonnarrative interpolations, may reiterate the statement made by the narrative, or may be ineffective substitutes for the narrative. Even when functionally defensible, they may be either apt or heavy. In noting that Farfrae's success somewhat diminishes his charm for the people, Hardy adds, "Hence the anxiety to keep him from annoyance showed not quite the ardor that would have animated it in former days" (37). Shrewd enough, but the four key words of Latin origin, alliterated and symmetrically arranged, contribute some slight excess of gravity. Compare a partly similar note on motives: "for in such cases we attribute to an enemy a power of consistent action which we never find in ourselves or in our friends; and forget that abortive efforts from want of heart are as possible to revenge as to generosity" (35). Despite the formal balance and the touches of alliteration, the sentence is not protuberant; pace and words seem right to transmit a mature perception. Sometimes, as commentator, Hardy acts with an especially fine, untrimmed despatch: "He was getting on towards the dead level of middle age, when material things increasingly possess the mind" (22).

Problems of style and method (the author's sense of his role) are interwoven in the consideration of Hardy's ex cathedra remarks. In dialogue, however, the matter is one of style alone. For servants, workers, and townspeople generally Hardy writes dialogue that reflects a very good ear—an ear for the idiom (proverbial, imagistic) and for the rhythms of spoken English. All these lines are from one passage (13): "Ay. Where the pigs be many the wash runs thin"; "for I was getting up husband-high at that time"; "such doggery as there was in them ancient days, to be sure"; "She'll wish her cake dough afore she's done of him. There's a bluebeardy look about 'en; and 'twill out in time"; "Stuff—he's well enough! Some folk want their luck buttered. . . . A poor twanking woman like her—'tis a godsend for her, and hardly a pair of jumps or night-rail to her name."

One could quote pages of such talk and come up with scarcely a false note. Hardy's inconsistency in dialogue appears rather in the speech of his principals, who at moments of intensity may speak with a convincing plainness or with an artificially ordered syntax that is gratingly inappropriate. At the bankruptcy hearing Henchard offers his watch and purse to help settle claims, saying, "It all belongs to ye, as much as everything else I've got, and I don't wish to keep it from you, not I. . . . There, now you have all I've got in the world. . . . And I wish for your sakes 'twas more." Farmer Everdene replies, "No, no, Henchard. . . . We don't want that. 'Tis honorable in ye; but keep it. What do you say, neighbors—do ye agree?" (31). The vocabulary, the constructions, and the length of units are right, and the result is a combination of feeling and dignity that avoids equally the bathetic and the high-toned. Hardy often gets a maximum effect out of the simple and compressed. When Henchard is working upon his scheme to beat Farfrae in a fight, he speaks to himself "aloud"—"I'm stronger than he" (38), words that wholly sum up his feeling and his plan. Then he says to Donald, "Now . . . we stand face to face—man to man." Simple and natural as the words are, they communicate the ominousness of a malicious man concealing his physical superiority, meant for murder, behind a façade of ultimate equality.

But just a few lines later Henchard says to Farfrae: "I've stood your rivalry, which ruined me, and your snubbing, which humbled me; but your hustling, that disgraced me, I won't stand!" Hardy has suddenly shifted to an elaborate rhetorical organization that suggests the calculation of public oratory rather than the spontaneity of private feeling. He makes Henchard speak similarly just after, at his command, the choir has played and sung Psalm 109: "But the bitter thing is, that when I was rich I didn't need what I could have, and now I be poor I can't have what I need!" (33). The epigrammatic balance belongs to Hardy rather than Henchard. Again, when Elizabeth rebukes Henchard in her last words to him, Hardy saddles her speech with chiastic balance, with parallel structure, with parataxis, with a complex appositive, and with an intermingling of careful subordinate clauses: "But how can I when I know you have deceived me so—so bitterly deceived me! You persuaded me that my father was not my father—allowed me to live on in ignorance of the truth for years; and then when he, my warm-hearted real father, came to find me, cruelly sent him away with a wicked invention of my death, which nearly broke his heart. O how can I love as I once did a man who has served us like this" (44). This is a written style that used to appear, and perhaps still does, in Sunday school plays.

Thus in one direction Hardy veers from the live spoken language to devices of traditional rhetoric that are related to what we have called his "quasi-classical" manner. In another direction he veers toward a flat, mechanically organized language of a journalistic cast. At their first meeting after twenty years, Henchard tells Susan, "These things, as well as the dread of the girl discovering our disgrace, makes it necessary to act with extreme caution" (11). This sounds less like a character taking part in a situation than it does like an author summarizing it or an editor explaining it. Repeatedly Hardy closes his ear and writes this sort of thing.

vi

My quotations constitute a rather extraordinary florilegium from a distinguished novelist's best novel—one that could hardly be duplicated by a search through a single novel by any other major novelist. The passages alluded to or cited are rather evenly distributed throughout the volume; this may strengthen somewhat their claim to representativeness.[2] They reveal that the problem of Hardy's style is its inconsistency. Hardy can be admirably concrete, and yet fall into abstractions even when his purposes demand specification. He can be crisp and pungent, and yet sink into the flaccid and flat. He can be direct and well organized, and yet in many sentences drift into the circuitous and the syntactically muddled. He may shift unpredictably from the flashing to the grinding, from the quick or the steady-paced to the stumbling.

To a slight extent the stylistic variation is related to a shifting of roles: at different times Hardy is poet, inventory taker, and explicator. "Poet" obviously implies the compact, the quick unrepeated strike, an unshuffling leap to the heart of the matter; the latter two roles imply explicitness and elaboration, which may be done neatly and surely, or may decline into the sprawling, roundabout, prolix, dragging, and generally tasteless. Hardy has also a fourth role, that of dialogue-maker; in this, the instability of manner that we have noted is indicative in a general way. At the beginning I said that Hardy writes at times like a man of good ear, at other times like a man with no ear at all. Let me rephrase this. At times Hardy writes like a man who has spent years listening to the actual speech of a variety of people—to their vocabulary, idiom, constructions, intonations, and color; while at others he writes as if he had listened only to secondary-school debates, Sunday school dramas, and the reading aloud of government bulletins, learned journals, accountant's reports, and inferior news dispatches. He seesaws back and forth between what is right and convincing, and what is so full of artifice, or of artifice and banality, that these seem not to come from the same writer. In Hardy the inconsistency is not just another case of "normal" inconsistency, such as may be found in many minds and personalities; rather it is a special inconsistency produced by the co-presence of strongly marked elements that seem wholly incompatible. He writes now like an unlearned man, now like an overlearned one; now like a man who has had no contact at all with accomplished writing, now like a man whose life has been centered in a strained bookishness; in a word—now like a peasant, now like a pedant.

Not only are the two extremes of Hardy's manner ones which it is hardly credible to find together, but Hardy's uncouth side is one which is hardly credible in a professional writer. For this side borders on the semiliterate. Here he gives us almost everything proscribed in rhetoric books: disorderly heaps of modifiers, relative clauses with unclear antecedents, upside-down *when* clauses, an excess of participial constructions, awkward absolute and gerund constructions, dangling modifiers of various kinds, faulty parallelism, clumsy passives, separation of related elements, confused pronoun reference. These suggest lack of experience with prose norms and insensitivity to the logic and grace of good prose. (Yet we know that he was exceptionally well read and did much rewriting.) Ironically, a writer of such habits will now and then come up with a strained correctness, or struggle into a kind of vulgar elegance: having heard that *me* is sometimes not the right word, he will cautiously use *I* everywhere, and especially after prepositions. Hardy is working in this way when, in describing a garden, he mentions "the flowers which smelt so sweetly" (12).

We are constantly surprised by Hardy. We are surprised to find these gaucheries present. We are further surprised to find them side by side with a vocabulary and artifice that suggest a self-conscious frequenter of libraries, to find the ill-bred, so to speak, hand in hand with the too well bred, the apparently untutored with the quasi-classical. The ultimate surprise is that both these polar imperfections accompany excellences that one would hardly expect to find with either—directness and fluency of statement, a telling concreteness, a fullness and variety of imagery ranging in effect from the suggestive to the striking and powerful, penetration and precision in analytical language, and richness and originality in imagination. No other writer shifts so patently from the unread man to the man who seems to have read only imitations of Cicero and Samuel Johnson, and from this two-headed monster to the man who has successfully fused the colloquial, the biblical, and the Shakespearean; who shifts from the laborious investment to the quick illumination, and from the intellectual self-made man to the moving and unseen artist.

The imperfections and the excellences are not really unrelated. They are rooted eventually in the unique constitution of Hardy. He is both "common man" and "uncommon man," and each of these elements in his personality imposes a burden and contributes a gift. As common man he is awkward, heavy, inept, but he is also direct, concrete, in contact with an immediate world in all its facets. As uncommon man he is donnish, formalistic, abstract, but he has a superior intuition of the nature of reality and an unusually free imagination. The various separate and contrasting vices we have cataloged. The virtues of the common man and the uncommon man are fused in the particular Hardian excellence that evokes such identifying terms as strength, integrity, and vision.

■ 18 ■
A Singular Element in D. H. Lawrence's Style

IN HIS BOOK about D. H. Lawrence the good critic Eliseo Vivas does not offer much formal discussion of Lawrence's style. He mentions stylistic slumps now and then—the flatness of the writing in *Aaron's Rod*, the vagueness of that in *St. Mawr* (with a delightful note on how bad Lawrence is when he "of-it-alls us"). In the main he admires Lawrence for "his superb mastery over language." Of Lawrence's ability to actualize certain scenes—nature generally, flora and fauna, the appearance of people, erotic and other emotional states, and the instability of these—by original image, figure, and verbal arrangement there is no doubt. Along Willey Water "There was a rousedness and a glancing everywhere"; "Something in him, inhuman and unmitigated, disturbed her"; "dangerous flamy sensitiveness"; "Her face . . . full of baffled light"; "the night smashed."

Along with such freshness, however, there is a great deal of mawkishness: sentimental diminutives, and so on. In general, there are two serious problems in Lawrence's style: one, repetitiousness, has often been noted; the other, though it is hinted at by Herbert Read and Edward Dahlberg, is less recognized. I refer to a recurrent effeminacy; the stylistic aspect of a persistent incoherence in Lawrence is that often one page seems to have been written by a man, the next by a woman. This appears not only in style but in aspects of method; a female point of view is used more often than a male, which can be an indication of imaginative skill, of course, but which can become quite distracting when what I have called "the mystique of the soma," a Lawrence basic, informs the occasion. After *Sons and Lovers*, in which Paul actually notices Clara's breasts several times, and a scene or two in *Rainbow*, women hardly become physiologically real at all; but with disconcerting frequency the reader is put in the position of a woman gazing erotically at a man and tingling to his navel-to-knees equipment. The candid camera shots of men's life-giving loins, powerful buttocks, and thrilling thighs (always in tight pants in *The Plumed Serpent*) induce a "What goes on here?" state of mind that somewhat interferes with "intransitive" attention, Vivas's term for the proper response to literary art. Lawrence's

260

endeavor to actualize the transcendental revealed in coitus or other physical engagements often suggests the language of the seance or the "religious" advertisement that says, "Is your vital power attuned to the beyond?" Of a piece with his addiction to the female perspective is his persistent dropping into an effeminate vocabulary: the pervasive use of "so" as an intensive ("so glad," "so nervous"), of such adjectives as "pure," "real," "strange," and especially "horrible"; of "mystery" and "ecstasy," "trance" and "lapse" and "swoon." The Laurentian concordance of swoonerisms reflects a persistent collapsibleness, a softness of texture, an excess of fold and give. I am not sure that it is balanced by the constant echo of "potent male," "cruel," "hate," and "murder." Such "strong words" denote other moods: lunges out of swoons toward power, bursts into violence, often closer to tantrums than vigor. There is the quick impulse, the plunge, not steady strength and ordered movement.

To avoid overstatement, I must interpose the reminder that in Lawrence there is a large body of live, creative language that does not fall into such categories. But there is the problem of the obsessive repetition. Two kinds of repetition must be distinguished: the repeating of key words within a single passage, and the repeating of a couple of hundred basic words throughout a book and in book after book. The former seems to me almost uniformly successful; it provides a rhythmic emphasis that helps complete the scene. When it comes to the wholesale repetitions, we could distinguish several vocabularies that blossom widely: that of rather ordinary adjectives that can lead to flatness and slackness ("wild," "bright," "quick," and so on, as Dahlberg points out); the biblical images, allusions, paraphrases, and rhythms; the Lawrence trademark wordhoard. The ubiquitous biblical should repay study: by it Lawrence often appears to be drawing on a traditional dignity and resonance to enhance events and feelings that lie outside of or even are counter to the tradition. The Lawrence specialties begin by catching the eye, challenging, puzzling, promising secrets; familiarity transforms them into idiom, an accepted argot divested of mystery; idiom sinks into cliché, but cliché that calls attention to itself, that is, mannerism. The prevalence of hyperbole in this private fashion prompts one involuntarily to frame a glossary: "annihilated" means "diminished," "dead" means "mortified," and so on. It will almost do, but not quite; though one can't help doing a lot of such scaling down as he goes along, the original is a little more than a trope of emphasis. But one nibbles at the problem of mannerisms and morals (which, for what it is worth, appears only slightly in *Sons and Lovers*, but keeps growing thereafter). What can one make of a world in which such substantives as these do the big business, ceaselessly hurtling at one like hard-sell entrepreneurs: *blood, will, power, violence, ma-*

levolence, contact, potency, maleness, trance, nullity? When almost every state or condition that becomes dramatically significant is presented in tireless adjectives such as these: *pure, naked, essential, electric, black, sensual, mental, proud, insolent, terrible, erect* and *prone, male* and *passive, potent, convulsive, willful, corrupt, cruel, insidious, sinister?* But above all, *dark, mad,* and *mindless* (the infinitely tedious *mindless,* which occurs scores of times to dozens of the others)? When the past participle is the queen verbal form, so that the focus is on the character to whom something is happening or being done: if he is doing well—*fulfilled, completed, perfected, half-created* or *created, translated, transfigured, transported;* if he is less well off—*inchoate, suspended, unfulfilled, uncreated, convulsed, dazed, stunned, crushed, stupefied, nullified, destroyed, obliterated, disintegrated?* Significantly, transitive verbs in active voice rarely become clichés: *hate* and *have power over* are among the few. In this world, the spontaneous and the masculine that are the proclaimed values are oddly infected with the feminine, the automatic, the passive, the categorical, the spasmodic and involuntary, with a queer mixture of the mechanical and the excessive, with the nonhuman. However one may characterize the moral quality of the world depicted, the depicting mannerisms reveal an obsessive attachment to this world—an unwillingness or inability to enlarge, complicate, enrich, or criticize it. Such steps would lead to a constantly extending freedom of vocabulary.

■ V ■
HARDY PERENNIALS

■ 19 ■
Sue Bridehead: A Brilliant Portrait

IN *JUDE THE OBSCURE*, a novel in which skillful characterization eventually wins the day over laborious editorializing, Thomas Hardy comes close to genius in the portrayal of Sue Bridehead. Sue takes the book away from the title character, because she is stronger, more complex, and more significant, and because her contradictory impulses, creating a spontaneous air of the inexplicable and even the mysterious, are dramatized with extraordinary fullness and concreteness, and with hardly a word of interpretation or admonishment by the author. To say this is to say that as a character she has taken off on her own, sped far away from a conceptual role, and developed as a being whose brilliant and puzzling surface provides only partial clues to the depths in which we can sense the presence of profound and representative problems.

Sue's original role, of course, is that of counterpoint to Arabella: spirit against flesh. Sue and Arabella are meant to represent different sides of Jude, who consistently thinks about them together, contrasts them, regards them as mutually exclusive opposites (see III, 9, 10; IV, 5; references are to parts and chapters). Early in their acquaintance he sees in Sue "almost an ideality" (II, 4), "almost a divinity" (III, 3); the better he gets to know her, the more he uses, in speech or thought, such terms as "ethereal" (III, 9; IV, 3; VI, 3), "uncarnate" (III, 9), "aerial" (IV, 3), "spirit, . . . disembodied creature . . . hardly flesh" (IV, 5), "phantasmal, bodiless creature" (V, 1), "least sensual," "a sort of fay, or sprite" (VI, 3). She herself asks Jude to kiss her "incorporeally" (V, 4), and she puts Mrs. Edlin "in mind of a sperrit" (VI, 9).

The allegorical content of Hardy's delineation of Sue has also a historical base: she is made a figure of Shelleyan idealism. When Phillotson describes the rather spiritualized affinity that he perceives between Jude and Sue, Gillingham exclaims "Platonic!" and Phillotson qualifies, "Well, no. Shelleyan would be nearer to it. They remind me of Laon and Cythna" (IV, 4), the idealized liberators and martyrs in *The Revolt of Islam* (which is quoted later in another context [V, 4]). Sue asks Jude to apply to her certain lines from Shelley's "Epipsychidion"—"a Being whom my spirit oft / Met on its visioned wanderings far aloft. . . . A seraph of Heaven, too gentle to be human" (IV, 5)—and Jude later calls Sue a "sensitive plant" (VI, 3).

Deliberately or instinctively Hardy is using certain Romantic values as a critical instrument against those of his own day, a free spirit against an oppressive society, the ethereal against commonplace and material. But a very odd thing happens: in conceiving of Sue as "spirit," and then letting her develop logically in such terms, he finds her coming up with a powerful aversion to sex—in other words, with a strong infusion of the very Victorianism that many of her feelings and intellectual attitudes run counter to. On the one hand, her objection to allegorizing the Song of Solomon (III, 4) is anti-Victorian; but when, in refusing to have intercourse with Jude, she says, "I resolved to trust you to set my wishes above your gratification," her view of herself as a suprasexual holder of prerogative and of him as a mere seeker of "gratification" is quite Victorian. She calls him "gross," apparently both for his night with Arabella and for desiring her physically, and under her pressure he begs, "Forgive me for being gross, as you call it!" (IV, 5). Again, he uses the apologetic phrase, "we poor unfortunate wretches of grosser substance" (V, 1). All of Sue's terms for Arabella come out of middle-class propriety: "fleshy, coarse woman," "low-passioned woman," "too low, too coarse for you," as does her argument that Jude should not go to help her because "she's not your wife." Jude is not entirely pliant here; in fact, there is some defiance in his saying that perhaps he is "coarse, too, worse luck!" But even while arguing against her refusal of sex he can say that "your freedom from everything that's gross has elevated me," accepting the current view of the male as a lower being who needs to be lifted up to a higher life (V, 2). Even when, near the end, he is vehemently urging Sue not to break their union, he can entertain the possibility that in overturning her proscription of sex he may have "spoiled one of the highest and purest loves that ever existed between man and woman" (VI, 3); the "average sensual man" all but gives up his case to a conventional opinion of his own time. Other aspects of Sue's vocabulary betray the Victorian tinge: when she first calls marriage a "sordid contract" (IV, 2) it seems fresh and independent, but the continuing chorus of "horrible and sordid" (V, 1), "vulgar" and "low" (V, 3), "vulgar" and "sordid" (V, 4) suggests finally an overnice and complacent personality. The style is a spontaneous accompaniment of the moral elevation which she assumes in herself and which in part she uses—Hardy is shrewd in getting at the power-sense in self-conscious "virtue"—to keep Jude in subjection.

There is a very striking irony here: perhaps unwittingly Hardy has forged or come upon a link between a Romantic idea of spirit (loftiness, freedom) and a Victorian self-congratulatory "spirituality"—a possibly remarkable feat of the historical imagination. But above all he has given a sharp image of inconsistency in Sue, for whatever the paradoxical link between her manifestations of spirit, she nevertheless appears as the special outsider on the one hand and as quite conventional on the other. In this he continues a line of characterization that he has followed very skillfully from the beginning. Repeatedly he uses such words as "perverseness," "riddle" (III, 1), "conundrum" (III, 2), "unreasonable . . . capricious" (III, 5), "perverse," "colossal inconsistency" (III, 7), "elusiveness of her curious double nature," "ridiculously inconsistent" (IV, 2), "logic . . . extraordinarily compounded," "puzzling and unpredictable" (IV, 3), "riddle" (IV, 4), "that mystery, her heart" (IV, 5), "ever evasive" (V, 5). With an inferior novelist, such an array of terms might be an effort to do by words what the action failed to do; here, they only show that Hardy knew what he was doing in the action, for all the difficulties, puzzles, and unpredictability have been dramatized with utmost variety and thoroughness. From the beginning, in major actions and lesser ones, Sue is consistently one thing and then another: reckless, then diffident; independent, then needing support; severe, and then kindly; inviting, and then offish. The portrayal of her is the major achievement of the novel. It is an imaginative feat, devoid of analytical props; for all of the descriptive words that he uses, Hardy never explains her or places her, as he is likely to do with lesser characters. She simply is, and it is up to the reader to sense the inner truth that creates multiple, lively, totally conflicting impressions. With her still more than with the other characters Hardy has escaped from the allegorical formula in which his addiction to such words as *spirit* might have trapped him.

From the beginning her inconsistency has a pattern that teases us with obscure hints of an elusive meaningfulness. Her first action characterizes her economically; she buys nude statues of classical divinities, but "trembled," almost repented, concealed them, misrepresented them to her landlady, and kept waking up anxiously at night (II, 3). She reads Gibbon but is superstitious about the scene of her first meeting with Jude (II, 4). She criticizes unrestrainedly the beliefs of Jude and Phillotson, but is wounded by any kind of retort (II, 5); repeatedly she can challenge, censure, and deride others but be hypersensitive to even mild replies, as if expecting immunity from the normal reciprocities of argument and emotion (III, 4; IV, 5; VI, 3, 4, 8). She reacts excessively to the unexpected visit of the school inspector, snaps at Phillotson "petulantly," and then "regretted that she had upbraided him" (II, 5). Aunt Drusilla reports that as a girl Sue was "pert . . . too often, with her tight-strained nerves" and an inclination to scoff at the bylaws of modesty; she was a tomboy who would suddenly run away from the boys (II, 6).

These initial glimpses of Sue prepare for the remarkable central drama of the novel: her unceasing reversals, apparent changes of mind and heart, acceptances and rejections, alternations of warmth and offishness, of evasiveness and candor, of impulsive acts and later regrets, of commitment and withdrawal, of freedom and constraint, unconventionality and propriety. She is cool about seeing Jude, then very eager, then offish (III, 1). She escapes from confinement at school but appears increasingly less up to the exploit already concluded (III, 3–5). She tells Jude, "You mustn't love me," then writes "you may," quarrels with him, and writes, "Forgive . . . my petulance" (III, 5). Before and after marriage she resists talking about Phillotson ("But I am not going to be cross-examined") and then talks about him almost without reserve (III, 6, 9; IV, 2). Again she forbids Jude to come to see her (III, 9), then "with sweet humility" revokes the prohibition (III, 10), is changeable when he comes, invites him for the next week (IV, 1), and then cancels the invitation (IV, 2). She "tearfully" refuses to kiss Jude, and then suddenly kisses him (IV, 3). Hardy identifies, as a natural accompaniment of her shifting of attitude and mood, a tendency to shift ground under pressure. Since she dislikes firm reply, argument, or questioning from others, she may simply declare herself "hurt." Another ploy is to make a hyperbolic statement of desolation or self-condemnation. "I *wish* I had a friend here to support me; but nobody is ever on my side!" (III, 5); "I am in the wrong. I always am!" (IV, 3); "I know I am a poor, miserable creature" (IV, 5). Another self-protective, situation-controlling move is to fall back directly on her emotional responsiveness to a difficult moment. She will not sleep with Jude but is jealous of Arabella; so she simply tells Jude, "I don't like you as well as I did!" (IV, 5). When she will not acknowledge loving him and he remarks on the danger of the game of elusiveness, her reply, "in a tragic voice," is, "I don't think I like you today so well as I did" (V, 1). For all of her intellectual freedom, she seems to accept the ancient dogma of "women's whims" (IV, 5) and calls Jude "good" because "you give way to all my whims!" (V, 4)

Through all the sensitivities, fragility, and caprice there appears an impulse for power, for retaining control of a situation, very delicately or even overtly, in one's own terms. The Victorian acceptance of woman's pedestal implies a superiority to be acknowledged. Early in the story, just after Jude sees "in her almost a divinity" (III, 3), Sue states candidly that she "did want and long to ennoble some man to high aims" (III, 4)—which might be pure generosity or an idealism infected with egoism. She trusts Jude not to pursue her with a desire for "gratification" (IV, 5). She would rather go on "always" without sex because "It is so much sweeter—for the woman at least, and when she is sure of the man" (V, 1).

The reappearance of Arabella so disturbs Sue's confidence in owner-ship that she tries to get rid of Arabella without Jude's seeing her, and when that fails, accepts the sexual bond only as a necessary means of binding Jude to her (V, 2). This gives her new confidence—"So I am not a bit frightened about losing you, now"—and hence she resists marriage (V, 3). Behind this near-compulsion to prescribe terms is a need that Sue states three different times: "Some women's love of being loved is in-satiable" (IV, 1); "But sometimes a woman's *love of being loved* gets the better of her conscience" (IV, 5); "the craving to attract and captivate, regardless of the injury it may do the man" (VI, 3). Here again Hardy avoids both allegory and the idealizing of a character whom her own associates find it easy to idealize.

At the center of hypersensitivity he perceives a self-concern that can mean a high insensitivity to others and hence a habit of hurting them that may actually embody an unconscious intention (another version of the power-sense). Despite her formal words of regret and self-censure, Sue seems almost to relish the complaint of the student that she "was breaking his heart by holding out against him so long at such close quar-ters" (III, 4). Though she resents criticism of or even disagreement with her, all that Jude believes in and holds dear she attacks with an unre-straint that ranges from inconsiderateness to condescension to an out-right desire to wound—the church, the university, and their traditions (III, 1, 2, 4). Always careless of Phillotson's feelings, she does not even let him know about her expulsion from school (III, 6). Hardy presents her desire to leave Phillotson as understandable and defensible, but at the same time he portrays her style with Phillotson as fantastically incon-siderate. For instance, as he "writhed," she upbraided him in a doctri-naire style for not having a free mind as J. S. Mill advised (IV, 3); later, he lies "writhing like a man in hell" (IV, 6) as she lets him think that her relation with Jude is adulterous. She is indifferent to Jude's feelings when she refuses to have sexual intercourse with him. She insists that Jude must "love me dearly" (V, 3), but when he gives her an opening for speaking affectionately to him, she says only, "You are always trying to make me confess to all sorts of absurdities" (V, 5). She moves variously toward self-protection, self-assertion, and self-indulgence. One of the most remarkable cases of giving way to her own feelings in complete disregard of their impact on others is her telling Father Time, "vehe-mently," that "Nature's law [is] mutual butchery!" (V, 6)—a view that with any imagination at all she would know him utterly unfitted to cope with. It prepares for her thoughtless reply of "almost" to his statement that it "would be better to be out o' the world than in it" and for her total ineptitude in dealing with his surmise that all their trouble is due to the children and with his desperation in finding that there is to be another child. Sue actually provides the psychological occasion, if not the cause, of the double murder and suicide (VI, 2)—the disasters that, with massive irony, begin her downward course to death-in-life.

The final touch in Sue as Victorian is her "I can't explain" when Father Time is driven frantic by the news that there will be another child. This is a lesser echo of Sue's embarrassment in all matters of sex—a disability the more marked in one who enters into otherwise intimate relations with a series of men. In her feeling free to deny the very center of the relationship, what looks like naiveté or innocence masks a paradoxical double design of self-interest: she wants to be sexually attractive and powerful but to remain sexually unavailable. Sue has something of la belle dame sans merci, leaving men not "palely loitering" but worse off than that: of the three men who have desired her, one finally has her but only as a shuddering sacrificial victim, and the other two die of "consumption," often thought to be of psychosomatic origin. She does give in to Jude, indeed, but immediately begins campaigning against marriage, and in terms so inapplicable—she repeatedly argues from the example of their earlier marriages, which are simply not relevant (see V, 4)—that they exist not for their own sake but as a symbolic continuation of the resistance to sex. They secretly help to prepare us for her eventual flight from Jude, and to keep us from crediting her later statement that she and Jude found a pagan joy in sensual life (Hardy's belated effort to do something for sex, which he has hardly moved an inch from the most conventional position). True, she declares, just before resuming sexual relations with Phillotson, "I find I still love [Jude]—oh, grossly!" (VI, 9), but at this time the words seem less an intuition of truth than a reaction from the horror of her penitential life; and it is noteworthy that, in whatever sense they may be true, they are spoken by her only when the action they imply is now finally beyond possibility.

La belle dame sans merci cannot practice mercilessness without being belle—beautiful, or charming, or fascinating. Though Sue may be, as Arabella puts it, "not a particular warm-hearted creature" and "a slim, fidgety little thing" who "don't know what love is" (V, 5), even Gillingham feels what the three men in her life respond to, her "indefinable charm" (VI, 5). She is always spontaneous, often vivacious, occasionally kindly and tender. More important, Hardy has caught a paradoxical and yet powerful kind of charm: the physical attractiveness of the person who seems hardly to have physical existence and hence evokes such terms as *aerial* and *ethereal*. The possibility that she unconsciously holds out to men is the enrichment of the ordinary sensual experience by its very opposite: all modes—or rather, the two extremes—of relationship are present at once in an extraordinary fusion. But this special charm is tenuously interwoven with the much more evident charm, the sheer power to fascinate, of an unpredictable personality. Though Sue may, as she herself theorizes, get into "these scrapes" through "curiosity to hunt up a new sensation," she does not have in her very much of the cold experimenter. Jude senses sadistic and masochistic elements in her (elements much noted by more recent critics). He theorizes that she "willfully gave herself and him pain" for the pleasure of feeling pity for both, and he suspects that she will "go on inflicting such pains again and again, and grieving for the sufferer again and again" (III, 7). Her selfishness is never consistent; she can be virtually ruthless in seeking ends, and then try to make reparation. She can be contemptuous and cutting, and then penitent and tearful. She can be daring and then scared (*scared* and *frightened* are used of her repeatedly); inconsiderate, and then generous; self-indulgent, and then self-punishing; callous, and then all but heartbroken—always with a kind of rushing spontaneity. Such endless shifts as these, which Hardy presents with unflagging resourcefulness, make Jude call Sue a "flirt" (IV, 1). Jude merely names what the reader feels on page after page: the unconscious coquetry that Sue practices. The novel is, in one light, a remarkable treatment of coquetry, for it implicitly defines the underlying bases of the style. The ordinary coquette may tease and chill by plan, invite and hold off deliberately, heighten desire by displaying readiness and simulating retreat: the piquant puzzle. This is what Arabella offers with great crudity in the beginning: Hardy's preparation, by contrast, for the brilliant unconscious tactics of Sue.

The true, ultimate coquette, the coquette in nature, has no plans, no deliberations, no contrived puzzles. Her inconsistency of act is the inconsistency of being. She goes this way, and then that way, for no other reason than that she cannot help it. She acts in terms of one impulse that seems clear and commanding, and is then pulled away by another that comes up and, though undefined, is not subject to her control. On the one hand, she freely puts conventional limitations behind her; on the other, she hardly comes up to conventional expectations. She has freedom of thought but not freedom of action and being. She is desirable but does not desire. She wishes to be desirable, which means making the moves that signify accessibility to desire; the cost of love is then a commitment from which she must frantically or stubbornly withdraw. She is thoughtless and even punitive, but she has pangs of conscience; yet to be certain that she has conscience, she must create situations that evoke pity for others and blame of self. Hardy catches very successfully the spontaneity of each of her acts and gestures; they are authentic, unprogrammed expressions of diverse elements in her personality. Coquetry is, in the end, the external drama of inner divisions, of divergent impulses each of which is strong enough to determine action at any time, but not at all times or even with any regularity. The failure of unity is greater than that of the ordinary personality, and the possibilities of trouble correspondingly greater. If the coquette is not fortunate in finding men with great tolerance for her diversity—and ordinarily she has an instinct for the type she needs—and situations that do not subject her to too great pressure, she will hardly avoid disaster.

The split that creates the coquette is not unlike the tragic split; the latter, of course, implies deeper emotional commitments and more momentous situations. Yet one might entitle an essay on Sue "The Coquette as Tragic Heroine." Because she has a stronger personality than Jude, has more initiative, and endeavors more to impose her will, she is closer to tragic stature than he. Like traditional tragic heroes, she believes that she can dictate terms and clothe herself in special immunities; like them, she has finally to reckon with neglected elements in herself and in the order of life. If the catastrophe that she helps precipitate is not in the first instance her own, nevertheless it becomes a turning point for her, a shock that opens up a new illumination, a new sense of self and of the moral order. After the death of the children Sue comes into some remarkable self-knowledge. She identifies precisely her errors in dealing with Father Time (VI, 2). Her phrase "proud in my own conceit" describes her style as a free-swinging critic of others and of the world. She recognizes that her relations with Jude became sexual only when "envy stimulated me to oust Arabella." She acknowledges to Jude, "I merely wanted you to love me . . . it began in the selfish and cruel wish to make your heart ache for me without letting mine ache for you." Such passages, with their burden of tragic self-understanding, predominate over others in which Sue looks for objects of blame, falls into self-pity, or frantically repeats her ancient self-protective plea, "Don't criticize me, Jude—I can't bear it!" (VI, 3).

But the passages that indicate growth by understanding are predominated over, in turn, by others in which Sue violently and excessively blames herself and pronounces on herself a life sentence of the severest mortification that she can imagine. Under great stress the precarious structure of her divided personality has broken down, and it has been replaced by a narrow, rigid unity under the tyrannical control of a single element in the personality—the self-blaming, self-flagellating impulse which Sue now formulates in Christian terms but which has been part of her all along. In place of the tragic understanding there is only black misery. Hence she ignores all Jude's arguments; Hardy may sympathize with these, but he knows what development is in character for Sue. A basic lack of wholeness has been converted, by heavy strains, into illness. Not that an imposition of a penalty is in itself pathological; we see no illness in the self-execution of Othello or, more comparably, in the self-blinding of Oedipus. Facts become clear to them, and they accept responsibility by prompt and final action. Sue not only judges her ignoble deeds but undiscriminatingly condemns a whole life; she converts all her deeds into vice, and crawls into an everlasting hell on earth. Remorse has become morbid, and punishment seems less a symbolic acknowledgment of error than the craving of a sick nature.

The problem is, then, whether the story of Sue merely touches on tragedy, with its characteristic reordering of a chaotic moral world, or becomes mainly a case history of clinical disorder, a sardonic prediction of an endless night. As always, the problem of illness is its representativeness: have we a special case, interesting for its own sake, pitiable, shocking, but limited in its relevance, or is the illness symbolic, containing a human truth that transcends its immediate terms? There is a real danger of reading Sue's story as if its confines were quite narrow. If she is simply taken as an undersexed woman, the human range will not seem a large one. If she is simply defined as "sadomasochistic," we have only an abnormality. If she appears only as the victim of conventions that the world should get rid of, the romantic rebel unjustly punished, the intellectual range will seem too narrow, wholly without the comprehensiveness of George Eliot, who could see at once the pain inflicted by, and the inevitability of, conventions. If she seems simply a person of insufficient maturity—and Hardy uses the words *child* and *children* repeatedly of Jude and Sue, and makes Sue say, "I crave to get back to the life of my infancy and its freedom" (III, 2)—we will seem to have only the obvious truth that it is risky for a child to be abroad in an adult world. If she seems simply an innocent or idealist done in by a harsh world, the story will seem banal, if not actually sentimental. A Christian apologist might argue that her history shows the inescapability of Christian thought; an anti-Christian, that she is the victim of wrong ideas without which she would have been saved. The answer to the former is that such a Christian triumph would be a melancholy and hardly persuasive one, and to the latter that Sue's nature would find in whatever system of values might be available, religious or secular, the doctrinal grounds for acting out her own disorder.

She does not strike us, in the end, as of narrow significance. She is the rather familiar being whose resources are not up to the demands made upon them. This is not so much a matter of weakness and bad luck as it is of an impulsiveness and willfulness that carry her beyond her depth;

even as a child she shows signs of strain and tension. She has many of the makings of the nun, but she wants the world too; she is peculiarly in need of protection, but she wants always to assert and attack. She works partly from an unrecognized egoism, sometimes from an open desire to wound and conquer; her aggressiveness leads her into injurious actions not unlike those of tragic protagonists. Aside from inflicting unfulfilled relationships upon three men, she does a subtler but deeper injury to Jude: with a mixture of the deliberate and the wanton she helps undermine the beliefs that are apparently essential to his well-being; she cannot stand that he should have any gods but her own. She has the style of the bluestocking who has found a new key to truth and is intolerant of all who have not opened the same door. Though she is sympathetic with Jude in many ways, she lacks the imagination to understand the real needs of his nature; instead of understanding either him or her substantial indifference to his well-being, she volubly pities him because the university and the world are indifferent to him. Having lost his faith and hope, he leans heavily on her; then she takes that support away when her own needs set her on another course. Symbolically, she comes fairly close to husband-murder.

In the pair Hardy activates two important, and naturally hostile, strains of nineteenth-century thought and feeling. Jude is under the influence of the Tractarian Movement, which, appealing to some of the best minds in university and church, displayed great vitality in pursuing its traditionalist and anti-liberal aims. Yet his allegiance does not hold up under the blows of Sue's modernist criticism; she looks at Jude as a sort of archaeological specimen, "a man puzzling out his way along a labyrinth from which one had one's self escaped" (III, 2), and refers sarcastically to his "Tractarian stage" as if he had not grown up (III, 4). So he falls into a secular liberalism which simply fails to sustain him. Sue, on the other hand, has felt the influence of utilitarianism (she quotes Mill to Phillotson very dogmatically); but her skepticism wilts under catastrophe, and she falls into an ascetic self-torment that utterly distorts the value of renunciation (the reduction of hubris to measure). Sue often talks about charity, but, despite her moments of sweetness and kindliness, it is hardly among her virtues; as a surrogate for charity to others she adopts a violent uncharitableness to herself.

Hardy may be intentionally commenting on the inadequacy of two important movements, perhaps because neither corresponds enough to human complexity. But as novelist he is rather exhibiting two characters who in different ways fail, despite unusual conscious attention to the problem, to find philosophical bases of life that are emotionally satisfactory. They like to think of themselves as ahead of their times, but this is rather a device of self-reassurance in people who are less ahead of their times than not up to them. One suspects that in the twentieth century, which has done away with the obstacles that loomed large before their eyes, they would be no better off—either because they lack some essential strength for survival or because they elect roles too onerous for them. Hardy, indeed, has imagined characters who could hardly survive in any order less than idyllic.

In Sue the inadequacy of resources is a representative one that gives her character great resonance. The clue is provided by a crucial experience of her intellectual hero, John Stuart Mill: under the strain of a severe logical discipline he broke down, and this crisis led to his discovering the therapeutic value of poetry. Sue, so to speak, never finds a therapy. In all ways she is allied with a tradition of intellect; she is specifically made a child of the eighteenth century. She dislikes everything medieval, admires classical writers and architecture, looks at the work of neo-classical secular painters, conspicuously reads eighteenth-century fiction and the satirists of all ages. Jude calls her "Voltairean," and she is a devotee of Gibbon. She is influenced, among later figures, by Shelley as intellectual rebel, by Mill's liberalism, and by the new historical criticism of Christianity. Rational skepticism, critical intelligence are her aims; in his last interview with her, Jude attacks her for losing her "reason," "faculties," "brains," "intellect" (VI, 8). Much as she is an individual who cannot finally be identified by categories, she is a child of the Enlightenment, with all its virtues and with the liabilities inseparable from it. Hardy was very early in intuiting, though he did not expressly define it, what in the twentieth century has become a familiar doctrine: the danger of trying to live by rationality alone.

In Sue, Hardy detects the specific form of the danger: the tendency of the skeptical intelligence to rule out the nonrational foundations of life and security. Sue cuts herself off from the two principal such foundations—from the community as it is expressed in traditional beliefs and institutions and from the physical reality of sex. The former she tends to regard as fraudulent and coercive, the latter as "gross"; in resisting marriage she resists both, and so she has not much left. Her deficiency in sex, whatever its precise psychological nature, is a logical correlative of her enthroning of critical intellect; thus a private peculiarity takes on a symbolic meaning of very wide relevance. The rationalist drawing away from nonrational sources of relationship creates the solitary; Sue is that, as she implies when, considering marriage because of the arrival of Father Time, she remarks, sadly, "I feel myself getting intertwined with my kind" (V, 3). Precisely. But she is unwilling to be quite the solitary, and for such a person, the anchorite in search of an appropriate society, the natural dream is a private utopia—an endless unconsummated idyll with a single infinitely devoted lover.

At the heart of the drama of Sue is the always simmering revolt of the modes of life which she rejects, the devious self-assertion of the rejected values. Hence much of her inconsistency, of the maddening reversals that constitute a natural coquetry, the wonderfully dramatized mystery that simply stands on its own until the clues appear in the final section. Sue cannot really either reject or accept men, and in attempting to do both at once she leaves men irritated or troubled or desperate, and herself not much better off. She revolts against conventions, but never without strain; and here Hardy introduces an inner drama of conventions far more significant than the criticisms leveled by Jude and Sue. He detects in conventions, not merely inflexible and irrational pressures from without, but a power over human nature because of the way in which human nature is constituted. Sue is one of the first characters in fiction to make the honest mistake of regarding a convention as only a needless constraint and forgetting that it is a needed support, and hence of failing to recognize that the problem admits of no easy pros or cons. As a social critic Hardy may deplore the rigidity of conventions or the severity of their impact, but as an artist he knows of their ubiquity in human experience and of their inextricability from consciousness. They are always complexly present in the drama. At first Jude thinks that there is "nothing unconventional" in Sue (III, 2); then he decides that "you are as innocent as you are unconventional" (III, 4); still later he accuses her of being "as enslaved to the social code as any woman I know" (IV, 5). The Sue who is devastatingly witty about institutions finds herself constantly acting in terms of traditional patterns. On one occasion she assures Jude that "she despised herself for having been so conventional" (III, 10); on another she has to acknowledge, "I perceive I have said that in mere convention" (IV, 1); and above all she says to Phillotson, "I, of all people, ought not to have cared what was said, for it was just what I fancied I never did care for. But . . . my theoretic unconventionality broke down" (IV, 3). Then Jude, shocked when she joins him but will not sleep with him, finds relief in the thought that she has "become conventional" rather than unloving, "Much as, under your teaching, I hate convention" (IV, 5). Here she is not clear herself, and she falls back mainly upon a concept whose conventionality she appears not to recognize, "woman's natural timidity." It is then that Jude accuses her of being "enslaved to the social code" and that she replies, "Not mentally. But I haven't the courage of my views." Her words betray the split between reason and feeling, between the rational critique of the forms and the emotional reliance upon them. This steady trail of comments, clashes, and partial acknowledgments leads up to the key event: in Christminster, she catches sight of Phillotson on the street, and she tells Jude, "I felt a curious dread of him; an awe, or terror, of conventions I don't believe in" (VI, 1). It is the turning point; her suppressed emotions, her needs, so long harried by her "reason," are seriously rebelling at last. "Reason" can still phrase her assessment of the event: "I am getting as superstitious as a savage!" Jude can lament the days "when her intellect played like lambent lightning over conventions and formalities" (VI, 3) and somewhat complacently attack her for losing her "scorn of convention" (VI, 8). But the defensiveness behind these criticisms soon emerges: as the defender of reason, Jude has also failed to find emotional anchorage, and his new independence of mind has provided him with no sustaining affirmations; and so he must blame Sue for deserting him.

Hardy has faithfully followed the character of Sue and has not let himself be deflected by his own sermonizing impulses. From the beginning he senses the split in her makeup—between rejections made by the mind, and emotional urgencies that she cannot deny or replace. If she is an "epicure in emotions," it may partly be, as she says apologetically, because of a "curiosity to hunt up a new sensation" (III, 7), but mostly it is that a turmoil of emotions will not let the mind, intent on its total freedom, have its own way. Much more than he realizes Jude speaks for both of them when he says, "And [our feelings] rule thoughts" (IV, 1). Sue's sensitivity, her liability to be "hurt," is real, but she uses it strategically to cut off Jude's and Phillotson's thoughts when they run counter to those that she freely flings about; understandably Jude exclaims, "You make such a personal matter of everything!" (III, 4). Exactly; what appears to be thought is often personal feeling that must not be denied. Answerability, in ordinary as well as special situations, shakes her. On buying the Venus and Apollo she "trembled" and at night "kept waking up" (II, 3). When the school inspector visits, she almost faints, and Phillotson's arm around her in public makes her uncomfortable (II, 5). Repeatedly her feelings are very conventional: her embarrassment when Jude comes into the room where her wet clothes are hanging (III, 3), her discomfort after rebelling at school (III, 5), her jealousy of Arabella (III, 6; V, 2, 3). She is "evidently touched" by the hymn that moves Jude, she finds it "odd . . . that I should care about" it, and she continues to play it (IV, 1). She is "rather frightened" at leaving Phillotson (IV, 5). When she refuses to sleep with Jude, it is less that she is "epicene" and "boyish as a Ganymede" (III, 4) or that her "nature is not so passionate as [his]" (IV, 5) than that joining Jude is an act of mind, of principled freedom, that does not have emotional support. Hence her singular scruple that "my freedom has been obtained under false pretences!" (V, 1)—a rationalizing of feelings that, for all of her liking of Jude, run counter to their mode of life. Hardy rightly saw that only some very powerful emotional urgency could get her over the barrier between Jude and herself, and he supplies that in her jealousy of Arabella. It is a common emotion that her mind would want to reject; and it is notable that after giving in to Jude she gives voice to another conventional feeling—assuring him, and herself, that she is "not a cold-natured, sexless creature" (V, 2).

In a series of penetrating episodes whose cumulative effect is massive, Hardy shows that her emotions cannot transcend the community that her mind endeavors to reject. With a deficiency of the feeling needed to sustain the courses laid out by the detached critical intellect, she would predictably return under pressure to whatever forms of support were available, to those indeed to which, while professing other codes, she has regularly been drawn. Though it would not take too much pressure, Hardy serves several ends at once by introducing the violent trauma of the death of the children. From here on he has only to trace, as he does with devastating thoroughness and fidelity, the revenge of the feelings that, albeit with admirable intellectual aspirations, Sue has persistently endeavored to thwart. They now counterattack with such force that they make her a sick woman. Although her self-judgments take the superficial form of tragic recognition, what we see is less the recovery that accompanies the tragic anagnorisis than the disaster of a personality distorted by the efforts to bear excessive burdens and now blindly seeking, in its misery, excessive punishments. Illness is something other than tragic.

Whatever Hardy may have felt about the course ultimately taken by Sue, he was utterly faithful to the personality as he imagined and slowly constructed it. That is his triumph. His triumph, however, is not only his fidelity to the nature of Sue, but the perception of human reality that permitted him to constitute her as he did. We could say that he envisaged her, a bright but ordinary person, attempting a career that would be possible only to the solitary creative intellect, the artist, the saint, whose emotional safety does lie in a vision somewhere beyond that of the ordinary community. Sue does not have that vision; she is everyman. She is everyman entirely familiar to us: her sense of the imperfections around her leads her into habitual rational analysis that tends to destroy the forms of feeling developed by the historical community and make her unable to find a replacement for them. The insistence on the life of reason has become increasingly emphatic in each century of modern life, and Sue as the relentless critic of institutions incarnates the ideal usually held up to us in abstract terms. On the other hand, as if in defiance of rationalist aspirations, the twentieth century has seen destructive outbreaks of irrational force that would have been supposed incredible in the nineteenth. But a still more impressive modern phenomenon, since it entirely lacks the air of aberration, is a growing concern with the threat of intellect to the life of feelings and emotions. From some of the most respected guides of modern thought come warnings against arid rationality, and visions of a reconstructed emotional life essential to human safety and well-being. The present relevance of such cultural history is that it contributes to our understanding of Hardy: in *Jude the Obscure*, and primarily in the portrayal of Sue, he went to the heart of a modern problem long before it was understood as a problem. Yet the "modern" is not topical, for the problem is rooted in the permanent reality of human nature. Neurotic Sue gives us, in dramatic terms, an essential revelation about human well-being.

■ 20 ■
"Intentions" in *The Mayor*

THE ARGUMENT over the author's "intention" once ranged between two extreme positions: from the disparaging of intention evident in W. K. Wimsatt and Monroe C. Beardsley's "intentional fallacy" to E. D. Hirsch's counterinsistence that intention was the only secure base for interpreters. By 1990 this debate yielded to other ones, and it may be possible to make a few observations on the general issue without seeming to intend a revival of the old battle. Intention, I believe, is significant but not necessarily determinative. In various prefaces Henry James pointed out how different works of his diverged from an original plan. But Thomas Hardy, I propose, gives us some more useful material on the issue. James was writing from memory; Hardy tells us what he is doing, or what he thinks he is doing, while he is doing it. Closer to standard Victorian practices, Hardy was a talkative author, constantly acting as emcee, cicerone, and commentator. He provides program notes and pushes ideas, sometimes, alas, in a rather cracker-barrel way. He tells us that he is presenting a character of a certain kind, and a universe in which things of a certain sort happen to characters. He does this in *The Mayor of Casterbridge*, *The Return of the Native*, *Tess of the D'Urbervilles*, and *Jude the Obscure*. Of these, *The Mayor* provides the best material for closer inspection; the almost paradoxical reason is that in a talkative world it is rather less talkative than the others. Hardy "talks" more in *Tess* and *Jude*; especially in *Jude* he lectures constantly, and not always consistently. *The Mayor* has more of a look of being better ordered, of knowing where it is going, and of getting there. If, then, it has discrepancies between apparent intention and apparent execution, these will be especially significant.

Many readers tend to take at face value various observations about the world and human beings that Hardy makes as he carries his story along. Our problem is to see whether these observations square with the dramatic evidence, with what the narrative itself is "doing" or "saying." In a word, I want to compare the "intellectual intention" with the "imaginative intention." These terms, I hope, will be useful in a consideration of the old problem of intention.

ii

In three elements in *The Mayor* Hardy is explicit about his "intentions." The first is the characterization of Susan Henchard, the wife whom Michael Henchard sells to Newson at the outset and later, when he is mayor, "remarries"; the second, the characterization of Elizabeth-Jane, the daughter of Susan and Newson who Henchard first thinks is his own daughter and whom he later deceives about her parentage; the third, certain philosophic assessments of Elizabeth's life and, by extension, of the human condition generally.

In talking about Susan analytically, Hardy is virtually condescending. His characteristic phrases are: "her simplicity," "meek conscience," "poor forgiving woman," "poor woman," "had no practical hand at anything," and "extreme simplicity of her intellect." There is no evidence that he disagrees when Henchard complains of her "idiotic simplicity," or when Henchard and Newson agree that she was "simple-minded" (with respect to the sale) and "warmhearted, homespun . . . not what they call shrewd or sharp at all." The characterizing phrases that come directly or implicitly from the author's pen reveal that he intends to make Susan mild, nice, mousy, confused, and dull to the verge of stupidity. But aside from telling the reader directly what he wants Susan to be, Hardy also gives us a full picture of Susan in action. And what is little short of amazing is that the character revealed in action is sharply at variance with the character that Hardy intends, that is, describes for us in analytical terms. For Susan does the following things. When she sees that Henchard really means to sell her, she leaves him with a real dash of independence. She has so much force of character that, once she comes to believe that living with Newson is wrong, her distress leads him to stage a fake drowning to free her. She successfully keeps the vital elements in the family history from a daughter said to be above average in intelligence and inquisitiveness. To provide for Elizabeth, Susan plans to recapture Henchard; she is shrewd enough to begin her search at the very spot where she was sold, to avoid getting overcommitted to Henchard until she can learn how he is doing, and through Elizabeth to make a very skillful approach to him. She now makes her second successful concealment in a crucial matter: she hides from Henchard the parentage of Elizabeth that might forestall the reunion and his care of Elizabeth. She stalls off Henchard's proposal for calling Elizabeth "Henchard" without arousing his suspicion, and subtly induces Elizabeth to resist the proposed name change without arousing Elizabeth's suspicion that deception is involved. To save her honor she plans ultimately to reveal Elizabeth's parentage to Henchard, and she shows something akin to genius in timing thc revelation for Elizabeth's wedding day, since this will involve least risk to Elizabeth (who will be safe in the hands of her husband) and least pain to Henchard (who will have "lost" Elizabeth anyway). She observes the compatibility between Elizabeth and Farfrae, senses the desirability of Farfrae, and devises an unusual rencontre to set off currents between them. It is not her fault that the timing of the revelation to Henchard misfires, and that Lucetta deflects Farfrae from Elizabeth. Yet despite these accidents, Susan has her way in more matters than most people ever do: she gets rid of a no longer satisfactory mate, she captures a former mate, she secures his devotion to the other one's daughter, and she works for a marriage that eventually does come to pass. Hardy might well have talked to us about Susan's energy, determination, resourcefulness, shrewdness, amounting at times to foxiness, and managerial skill verging on brilliance.

Hardy "intends" Susan to be one thing, and he tells us just what that is; but then his imagination begins working, and he "presents" her as something else. This gives us a choice of two conclusions. We can say that as a guide to understanding Susan's character, Hardy's stated "intentions" are worthless. Or we can say that, through some other agency than the rational consciousness that lays out overt plans, Hardy conceived of the situation differently and hence, in effect, really formulated other "intentions" than those which he literally specifies, and that these other intentions are knowable only through the literary structure that executes them. We will return later to this option.

Let us now pass on to the second case. In telling us directly what he intends Elizabeth to be—that is, in making nondramatic, analytical assertions about her qualities—Hardy claims for her a profusion of attributes that can hardly be brought together into a unity. He speaks of her in general as a poor girl without advantages or a knowledge of conventions, but gives her extraordinary endowments—"great natural insight," "innate perceptiveness that was almost genius," "wisdom." She dresses plainly and modestly, but is also several times drawn into extravagance, and on one occasion of enjoying her "finery" suspects that she is "setting up as the town beauty"; yet at another time she is said to be "comparatively indifferent . . . to dress." Hardy refers to "her simplicity" and terms her "a dumb, deep-feeling . . . creature"; but he also calls her "subtle-souled" and makes her ask and debate questions suitable for professional philosophers, as when she speculates on "that chaos called consciousness." On the one hand she is very informal with the help and uses enough dialectical words to irritate her unlearned stepfather; on the other hand she is a bluestocking who "read omnivorously," "read and took notes incessantly," and studies "unremittingly." On the one hand she is a craftsman with "a wonderful skill in netting of all sorts," and on the other a bookworm who bones up Latin unaided, makes a sophisticated disparagement of her "wretched bit of Latin," and later pedantically quotes Ovid, in the original, to Lucetta. This medley of ignorant sailor's daughter, town beauty, wise but simple woman, hand-icraft expert, and scholarly intellectual has to be taken almost entirely on Hardy's unsupported word, which specifically names not one inten-tion but actually a number of different intentions. He offers us, to put it mildly, a major problem. But there is almost no problem if we rely on the picture of Elizabeth as Hardy has "presented" her in the dramatic ac-tion. In his proper role as narrator of what has happened he has appre-hended her fully and consistently; what comes through to us is an ample and convincing picture of Elizabeth as a plain, sensible, loyal, self-effac-ing Good Samaritan, firm in judgment and decision but not very force-ful in her impact on others, mild in manner but energetic and devoted as a helper.

In dealing with Susan, Hardy exhibits one kind of discrepancy be-tween intention and performance; in dealing with Elizabeth, another. With Susan, his intuition of character saves him by making her more complex than he directly asserts her to be; with Elizabeth, his intuition of character saves him by making her less complex, that is, more pulled together into a unity, than he formally asserts her to be. He reverts from design to nature in two opposite ways, losing sight of two intentions that come from quite different motives. In intending Susan to be a simple-ton, he evidently meant to justify her acquiescing in the wife-sale, which he appears to have felt was improbable, since in the text itself he takes pains to explain that such dealings were occasional facts of Wessex life. In ascribing an incredible diversity of qualities to Elizabeth, Hardy be-trayed an unconscious longing for a "dream girl"—a prize package of beauty, brains, craftsmanship, and a cool, selfless hand for every fevered brow. The intention for Susan shows Hardy on his technical side; that for Elizabeth shows him on his sentimental side.

The sentimental side appears more massively in the third area where performance diverges from intention—his evaluation of Elizabeth's life as representative of human experience generally. He calls Elizabeth a "lonely girl," naming a pathetic condition that is not at all verified in the action. He says that she learned "the lesson of renunciation" and was "familiar with the wreck of each day's wishes"; true, Farfrae's attention has temporarily shifted to Lucetta, but still *renunciation* and the *wreck* phrase are emotion-begging terms for a well-organized girl's temporary disappointment before her eventual marriage, with virtual popular-fic-tion splendor, to the mayor and the richest man in town (the local catch for whom nineteen other rivals had been competing). Some compulsion makes Hardy want to convert almost any serious human experience into a sad hard-luck story. When Elizabeth leaves Henchard's house to become a companion to the wealthiest woman in town, Hardy calls it a change from "gay independence to laborious self-help," as if she were going to become a field hand or a kitchen scullion. This is consistent with his references to her pre-Casterbridge past, which sound like an editorial on the underprivileged and mistreated. Consider the following phrases and statements: "casual disfigurements . . . from straitened circumstances"; "carking accidents of her daily existence"; "that strait-waistcoat of poverty from which she [Susan] had tried so many times to be delivered for the girl's sake"; "strictest economy was indispensable." Elizabeth felt that "life and its surroundings . . . were a tragical rather than a comic thing"; "who had known so little friendship"; "early habituated to anxious reasoning." "Like all people who have known rough times, lightheartedness seemed to her . . . a reckless dram"; she had "that fieldmouse fear . . . which is common among the thoughtful who have suffered early from poverty and oppression." One would think she had been a solitary pauper in a slum, or a slave in a sweatshop. But when we turn from these gloomy evaluations to the facts of the story, we find something quite different. For almost two decades Susan and Elizabeth had lived most happily with Newson, to whose kindness Elizabeth testifies repeatedly and unreservedly; when Newson shows up at the end, he is hearty, amiable, generous, and forbearing to an almost allegorical extreme. What is more, he appears very close to well-to-do, and we assume that this could not have come about all at once. We know that at one time the Newson family was not on easy street, and that Susan and Elizabeth both were regular and perhaps hard workers; but still there is no evidence at all of the abject poverty that Hardy keeps nagging us about. After Newson's supposed death, there was only "a month or so" of "working twine nets" (at which Elizabeth was so gifted that it can hardly have been a form of slavery) before they set out to look for Henchard; and if they had to watch their purses on the trip, this is a not unfamiliar human experience, and Hardy offers no evidence that they were unpresentably clad or undernourished. Then they quickly find a generous welcome from and an unusually comfortable home with the rich mayor, Henchard.

The divergence of narrative fact from formal, expressed purpose is little less than shocking. It is as if there were two Hardys, one a spontaneous, adequately complex, untheorizing storyteller, the other a rigid man of doctrine "intending" to force upon us a dour view of oppressive circumstance. This sentimental intention has a final fling on the last page. Here the doctrinaire Hardy imposes upon Elizabeth, whom we are quite unable to credit with such ideas, the belief that life is a "brief transit through a sorry world," and insists irreconcilably that, though she is now tranquil (it is difficult to avoid remarking that this unfair trick of hers is very annoying to the author), her "youth had seemed to teach that happiness was but the occasional episode in a drama of pain." This grim coda is entirely out of line with the composition as a whole. "Sorry world" and "drama of pain" do not apply at all to their alleged formulator, Elizabeth, or to Farfrae, since both come to a fine triumph; hardly apply to Susan; and, insofar as they suggest external conditions of which man is the victim, are not applicable to the sorrows of Lucetta and Henchard. But Hardy is determined on his side-mouth observations and sour obiter dicta. These may be sarcastic potshots at young ladies' conduct in Casterbridge (overdressing, chasing Farfrae), notations on the doleful history of the Amphitheatre (so overwhelming that we are surprised that, after they have met there, Henchard and Susan make a quite tolerable go of it), or a harsh insistence that "woman's eye" is "ruled . . . so largely by the superficies of things" and that marriage produces an "atmosphere of stale familiarity." Or he can come up with a more disillusioned generalization, such as that Susan had learned from "civilization" to expect anything from "Time and Chance, except, perhaps, fair play" or that Henchard is kept from starting out all over again by "the ingenious machinery contrived by the Gods for reducing human possibilities of amelioration to a minimum."

We need no further documentation for the view that in Hardy there is a sharp hiatus between what as interpreter he says to us directly (intention) and what the story says (artistic performance). Although our primary concern is with the light that his work sheds on a theoretical problem, we may make two comments on Hardy himself. One is that while readers are generally not thrown off the track by what Hardy asserts about the makeup of his characters but do get an adequate sense of the characters from the purely dramatic presentation of them (as with Susan and Elizabeth), most readers tend on the other hand to pay excessive attention to Hardy's nobody-can-fool-me and even querulous philosophic asides, which fall very little short of suggesting an immature distaste for the way things are. If *Tess* is the subject, one is likely to hear much more about Hardy's sardonic aphorism, "the President of the Immortals . . . had ended his sport with Tess," than about the genuine complications of character in this book. Such caustic saws are much simpler to deal with than artistic wholes; easy to snatch out of context and fix in mind, they give a quick sense of having mastered the work and placed the author. But readers who rely on these intrusive marginalia get a distorted sense of Hardy's vision of reality, and they seriously diminish his stature by seeing in him only the disillusioned portrayer of the cosmos as infernal machine giving ever sharper turns of the screw to hapless humanity. This view, which is seductive not only because it is intellectually easy but also because it nourishes all our inclinations to self-pity, simply is not sound. Hardy treats characters far less as victims than as moral beings whose histories are congruent with their natures, and his sense of characters is profound and many-sided enough to forbid any inference of a rigid, single-valued cosmology. Hardy's ultimate reliance on character, as opposed to a theory of inimical circumstance, is made clear precisely where it might seem least probable—in *Jude.* Here he sets out to blast the institutions of marriage and education by exhibiting their damaging effect upon superior individuals; but what he actually does, in a conspicuous act of fidelity to the character principle that cuts athwart his "design," is to pick as victims people of such intense inner discords and disturbances that they are inevitable victims who would go down in any system less than utopian.

My second comment on Hardy is perhaps no more than a restatement of the first with a shift in emphasis: Hardy's stature as artist is a function of the discrepancy between intention and performance. Had he actually made his characters conform to his doctrines, they would hardly have had life enough to survive as long as this. Fortunately his imagination was under no bond to his ponderings about the Immanent Will, and his characters are truly impressive when they are, as it were, acting on their own instead of standing still and submitting to his pedagogical pointer and his theoretical anatomizing. Hardy indulges himself in enough glum ironies about the human condition to permit our saying that he "asked for it" when he was assailed by the charges of "pessimism" that so annoyed him and that have so long befogged the interpretation of his work. By way of getting himself out of a philosophic box he insisted that his novels were simply rendering "impressions." He made this remark, which is sound enough, in 1892, when he was looking back on his novels and had only one more to write. More than a decade later, in *The Dynasts,* his metaphysical intentions were so thoroughly in control that few "impressions" broke through to vitalize the work. It is when his impressions escape from all demonstrative intentions that he is great.

iii

Hardy presents us, then, with that remarkable situation in which, in the very course of a work in progress, a writer specifically indicates various intentions and then, as the autonomous creative activity takes over, does something else. We see him for technical reasons intending that a character appear in a certain light (Susan as dully acquiescent) but unconsciously permitting a person of quite different mind and character to develop; for emotional reasons, about which we can only guess (a wish that the first Mrs. Hardy were a less narrow person?), intending to endow a character with extraordinary charms and talents (Elizabeth as beautiful, learned, and so forth) but failing in that intention and successfully creating, instead, a more substantial and limited character; and finally, because of a philosophical penchant, intending that the reader see certain careers, Elizabeth's in particular, as evidence of a badly planned universe by which man is irrationally pushed around or even doomed, but as storyteller portraying a life in which man's own nature is the major influence toward the good or evil that he experiences.

If we want to salvage the concept of intention, we can do it by making a distinction between two modes of intention. We can bring into play what I have called the "intellectual intention" and the "imaginative intention." The intellectual intention is the a priori design, the conscious plan, the product of full consciousness aimed at the raw materials. The imaginative intention may hardly get into the writer's official consciousness at all, except perhaps retrospectively. Though the former may have to be discarded, the latter is a metaphorical way of defining the creator's powers; it is a reminder of the genetic aspects of the work and of the fact that it bears the impress of one personality rather than another. "Imaginative intention" would not refer to any conceptual resolve such as may be expressed either in the formula "I will do so and so" or in analytical assertions of the Hardian sort. It would refer rather to the subtle, nearly or actually subliminal decisions that constitute a great deal of the composing process; to the innumerable back-and-forth mediations between forming mind and substance achieving form; to the tentative steps from hypothesis, or the arbitrary leaps in the dark, by which incremental advances are made, advances that then undergo assaying, possibly by overt examination, more probably by an intuitive feeling-out of an almost formless sort, and eventual acceptance, modification, or rejection; to the making of commitments and the recognition of their consequences, that is, the acquiescing, with whatever degree of consciousness, in the necessary adjustments of what we might call the "inaugural stance" (Hardy lets Susan "get her head" and become a planner rather than a pushover). A case might be made for "intention" in this sense: as the sum of the multiple and hardly discriminable activities of the creative spirit at work in the complex interplay between the molding imagination and the resistant materials. It enables us to conceive of a "guiding vision" without eliminating the "autonomy of the work." The former—

"guiding vision"—is the writer's unique apprehension of the materials; the latter—"autonomy of the work"—is an indispensable figure for that intrinsic character of the materials that cannot finally be constrained by the intellect or will of the writer. (As a man of imagination Hardy perceives in the moral constitution of his personae the strongest influence upon their destinies; this cannot be constrained by repeated efforts of his intellect and will to prove that certain immortals are palming off a pretty unsavory destiny on passive personae.)

"Intention," then, becomes a figure for those ultimate operations of the artist's spirit that make the work what it is. Robert Penn Warren put it thus: "The poet intends what the work says." W. H. Auden elaborated: "How do I know what I think till I see what I've said?" In this view, the only evidence for the intention is the way it has come out in the text; whatever its usefulness, intention is to be inferred from its effects.

Whether one wants to save the concept of intention, however defined, may depend a little upon the times. One may well be dubious of intentionists when they seem to overstress external forces at the expense of inner realities—structure, style, and so on—and insist that the former dictate the reading of the work. But that is hardly a danger now. In latter days one might even want to rescue registered intention as a bulwark against wild readings by self-absorbed readers not mature enough to concede the authority of the text, or against theory-formed readers who believe that the text has no authority and hence is in effect created by their own interpretative gymnastics. The problem is always to find a workable middle ground—a body, as it usually is, of readings that, however they differ in detail, still reveal a basic fidelity to the text—a middle ground lying between two extremes: the enforced single reading, dictated by genetics or intention or some other supposed and independent external force, and, opposite it, the view that any reading goes because the text has no reality beyond its role as stimulus to the critic's virtuosity. Of course we live in an era—the latter decades of the twentieth century—in which a plurality of readings is standard fare. These at least serve to reveal something of richness in the work of the writer who stirs multiple readings. But we need some kind of barrier against the threatened situation in which every solipsistic exercise danced upon the text is taken to be as valid as any other. That essential barrier may be the concept of the ideal reading, the reading made, as it were, by the mind of God. Since even literary critics do not easily achieve divine insight, the ideal reading may long be elusive. But the struggle toward it is the only justification of critical exercises. Nor is that struggle totally foredoomed. In interpretation, such endowments as experience, maturity, and taste will eventually pay off. To say this is to imply the existence of human constants that will in time react against the irresponsible and the eccentric in interpretations, against the self-indulgent and the aridly logical. Indeed, the relationship between the literary work and its readers is essentially a relationship between underlying constants in form and meaning, whatever the novelties of perspective and the historical individuality of presentation, and constants of apprehension, whatever the variables that enter through personal idiosyncrasy and the periodic emergence of new descriptive and analytical tools. This is the final safeguard against chaos.

■ 21 ■
The Dictatorial Idea:
Hardy and Some Late Characters

i

IN HIS FICTION and in his criticism Robert Penn Warren has meditated about "the idea," roughly the conceptual or theoretical apparatus that in some men determines the key actions of their lives. The idea may "redeem" conduct, that is, infuse it with a value that rescues it from pointlessness, makes it more than the product of some thoughtless drive or other. But on the other hand the idea may be a compelling abstraction that tends to ignore, oversimplify, or contort the complexities of actuality. (When the dictatorial idea generates a system, we call it an "ideology," that is, a program to which reality must be made to conform.) Thus Warren formulated a problem that had come up, in various ways, in the works of earlier novelists—in Meredith, for instance, and Conrad and Hardy.

Thomas Hardy did not employ a specific term for this problem, but it was very much present in his imagination when he wrote certain novels, notably those of his later or "major" period. Michael Henchard, the title character in *The Mayor of Casterbridge* (1886), is dominated, after his success, by the idea of himself as the preeminent figure in Casterbridge, as the leader who is bound to triumph in all matters to which he puts his hand. He tries to rule history, to make the facts fit the idea, but the outcome, of course, is his defeat. In *Tess of the D'Urbervilles* (1891) Angel Clare has a rigid idea of the behavior appropriate to the woman one loves, and he applies it with such rigor that his new wife undergoes immense suffering, commits a murder, and is hanged. In *The Well Beloved* (1892) the sculptor Jocelyn Pierston is ruled by an "Idea" of beauty (he once calls it "Platonic" and regularly refers to it as his "Well Beloved") which determines his art and seems embodied in a series of women whom he believes himself in love with and wants to marry—notably, in succession, an Avice Caro and her daughter and granddaughter. In an overplotted and laboriously ironic tale, this version of Pygmalion finally gives up art and in his sixties makes a calm *mariage de convenance* with an equally aged former embodiment of the Idea. (In Shaw's version of the myth, Pygmalion loves the idea of the creative process but is incapa-

290

ble of responding to the created being.) Jude Fawley, the title character of *Jude the Obscure* (1895), has so exclusive an idea of the inherent excellence or superiority of academic/intellectual life that he is a poor bet as husband and father; on a crucial occasion he behaves so thoughtlessly that he sets off a ruinous series of events. His wife, Sue, is likewise dominated by an idea, the idea of anti-institutional, anti-traditional freedom; it is disastrously unsuited to the needs of her own nature.

Thus in four of his last six novels Hardy focuses attention on characters who are in different ways subject to dictatorial ideas. Yet that theme is not simply a discovery of the late period: it first appears almost a decade earlier in *The Return of the Native* (1878). *The Return* is outstanding among the nine novels published between 1871 and 1882, most of which belong to the classes that Hardy called "Romances and Fantasies" (*A Pair of Blue Eyes*, *The Trumpet Major*, and *Two on a Tower*) and "Novels of Ingenuity" (*Desperate Remedies*, *The Hand of Ethelberta*, and *A Laodicean*). One might say that Hardy, aged thirty-eight in 1878, was discovering the type of character that would grip his imagination in his major work. Perhaps his exhaustion of the theme was a contributory factor to his giving up novel-writing at age fifty-five.

In fact, the link between *The Return* and the later novels is twofold. The most conspicuous tie, of course, is the centrality of the stiff-necked man with the single-track mind, the idée fixe. Then in three of the novels the human scene of action of the fixed-idea man is marriage. In *The Well Beloved*, of course, the marriage is a nonevent until the Idea, and with it all passion, is spent, and in *The Mayor* the marriage is not at the center, although it could be at the center if Hardy had chosen to emphasize the contrast between the wife's immense adjustability to the world and her husband's growing rigidity. But in the other three novels we see the marriage relation as it is influenced by the idea-possessed characters. In *Tess* the husband of rigid mind drives away a devoted bride who means to adjust to a world of which he will be the center. In *Jude*, as we have seen, each spouse has a worldview which contradicts that of the other; though they are held together by sexual attraction and a kind of devotion that somehow survives the idée fixe, each is in time undone primarily by his worldview. In some ways the most interesting variant of this scenario is the one in *The Return*: in part the marriage comes about because each partner, holding to an idea that is entirely at variance with that of the other, is persuaded that, once the marriage occurs, his own worldview will triumph and determine the scene and direction of married life. It is a fascinating story of the way in which a strongly held idea can deceive its holder.

One necessary point: to describe these novels in the terms I have used here might suggest that they are allegorical in manner and tone. In no way are the characters allegorical; they have humanity enough. To that humanity belong the preconceptions that damage or destroy the human beings. Still, it may be a little surprising that the characters do not become allegorical, since they are so much subject to pressure from Hardy's own ideas about life. But his intuition of characters is almost invariably reliable, and his tendency to push a character in one direction or another—at least by his formal interpretations, his theoretical ideas about the state of human affairs—does not really skew his presentation of human reality. To say this much, of course, is to acknowledge that Hardy's management of narrative has its ups and downs. These are worth a little further inspection. Since I have already partially dealt with the matter in commenting on other novels, I will restrict this discussion to *The Return of the Native*. Now and then Hardy's technical art does not match his intuition of the workings of humanity or of the deformation of characters' lives by the idea that they want to impose on reality.

Insofar as Hardy is making rational judgments rather than relying on his artist's sixth sense of things, he is likely to be unreliable. This is quite apparent in his formal condemnation of the "happy ending" that he added in a later edition of *The Return of the Native*—the marriage of the lesser characters Thomasin Yeobright and Diggory Venn. In the original version his final emphasis was upon the deaths of Eustacia and Wildeve; Thomasin remained a widow, and Venn disappeared. In Hardy's view, the earlier version represented an "austere artistic code," a "more consistent conclusion," and the "true one." This simply is not true. All Hardy's repudiation of the earlier ending means is that for some reason he wants to stick to his darker view of things—his "idea"—and deny his sound imagining of the terms in which some human beings work things out with reasonable satisfactoriness. He sees that some people fail by wanting to dictate reality, but he also sees that there are some people who do keep their feet on the ground (that is, have good sense and reasonable expectations), who do effect an accommodation with reality, who do manage to like suitable members of the opposite sex and find adequate lives with them. Thomasin and Diggory earn each other; it is not a case of Hardy's interfering and giving each one to the other to gratify a public not up to his grimmer idea of reality. The final evidence of the truth of this relationship is the naturalness, spontaneity, and vivacity of the chapters in book VI. They work; they are not forced, casual, or flatly dutiful. Hardy's art contradicts his official opinion of the cosmos, but it does not betray his insight. His imagination embraced a fuller reality than he supposed.

And that is the source of the real strengths of *The Return*.

ii

Hardy's unsure formal judgments perhaps stand out more clearly than the artistic decisions that he makes along the way. But the artistic choices are interesting: though they may not involve a clash between a formal idea and an instinct, they do seem to represent a comparable split between, so to speak, an automatic or mechanical way of doing things and a sure sense of human beings in action. Thus Hardy varies between an apparently effortless and convincing narrative and awkwardnesses that spur the involuntary retention, rather than the willing suspension, of disbelief.

We probably cannot say that Hardy had a definite idea about the basic significance of his supporting cast of common folk, but he does appear to be hypnotized by their voices, and he lets them run on and on, excessively it seems. He does have a definite idea about the former jobs of Clym and Wildeve: he wants one to be the object of rejection, and the other to represent a better life from which there has been a conspicuous comedown. So both men are credited with having had positions which, given their personalities, seem highly improbable. Clym was "manager to a diamond merchant" and Wildeve an "engineer." Hardy evidently shares Clym's idea of the unworthiness of his Paris job, for he lets Clym run on about it, even to a most unlikely audience of rustics at a haircutting (III, 1; all references are to parts and chapters). Hardy wants Clym to go nearly blind from study, but his art lags behind his idea, for he cannot provide the name of a single book that Clym reads (in contrast with the ample reading lists in *Jude*). The unchecked reportorial flux in Hardy's representation of rustics appears again in his treatment of the to-do that Clym and his mother make about the Thomasin-Wildeve wedding: thus the newlyweds come into apparent narrative significance, but Hardy drops them cold until he can use them in the Clym-mother-Eustacia conflict. He suddenly shifts from documentation to design—a rather characteristic leap.

The impact of an idea appears in Hardy's introductions of Clym and Eustacia. He thinks of them, at least initially, in very grand terms, and he writes rather windily in the early set-piece descriptions that, though much noticed, simply do not hold up when we see the individuals in action. The famous idea that "thought is a disease of flesh" (II, 6) is of such beguiling novelty that we may not notice its inapplicability to Clym. Though Hardy prophesies that Clym's "beauty . . . would in no long time be overrun by its parasite thought" and asserts that he has "a wearing habit of meditation," the character presented dramatically reveals neither a philosophic bent nor a suffering from "a full recognition of the coil of things." Clearly Hardy is pushing his "idea." Hardy goes from inapplicable theory (and surely erroneous theory: who has not seen deeply lined faces that go with conventional well-being, and recognized truly philosophic minds behind bland faces? I once heard Eric Voegelin, a truly profound thinker, say that he had a "silly face") to half-truth when he declares that Clym's "look . . . was a natural cheerfulness striving against depression from without, and not quite succeeding." There is no sign of depression in newly arrived Clym, but much of "natural cheerfulness."

Hardy's set portrait of Eustacia (I, 7), once thought a great description, conforms a little better to the Eustacia developed dramatically, for Hardy's formal idea of her is partly modified by his imagination of her. A beautiful woman, alluring in a rural environment where she seems exotic, she is intense, romantic, willful, yearning, and resentful; Hardy says this, and he makes it good in the story (though one wonders why she fails to resist the hated heath-bound life imposed on her by her grandfather, who seems less a man of iron than a Smollett-Dickens nautical humor apparently manageable by an energetic woman whom Hardy calls an "absolute queen" [I, 6] at home). What she cannot sustain is the implied comparison with Clotho, Lachesis, and Atropos, with Artemis, Athena, and Hera, with Heloise and Cleopatra; nor the assertion that her style resembled "the comprehensive strategy of a general" and that she "could utter oracles of Delphic ambiguity." Partly Hardy has fallen in love with her, partly he uses her to express another "idea" of his—namely, heavenly mismanagement and hence the "inequality of lot" and "captious alternation of caresses and blows that we endure now." In no way is Eustacia "the raw material of a divinity"; rather than a goddess manquée she is, as various readers have noticed, a full achiever in a human mode identified in 1856—bovarysm. Eustacia is sharper than Emma, but the kinship is there.

Hardy's sense of the inner realities of developing relationships is excellent, but his external ways of bringing about change and crisis often raise eyebrows. His narrative represents the interplay of two basic ideas of his: the dominant one is that things will go wrong most of the time, and the lesser one is that the inevitable downward spiral of human lives is sometimes temporarily checked by a sort of *deus-ex-machina* event. When the appointed *deus* needs help, Hardy can drag in the machinery in defiance of all probability. For instance, to provide a possible savior with needed information, Hardy arranges the most fantastic overhearing since Pamela Andrews picked up whole paragraphs of praise of herself from locations anywhere near the unnoticing speakers. To serve as secret protector of Thomasin, Diggory must know what Wildeve and

Eustacia are up to. Hence in the open heath he pulls off a remarkable feat of eavesdropping, creeping up unheard, and unseen under a couple of "turves," to monitor a long conversation (I, 9). The coincidences that are standbys in Hardy's technical supply-kit we partly accept—all critics insist on this—as symbolizations of the untowardness of things that, in Hardy's idea of life, afflicts humanity. However, his "life's little ironies" and "satires of circumstance" range from the heavy-handed and contrived to the convincing and revealing. Diggory's "van" is the Grand Hotel of Egdon Heath: everybody happens by there when a hiding place or a shelter or a meeting with Diggory will be of convenience to the narrative. Certain events do make it fairly plausible that Wildeve and Mrs. Yeobright embark on visits to the Clym-Eustacia home about the same time. But then Hardy gets into the act to make sure that things will go wrong: he has Wildeve and Mrs. Yeobright pick not only the same day for their visits but the same time of day. On the other hand, after such an enforced coincidence has set the stage, the crucial slip into disaster is plausible: we understand Eustacia's not answering her mother-in-law's knock at the door, and her thinking that Clym is waking up from a nap and will open the door himself (IV, 6). Then Hardy goes back to pure coincidence: Clym does not wake up but has a dream that is a singular mirror-image of current events; and Mrs. Yeobright, on her return trip, runs into Johnny Nunsuch, who can hear and report her bitter statements and thus contribute to the remorse of her son. And on her walk, finally, comes the ultimate turn of the screw by an almost indecently willful Hardy: he now inflicts upon her the bite of a poisonous adder (IV, 7). The Lear allusions are painfully clear.

Mrs. Yeobright picks an excessively hot August 31 for her six-mile walk. We can protest that a woman of such practical sense as she has been shown to have would surely postpone the expedition, or we can say that yes, once she has resolved on the initiative, she is so eager to get on with it that she is immune to the likely protests of good sense. However we settle that, we must also see this disastrous expedition in its unforced relationship to two others in which good intentions lead to a bad end. Here, Hardy's aesthetic sense rather than his ideas takes over: he manages effective structural repetitions so unobtrusively that critics may be slow to notice them.[1] Of the related expeditions, one takes place later, one earlier. The later one depends on one of the best ironies in the book: to please Eustacia, her young admirer Charlie lights another evening fire and thus summons Wildeve and prepares for Eustacia's final journey, which like Mrs. Yeobright's ends in a death assisted by the elements. The earlier expedition, on the contrary, is the product of one of Hardy's most mechanical devisings—ultimately of his idea that every-

thing will go wrong, despite occasional glimpses of a satisfactory outcome. On Clym's wedding day Mrs. Yeobright dispatches inheritances
of fifty guineas each to Thomasin and Clym. Obviously, Hardy wanted a
major break between Mrs. Yeobright and Eustacia, and a quicker action
than a plausible but slowly developing friction. So he imposed disaster,
as his idea demanded, by a preposterous series of events.

To carry the hundred guineas (a large sum in the 1840s), Mrs. Yeobright, though presented as a shrewd observer of the human scene, is
incredibly made to pick Christian Cantle, who, almost the village idiot,
is much too foolish, fearful, and fragile for such a mission. Only such an
incompetent bearer could be drawn into gambling and, of all things, losing the entire hundred to Wildeve (III, 7). But Hardy saves the day, momentarily: ever-present Diggory Venn spies on the whole thing, dashes
out, forces Wildeve into an unwilling resumption of the game, and wins
back the whole hundred (the last twenty-one by the light of thirteen
glowworms drafted by Venn to replace a lantern put out by a careless
moth). Only in popular melodrama could chance totally reverse itself
thus. Hardy simply imposes his idea of an effective scene. (Returning
home, the miserable Wildeve has to pass and see the happy newlyweds—a
heavy irony reversed when, at the lowest stage of her marital fortunes,
Eustacia, learning that Wildeve has inherited £11,000, has to be bad-
gered about her choice of men by her grandfather [IV, 8].) But happy
melodrama for the deserving is only temporarily permissible, and so
Venn erroneously delivers the whole hundred guineas to Thomasin.
With his dogmatic idea of unavoidable disaster, Hardy is upsetting the
peach basket again. For though Venn, spying on the Wildeve-Christian
gambling, has overheard so much that, when he is defeating Wildeve, he
can crow over him by repeating to him the exact words that Wildeve had
used to Christian, Hardy does not let him hear the key fact: that half the
guineas were to go to Clym (III, 8). Thomasin innocently keeps all the
guineas. Mrs. Yeobright, dismayed that she receives no thanks from
Clym, goes out to check up, and Hardy forces her into two serious mis-
steps. She does not inquire of friendly Thomasin, as would be probable.
Instead, she goes to Eustacia, and then sensible Mrs. Yeobright puts her
question in the one way bound to be irreparably offensive: "Have you
received a gift from Thomasin's husband?" (IV, 1). What is more, she
never explains what she means, even as Eustacia naturally falls into angry outbursts that seem bound to elicit a clarification. Thus has Hardy
made the breach irreparable. Next, Mrs. Yeobright tardily visits Thomasin
and learns what happened; Thomasin conveys guineas and facts to Clym;
but Clym does not pass the word on to Eustacia (IV, 2). Nor does Eustacia explain to Clym the grudge which she now nurtures. Rarely has

disaster been led up to by such devisings, in which Hardy reminds us of the unkind divinities upon whom he likes to cast aspersions. His idea about the irresistible darkness of life can at times produce resistible art.

iii

Yet happily that is less than half the story, for the true artist in Hardy—when the imagination supersedes the idea—has the larger voice. He is capable of superb narrative—for instance, the unstrained continuity of events on the evening of November 5. In an easy-flowing eight and a half chapters Hardy traces the events of a few hours in such a way as to introduce all the main and supporting characters (even the absent Clym by talk of his expected visit) and all the principal situations (Diggory's rejection by Thomasin, the aborted Thomasin-Wildeve wedding, Mrs. Yeobright's hand in these relationships, the Thomasin-Wildeve-Eustacia triangle). Hardy manages a very fluent movement from hour to hour, from scene to scene. In fact, long before films he hits upon a cinematic flow of episodes, and at times he uses a panning technique or a transition by contiguity: we move effortlessly, as if guided by a camera following people's steps and seeing through their eyes—a technique which he might have learned from George Eliot's *Middlemarch* of 1871–1872 (see essay 8 in this volume), though ironically he considered her less a storyteller than a voice of the idea. It is a truism that Hardy liked to open a novel with out-of-doors movement: *The Return* employs a virtuosity of functional motion. Hiking a heath road, Captain Vye catches up with Diggory Venn and his pony-drawn van; inside is the woman who we later learn is Thomasin. Vye moves on, Venn stops for a rest, and we follow his eyes as he looks up and sees a woman's figure atop the highest elevation (Rainbarrow). She leaves, and many people replace her, carrying faggots for fires. We pan to such fires all over the heath, and then settle into a long close-up on the major community fire on Rainbarrow. While they talk, the rustics several times look down to a light that comes from the Quiet Woman Inn, Wildeve's place to which he is supposedly returning with his new bride. Later, when their fire and others are dying, the rustics see one fire that remarkably maintains a steady brightness: they locate it at Captain Vye's place and decide that it is his granddaughter's work. Diggory Venn comes up, looking for the road to Mrs. Yeobright's. She herself stops by to check on the festivities. We follow her when she leaves, walks down off the hill, comes to Diggory's van, meets Thomasin, gets the story of the failed wedding, and goes to the inn to accost Wildeve. We are there when the rustics come down from Rainbarrow for the shivaree which they have been planning. During the activities they all look up at the Vye fire; Wildeve does too, and he starts to move in that direction. The camera now takes us back to deserted Rainbarrow: Eustacia, whom Venn had seen there earlier, returns, and we have a long close-up on her. As the others had done, she looks down at the Wildeve inn, and then she walks cross-heath to the bright fire we have seen several times—her own fire, of course. A wait, and then Wildeve, whom we have seen start, arrives. We get a sense of their relationship and then follow the homeward walk of Eustacia's fire-builder, the boy Johnny Nunsuch; he runs into Diggory, whom we have already seen twice, tells him about the Eustacia-Wildeve meeting, and thus inadvertently provides the information that determines Diggory's actions from then on. The sequence of actions which I have sketched should reveal Hardy's extraordinary skill in designing an easy flux of perspectives and scenes in which, without our ever having a sense of hiatus or of being arbitrarily placed by the author, or even of his steering presence, we glide among the many elements, animate and inanimate, that we must know.

This long night of November 5, brilliant as an introduction, is also important in the overall structure: it is balanced by the long night of the next year's November 6. The symmetry does not create a too-mechanical balance, however, for the account of the second long night is briefer and more intense; on one night, hope sets in, on the other it dies out. The ties are elemental too: on the first, the actions revolve about fires, symbols of cheer and well-being; on the second, the same scenes are swept by wind and rain, indeed a flood that destroys not a race but the self-chosen seeking escape (with a boat to France as ark). The compactness of the two long nights is matched by the compression of the overall story; taking place in just a year, it is tighter than *The Mayor* and *Jude*, which are life histories. The year has its own cycle of seasons: a November day of community pleasures and lovers' problems, a new love ready to be born at Christmas, spring courting, June wedding, dog-days crises, November disaster. These seasons enfold a cycle of experience from old love to new, from new love to disillusion, from dreams to despair, from birth (Thomasin's baby, ironically named Eustacia) to death.[2]

iv

Narrative skills and structural felicity are the external manifestations of the fictional essence in which lies the strength of *The Return*. The essence is the human reality that Hardy gets hold of when his imagination supersedes his idea-pushing. Initially he uses an unostentatious contrast; it is voiced by Eustacia when Diggory tells her that if he cannot have Thomasin he will do his "duty in helping her to get [Wildeve], as a man ought." Eustacia is incredulous. "What a strange sort of love, to be entirely free from that quality of selfishness which is frequently the chief constituent of the passion, and sometimes its only one!" She hardly understands this, "and she almost thought it absurd" (II, 7). Hardy can imagine the love that serves as well as the love that grasps; it is a skillful hedge against sentimentality to see the former through the latter. Eustacia's "absurd" has another value too: in thus calling Diggory irrational, she establishes a subtle link with the loves of Wildeve, Clym, and herself. For the two men and she are, above all, irrational, and driven. And so is Mrs. Yeobright in her own way. Hardy sees in them a compulsiveness that would lead all but very lucky people into disaster.

In Mrs. Yeobright Hardy gets hold of interesting ambiguities. As an influence on Thomasin she reveals conventionality of values, some perceptiveness, and some power of accommodation. She encourages Thomasin to think Diggory lacking in the status her suitors should have (I, 9), and she is right in seeing that Wildeve is not good marital material; then, having given in, she is as insistent on Wildeve's following through as she was once set against him (I, 5, 11), even though she feels an intelligent skepticism about his motives (II, 8). Vis-à-vis Clym and Eustacia, she is shrewd in perception but weak in accommodation. If it is snobbery or a superficial notion of "success" that makes her want Clym to stay on in Paris (III, 2), she is accurate in treating his educational evangelism as one of his "new crotchets," as "wasting your life here," as "the folly of such self-sacrifice," as "a castle in the air" (III, 3). We are convinced early on of what Hardy calls her "singular insight into life" and of the limitations that he ascribes to her (III, 3). He sees clearly her mixed emotions. While she was jealous for Thomasin, she is jealous of Clym and Eustacia—the displaced mother. So she errs in making Eustacia the cause of Clym's conversion, and she condemns Eustacia too harshly. She is sound in insisting that Eustacia is not the right girl for Clym, but the shrill derogatory style that comes out of her defensive motherhood and sense of defeat contributes ironically to the outcome that her insight leads her to oppose—Clym's marriage (III, 5, 6). All this Hardy perceives brilliantly. He skillfully uses Mrs. Yeobright's point of view on the wedding day, and compresses the ambiguities of her feeling into a single sad comment: "O, it is a mistake! . . . And he will rue it some day, and think of me!" (III, 7).

The heart of the story is the Clym-Eustacia relationship, and here is Hardy's great strength. Though the grander things that Hardy claims for them—the divine and the Promethean—are not there, they are not essential to fictional magnitude. The big and impressive truth is the nature of the attraction between them and the compulsive inability of each to grasp the evidence that could modify the attraction. Hardy's extraordinarily late introduction of the title character as a physical presence (in the seventeenth of forty-eight chapters) is not only a rare technical tour de force in the Victorian novel but also a device that helps define the amatory relationship. For first we see fully the toying, the fencing, the sparring of Eustacia and Wildeve—an excellently imagined affinity in which there is mutual erotic responsiveness but not the felt irresistibility that induces total commitment. They make use of each other, perhaps less as sex objects than as ego-maintaining objects. Whether because he feels the incompleteness of Eustacia's devotion or because two girls are more gratifying than one, Wildeve gets engaged to Thomasin; then the love of power of which Hardy is deeply aware makes Eustacia pull him back to her (I, 5), though she is a little embarrassed to discover "the dog in the manger" in herself (I, 11). Acknowledging the irrationality, she can tell him, "and yet I love you," and still always feel that in some way Wildeve is not good enough for her; hence it is natural for her to feel no more need of him once she has met Clym, the hero from Paris, and begins to nourish other hopes. Dismissed and fearing "to lose two women," Wildeve must salvage his ego by marrying Thomasin (and hoping thus to make Eustacia feel slighted). All this is very well done.

When Clym shows up, then, Eustacia is already known to the reader as a handsome woman who wants "to be loved to madness" (I, 7), who has a strong sense of her own status and value, and who has some instinct for and experience in the politics of emotion. Hardy carefully shows both parties drawn in by peripheral aspects of charm—the exotic, the unexpected, the preconceived—rather than by a center of congeniality. There is a touch of the Benedick-Beatrice psychology when Eustacia overhears rustics praising Clym and talking about a match between her and Clym; she adores the Paris that she assumes defines Clym—"like a man coming from heaven"; she begins to have "visions," a "day-dream" (II, 1), a "Great Dream," as Hardy puts it in the caption of the chapter in which he calls her "half in love with a vision" (II, 3); later she thinks of Clym as a deliverer (II, 5). She creates him out of her needs and desires rather than observes the actual creature before her. When she takes a part in the mummer's play, Clym is struck by "a cultivated young woman playing such a part as this" (II, 6). Taken for a witch and pricked by a needle wielded by Susan Nunsuch, Eustacia becomes the victim bound to attract Clym's attention and sympathy; and each expresses concern for the other's risk of injury at the bucket-raising—a "Timeworn Drama" as Hardy almost jestingly puts it in the caption (III, 3).

Earlier we saw Hardy, as narrator, working out from an "idea" of his own instead of trusting to his excellent imagination of human personality and conduct. Now, in his treatment of Eustacia and Clym, we see Hardy with wonderful accuracy detecting the controlling "idea" held by each character—the preconception, the idée fixe, the prior certainty that determines conduct and expectation. The idea cuts off a sense of reality that may be unpleasant but might be a lesser evil. From the time when Eustacia and Clym become aware of a strong attraction to each other, each fits the other into a system of preconceptions. They cease to take adequate account of human reality. Hardy masterfully records the way in which each one listens to himself and not the other. Eustacia is quite explicit in her disavowal of interest in schoolteaching, but Clym doesn't hear it or doesn't believe it. Likewise with her hatred of the heath that he loves. The intensity of her romantic fascination with Paris does not dawn on him. And he pays not the slightest attention when she says, testingly or coquettishly but still truthfully, "I shall ruin you. . . . Kiss me, and go away forever" (III, 4). So they get engaged, she thinking that she can get him out of teaching and back to Paris, and he sure that they'll be happy in love and in improving heath-life. Despite their moments of doubt, the egoism of passion, which Hardy entirely understands, carries them ahead into marriage. The hubris of each is to think that the loved one can be subsumed under, or co-opted into, the social passion of the lover. Neither surrenders his master idea.

Once the initial excitement is over, their minds and feelings are more than ever back on their single tracks. One might wish that Hardy, evidently with the epic year in mind, had not chosen to speed disaster by making Clym go nearly blind (mildly prepared for by brief references to eyestrain), by inventing the plot of the misdirected guineas, and by employing the adder to make sure that Mrs. Yeobright does not survive, but they are his way of reducing the inevitable to plot-form. What is unexceptionable is the tracing of the life within as it issues in visible conduct—Eustacia's seeking a little excitement with Wildeve, her concealment of his presence on the day Mrs. Yeobright calls, Clym's breakdown after her death, the self-righteousness of his fury against Eustacia when he learns the whole story, the mutual recriminations, Eustacia's mixture of almost unconscious footwork and desperation. What is especially good is Hardy's perception of the egoism that runs through the grief and despair on both sides, of the interplay, in both characters, of tragic sense of guilt and a strange *amour propre* that clings to intensity of blame, of others or obdurate circumstance or even of oneself. "But I don't want to get strong," complains Clym at one point (V, 1)—a key point in a continuing self-flagellation that borders on the self-indulgent. On the other hand, when he can say, after Eustacia's death, "She is the second woman I have killed this year" (V, 9), his words lack the theatrical and hysterical note: here is the endured self-knowledge of tragic experience, a surrender of the idea to a perception of reality.

Likewise, on learning of Mrs. Yeobright's death, Eustacia can be toughly clearheaded for a moment: "I am to blame for this. There is evil in store for me" (IV, 8). But she cannot tell Clym the truth; he ferrets it out and rages, and her awareness turns self-defensively from what she has done to what has been done to her, and to bitterness. At one moment Hardy can look at her with his tragic sense; at another shows his sympathy with a woman who finds it easy to believe herself an undeserving victim. As tragic observer he remarks that "instead of blaming herself for the issue she laid the fault upon the shoulders of some indistinct, colossal Prince of the World, who had framed her situation and ruled her lot" (IV, 8). There he virtually spots in her a habit of his own mind: the flight from tragic awareness to the laying of blame on outer forces. She oscillates as he does—between the idea and the deeper awareness of reality. How well he imagines the anguish of the self that feels at once immaculate and preyed upon by an uninvited fate. Eustacia can perceive the difference between fact and hope (if not the illusion that feeds the hope): Wildeve is "not *great* enough for me to give myself to—he does not suffice for my desire!" (V, 7). She goes on in a rage of unearned defeat: "How have I tried and tried to be a splendid woman, and how destiny has been against me! . . . O, how hard it is of Heaven to devise such tortures for me, who have done no harm to Heaven at all!" Hardy catches beautifully the ecstasy of self-love and self-pity, a force as dangerous to the psyche as a suicidal guilt neurosis. It is the last of the governing irrationalities that he portrays with a vitalizing mastery (and by which he makes us all but forget the artifices of the mediating actions).

v

If in *The Return* Hardy treated brilliantly a theme to which he would return in later works—the simple idea versus complex reality—he also hit upon certain narrative devices that he would use again. Clym's letter urging Eustacia to return fails of delivery, as does Tess's letter explaining her past to Angel; both might have changed the course of action. The heavy rains of November 6 appear again in *The Mayor* to compound Henchard's difficulties, and in *Jude* to amplify the troubles of the return to Oxford. Hardy begins to use preaching as an index of personality: Clym slowly finds it a way of life, Alec d'Urberville finds it a temporary satisfaction, and Angel Clare renounces it. Eustacia's dislike of Clym's reading is interestingly duplicated in Arabella's attitude to Jude's learning and books. Eustacia's and Clym's opposite attitudes to Parisian life are deepened in the opposition between Sue's rationalism and Jude's faith, the latter opposition ironically reversed. A subtler anticipation: when Eustacia handles searching questions of Clym by saying, "Dearest, you must not question me unpleasantly, or it may make me not love you," and by using several similar ploys (IV, 2), Hardy is discovering a kind of female strategy that he will explore more fully in Sue Bridehead. Eustacia is a forerunner of Sue in that both are willful and crave power without defining power as a conscious end. Eustacia, however, has read travel books and comes up with a conventional desire for self-gratification in a glamorous city, whereas Sue wants to be the ruling divinity only in the life of one unglamorous man. In Clym, Hardy is getting into two aspects of human nature that later he would carry into further implications. After his mother's death Clym clings to a sense of guilt that borders on the pathological, but he does come around; after the death of her children, on the other hand, Sue falls into a sense of guilt that, as Hardy well sees, has such deep roots in her personality that it must intensify into an illness beyond therapy. When Clym finally learns the death-day facts that Eustacia has not told him, his verbal chastising of her contains a good deal of self-righteousness. Likewise Angel Clare's reaction when he learns facts about his wife's past: wounded ego, censoriousness, self-righteousness. But just as Sue's guilt is deeper than Clym's, so is Angel's punitiveness.

If such partial duplications tell us something about continuities and developments in Hardy's imagination, some comparisons outside the Hardy oeuvre[3] may help place the range and depth of his perceptiveness. Like *The Mayor*, which reminds us of *Oedipus*, and *Jude*, which anticipates some character developments of the twentieth century, *The Return* looks beyond its own time. Mrs. Yeobright is the possessive mother who is a fixture on the twentieth-century stage, though she is a larger character than many of her successors because of her intelligent grasp of the world in which she lives. Eustacia looks both backward and forward in time. As a sister of Emma Bovary she so yearns for an overpowering romance that any available life is not going to satisfy, though she is complicated by a precocious sense of the transitoriness of things (a Hardy "idea" again) that makes her doubt the relationship with Clym before its insufficiency has become evident. In the next century Eustacia's longing to be whirled away by some more than life-size force might lead to the beds of presidents or prime ministers, to drugs, or to political adventurism of a millennial coloring. Yet in all these courses there is an infusion of the vulgarity that Eustacia, whose taste is insecure, would avoid if she could, witness her final judgment of Wildeve.

Though Clym is never the thinker that Hardy asserts him to be, he is a very successful character: in him Hardy catches the archetypal lineaments of what we now call the do-gooder, and he anticipates the ironic treatment of the type in Dorothy Sayers's *The Devil to Pay* (1939) and

Friedrich Dürrenmatt's *An Angel Comes to Babylon* (1953). Clym is sure that "with my system of education, which is as new as it is true, I shall do a great deal of good to my fellow-creatures" (III, 5). By a do-gooder we mean a theorist in benevolence who pays little attention to human actuality and who hence may be a fantast, a busybody, or an enforcer (the man of good will whose will is to impose his good on man). There is a nice structural interplay between Clym and Diggory Venn, who does good as it may be done: he consults the will of a specific person, learns her specific desire, and does his best to see that it is satisfied. But Clym is a man of the idea: he knows what is good for local humanity generally— "instilling high knowledge into empty minds without first cramming them with what has to be uncrammed again before true study begins" (III, 5). It sounds noble, but it is hard to tell what it means. If as observer of education Hardy approves of Clym's idea, as artist he is unable to come up with a single concrete formulation that would give life and meaning to the theoretical program. Clym does seem to think that Susan Nunsuch's anti-witch operation—sticking Eustacia with a needle— proves the need of a new education, but Hardy gives no sign of sharing the belief. In fact, Hardy rather enjoys setting it off against furze-cutter Humphrey's view that some such "rum job or other is sure to go on" whenever anyone from Egdon goes to church (III, 2).

Hardy portrays, not a period freak, but the a priori, dogmatic improver who belongs to every age. This type pays no attention to conditions and possibilities. These are implicitly recorded by local observers when Clym announces his desire for a "rational occupation among the people I [know] best": Timothy Fairway is sure that "In a few weeks he'll learn to see things otherwise," and "another" that "he had better mind his business" (III, 1). The Clym type pays no attention to historical appropriateness; Hardy himself notes that the "rural world was not ripe for him" and that his "mind" was not "well-proportioned." This type pays no attention to lack of appropriate experience; Clym does not listen when his mother says, "The place is overrun with schoolmasters. You have no special qualifications" (III, 5), and when she prophesies accurately, "Your fancies will be your ruin" (III, 2). In a particularly shrewd perception Hardy sees that the type absolutizes personal philosophical ideas and regards them as a sound center for reform: "teach them ["half the world"] how to breast the misery that they are born to." The type is ascetic, immune to the pleasures made available by culture: "I cannot enjoy delicacies; good things are wasted upon me." The type instinctively subsumes persons and relationships to the mission; Hardy does very well to have Clym ask the turf-cutter whether Eustacia "would like to teach children" (III, 2) and pay no attention to the answer. He hardly takes it in when she wants to talk about Paris; he categorically refuses to return there because "it would interfere with my scheme" and feels he can command her, "Don't press that, Eustacia"; he doesn't really listen when she accepts his proposal on the ground that "You will never adhere to your education plan" (III, 4); and when, after their marriage, she makes an effort to get Paris into their plans, he is shocked and responds by working harder than ever at his books (IV, 2). Eustacia learns the approximate truth of what Mrs. Yeobright has told her, that Clym "can be as hard as steel" (IV, 1). Clym may look less like the rigid ideologue when, nearly blind, he takes to the rough life of the furze-cutter and thus seems to make peace with actuality instead of seeking a way to compel it. But in finding his way out of difficulty, he pays no attention to his wife; he arbitrarily rejects the financial help that could come from Captain Vye, and in his relative contentment he is insensitive to Eustacia's grave discontent (IV, 2); he is almost resentful that she can "cling to gaiety so eagerly as to walk all the way to a village festival in search of it," although he does finally tell her to go (IV, 3); the egoist inside the relentless idealist bursts out fully when Clym, sure of grave misdeeds by Eustacia, attacks her with the crude fervor of a prosecuting attorney (V, 3).

To show that Clym, despite basic decency and good intentions, is not a very good matrimonial risk (a social scientist informs me that the domestic-success rate for cause-addicts is low; the excitement of battling conspicuous evil reduces the capacity for doing humble good, *vide* Dickens's Mrs. Jellyby, the archetype) is to round out the portrait of the strong-willed do-gooder that transcends historical boundaries. In the final stroke in that portrait Clym appears as itinerant preacher—exactly the right outcome for the character as created. It would be less so if Clym had a strong sense of actuality (human habits and needs) and a talent for collaboration and what we now call organization. But his bent is toward the prophetic voice, the unclear saving vision, and solitary summons to better things that have become present to him after he has read a book and looked outward through the interstices of daily routines. A gentle egoist with a flair for moral theater, he needs only a little ladder and a Hyde Park, and Clym finds his on Rainbarrow and elsewhere in Wessex.

vi

Clym, as we have seen, is chronologically the first Hardy version of the human being ruled by the idea—a type also present in Eustacia and later in Michael Henchard and studied more literally in Angel Clare, Jude Fawley, and Sue Bridehead. Though Clym survives in an itinerant public life, he has failed in personal life. The failures of his successors in the later Hardy novels are more drastic. In all of these men and women we see preconceptions that do not take adequate account of human reality.

What is fascinating about this history is that Hardy himself was, at least part of the time, a man of the idea. Hence it is possible to think of a number of his major characters as versions of himself (indeed there are biographical parallels between Jude's life and his own). In these very novels he complains that something is wrong with the universe, some basic indecency that victimizes innocent men. Clym thought he could use education against it, Jude inveighed against it, and Hardy himself accused the gods of doing in Tess. Hardy loved to heckle the gods, hector apparent happiness, carp at inequities, and pummel the universe generally. The habit grew on him in the later novels. He often talks as if there ought to be some universal guarantee of human felicity out there, and he castigates the powers divine or societal because there is not. That was his idée fixe.

But that idée fixe could produce, from a writer, only pamphlets or satires, not major novels. The great thing is that as novelist Hardy transcended his persistent idea: he wrote not from it but from a profound imaginative insight into human reality. He intuited the limitations of the single-idea people who were deprived of such an insight into human reality. It is not that their ideas are necessarily wrong, but that they obscure other matters that must be taken into account. Hardy's characters are done in not by malicious circumstances, though Hardy as idea-man would like to see them as victims, but by defects of their own beings. As novelist, Hardy undercut his ruling idea by imagining, in his characters, the disastrous limitations imposed by their ruling ideas. His feat was to see in his characters a habit of his own, and thus to transcend it.

■ VI ■
QUEST AND DISORDER:
LARGELY AMERICAN

■ 22 ■
Hawthorne's "The Birthmark": Science as Religion

HAWTHORNE'S "THE BIRTHMARK" has been called, not inappropriately, a parable. The "truth" that it aims to set forth can be disengaged from the narrative: in a rational attempt to "perfect" nature man may destroy the organic life from which the imperfection is inseparable. But it is necessary to guard against an oversimplification of what the story says, to guard particularly against converting even a parabolic drama into melodrama. Aylmer, the overweening scientist, resembles less the villain than the tragic hero: in his catastrophic attempt to improve on human actuality there is not only pride and a deficient sense of reality but also disinterested aspiration. The story does not advocate total resignation or a flat acquiescence in the immediate state of affairs. Despite its firm expository conclusion, "The Birthmark" hardly advocates at all; it enters the neighborhood of greatness because it has a great theme, but is not tempted into pat answers. The theme which Hawthorne explores may be defined as the problem of mediating between irrational passivity and a hyperrational reorganization of life. Failure in this problem, as in others, may coincide with urgent good will; this is the formulation of the tragic actor which Hawthorne adopts, in contrast with the tragic structure in which an evil or perverted will is joined to saving qualities such as the capacity for repentance. But Hawthorne makes a more precise definition of the tragic error—one that is worth a brief examination.

This definition is made implicitly in the language-pattern of the story—language that may be either literal or figurative but in either case has influential overtones. What we find recurrently in "The Birthmark," and therefore insistently asking to be taken into account, is the terminology and imagery of religion. Specifically religious problems are not overtly introduced into the story, but the language of religion is there so unfailingly that, like iterative imagery in drama and poetry, it must be closely inspected if a final reading of the story is to be complete. What it does is create a story that transcends the parabolic: the foreground parable concerns man's relations with nature, but the immanent story is about man's conceptions of evil. The further we trace the implications of language, the less simple we discover Hawthorne's tale to be.

The scientific progress of Aylmer's day, we are told, "seemed to open paths into the region of *miracle*"; scientists are called *votaries*; Aylmer may have shared their "*faith* in man's ultimate control over Nature." The subjects of their study are called *secrets*, but also, repeatedly, *mysteries*; at the end, the "*mysterious* symbol had passed away," but it had been inseparable from the very "*mystery* of life." When Georgiana and Aylmer's union has been virtually identified with the scientific effort to remove the birthmark, Georgiana thinks of Aylmer's devotion to her— to the perfected her—as "*holy* love." What is made clear by such terms, which function precisely like poetic images, is that science itself has become religion, able to provide an ultimate account of reality and therefore to exact complete human dedication. It has become religion not only for Aylmer but also for Georgiana—"she *prayed* that, for a single moment, she might satisfy his highest and deepest conception." Indeed, her taking of Aylmer's final potion, which is to effect her transformation, is recorded in terms which make it virtually a Christian act. The drink is "bright enough to be the draught of *immortality*"; to Georgiana it is "like water from a *heavenly* fountain," and it will allay "a feverish thirst that had parched me for many days." Since biblical language makes frequent use of metaphors of thirst to express spiritual yearnings, it is difficult not to read in such a passage a reminiscence of John 4:14— "whosoever drinketh of the waters that I shall give him shall never thirst; but the water that I shall give him shall be in him a well of water springing up into everlasting life."

The question, of course, is whether Georgiana's draught is really heavenly and has the power to allay the thirst that from the soul doth rise; whether, in other words, the auspices under which she drinks are spiritual principles. The irony of her illusion is subtly carried on by her blunt command, "Give me the goblet." At one level the analogy with communion is amplified; but *goblet* also has a metaphorical value, and we are inevitably reminded of the cup which is an ordeal: "the cup which my Father hath given me, shall I not drink it?" Georgiana has overcome her dread and has come to conceive of herself, at least in part, as a sacrifice. The end is the secular salvation of mortal man.

The cup has been given by Aylmer. The language pattern of the story indicates that in the religion of science Aylmer is less priest than God. The votaries believed, Hawthorne records, that the scientist would "lay his hand on the *secret of creative force* and perhaps *make new worlds* for himself." The word *wonders* is used repeatedly to describe what Aylmer and other scientists achieved. Aylmer, though he speaks jokingly, does apply the term *sorcerer* to himself; a laboratory exploit of his is *magical*; he is confident that he can "draw a *magic* circle around her within which no evil might intrude." He could make, he intimates, an "*immortal* nostrum"; he has created an "elixir of *immortality*"; the potion which he prepares for Georgiana may be the draught "of *immortal* happiness or misery." Aylmer has given to the problems offered by the birthmark such deep thought that he feels almost able "to *create* a being less perfect" than Georgiana. He is sure that he can make her cheek *faultless*. And then he makes an allusion which contributes importantly to this part of the meaning: "Even Pygmalion, when his sculptured woman assumed life, felt not greater ecstasy than mine will be." Formally, Aylmer rarely fails to exhibit a consciousness of human limitations; but still he cannot discipline that part of himself which aspires to infinite power. At the conclusion of the experiment he exclaims spontaneously, "By *Heaven*! it is well nigh gone!" What is this Heaven? Has a superhuman power aided him? Or has his power itself seemed to go beyond the terrestrial? A minute later he lets "the light of *natural* day" enter the room, and Aminadab, "the *earthly* mass," chuckles grossly. It is as though Aylmer has descended for a moment into another kind of reality from that which is proper to him. Indeed, he distinguishes two kinds of force which he declares have been at work: "Matter and spirit—*earth and heaven*—have both done their part in this!" But the question is whether Aylmer really accepts the dualism to which his words give expression.

In fact, we have almost a parody of the Father who gives the bitter cup to drink. Aylmer, as we have seen, is virtually translated into the godhead: His "*sorcerer's* book," Georgiana insists to him, "has made me *worship* you more than ever." The confusion of identities has spread to Georgiana. Aylmer's own confusion is shown further in his paradoxical inclination to adore as well as create: "the spectral hand . . . wrote mortality where he would fain have *worshiped*." Yet later, in a context which shows that his evaluation is moral, he assures her, "You are fit for heaven without tasting death!" Perhaps, then, she ought to be almost suitable for adoration, and the hand itself should seem a negligible flaw. Yet over it Aylmer is almost hysterical, while, as we shall see, he is blind to more serious flaws closer to home.

That Aylmer is a confused man has always been plain to readers of the story. But, when we examine it in detail, we discover that the language of the story defines his confusion very precisely—defines it as the mistaking of science for religion. The essential story, I have said, is about man's conception of evil: Aylmer does not, in the long run, regard evil as real. Without actually denying its reality, Aylmer in effect simplifies and attenuates it by treating it as manageable, subject to human control, indeed removable. Aylmer's religion reverses the Christian sense of the reality of evil—a reality which can ultimately be dealt with only by divine grace. Aylmer is a romantic perfectibilitarian, who suffers from a dangerous fastidiousness in the presence of complex actuality. "You are perfect!" he assures Georgiana—as she is dying. He believes in perfectibility without retaining the modifying concept of damnability. Man's confidence in his ability to deal with evil by some physical or psychological or social surgery makes him an earthly god: in his presumption he proposes to establish a heaven on earth. Thus, like Aylmer, man becomes committed to a hyperrational—that is, a shallowly grounded—reorganization of life. Hawthorne brilliantly summarizes the metaphysics of the scientific religion in Aylmer's explication of the series of steps in his rehabilitation of Georgiana. He tells her, "I have already administered agents powerful enough to do aught except to change your entire physical system. Only one thing remains to be tried"; "to change your entire physical system" is, in this cosmology, the equivalent of regeneration or conversion. Aylmer's faith becomes, in effect: improve the body, and you save the soul.

Hawthorne repeatedly underlines the error of Aylmer's ways. His confusion of values shows in the fact that his husbandly love can have strength only "by intertwining itself with his love of science." The birthmark that he proposes to remove is "fairy," "mysterious," "magic"— terms which indicate how much more is at stake than Aylmer suspects at his most acute. He accepts uncritically Georgiana's assurance that from his hand she is willing "to take a dose of poison," an ironic anticipation of the way in which his elixir actually does work. He demands complete "trust" and is angry when, following him into the laboratory, she throws "the blight of that fatal birthmark over my labors"—his own word, *blight*, having a summary accuracy of which he is ironically innocent. Aylmer accepts entirely his wife's passionate exclamation that if the birthmark is not removed "we shall both go mad!" What the reader must see in this madness is a simple inability to accept the facts of life. It is precisely this inability of which Hawthorne, throughout the story, keeps reminding us, almost overwhelmingly.

Hawthorne could hardly have found a better symbol than the birthmark, which speaks of the imperfection born with man, with man as a race. Here is original sin in fine imaginative form. Aylmer does not altogether fail to see what is involved; he is not crudely stupid; but his sense of power leads him to undervalue the penalties of life. His tragedy is that he lacks the tragic sense; he is, we may say, a characteristic modern, the exponent of an age that has deified science and regards it as an irresistibly utopianizing force. His tragic flaw is to fail to see the tragic flaw in humanity. Hawthorne never lets the reader forget the deep significance of the "human hand" that scars Georgiana. He comments ironically on the lovers who hoped to see "one living specimen of ideal loveliness without the semblance of a flaw," a suggestion of a common attitude for which Aylmer speaks. The birthmark is a "symbol of imperfection," "the spectral hand that wrote mortality," the "sole token of human imperfection." This "fatal flaw of humanity"—the terms are virtually Christian—implies that all the productions of nature are "temporary and finite" and that "their perfection must be wrought by toil and pain." For spiritual discipline Aylmer wants to substitute magic—not quite push-button magic perhaps, but still a shortcut, a kind of prestidigitation. It is not that he is ignorant in a gross way; he sees much, but his premises stop him at the threshold of wisdom. He recognizes that the blemish on Georgiana's face is a "mark of earthly imperfection"; he even selects it "as the symbol of his wife's liability to sin, sorrow, decay, and death." The frequency of images of death in the story is a thematic reminder of the reality from which Aylmer doggedly turns away. Although here he actually puts his finger upon the realities which the mature man must come to terms with, his faith leads him to feel, as we have seen, "that he could draw a magic circle round her within which no evil might intrude." Evil is manageable: the symbol itself has become the reality.

What we finally come to is the problem of spirit, and the test of Aylmer's creed is the kind of spiritual values it embodies. We hear repeatedly about Aylmer's spirit and his interest in the spiritual. He had "attempted to fathom," we learn, "the very process by which Nature assimilates all her precious influences from earth and air, and from the *spiritual* world, to create and foster man, her masterpiece." Aminadab represents "man's physical nature"; in Aylmer we see "the *spiritual* element." Georgiana is almost convinced "that her husband possessed sway over the *spiritual* world." As she reads his record of experiments, the author, apparently speaking for her, comments: "He handled physical details as if there were nothing beyond them; yet *spiritualized* them all, and redeemed himself from materialism by his strong and eager aspiration towards the *infinite*. In his grasp the veriest clod of earth assumed a *soul*." His failures are those of "the *spirit* burdened with clay and working in matter"; "his *spirit* was ever on the march, ever ascending"—the spirit, one is tempted to say, of progress. But as a result of this spiritual yearning of his, another's "angelic spirit" leaves on its "heavenward flight."

At the end Hawthorne, distinguishing "mortal" and "celestial," reaffirms a dualism which he has insisted upon throughout the story and which, as various words of theirs make clear, is formally assented to also by Georgiana and Aylmer. But the first defect of Aylmer's religion, as the drama makes clear, is that in practice he does not accept dualism at all: for him, spirit is not distinct from matter but is the perfecting of matter. The material stigma that shocks him he is said, just once, to regard as symbol; but his efforts at amelioration are directed wholly at the symbol, not at its antecedent substance. Aylmer is actually symptom-doctoring and is unaware that the locus of the disease is elsewhere. His creed is secular and monistic. All the talk about spirit is an ironic commentary upon his essential lack of insight into real problems of spirit.

The story specifies what level of spiritual comprehension Aylmer does reach. He aspires, and his aspiration is presented with a good deal of sympathy, as is just. Between aspiration and passivity, the choice is, in the main, clear; but a judgment must be made between one kind of aspiration and another. So the question becomes: how, and toward what, does Aylmer actually aspire? Does he, for instance, aspire toward better insight? Toward charity? Toward wisdom? Or is it not rather that his aspiration is inextricably involved with the exercise of power? "There is no taint of imperfection on thy spirit," he tells Georgiana. Why? Because Georgiana has just indicated an unreserved willingness to accept his potion; her faith in him is total. He is not content with her perfection of "spirit." For him, immense knowledge is a means of doing things, of achieving physical, visible ends. We see in him no evidence of concern with the quality of his own life, or perception, or thought.

In this man of science divine discontent is with others; as Georgiana puts it, his love "would accept nothing less than perfection nor miserably make itself contented with an earthlier nature than he had dreamed of." It is of course Georgiana who shall be "all perfect." The romantic scientist has no thought of the problem of perfecting himself; indeed, his spiritual perception is very close to that of uplift and do-goodism. He begs the real problem of spirit and is fanatical about the shortcomings of the world. Hawthorne is very acute in analyzing further the especial quality of Aylmer's outward-bound perfectionism and in discerning in it a core of intense fastidiousness. This hypersensitivity rushes in, indeed, at the very moment at which Aylmer fleetingly achieves a kind of wholeness of response to Georgiana, an acceptance of her that implies a spiritual modification of himself. "Yet once, by a strange and unaccountable impulse, he pressed it [the birthmark] with his lips." Here is virtually a redefinition of his love. But immediately his fastidiousness reasserts itself and gives the parting tone to the action: "His *spirit* recoiled, however, in the very act." That is his spirit: a primary awareness of the flaws of others and of the demand which they appear to make for remedy from without.

The heir of Prometheus kills his beneficiary, not by conferring a single blessing, but by endeavoring to eradicate the imperfections humanity is heir to. Upon this aspiration to divinity Hawthorne comments in

his account of Aylmer's library, of the works of "these antique naturalists" who "perhaps imagined themselves to have acquired from the
investigation of Nature a power above Nature, and from physics a sway
over the spiritual world." Hawthorne has already remarked that the "great
creative Mother . . . is yet severely careful to keep her own secrets."
What Hawthorne has done, really, is to blueprint the course of science
in modern imagination, to dramatize its persuasive faith in its omnipo-
tence, and thus its taking on the colors of religion.

This very formulation commits Hawthorne to a critique—a critique
which he makes by disclosing the false spirituality of Aylmer. It is the
false spirituality of power conjoined with fastidiousness, of physical improvement, of external remedy, of ad hoc proscriptions, of reform: Aylmer's surgery is an accurate symbol for a familiar code. Yet the code
would have only an innocuous life in a museum case if it did not gain
converts. Thus we have Georgiana's very important role in the story:
she is less the innocent victim than the fascinated sharer in magic who
conspires in her own doom. Georgiana, the woman killed with kindness
by the man who would be God, is really humanity—with its share of the
heroic, its common sense, which enables it to question heroes, and yet
its capacity for being beguiled, for combining good intention, devotion,
and destructive delusion. In the marriage of science and humanity we
see the inevitably catastrophic interaction of a mechanical perfectionism and the "birthmark of mortality." Science has no way of coming to
terms with human imperfection, and humanity, tutored by science, can
no longer accept its liability to sin and death.

Ironically, it is Georgiana who cuts off, or at least helps cut off, a final
path of spiritual rectification for Aylmer. "Do not *repent*," she says, "that
. . . you have rejected the best earth could offer." Not only is Aylmer's
definition of "the best" inadequate, but he is encouraged in a hardening
of spirit which precludes his entering upon a reconsideration of values.
His religion offers no way of dealing with his pride. And his pride—with
its intense demand that the world submit itself to his limited criteria—
gives us another definition of the spiritual defect of this man who is so
convinced that spirit is his concern. When Georgiana confesses her desire to worship him more fully, he scarcely bothers to be deprecatory:
"Ah, wait for this one success, . . . then *worship* me if you will. I shall
deem myself hardly unworthy of it." These are the ultimate marks of his
moral infatuation.

The critical problem in "The Birthmark" has to do with the kind of
mistake Aylmer makes. Hawthorne's language tells us, subtly but insistently, that Aylmer has apotheosized science; and the images and drama
together define the spiritual shortcoming of this new revelation—its be-

lief in the eradicability of evil, its Faustian proneness to love power, its incapacity to bring about renunciation or self-examination, its pride. I once thought that Hawthorne had stopped short of the proper goal of the story by not including the next phase of Aylmer's experience—the phase in which, if the tragic view of Aylmer were to prevail, Aylmer would entertain the Furies. But the summation of Aylmer's defects is that he cannot see the Furies. The story stops where it must.

■ 23 ■
Trouble in Eden: James's *The Turn of the Screw*

i

HOW ONE INTERPRETS Henry James's *The Turn of the Screw* depends primarily upon how one reads the public story.[1] I take it to mean just what it says. At Bly there are apparitions which the governess sees, which Mrs. Grose does not see but comes to believe in because they are consistent with her own independent experience, and of which the children have a knowledge that they endeavor to conceal. These dramatic circumstances have an import which is not too mysterious: the ghosts are evil, evil which comes subtly, conquering before it is wholly seen; the governess, Cassandra-like in the intuitions which are inaccessible to others, is the guardian whose function it is to detect and attempt to ward off evil; Mrs. Grose—whose name, like the narrator's title, has virtually allegorical significance—is the commonplace mortal, well intentioned, but perceiving only the obvious; the children are the victims of evil, victims who, ironically, practice concealment—who doubtless must conceal—when not to conceal is essential to salvation. If this reading of the symbolism be tenable, we can understand in part the imaginative power of the story, for, beneath the strange and startling action-surface, we have the oldest of themes—the struggle of evil to possess the human soul. And if this struggle appears to resolve itself into a Christian form, that impulse, as it were, of the materials need not be surprising.

But the exceptionally vivid action is only one of the means by which James sets forth his meaning. Another tool, and a very effective one by which he stirs our imaginations, is a highly suggestive, and often symbolic, language, one permeating the entire story. Indeed, he uses recurrent imagery as poets and dramatists (Shakespeare, for example) often do. By iterative imagery and unobtrusive symbols James has richly qualified the bare narrative and influenced the tone and meaning of the story. If he has not defined outright the evil which, as he specified, was to come to the reader as something momentous and unidentified, he has at least set forth the mode and terms of its operation with extraordinary fullness.

If *The Turn of the Screw* is, as it has been called, a "horror story," the

317

center of horror is not the apparitions themselves, uniquely disturbing as their manifestations are, but the children, and our sense of what is happening to them. What is happening to them is Quint and Jessel: the governess's awareness of the apparitions is her awareness of a change within the children; the shock of ghostly appearances is the shock of evil perceived unexpectedly, suddenly, after it has secretly made inroads (compare, in our own day, the discovery of drug addiction in a youngster apparently innocent). For some readers this has been a difficult dish. There are two reasons for the difficulty: the widespread sentimentalizing of children, and the tendency to think of evil only as melodramatic— that is, the exclusive possession of wrongdoers who can be handled by the police. James is not disposed to make things easier; he emphasizes that it is the incorruptible who have taken on corruption.[2] He introduces no mere pathos of childhood catastrophe; his are not ordinary children. He is at pains to give them a special quality—by repetition which in so careful an artist can hardly have been a clumsy accident. As the repeated words achieve a cumulative tonal force, we can see the working of the poetic imagination.

Flora has "extraordinary charm," is "most beautiful." Miles is "incredibly beautiful." Both have "the bloom of health and happiness." Miles is "too fine and fair" for the world; he is a "beautiful little boy." The governess is "dazzled by their loveliness." They are "most loveable" in their "helplessness." Touching their "fragrant faces" one could believe only "their incapacity and their beauty." Miles is a "prodigy of delightful, loveable goodness." In midstory Flora still emerges from concealment "rosily," and one is caught by "the golden glow of her curl," by her "loveliest, eagerest simplicity," by "the excess of something beautiful that shone out of the blue" of her eyes, by "the lovely little lighted face." In both, "beauty and amiability, happiness and cleverness" are still paramount. Miles has still the "wonderful smile" and the "beautiful eye" of "a little fairy prince." Both write letters "too beautiful to be posted." On the final Sunday the governess still sees Miles's "beautiful face" and talks of him as "beautiful and perfect"; he smiles at her "with the same loveliness" and spars verbally with "serenity" and "unimpeachable gaiety." Even after Flora is gone, Miles is "the beautiful little presence" as yet with "neither stain nor shadow"; his expression is "the most beautiful" the governess has ever known.

James devotes an almost prodigal care to creating an impression of special beauty in the children, an impression upon which depends the extraordinary effectiveness of the change that takes place in them. In such children the appearance of any imperfection is a shock. The shock is emphasized when the governess wonders whether she must "pronounce their loveliness a trick of premature cunning" and reflects upon the possibility that "the immediate charm . . . was studied"; when Miles's "sweet face" must be described as a "sweet ironic face"; when his "happy laugh" goes off into "incoherent, extravagant song"; and when, above all, the governess must declare with conviction that their "more than earthly beauty, their absolutely unnatural goodness [is] a game, . . . a policy and a fraud."

Is James, then, laboriously overusing the principle of contrast, clothing the children with an astonishing fascination merely to accentuate the shock of their being stripped bare? Obviously not. Beneath the superficial clash we can already sense a deeper paradox. When James speaks of Miles's "beautiful fevered face" and says that he "lives in a setting of beauty and misery," he puts into words what the reader has already come to feel—that his real subject is the dual nature of man, who is a little lower than the angels, and who yet can become a slave in the realm of evil. The children's beauty, we have come to feel, is a symbol of the spiritual quality that is open to man, whether or not he seeks it. Of course the search for it may go awry, as in Hawthorne's "The Birthmark" (see the preceding essay).

ii

When James speaks of "any clouding of their innocence," he reminds us again of a special quality in their beauty which he has quietly stressed with almost thematic fullness. The *clouding* suggests a *change* in a characteristic brightness of theirs, a brightness of which we are made aware by a recurrent imagery of light. Flora, at the start, "brightly" faces the new governess; hers is a "radiant" image; the children "dazzle" the governess; Flora has "a lovely little lighted face," and she considers "luminously"; in his "brightness" Miles "fairly glittered"; he speaks "radiantly"; at his "revolution" he speaks with "extraordinary brightness." This light-giving quality of theirs is more than a mere amplification of a charm shockingly to be destroyed; it is difficult not to read it as a symbol of their being, as it were, at the dawn of existence. For they are children, and their radiance suggests the primal and the universal. This provisional interpretation is supported by another verbal pattern that James uses to describe the children. Miles has a "great glow of freshness," a "positive fragrance of purity," a "sweetness of innocence"; the governess comments again on the "rose-flush of his innocence"; in him she finds something "extraordinarily happy, that . . . struck me as beginning anew each day"; he could draw upon "reserves of goodness." Then, as things change, the governess remarks, on one occasion, that he "couldn't play any longer at innocence," and mentions, on another, his pathetic struggles to "play . . . a part of innocence." To the emphasis upon beauty, then, is added this emphasis upon brightness and freshness and innocence. What must come across to us, from such a context, is echoes of the Garden of Eden; of mankind at its first radical crisis; Miles and Flora become the childhood of the race. They are symbolic children as the ghosts are symbolic ghosts. Even the names themselves have a representative quality as those of James's characters often do: Miles—the soldier, the archetypal male; Flora—the flower, the essential female. Man and woman are caught even before the first hint of maturity, dissected, and shown to have within them all the seeds—possible of full growth even now—of their own destruction.

James's management of the setting and of other ingredients in the drama deepens one's sense of a story at once primeval and eternal, lurking beneath the surface of the action. Bly itself is almost an Eden with its "lawn and bright flowers"; the governess comments, "The scene had a greatness." Three times James writes of the "golden" sky, and one unconsciously recalls that Flora was a "rosy sprite" with "hair of gold." Miss Jessel first appears "in the garden," where "the old trees, the thick shrubbery, made a great and pleasant shade." Here, for a time, the three "lived in a cloud of music and love"; the children are "extraordinarily at one" in "their quality of sweetness." Now it is significant that James uses even the seasons to heighten his drama: the pastoral idyll begins in June, when spring is at the full, and then is gradually altered until we reach the dark ending of a November whose coldness and deadness are unobtrusively but unmistakably stressed: "the autumn had dropped . . . and blown out half our lights" (a variation of the light pattern); the governess now notices "grey sky and withered garlands," "bared spaces and scattered dead leaves." What might elsewhere be Gothic trimming is here disciplined by the pattern. When, on the final Sunday night, the governess tries hard to "reach" Miles, there is "a great wind"; she hears "the lash of the rain and the batter of the gusts"; at the climax there is "an extraordinary blast and chill," and then darkness. The next afternoon is "damp and grey." After Flora's final escapade at the pond, James stresses the governess's feelings at the end of the day; the evening is "portentous" without precedent; she blows out the candles and feels a "mortal coldness." On the final day with Miles she notices "the stupid shrubs," "the dull things of November," "the dim day." So it is not merely the end of a year but the end of a cycle: the spring of gay, bright human innocence has given way to the dark autumn—or rather, as we might pun, to the dark *fall*.

And in the darkness of the latter end of things we might note the special development of the light which, to the sensitive governess, the children seem actually to give off. It is, I think, more than a coincidence that, when the governess mentions Miss Jessel, Flora's face shows a "quick, smitten glare," and that, in the final scene, Miles is twice said to be "glaring"—the same verb that has been used to describe Quint's look. All three characters, of course, look with malevolence; yet *glare* must suggest, also, a hard, powerful, ugly light—an especially effective transformation of the apparently benign luminousness of the spring.

The same movement of human experience James portrays in still another symbolic form. As the light changes and the season changes and the children's beauty becomes ambiguous, another alteration takes place in them. Their youth, of course, is the prime datum of the story, and of it we are ever conscious; at the same time we are aware of a strange maturity in them—in, for instance, their poise, their controlled utilization of their unusual talents to give pleasure. Our sense of something that transcends their youth is first defined overtly late in the story when the governess speaks of her feeling that Miles is "accessible as an older person." Though she does not speak of change, there is subtly called forth in us a conviction that years have been added to Miles. So we are not surprised when the governess assures Mrs. Grose, and goes out of her way, a little later, to remind her of the assurance, that, at meetings with Miss Jessel, Flora is "not a child" but "an old, old woman"—an insight that receives a measure of authentication, perhaps, by its reminiscence of the Duessa motif. The suggestion that Flora has become older is skillfully conveyed, in the pond scene, by her silence (and silence itself has an almost symbolic value throughout the story), by her quick recovery of her posed gaiety, and especially by the picture of her peeping at the governess over the shoulder of Mrs. Grose, who is embracing her—the first intimation of a cold adult calculatingness that appears in all her remaining actions. The governess says, "her incomparable childish beauty had suddenly failed, had quite vanished . . . she was literally . . . hideously hard; she had turned common and almost ugly." Mrs. Grose sums up, "It has made her, every inch of her, quite old." More effective, however, than any of this direct presentation of vital change is a delicate symbol which may pass almost unnoticed: when she is discovered at the pond, Flora picks up, and drops a moment later, "a big, ugly spray of withered fern"— a quiet commentary on the passage of symbolic spring, on the spiritual withering that is the story's center. When, at the end of the scene, the governess looks "at the grey pool and its blank, haunted edge," we automatically recall, "The sedge has withered from the lake"—the imagery used by Keats in his account of an ailing knight-at-arms in another bitter autumn.

Besides the drying of foliage and the coming of storms and darkness there is one other set of elements, loosely working together and heavy with implications, which suggest that this is a story of the decay of Eden. At Quint's first appearance Bly "had been stricken with death." After Miles's nocturnal exploit the governess utters a cliché that, under the influence of the context, becomes vigorously meaningful: "you . . . caught your death in the night air!" There are, further, some arresting details in the description of Quint: "His eyes are sharp, strange—awfully; . . . rather small and very fixed. His mouth's wide, and his lips are thin." These are unmistakably the characteristics of a snake. James, of course, does not press the point, but, as he has shaped the story, the coming of Quint is the coming of the serpent into the little Eden that is Bly. (Both Katherine Anne Porter and Allen Tate have noted other physical characteristics of Quint which traditionally belong to the devil.) Quint's handsomeness and his borrowed finery, by which he apes the gentleman, suggest, perhaps, the specious plausibleness of the visitor in the Garden. As for the "fixed eyes": later we learn that Miss Jessel "only fixed the child" and that the apparition of Quint "fixed me exactly as it had fixed me from the tower and from the garden." Of Quint's position at Bly, Mrs. Grose says, "The master believed in him and placed him here because he was supposed not to be well and the country air so good for him." The master, in other words, has nourished a viper in his bosom. The secret influence upon Miles the governess describes as "poison," and at the very end she says that the demonic presence "filled the room like the taste of poison." In the first passage the governess equates "poison" with "secret precocity"; toward the end she emphasizes Miles's freedom and sorrowfully gives up "the fiction that I had anything more to teach him." Why is it a fiction? Because he already knew too much, because he had eaten of the fruit of the tree of knowledge? We have already been told of the "dark prodigy" by which "the imagination of all evil *had* been opened up to him," and of his being "under some influence operating in his small intellectual life as a tremendous incitement."

iii

We should not press such analogies too hard, or construct inflexible parables. Our business is rather to trace all the imaginative emanations that enrich the narrative, the associations and intimations by which it transcends the mere horror story and achieves its own kind of greatness. But by now it must be clear from the antipodal emphases of the story that James has an almost religious sense of the duality of man, and, as if to manifest an intention, he makes that sense explicit in terms broadly religious and even Christian. The image of Flora's "angelic beauty" is "beatific"; she has "the deep, sweet serenity . . . of one of Raphael's holy infants"; she has "placid heavenly eyes." In Miles there is "something divine that I have never found to the same degree in any child." In a mildly humorous context the children are called "cherubs." Seeing no signs of suffering from his school experience, the governess regards Miles as an "angel." Mrs. Grose imputes to Flora a "blessed innocence," and the governess surrenders to the children's "extraordinary childish grace"—a noun which in this patterned structure can hardly help being ambivalent. In midstory Flora has still a "divine smile"; both children remain "adorable." This verbal pattern, which is too consistent to be coincidental, irresistibly makes us think of the divine in man, of his capability of salvation. Now what is tragic and terrifying in man is that to be capable of salvation is to be capable also of damnation—an equivocal potentiality suggested early by the alternation of moods in the newly arrived governess, who senses immediately a kind of wavering, a waiting for determination, at Bly. And James, to present the spiritual decline of the children, finds terms which exactly balance those that connote their spiritual capabilities.

We are always compelled to see the apparitions as moral realities. Miss Jessel is a figure of "unmistakeable horror and evil . . . in black, pale and dreadful." She is a "horror of horrors," with "awful eyes," "with a kind of fury of intention," and yet "with extraordinary beauty." Again she is described as "Dark as midnight in her black dress, her haggard beauty, and her unutterable woe." It is brilliant to give her beauty, which not only identifies her with Flora and thus underscores the dual possibilities that lie ahead of Flora, but also enriches the theme with its reminder of Milton's fallen angels who retain something of their original splendor—"the excess / Of glory obscured." So, with the repeated stress upon her woe, we almost expect the passage which tells us that she "suffers the torments . . . of the damned": she is both damned and an agent of damnation—another reminiscence of the Miltonic myth. She is called later a "pale and ravenous demon," not "an inch of whose evil . . . fell short"—which reminds us of James's prefatory insistence that the apparitions were to be thought of as demons. Again, she is "our infernal witness"; she and Quint are "those fiends"; "they were not angels," and they could be bringing "some yet more infernal message." "And to ply them with that evil still, to keep up the work of demons, is what brings the others back." They are "tempters," who work subtly by holding out fascinating "suggestions of danger." In the last scene Quint presents— the phrase is used twice—"his white face of damnation."

By this series of words, dispersed throughout the story yet combining in a general statement, James defines as diabolic the forces attacking the children of whose angelic part we are often reminded. Now these attacking forces, as often in Elizabethan drama, are seen in two aspects. Dr. Faustus has to meet an enemy which has an inner and an outer reality— his own thoughts, and Mephistopheles; James presents evil both as agent (the demons) and as effect (the transformation in the once fresh and beautiful and innocent children). The dualistic concept of reality appears most explicitly when Mrs. Grose asks, "And if he was so bad there as that comes to, how is he such an angel now?" and the governess replies, "Yes, indeed—and if he was a fiend at school!" By the *angel-fiend* antithesis James underscores what he sees as a central human contradiction, which he emphasizes throughout the book by his chosen verbal pattern. The governess speaks of the children's "love of evil" gained from Quint and Miss Jessel, of Miles's "wickedness" at school. In such a context the use of the word *revolution* to describe Miles's final taking up of matters with the governess—a move by which, we should remember, he becomes completely "free"—cannot help calling to mind the Paradise and Eden revolutions of Judeo-Christian mythology. The revolutionary change in character is nicely set forth by the verbal counterpoint in one passage. "He found the most divine little way," the governess says, "to keep me quiet while she went off." "Divine?" Mrs. Grose asks, and the governess replies, "Infernal then!" The divine has paradoxically passed into the infernal. Then we see rapidly the completed transition in Flora: she turns upon the governess an expression of "hard, fixed gravity" and ignores the "hideous plain presence" of Miss Jessel—"a stroke that somehow converted the little girl herself into the very presence that could make me quail." In Miles, by contrast, we see a protracted struggle, poignantly conveyed by a recurrent metaphor of illness. Early in the story Miles is in "the bloom of health and happiness," but near the end he seems like a "wistful patient in a children's hospital," "like a convalescent slightly fatigued." At the end he shows "bravery" while "flushing with pain"; he gives "a sick little headshake"; his is a "beautiful fevered face." But the beauty goes, the fever gains; Miles gives "a frantic little shake for air and light"; he is in a "white rage." The climax of his disease, the binding together of all the strands we have been tracing, is his malevolent cry to the governess—"You devil!" It is his final transvaluation of values: she who would be his savior has become for him a demon. His face gives a "convulsive supplication"—that is, actually, a prayer, for and to Quint, the demon who has become his total deity. But the god isn't there, and Miles despairs and dies. We need not labor the dependence of this brilliant climax upon the host of associations and evocations by which, as this outline endeavors to show, James prepares us for the ultimate resolution of the children's being.

There are glimmerings of other imaginative kinships, such as that already mentioned, the Faustian. Miles's "You devil" is in one way almost identical with Faustus's savage attack, in Marlowe's play, upon the Old Man who has been trying to save him; indeed James's story, in its central combat, is not unlike the Faustus story as it might be told by the Good Angel. But whereas Dr. Faustus is a late intellectualist version of Everyman, James, as we have said, weaves in persuasive hints, one after another, of mankind undergoing, in its Golden Age, an elemental conflict: thus we have the morality play, but in a complicated, enriched, and intensified version. When the governess first sees Quint, she is aware of "some challenge between us"; the next time it seems "as if I had been looking at him for years and had known him always"; near the end she says, "I *was* . . . face to face with the elements," and, of the final scene, "It was like fighting with a demon for a human soul."

iv

What, then, does the story say about the role of the governess, and how does this contribute to the complex of impressions built up in part by James's language? From the start the words used by the governess suggest that James is attaching to her the quality of savior, not only in a general sense, but with certain Christian associations. She uses words like "atonement"; she speaks of herself as an "expiatory victim," of her "pure suffering," and at various times—twice in the final scene—of her "torment." Very early she plans to "shelter my pupils," to "absolutely save" them; she speaks variously of her "service," "to protect and defend the little creatures . . . bereaved . . . loveable." When she fears that she cannot "save or shield them" and that "they're lost," she is a "poor protectress." At another time she is a "sister of Charity" attempting to "cure" Miles. But by now what we cannot mistake is the relation of pastor and flock, a relationship that becomes overt when the governess tells Miles, "I just want you to help me to save you." It is in this sense that the governess "loves" Miles—a loving which must not be confused, as it is confused by some critics, with "making love to" or "being in love with" him. Without such pastoral love no guardian would consider his flock worth the sacrifice. The governess's priestly function is made still more explicit by the fact that she comes ultimately to act as confessor and to use every possible means to bring Miles to confession; the long final scene really takes place in the confessional, with the governess as priest endeavoring, by both word and gesture, to protect her charge against the evil force whose invasion has, with consummate irony, carried even there. In one sense the governess must elicit confession because, in her need for objective reassurance, she will not take the lead as accuser. But securing the confession is, more importantly, a mitigation of Miles's own pride, his self-will; it could soften him, make him accessible to grace. The experience has a clear sacramental quality: the governess says that Miles senses "the need of confession . . . he'll confess. If he confesses, he's saved." It is when he begins to break and confess that "the white face of damnation" becomes baffled and at a vital moment retreats; but it returns "as if to blight his confession," and it is in part through the ineptitude of the governess-confessor-savior, we are led to understand, that Miles is lost.

It is possible that there are even faint traces of theological speculation to give additional substance to the theme of salvation and damnation which finally achieves specific form in the sacramentalism of the closing scenes. Less than halfway through the story the governess refers to the children thus: "blameless and foredoomed as they were." By "blameless" she can only mean that she does not have direct, tangible evidence of voluntary evildoing on their part; they still look charming and beautiful; she does not have grounds for a positive placing of blame. Why, then, "foredoomed"? May this not be a suggestion of original sin, an interpretation consistent with the view of Bly as a kind of Eden? Three-quarters of the way through the story the governess again turns to speculation: "I constantly both attacked and renounced the enigma of what such a little gentleman could have done that deserved a penalty." "Enigma" is perhaps just the word to be applied to a situation, of which one technical explication is the doctrine of original sin, by an inquiring lay mind with a religious sense but without precise theological tools. What is significant is that the governess does not revolt against the penalty as if it betokened a cosmic injustice. And original sin, whether it be natural depravity or a revolt in a heavenly or earthly paradise, fits exactly into the machinery of this story of two beautiful children who in a lovely springtime of existence already suffer, not unwillingly, hidden injuries that will eventually destroy them.

v

This summary of the imaginative overtones in *The Turn of the Screw* has taken us rather deeply into a view of the book as strongly religious in cast. Yet this very moving impression is produced by agencies that quietly penetrate the story, not by devices that stick out of it, so to speak, and become commanding guideposts. There are no old familiar signs announcing a religious orientation of experience. There is nothing of the Bible overtly; there are no texts, no clergymen; there are no conventional indices of religious feeling—no invocations or prayers or meditations; all there is is a certain amount of churchgoing of a very matter-of-fact sort, and otherwise the context is ostensibly secular. Thus the story becomes no bland preachment; it simply "has life"—to use James's criterion of excellence—and it is left to us to define the boundaries and extensions and reverberations of that life. Right where we might expect the most positive assistance, perhaps, in seeking that definition, we find least. Yet even in a few dry and casual ecclesiastical mementos we sense some ever-so-mild symbolic pressures, as of a not-very-articulate wispish presence that quietly makes itself felt. These intimations of a presence would not be magnified into a solid "character" who demands our attention. But in their small way they collaborate with other intimations. The reading of the story, for instance, takes place during the Christmas season, the framework action begins on Christmas Eve. Quint appears for the second time on a Sunday, a gray, rainy Sunday, just before the governess is about to go to the late church service with Mrs. Grose; after that she is, she says, "not fit for church"; and their only service is then "a little service of tears and vows, of prayers and promises." This is the important occasion on which Mrs. Grose identifies the apparition with Quint. As the governess reflects on the situation, she speaks of the "inconceivable communion" of which she has learned—a Black Mass, as it were. The event next in importance to the identification of Quint also occurs on a Sunday—Miles's "revolution." Miles and the governess are "within sight of the church"; she thinks "with envy" of the "almost spiritual help of the hassock." After they enter the churchyard gate, Miles detains her "by a low, oblong, table-like tomb"—a reminder that Bly was "stricken with death" on the first appearance of Quint. Then Miles threatens to bring his uncle down, and it is he, with fine irony, who "marched off alone into church," while the governess can only walk "round the church" and listen "to the sounds of worship." Here, for once, what we may call the Christian apparatus is out in the open, with a clear enough ironic function. From this we go on to the most tantalizing body of suggestion in the whole book, less a body than a wraith, indeed, and yet the more urgent for its not falling within the everyday commonplaces of fictional method. Miles's revolution introduces a straight-line action which continues with remarkably increasing tension to the end of the story. James allots 40 percent of his total space to this action, which—and here is the notable point—takes only three days. Thus he puts the heaviest emphasis on those three days—Sunday, Monday, and Tuesday. During those three days the governess, the clergyman's daughter, undertakes her quasi-priestly function with a new intensity and aggressiveness. On Sunday night she enters upon a newly determined, if still cautious, effort to bring Miles to confession; she openly asserts her role as savior. On Monday she tries to shock Flora into spiritual pliability—and fails. All her will to redeem, she now turns upon Miles; in the final scene she fights the adversary directly. She succeeds to an extent: Miles cannot see Quint. But the end of the climactic triduum of her ordeal as savior is failure: Quint comes again, as if to "blight" Miles's confession; Miles still cannot see him—and dies. The would-be redeemer of the living is called "devil"; in Quint we see one who has risen again to tempt the living to destruction—that is, the resurrection and the death. Here, Sunday does not triumphantly end a symbolic ordeal that had begun in apparent failure on Friday; rather it hopefully initiates a struggle which is to end, on the third day, in bitter loss. We have, then, a modern late-fall defeat patterned on the ancient springtide victory. To transmit its quality and to embrace all of its associations, may we not call it a Black Easter?

vi

If this interpretation will hold up, it will crown the remarkable associational edifice which is both a part of and an extension of the dramatic structure of the story, an edifice which figures forth man's quality, his living, so to speak, as a potentiality which may be fulfilled or may paradoxically be transformed into its radical opposite. This we are told, by implication, through the beauty which can become ugliness, the brightness which becomes darkness, the innocence which can become sophistication, the spring which becomes fall, the youth which becomes age, the Eden which can be stricken with death, the angelic which becomes diabolic; and through the pictured capacity, whether it be understood as original sin or otherwise, for revolt, for transvaluation of values, for denial of the agency of salvation. And this truth comes to us with peculiar shock because we see enacted, not that imperceptible movement by which man's advance in age and in corruption becomes endurable, but the transformation from one extreme to the other in pure state, in essence, in symbolic immediacy. In this study of evil, youth is age.

James chose to omit certain matters from his narrative statement. But by a poetic use of language he elaborated upon his story and gave adequate clues to the metaphysical foundations of his plot. The felt substance that has stimulated many critics is the Judeo-Christian myth of good and evil; this substance James projected by image and figure into numerous details of language and action. James's statements are not overt; he proceeds not by conventional prose logic but by endowing his tale with an atmosphere in which we sense the pressure of a greater imaginative force than meets the casual fiction-reading eye. In defining the origins of the pressure, we may fall into statements that are too blunt, for example, that Bly "becomes" a Garden of Eden. But while backing off from such exact equivalents, we should retain a sense of parallels, analogies, intimations; they are the key to the tonal richness of the story. In accounting for tone, we move toward a definition of structure, which is partly determined by verbal and imagistic patterns. The intimations of language that acts poetically collaborate with the larger structural units—the narrative elements as such—in defining this version of the struggle between good and evil.

■ 24 ■
The Possessed Artist and the Ailing Soul:
Lowry's *Under the Volcano*

i

IF A HISTORIAN LEAFED through the journals of 1947 and noted the new novels reviewed, he would not find another one written in English, I surmise, that has achieved a more durable quiet esteem than Malcolm Lowry's *Under the Volcano* (I exclude Thomas Mann's *Doctor Faustus*, to which I shall return later). It has survived in a "population" where the normal death rate is close to 100 percent. A minor irony: in America it has survived its own publishing house. It has survived, as we have noted, an apparent smallness of canvas, and it has also survived a quite opposite difficulty: a fecundity of suggestive detail that tends to overstimulate the imagination, that is, to set it off in more ways than can be decently encompassed within an overall design. Something survives beyond the sense of chaos that the fecundity is in danger of creating, beyond an impression of a tropical creative richness (this in itself, of course, is not to be disparaged, even when it is imperfectly controlled). What survives, again, is something beyond the quality usually called "intensity," though the stresses that Lowry images, luxuriantly and often fantastically, do induce the severe tautness that marks some kinds of aesthetic experience. Intensity is really a secondary virtue; it can be attached to superficial forms of action (of the order of fisticuffs, for instance), just as more profound experience can be transmitted in relatively untaut moods such as the contemplative. The criterion is not the presence of intensity but the depth of the concern—the spiritual burden—that intensity accompanies. The less substantial the matter, the more the hard and gemlike flame will resemble ordinary flushed cheeks and fever that can be aspirined away. The fire in *Under the Volcano* is not easily put out.

The sense of a largeness that somehow bursts out of the evident constriction, the fertility that borders on the excessive and the frenzied, the intensity that is not a surrogate for magnanimity, and finally an apprehension of reality so vivid that it seems to slide over into madness— these are symptoms of the work of the "possessed" artist. If he has not quite achieved majority, Lowry belongs to the possessed novelists, among whom the great figures are Dostoyevsky and Melville and, some of the

330

time, Dickens. They may be distinguished from the "self-possessed" artists: Thackeray and Trollope and, more recently, C. P. Snow. Or, since
Lowry's theme is human disaster, a grievous, driving, frenetic disaster,
let us take for contrast Hardy: he seems calmly to organize and impose
disaster as if he were seated at some cosmic control panel. In an older
writer like Hawthorne or a modern one like R. P. Warren, there is somewhat of a conflict, or even an alternation, of possession and self-possession, of an unbridled urgency and a controlling will. The possessed artist
is in the tradition of Plato's Ion, and at the risk of too neat a polarity, it
may be hazarded that the self-possessed artist has ties with Aristotle's
Poetics: rational analyzability of form appears to imply rational creatabil-
ity of form. It is not altogether a parody to picture the self-possessed
artist, deep browed at his drawing board, coolly planning plot and catharsis. In C. P. Snow the key line, a recurrent one, is surely, "May I have
a word with you, Lewis?" "A word"—a council—a plan—logos and logis-
tics: life is ordered, or, if it does not wholly accede to the order designed
for it, what dissidence there is is reflected, not in unruly surges of action
that in their way elude the author and his decorous creatures, but through
the rational comment of observers. Things never get out of hand; no
wild dogs tear at the trainer's leash. Perhaps the ultimate figure in the
world of self-possession is Arnold Bennett: one of his major aims seems
to have been to keep his characters down, to remain the unyielding bai-
liff on his huge Five Towns estate. Was not this—that he would never
"let go"—a subtle ingredient in what Virginia Woolf had against him?
That, really, he saw Mrs. Brown only in terms of attributes that were at
his beck and call? Bennett illustrates the intimate relationship, the virtual identity, between self-possession and the rigorous domination of
character and scene (or at least the air of this). In some way his sense of
security seems to have been involved in his paternal tyranny: for his
creatures, no out of bounds, no fractiousness, no unpredicted courses,
no iddish cutting loose. And if V. S. Pritchett is right, Bennett suffered
accordingly: his self-possession was close to suicidal.

ii

Such comparisons help us to place Lowry. In sum: the self-possessed
artist—the one who uses his materials as an instrument. The possessed
artist—the materials appear to use him as an instrument, finding in him,
as it were, a channel to the objective existence of art, sacrificing a minimum of their autonomy to his hand, which partly directs and shapes
rather than wholly controls. This is how it is with Lowry. The possessed
artist works in a more dangerous terrain than the self-possessed artist.
Possessed work may open up any depth before us, any abyss in other

personalities or in our own. Though it may contemplate an ailing world, its obsessive theme is the ailing soul. It is an ancient theme whose history concerns us here only in that in our day the theme is used with extraordinary frequency. Whether it is that illness is especially attractive to us because we find in it a novel window to reality, or an apparently better window to reality, than the less clinical ones that we have principally relied on; or that the culture is sick, as some critics aver with almost tedious constancy, and that as a consequence we must, to avoid self-deception and serve truth, contemplate only sickness—these differing conclusions are arguable.

In the contemporary use of illness, at any rate, we find quite different perspectives. In *Sound and Fury* there are various ailing souls: through them we have a complex view of decadence and of a contrasting vitality. In Alain Robbe-Grillet's *Voyeur* clinical disorder of personality is itself the aesthetic object: despite all that has been said about Robbe-Grillet's innovations in the vision of reality, the final effect is one of a disturbingly ingenious tour de force. In *Magic Mountain* the ailment of the soul is intricately intertwined with that of the body; a host of theoretical salvations are examined, and the final note is one of hope through a surprisingly simple practical therapy. But in *Doctor Faustus* there is a more fundamental and violent illness of soul, a counterpart of a more fundamental and violent illness of body, one that is in effect chosen; we see a sick person and a sick era, sick thought that is a culmination of a tradition; yet a tradition in which the paradoxical affiliation of the destructive and the creative is terrifying.

Doctor Faustus offers some instructive parallels with *Under the Volcano:* both works belong to 1947; both recount the spiritual illness of a man that is in some way akin to the illness of an age; both glance at the politics of the troubled 1930s, but both are artistically mature enough to resist the temptations always offered by the political theme—the polemic tone, the shrill "J'accuse." Instead they contemplate the failures of spirit of which the political disorders are a symptom. They do this differently. Though both draw on the Faustian theme, Lowry introduces it less directly than suggestively, as one strand in a mythic fabric of considerable richness. Mann, by now an old hand at mythic reconstructions, revives Faustus in the grand manner. The mode of evil is affirmative: demonic possession, a rush into destruction in a wild flare of self-consuming, power-seizing creativity. In demonic possession there is a hypertrophy of ego; Lowry's hero, on the contrary, suffers from a kind of undergrowth of soul. One leaps on life rapaciously; the other falls short of the quality that makes life possible. Both the rape and the agonizing insufficiency are done with hair-raising immediacy. But Mann's style is heroic, whereas Lowry's stage is domestic. Geoffrey Firmin (the infirm Geoffrey) is more of a private figure than Adrian Leverkühn; his life has less amplitude in itself; in the concrete elements of it there is not the constant pressure toward epical-allegorical aggrandizement. But this is a statement of a difference, not of a deficiency. Both novelists are possessed; both seem to be the instruments of a vision whose autarchy they do not impair as they assist its emergence into public form. This is true of Mann, despite his usual heavy component of expository pages; it is true of Lowry, despite some artifice and frigidity in the narrative arrangements.

If Lowry's work is, compared with Mann's, "domestic," nevertheless the implied analogy with domestic tragedy is slight at best. To make one important contrast: Lowry has a range of tone that household drama never had. In fact, even in the orbit of possessed artists, his range is unusual: in recording a disaster of personality that is on the very edge of the tragic, he has an extravagant comic sense that creates an almost unique tension among moods. Desperation, the ludicrous, nightmare, the vulgar, the appalling, the fantastic, the nonsensical, and the painfully pathetic coexist in an incongruous mélange that is still a unity. The serious historian of the ailing soul may achieve the bizarre, but he rarely works through humor or finds the Lowry fusion of the ridiculous and the ghastly. With Lowry, the grotesque seems always about to trip up the catastrophic, the silly to spike the portentous, the idiotic to collapse the mad. When evil is present, it is more likely to be nasty than sinister. The assailing demons tend to be mean little gremlins; in a way, Geoffrey's disaster is the triumph of meanness, not as a case history of an eccentric flop, but as a universal image of man in the smallness to which he is always liable. This can take on its own dreadfulness, partly because petty vice contains echoes of major failures, partly because nemesis is not trivial, and partly because there is always maintained a touching nostalgia for a large and noble selfhood. In *Lady Windermere's Fan* there is a very bad line about man's being in the gutter but looking at the stars; it is bad because the play contains no vestige of real gutters or real stars, so that words alone are being exploited. But these antithetical images could be used of *Under the Volcano* without bathos, for it contains some of the more plausible gutters in modern fiction while portraying the survival, even in them, of a dim and struggling consciousness of other worlds. Lowry is quite lucid about what is sickness and what is health, rather more so, indeed, than another possessed novelist usually credited with expertise in these polar states, D. H. Lawrence.

iii

Lowry does not manage the cosmic texture of events that we find in *Doctor Faustus,* but there is an extraordinary texture of symbol and allusion. It is doubtless natural for the possessed novelist to call on many of the resources of poetry. The self-possessed novelist is not necessarily prosaic or shallow or one-dimensional, witness Henry James; but in the main we image him as forging steadily or deliberately ahead, on the direct prose route to his end. The possessed writer has an air of battling, not quite successfully, with a multitude of urgencies that come at him from all sides and fling off again on their own, not always forced into a common direction. If the overt action of *Under the Volcano* is slight, the metaphorical action is intense. Numerous objects, properties, occurrences, and even ideas, recollections, and observations not only exist in their own right but also work figuratively or symbolically. The nexuses are imaginative rather than causal, or logical, or chronological; hiatuses compel a high attention; dextrous leaps are called for. In such a sense the novel is "poetic."

The "story," as I have said, is slight: Yvonne, the wife of alcoholic Geoffrey Firmin, returns, after a year's separation, to her husband in Mexico. The events all take place on the day of her return. Geoffrey's passing desires to pull out with Yvonne are overcome by a far more urgent passion for alcohol. A French movie producer, former lover of Yvonne, is with them for a while and incredulously lectures Geoffrey. Geoffrey's brother Hugh, ex-reporter and sailor, now about to run arms to the Spanish loyalists, in love with Yvonne, spends the day with them. The chief event is an outing by bus—Lowry's own wayward bus ("making its erratic journey"), which stops for a while near a wounded Indian left by the roadside but leaves without anybody's having done anything. Late in the day Geoffrey, who has constantly been getting separated from Hugh and Yvonne, outrageously abuses Yvonne and runs into the woods near Popocatepetl. Yvonne and Hugh pursue. Yvonne and Geoffrey lose their lives by means symbolically associated with the episode of the unattended roadside Indian.

Hugh makes his boat for Spain: this we have learned from a retrospective prologue—the contents of which are certain words and thoughts of the French producer a year after the day of the main story. This prologue is supposed to introduce all the main themes; but there is too much there to assimilate, especially since most of the material is not dramatized. It is a cold beginning, and then one has to keep going back to it as to a table of contents—which is not the kind of rereading that a concentrated book may legitimately demand. Further, on technical matters: the retrospects on which a one-day story must rely tend to be flaccid in style (Hugh's) or foggy in detail (Yvonne's); and coincidence has a fairly large hand in things. But, once into the story, one is less aware of these things than of the imaginative richness. The minds of the characters are sensitive recording instruments, tenacious alike of facts and of their suggestive value. The book is a cornucopia of images; both the psychic and the outer world have a tangibility which a thoughtless slice of realism could never produce; humor and horror are never alleged but are molded into a hard and yet resilient narrative substance. Always one is driven to follow through on the evocations that trail off behind the foreground facts.

So, besides reading the story as story, we are always aware of a multitude of implications which, in their continual impingement upon us, remind us of the recurrent images of Shakespeare. The action takes place in November, on the Day of the Dead; Geoffrey feels his "soul dying"; a funeral takes place; burial customs, the shipping of a corpse are discussed; an earlier child of Yvonne's is dead; Geoffrey thinks he is seeing a dead man; a cantina is called La Sepultura; Geoffrey recalls Dr. Faustus's death; a dead dog is seen in a ravine; a dying Indian is found by the roadside. Always there are vultures, pariah dogs, the noise of target practice. There are a decaying hotel, a reference to the House of Usher, the ruins of the palace of Maximilian and Carlotta. Geoffrey's soul appears to him "a town ravaged and stricken"; an imaginary "little town by the sea" burns up. Frustrations and failures are everywhere—engagements are missed, the light fails in a cinema. Always we are reminded of the barranca or ravine, near the town—a fearful abyss. Once it is called "Malebolge"; there are various allusions to Dante's *Inferno*; Geoffrey feels he is in hell, quotes Dante on sin, looks at Cocteau's *La Machine Infernale*, takes a ride in a Maquina Infernal, calls ironically-defiantly, "I love hell"; at the end he is in a bar "under the volcano." "It was not for nothing the ancients had placed Tartarus under Mt. Aetna." There are continual references to Marlowe's Faustus, who could not pray for grace, just as Geoffrey cannot feel a love that might break his love for alcohol, or rather, symbolize a saving attitude; as in the Faustus play, *soul* is a recurrent word. There is an Eden-Paradise theme: a public sign becomes a motif in itself, being repeated at the end of the story: "Do you enjoy this garden, which is yours? Keep your children from destroying it!" Geoffrey once mistranslates the second sentence: "We evict those who destroy." Geoffrey's own garden, once beautiful, has become a jungle; he hides bottles in the shrubbery; and once he sees a snake there.

The lavish use of such rich resources reveals the possessed artist. They might serve, perhaps, only to create a vivid sequence of impressions, feelings, and moods. But Lowry is possessed by more than sensations and multiple associations; there is a swirl of passionate thoughts and ideas as well as passions; thought and feeling are fused, and always impressions and moods seem the threshold to meanings that must be entered. It seems to me that he seizes instinctively upon materials that have both sensory and suprasensory values. How present the central conception—that of the ailing soul? There are endless symbols for ill-being, from having cancer to taking dope. But Geoffrey's tremendous drinking is exactly the right one, or by art is made to seem the right one. In greater or lesser extent it is widely shared, or at least is related to widely practiced habits; it is known to be a pathological state; it may be fatal, but also it can be cured. It lacks the ultimate sinisterness of dope, the irresistibility of cancer; hence it is more flexible, more translatable. And Lowry slowly makes us feel, behind the brilliantly presented facts of the alcoholic life, a set of meanings that make the events profoundly revelatory: drinking as an escape, an evasion of responsibility, a separation from life, a self-worship, a denial of love, a hatred of the living with a faith. (There is an always pressing guilt theme: Geoffrey, who was a naval officer in World War I, is a kind of sinning Ancient Mariner, caught by Life-in-Death, loathing his slimy creatures, born of the d.t.'s, whom he cannot expiatorily bless but must keep trying to drink away.) The horror of Geoffrey's existence is always in the forefront of our consciousness, as it should be; but in the horror is involved an awareness of the dissolution of the old order, of the "drunken madly revolving world," of which Hugh says, "Good god, if our civilization were to sober up for a couple of days, it'd die of remorse on the third." At the end Geoffrey, unable by act of will to seize upon the disinterested aid of two old Mexicans, is the victim of local fascists: fascism preys upon a world that has already tossed away its own soul.

The episode that most successfully unifies the different levels of meaning is that of the Indian left wounded by the roadside. He is robbed by a Spanish "pelado," a symbol of "the exploitation of everybody by everybody else." Here we have echoes of the Spanish Conquest and a symbol of aggression generally. Yvonne can't stand the sight of blood: it is her flaw, her way of acquiescing in the de facto. Geoffrey finds rules against doing anything; everyone feels that "it wasn't one's own business, but someone else's." It is modern irresponsibility and selfishness; the reader is prepared also to think of the "nonintervention" policy by the refrain that echoes throughout the book, "they are losing on the Ebro." But above all this is the story of the Good Samaritan—only there is no Samaritan. Devil take the least of these. (Geoffrey's ship, a gunboat disguised as a merchantman, has been named the *Samaritan*—a comment upon modern Samaritanism.)

Hugh, held back by Geoffrey, is almost the Good Samaritan—Hugh who is going to run arms to Spain. To Geoffrey and Yvonne, he is "romantic"; doubtless he is, and he has his own kind of guilt; but at least he insists on action, disinterested action. Here we come to what is apparently the basic theme of the book: man, in the words of a proverb repeated chorally, cannot live without love. Lowry flirts with the danger of the topical: the Spanish war might give the novel the air of a political tract. But ultimately, I think, the author does succeed in keeping the political phenomena on the periphery of the spiritual substance, using them for dramatic amplification of his metaphysic. It would be possible to read Geoffrey, always impersonally called the Consul, as dying capitalism, as laissez-faire, or as sterile learning, like the speaker in Tennyson's *Palace of Art*. But such readings, though they are partly true, too narrowly circumscribe the total human situation with which Lowry is concerned.

iv

The Consul's climactic acts of hate are a world's confession. Yvonne thinks of the need "of finding some faith," perhaps in "unselfish love." Whence love is to be derived, or how sanctioned and disciplined, is a question which the symbols do not fully answer. Yet it is the effect of Lowry's allusions—Dante, Faustus—to push the imagination toward a final reality that transcends all historical presents, however much each present may comment upon and even modify it. Most of all this effect is secured by his constant allusion to Christian myth and history—the Crucifixion, Golgotha, the Last Supper, original sin. Lowry is hardly writing a Christian allegory; indeed, some of the Christian echoes are decidedly ironic. But his whole complex of image and symbol is such as to direct a dissolving order, in search of a creative affirmation, toward that union of the personal and the universal which is the religious.

The two extremes that are the technical dangers of this kind of work are the tightly bound allegory, in which a system of abstract equivalents for all the concrete materials of the story constricts the imaginative experience, and a loose impressionism, in which a mass of suggestive enterprises sets off so many associations, echoes, and conjectures that the imaginative experience becomes crowded and finally diffuse. It is the latter risk that Lowry runs. For the present account, to avoid excessive length, consistently oversimplifies the ingredients that it deals with, and it fails to deal with many other ingredients—for instance, the guitar motif, the cockfight motif, the theme of mystics and mysteries, the recurrent use of Indians, horses, the movie *The Hands of Orlac*, and so on. Lowry has an immensely rich and vigorous imagination, and he never corks his cornucopia of evocative images and symbols. Some disciplinary rejections, some diffidence in setting afloat upon the imagination every boat that he finds upon a crowded shore, would have reduced the distractedness to which the author is occasionally liable and would have concentrated and shaped the author's effect more clearly. This is to say, perhaps, that the possessed artist might at times borrow a little from the soul of the self-possessed artist. But if one might wish for a more ordered synthesis of parts, one would never want a diminution of the power of Lowry's possessed art. There is great life in what he has written—in his solid world of inner and outer objects in which the characters are dismayed and imprisoned as in Kafka's tales; and in the implicit coalescence of many levels of meaning that we find in Hermann Broch. Such a multivalued poetic fiction, with its picture of the ailing soul, its sense of horrifying dissolution, and its submerged, uncertain vision of a hard new birth off in clouded time, is apparently the especial labor of the artistic conscience at our turn of an epoch.

The Western Theme: Exploiters and Explorers

i

IF WESTERN KANSAS and eastern Colorado are not quite in the heart of the West, and if buffalo hunting is only a third or fourth cousin to westering, nevertheless the scene and the foreground action of John Williams's *Butcher's Crossing* (1960) inevitably bring to mind the problems of the writer who would make art out of the history of the West. It has been the fate of the American West to beget the stereotypes that belong to pseudo art before it has yielded up the individualized types that belong to art proper. A natural history of stereotypes would reveal, I surmise, that they come into being in two opposed ways. One of these involves the familiar death-in-life paradox: the stereotype is the devitalization of a once strong life that, since other writers cannot reproduce it, continues to drag on in pale likenesses. There were, for instance, the Pamelas that resisted men, the Tom Joneses that did not resist women, and the Yoricks that resisted no vibrations, however minute, of delight and pity—mechanical imitations that crowded through fiction until almost 1800. An innovator of genius (and genius may not always mean greatness) forms a taste, and camp-followers, mastering expected motions, gratify it. From the 1880s on, Conan Doyle created an influential image in detective fiction; from 1895 on, H. G. Wells in science fiction; from 1936 on, *Gone with the Wind* in the lusty-busty historical. If we think of "grades" of stereotype, we can perhaps identify an upper-level form which we call, less condescendingly, "vogue" or, even honorifically, a "style." Zola created a pattern with such limitations that it has come close to seeming a stereotype, and this may well be the fate of the *roman nouveau* and minimalism. When the innovator is not so much providing a re-illumination of constants as he is catching a particular note of his own time, the likelihood of the stereotype is greatest.

The stereotypes of the West, however, do not represent a decay or a degenerative hardening of what once was a living form, or a sterile mimicking of earlier creative acts. There are no reminiscences of a former greatness in the good and bad men, sheriffs and Indians, pioneers and profiteers, pardners and skunks, cowboys and emigrants, girls and gamblers, patriots and holdup men, those scarcely human molds into which simulated life-fluid is habitually poured by practiced script writers who never spill a drop that would mess up the neat little reception rooms in their readers' nervous systems. These standardized reductions of human variety have a contrary genesis: they spring into their nonvital life in response to large and striking real-life events that the mature imagination has not yet taken the measure of and assimilated. The first stereotype that I have identified has its origin in literary innovation, the second in historical "innovation." In literary innovation a creative mind, whose products may or may not turn out to be great, discovers a new style or a new method or a new emphasis for which an age is in some way "ready"; hence the strength of its impact, and hence the string of successors who repeat what it has done and feed it to those ever hungry for the repetitions. In historical innovation some crisis, some discovery, some great expansive movement, some surprising reconstruction of the known, some overturning of the accepted strikes its age like a blow; we are incapable of not making art of it, but equally incapable—perhaps for a century—of making art of it. In come the stereotypes, the simplest responses possible in terms of contemporary habits of feeling, to provide some substitute for that aesthetic experiencing and confrontation of newness in the world that we appear to seek instinctively. The most obvious example in the latter part of the twentieth century is space fiction.

The historical innovation, be it breakthrough or breakdown, comes soonest to the embrace of adult art when it is primarily a phenomenon of human behavior, in the sense that it results from interactions within the human community rather than from the discovery and exploitation of things, objects, or nature. The great wars of the twentieth century, for all of their novelties of magnitude and weapon and threat of global destruction, could be felt as rooted in human personality; hence, whatever their shock value, they have not had to be encountered by that application of formulas that is the surrogate for true artistic exploration. Sober and talented writers have dealt with both wars, and I will venture that there is an inverse proportion between the quantity of their work and the quantity of stereotype treatments of military themes. In the world of pulps there cannot help being an *Aviation Stories*, but there is probably not a *World War II Stories*.

Among innovations, it is things (objects, nature) that most readily evoke the formulas of pseudo art; formulas flourish when an adequate sense of human relevance is lacking, when objects do not impinge upon us as symbolizations of human motive and direction. The expansion of physical worlds is an affair of great things, of stages and properties so large that the human actor hardly seems significant at all. It becomes the business of journalism and of the conventions of melodramatic art. The actual history of New World conquests never became the material for a major work of European literature. Though in scores of works one can dig up stereotypes of noble and ignoble savages, pioneering heroism, exotic romance, and patriotic endeavor, the notes of greatness in some way traceable to Renaissance voyaging are infrequent: Panurge's voyage, Caliban, Robinson Crusoe, Gulliver (*The Lusiads* is unique in modern literature as an epic celebration of an explorer). The last phase of the great westward movement—crossing America to the Pacific, and conquering and domesticating the trans-Mississippi country—is another affair of things: of great distances, obstacles, and prizes, and it has hardly yet come under the humanizing imagination. But no other historical innovation has been so surrounded, walled in, thatched, trammeled, concealed, and buried by multitudinous layers of a few simple stereotypes apparently taken, by their readers, for candid revelation. The voluminousness of the trade in these stereotypes is doubtless due in part to the historical accident that they became available when mass-entertainment industries not only made extraordinary circulation possible but also helped prepare a very large public for notably uncomplicated versions of actuality.

ii

In the realm of the West and of westering, the very prevalence of stereotypes tends to proliferate stereotypes. They appeal to the "commercial writer," who deals in printed matter precisely as he might in slot machines, panaceas, or other traps for the quick buck. He haunts writers' conferences, hoping that publishers' representatives will betray tricks that will enable him to "hit the stands," or secret recipes for next year's best sellers, or formulas that will lead to the lush rewards of TV or movie popularity. At home he has the ear of reporters, who describe his new works with the earnest enthusiasm accorded to symphony doings and market behavior, and who distinguish him from the "quality writer" only by liking him more. He himself will have nothing to do with literary men, even though they have names; he will not listen to them if they come to town to lecture, and he will not acknowledge their existence except by assuring you, with a matter-of-fact certainty, that they write for money too. Indeed, he rather likes to put on the vestments of the common man's defender against highbrows. This writer and the local status that he often achieves represent an odd mélange of local pride, naive regional consciousness, belief in salvation by works that pay, democratic or socioeconomic clichés, and an imagination stunted by a diet of stereotypes. As a westerner, he looks for western subjects, but he sees western history only through the formulas of popular art.

When the scriptwriter, a good term for the type, has a sort of squatter's rights over western themes, the territory may be less inviting to the genuine literary explorer. The art-writer has not only to face the exacting task characteristic of his own work, that of probing the territory with his own imagination; even before that, he has to fight his way into it through all the obstacles, traps, and distorting perspectives set up by the scriptwriter, through the camouflage of commonplaces that may effectively hide the existence of workable grounds. The art-writer may not want to use up energy in dispossessing the scriptwriter. Yet he does. In more than one age, indeed, we can find a historical pattern of development from initial, unskilled routines to distinction. Out of the banalities of Senecan imitations Shakespeare took the revenge tragedy into brilliance and profundity, and out of the Gothic mode in the eighteenth century, with its endless repetition of clumsy devices, there sprang the achievements of the romantic novel in the nineteenth century. This evolution, from conventional practices to gifted creation, is of course the antithesis of the movement we have already described: the decline from full-blown, successful innovation to the uninspired carrying-on of the new mode. Both patterns give useful clues to the history of generic forms.

The two activities of which we may speak as if they were independent—on the one hand, sidestepping, or passing through, the clichés of predecessors; on the other, making one's own definition of the material—do in one sense come together. Like all creative artists, the writer who is attracted by western themes must discover the form of, or the form proper to, the materials. He may be discovering a form in the pre-existing material, or imposing a form upon it. If making a work of art be considered as basically drawing upon some anterior reality, nevertheless the modifying power of the "making" is extraordinary; if it be considered essentially "creative," nevertheless its ties to preartistic models are unmistakable. Further, it is questionable whether any model, that is, any lump of material not yet transmuted into artistic form, is infinitely susceptible of being molded, reshaped, or radically transformed. It is just possible, for instance, that western themes—all the events of westering—have inner limitations that in some way encourage stereotypes and, conversely, impede the individualizing, depth-seeking imagination. If this were true, the art-writer would have to contend not only with the sterilities of the scriptwriter but also with a sterilizing force in the materials themselves.

On the face of it the western story offers hope and courage and en-

durance, some troubles and some failure, but overall an immense success. Though this may sound like rather a cornucopia for the artist, the
fact is that the annals of triumph, especially of triumph that is mostly
over things, are not easily conducive to greatness except perhaps in an
epic mode that is not congenial to our habits of feeling; unless an artist
could manage a heroic amplitude that would encompass all the erosion
and waste inseparable from triumph, such annals are most likely to lead
only to shallow waters beset by the dangers of self-congratulation. There
is an excess of triumph. One is tempted to say, indeed, that western
materials are simply defective in the tragic component, that they are too
exclusively a melodrama of victory.

This needs qualification. To postulate an absence of the tragic in the
western saga does not mean that one forgets the disasters of the last
century. Those who are at all aware of the West will think quickly of
such names as Custer, Donner, Sutter, and Whitman, and perhaps even
of the unheroic end of Meriwether Lewis; or of fire and quake and the
Mountain Meadows massacre. But there has been no major regional
disaster, no all-encompassing tension and destruction and fight for physical and moral survival: no Civil War. Here, men have been extraordinarily lucky; they have not had to face the bitter enveloping crises that
flow out of their own natures, out of conflicting passions, out of rifts in
personality and struggles for power. It is these experiences of tragic cast
that reveal depths and permit others to feel these depths; it is the presence of tragic splits that can break stereotypes, for stereotypes are the
patterns of surface life from which true anguish is excluded. Without
tragic suffering, stereotypes hang on more tenaciously.

If he is to do mature work, the artist must have the "right feeling" for
his material. What I have been getting at is that some kinds of material
encourage right feeling more than others. If the material does not openly encourage the deeper penetration of human personality, the artist
will have to have the greater transforming power. He will have to be
more than a scriptwriter to move beyond the clichés of energy and variety (the staples of A. B. Guthrie's second, and lesser, novel, *The Way
West*). He will have to be larger still to move beyond the clichés of endurance and heroism, for these, if the management of them passes to
any degree beyond the mechanical, may not be spotted as clichés at all.
But if his material provides him with large and palpable disasters, or
most of all with tragic errors, he is the more likely to have the "right
feeling" out of which, given adequate craftsmanship, may come adult
and individual art. For now he is committed to the most inclusive and
probing awareness of the human involvement: not only of the victory,
but of the cost of victory, or of the failure in apparent victory; of the

ambiguities of earning and learning; of the moral hazard, the moral doubleness; of the oblique motive or the evil deed in the very fabric of the pure intent, the struggle, the strenuous search.

iii

Some novelists have indeed triumphed over the scriptwriters. In *The Big Sky* A. B. Guthrie interprets the West as milieu, so to speak; he provides, not a pictorial tour, but a re-creation of a chosen milieu in all its particularity, neither sentimentalized nor rejected: presented through a human figure neither stereotyped nor highly individualized, but with a somewhat flattened representativeness that so interacts with the scene as to aid in giving it a personality and dramatic vitality. In *Ox-Bow Incident* Walter Van Tilburg Clark is also concerned with the milieu, though it is less the focus of drama than a stage for character, which requires this stage but is not circumscribed by it (I discuss Clark's novel in detail in the following essay). More recently Ivan Doig has been doing the western scene without cliché or stereotype.

John Williams belongs in this group in that he has the same artistic conscience and the same basic tack of working stubbornly through the milieu. Even when he is using the old theme of survival against nature, he does not fall back on clichés of language and situation; any "western"-glutton beguiled into this book by the buffalo on the jacket would not last for twenty-five pages. But that is misleading, for it may imply that *Butcher's Crossing* brushes off or condescends to the regional scene and event of which it is born, whereas it does no such thing. It makes the most of western plateau and of alpine meadow in the Rockies, and of a frenetic-epic-grotesque buffalo kill, but without being bound to its places and subjects; it is not fulfilling rigid expectations or playing for automatic responses. There is a good deal of life in the ordinary sense, and there is constant movement. Williams has unostentatiously introduced, while keeping it always subordinate to human concerns, a quantity of trail lore, mountain lore, buffalo lore, blizzard lore, and finally even economic lore; all this is vivid, but it never gets drafty or cute or "educational." Williams keeps himself out of it; without showmanship he puts his characters through an extraordinary range of physical settings and threats—flat plain and an obscure, almost unclimbable mountain pass; extremes of summer heat and winter cold; autumn drought and spring flood; scarcely endurable blizzard and maniac arson. In this inclusiveness, as well as in the subordination of this outer world to the actions of men, it reminds one of Conrad's *Youth* (nowadays too easily disparaged). Such kinds of life, not to mention various peaks of suspense and, near the end, the admirably held mystery of a town's decay, should make this book accessible to many readers, and that is to the good; yet if many things in the book do not engage a mass audience, it is not that Williams ever slips into preciousness or snob appeal, any more than he slips into an easy final note of elegy or resolve.

He simply has a mature interest in the interplay between certain men, between these men and nature, and between the grandeur of plan and the grossness of fact. However, the West is not felt primarily as the school of character: the issue is not really the growth or change of character under the stresses of ambition, turmoil, and setback. Nor is it precisely the theater of character—the historic platform on which we see revealed the diversity of human responses as men seek certain ends and meet the unsought. True, it is that in part: we see the various motives that bring men together on a great hunting gamble, and the radically different impacts of disaster—death, deadness, mania, and new knowledge. In the most essential narrative the West acts, perhaps, as the mirror of character: the very novelty of set and action serves to clarify to Andrews, the newly arrived easterner, the lineaments of his own nature. What he has seen and has been a part of reflect to him the insubstantiality of the passions that have mainly determined his own course. In others he has seen "emptiness," "nothingness," "hollow glint," "open despair," and these, held together in an unobtrusively punning sequence, he identifies with his own "vanity"—literally "emptiness," as we are reminded by the recurrent terms of vacuity. Yet the futility that mirrors his own futility teaches him not to return to the East but to move on westward; if Butcher's Crossing is dust and ashes, and "nothing beside remains," the very catharsis of an earlier self, we take it, is the paradoxical beginning of new growth.

In telling the story of Andrews, the easterner who experiences a self-defining in Kansas and Colorado, Williams has chosen a convention quite familiar in our day—the convention of minimalized sentience, expressiveness, and reflectiveness. The playing down of overt feeling and thought in the protagonist is accompanied, in the earlier parts of the book, by a rather sparse use of sensory images. As a result there is a kind of flatness of texture that the author evidently intends; he appears to be strongly determined on an "objective" presentation and on the avoidance of that inner flux of sensation, emotion, and consciousness which in the "psychological" tradition is made the center of reality. This may be either a self-imposed aesthetic discipline or a considered adaptation of style and method to the western theme, to a milieu of intransigent, often brutal, fact and happening in which men had better expend energy only in the primary physical activities of surviving and arriving. The method has certain disadvantages: human responses that seem inevitable are sometimes missing; the reduction of memory leaves us curious about the hero's past and its relation to the present; major choices are made in an apparently mechanical way that leaves a motive unclear, even though motive does not seem unimportant; and even the hero's final clarification is not entirely free of fuzziness. On the other hand, Williams makes the convention of the nonresponsive and apparently analgesic man serve an excellent effect by discarding it at key moments and shifting to the convention of full sensibility; reality is no longer centered in impersonal muscular transactions with an external world of things, but shifts to the realm of feeling and thought. By this break in method, notably employed during the slaughter of the buffalo herd and at the final collapse of the buffalo hunter's world, Williams dramatizes as sharply as possible the emergence of understanding: character and reader are thrust simultaneously into moments of enlightenment, of the appraisal of external phenomena by the sentient observer newly revealed as the human reality behind the façade of the automaton-like adventurer. The world of outer scene and action itself gains a new intensity through a greater frequency of sensory images, just as we draw away from it into a new knowledge of it. The density of things is greatest when we turn to their significance; the novel opens out most widely as it moves inward into consciousness.

Williams's instinct for playing down meaning except at moments of epiphany serves him well in a different area: it contributes to a laudable reticence in the symbolic overtones that, in an age when writers can hardly help being highly self-conscious technicians, are likely to become much too assertive. Perhaps most open to view is the hero's involvement with both love and death: his progress from a shrinking diffidence to a knowing and yet amateur participation, where custom and passion are oddly intermingled, and to an incipient maturity out of which, we assume, will develop better ways of coming to terms with both. Yet what he feels in himself is perhaps not the most profound source of what he knows; it is something of an echo of what he feels, perceives, recognizes in others to whom he is, for a time, bound. In the chief buffalo hunter Andrews discovers, as inner truth, an obsession with process that can come to rest only upon exhaustion of the materials: he sees a kind of totality that tends to make extermination the only possible end. In this there are suggestions, though only the subtlest suggestions, of political symbolism. But the leader is also engaged in economic enterprise, and the story somehow recapitulates the entrepreneurial myth—from the initial union of talented half-possessed idea-man and venture capitalist and salaried technician in a grandiose dream of the ultimate killing, to the eternal irrationality of natural event, overriding passion, and human fickleness that, despite fantastic struggle and endurance, can bring the dream to nought. Yet this economic symbolism is barely hinted. Fortunately for the novel, its concern is with neither the political nor the economic cycles whose shadowy presence one may feel there, lurking in the narrative as a subtle increment, but with what is prior to these—the ways of the human psyche. What Williams has caught sight of is the capacity deep in man for paradoxically combining automation and frenzy, for achieving, at the very summit of vital and passionate energizing, an insensate reduction of life to thingship. He has discerned, in the classical gestures of production, a latent impulse to destruction that, when the manic absorption in operations whirls the dream into nightmare, becomes the whole truth.

This is what the reader learns. But he learns it through Andrews, whose learning of it is the first step in his own growth. If the great adventure, whose greatness is closely allied with its sickness, kills one participant and maims two, it leads a fourth toward knowledge. That Williams sees certain terrifying depths, and that he sees that seeing these may mean, not despair, but a saving sense of reality, is an index of his range in apprehending what man can do. His range embraces the complementary insights that the dream may become twisted into the nightmare, but that man may come out of the nightmare and be the more capable of a decent working dream. This sense of possibility Williams reveals through a craftsmanship that justifies some examination. It is the craftsmanship of one who, working to make a familiar territory, the West, produce the best that it can, rejects the popular quick-profit single-crop system that requires only mechanical repetitions of familiar steps, and takes the hard way of surveying the land anew and exploring complex possibilities that are there only when they are seen.

■ 26 ■
Clark's Western Incident:
From Stereotype to Model

i

SOME YEARS AGO, when he was a boy of ten or eleven, my son occasionally, at the movies, would see some kind of action that he could not stand, and he would go out into the lobby for a brief respite. He was very tight-lipped about this; he did not explain what seemed unbearable. I was usually a little puzzled, for we did not take him to movies that might be expected to test his psychological stamina.

Yet his flight brought back memories—memories of my own responses to reading three decades earlier. In pretelevision days we read books over and over again. In certain books that I read more than once—boys' books that I can no longer identify, but also novels by Dumas and Henty—there were some scenes that I could hardly bear to live through again—scenes, I suppose, of suffering or potential disaster. I dreaded those scenes even when I knew that the key figures survived and things got better later. Hence, when I came to the scenes, I would skip outright, read very rapidly, or try to neutralize the painful episode by reminding myself, while agonizing through it, that life would soon look brighter.

I am not, however, substituting family history for literary discussion. On the contrary, the memory of a childhood dread leads right into my theme. When, in preparation for writing this essay, I was about to reread Walter Clark's *The Ox-Bow Incident*, I found myself experiencing something very like that strange anticipatory dread that I can hardly recall having known since the passionate reading of more than fifty years ago. I do not think I am a hypersensitive reader; I hope I am not an eccentric one; in general I am not much moved by the "literature of the victim," in which easy subject matter often stands in for hard mastery by the artist. I should like to think, then, that my spontaneous expectation of acute disquietude in the coming rerun was a tribute to Walter Clark's grasp of reality. I hope that, even though they might use different words, other readers can join me in finding an inner truth of the kind that evokes what I have called dread. I will try to put my finger on that truth.

The word *dread* of course designates an emotional response. In casting about for a term to denote the objective quality of the events that

348

cause such a response, I toyed with the word *inexorableness*—that is, fearful relentlessness. Yet as soon as we think of some inexorable forces— violent storms, earthquakes, even terminal diseases—we realize that we do face up to them as somehow in the nature of things. We may feel anger, terror, or despair; but not, I think, dread. Dread implies the presence, not only of danger, which can even be a stimulus, but of a peculiar ominousness; it connotes, not so much a recognizable eruption within the norms of existence, as a threat to the norms themselves. Furthermore, in *The Ox-Bow Incident* we do not really have an inexorable course of injustice. There is a powerful surge toward the murders, but there is also an observable resistance. It expresses itself in constant delays; one tension of the story lies in the possibility that the drift into delay may shape up as a decision to postpone. What causes dread is that the men may prefer the evil act. In the choice made, what is more, the voluntary is strangely compounded with the unwilling; the source of dread is the mysterious veto of a saving intuitive reluctance. But even this diagnosis is still on the surface, and we need to seek out the underlying reality.

ii

It is a critical truism that in *The Ox-Bow Incident* Clark showed what could be done with "the western"; he freed himself from a stereotype and came up instead with a model of fundamental human behavior. There is some obviousness in this approach, and it has been disparaged, but I choose it because I think it steers us to the heart of his achievement. What Clark did was to burrow more deeply into the stereotype and discover the secret bases of truth without which no stereotype could exist. A stereotype is not a falsification of reality but a sclerosis of reality: a pattern has become rigid instead of staying flexible and thus able to accommodate the inevitable varieties of unpredictable experience.

It is always interesting to try to define the kind of truth that is imprisoned in any stereotype. In approaching the western stereotype that concerns us here, I cannot help recalling the attitude of several British friends: they are devotees of the American western—not western literature as a reputable school, but actually the movie melodramas popular in England. There are varied motives for this fondness, which reflects a deeper passion old enough to deserve a name. I shall call it *hesperophilia*, or the love of things western.[1] In Europe hesperophilia is related to a persistent habit of feeling that dates at least from the Renaissance: enchantment with the exotic, be it oriental or occidental. In America, the only thing left that can be imagined to be exotic is the special life attributed to the West, and Englishmen (or Americans) may want to believe that there is such a special life because they cannot bear to be without exotic relief from the too-well-known that is every man's fate.

We come now, however, to a deeper issue. Into the long-lived European fascination with the American exotic there entered very early another motive: the exotic, being by definition little known and extraordinary, could readily connote a little-known and extraordinary condition: perfectibility, in either an Eden that could be recovered or a utopia that could be founded. The lure of the utopian quest was exported from Europe to America. Deriving moral energy from the Puritan conviction of God's presence within, dreamers or idealists could seek to institute a heaven upon earth, moving west for the indispensable exotic scene as the East became known. The most familiar term for their spirit is *millennialism,* and it lies deep within hesperophilia and its literary offspring, the western stereotype. And it is what Clark found and obliquely utilized in a dramatic narrative in which the power of the surface is matched by the complexity of inner force.

We have been looking for the qualities in *The Ox-Bow Incident* that could evoke what I call dread. I propose that an underlying theme of this tale is the millennial impulse. The millennial impulse and the feeling of dread: surely these are incompatible terms, except perhaps to a diabolical being for whom the most ominous evil would be the appearance of a heaven upon earth. I hope, however, not to be the devil's voice or, what is worse, to be attracting attention by a frantic paradox. So I will try to point out the quiet link between the apparently irreconcilable cause and result.

Millennialism can work in several ways. It may inspire a fierce total quest—that is, a campaign to root out or destroy evil in a grand way, literal or symbolic. This is a familiar American endeavor; it is what the governess does in *Turn of the Screw,* what Captain Ahab does in *Moby-Dick,* what Curt Bridges does in Clark's *The Track of the Cat*—what all prohibitionists do. In ordinary fictional western millennialism we find a simple pursuit of a readier, more decisive justice than the actual world seems to offer. Misconduct is clear-cut and tangible and hence vulnerable, like a body to a bullet. Though evil may cause damage, it finally gets run out of the county. This is a seductive goal for good men, doubtless persuasive even to those ordinarily suspicious of stereotypes. Quick, pure justice charms many who may feel immune to societal mirages but are gladdened by the doctrinaire's mirage, the Platonic idea clamped like a mold upon everyday experience.

This justice triumphant has another charm: it offers a utopia without doctrine, a heaven without theology. The implicit slogan is "We all know what justice is; let's execute it." Winder, anxious to be off on the hunt, is driven "wild" by the question posed by Davies: "I mean, if you had to say what justice was, how would you put it?" (46; page references are to the Signet edition, 1960). Winder, one of those more eager to execute justice, is like many for whom doctrine is always frustrating; it means laws, bylaws, rules, regulations—a maze where the noble ends that we all visualize seem hopelessly lost. Hamlet put the problem in a phrase we often quote, "the law's delay." The law's delay is rooted in procedure, and we tend to be of two minds about procedure, alternately valuing it as the safeguard of the innocent and disparaging it as the escape hatch of the guilty. In the last decade we have often had doubts about procedure, and they have arisen on both left and right. For the left, the law undergirds the status quo and especially its inequities; for the right, the law protects criminals instead of victims. To both, the procedure becomes what we might call undue process. The antidote is supposed to be direct action, and so from one side we get vigilantes, and from the other, revolutionary radicalism. And in the middle there is much of that representative activity of the middle—grumbling.

I am trying to set up a perspective for *The Ox-Bow Incident.* Some things that since the 1950s we have often seen before our eyes are what Clark got hold of in 1940. He has one character after another harp on the law's uncertainty. "If we wait for [Judge] Tyler," Bartlett says, "there won't be one head of anybody's cattle left by the time we get justice" (34). The theme is pounded home in a dozen such remarks. We can turn these complaints off as lynchers' rationalizations if we will, but we ought rather to recognize them as criticisms of courts such as we have made or might make ourselves, and certainly have heard made by angry people who are not extremists. The point, of course, is not that Clark is good because he anticipated a style often used in later decades; the point is rather that he speaks to us because he was accurate enough, when using a formula, to transcend it and catch a truth beyond history. That is, he dug deep enough into the stereotype to find there a perennial human reality that appears in the usual western, in his own special version of it, and in historical events at different times. He has authentically caught, in an actual antisocial outbreak, the tempting millennialism of "Come, we all know what the good and the true are, and let us establish them at once, for delay is unnecessary." Resentment against the law's delay is a quite literal thing, of course. But the law's delay is also a symbol of all the institutional habits that try our patience; we speak of bureaucracies, for instance, as if the word were a synonym of "law's delay."

iii

In the stereotype Clark not only found a residue of millennialism but also put a finger on something else of deep importance, and I turn to it now. It is a truism that the western excludes women or reduces them to marginal supporting figures: we all have seen the movie poster of the brave-faced blonde erectly outfacing danger from just behind the hero's shoulder blade on his trigger side as he blasts away at the enemy. Clark squeezes profits out of the stereotype, but with great originality. He keeps women peripheral, but they help clue us into another phase of the ideal essence that is reduced to a mechanism in the stereotype. Only one woman goes along with the manhunters, Ma Grier—a great big woman, "strong as a wrestler, probably stronger than any man in the valley except Gabe" (75): a man by another name and, "soiled and greasy," doubtless smelling unsweet enough to prevent confusion. The creature who spurs the men on to their hunt is a screaming harridan, Frena Hundel (the name means "frantic little bitch," which I suppose is not an accident), allegedly hating men because they found no female charms in her. The two appearances of Rose Mapen, the authentic female, and her new San Francisco husband seem like pointless intrusions from a softer, more convoluted world, in some way inferior because, in its less uncouth and more calculating style, it is out of harmony with the larger world of direct action in the name of justice.[2] The narrator's friend, Gil Carter, was in love with her, but this seems a mistake on his part, a deviation from the straight and narrow.

When we look beneath the stereotyped male world that Clark examines anew, we do not find, I am sure, anything so banal as sexlessness or homosexuality. On the contrary, we find another component of hesperophilia, a fantasy quite characteristic of heterosexual men: the fantasy of straightforward, uncomplicated action, aggressive, marked by physical rather than social ability, by blunt tactics rather than troublesome tact, by endurance rather than forbearance. It is uninhibited by the conflicting values of the whole world of men and women, but invigorated by an unmixed code that highlights the goal and the road toward it, and brings forth the heroic, in solitude or in comradeship—voyage, hunt, rescue, quest, crusade (the responses to the everlasting challenges of nature, beast, victim, grail, and pagan). Instance Walter Mitty, a westerner without a West. This powerful motive buried beneath the detritus of the stereotype is what Clark gets hold of: virtually all his men feel the lure of the search, in the dark and in a blizzard, for rustlers and a killer.

Yet the terms of this search are ambiguous, and hence the imperative is less absolute than a man wants it to be. So the more committed instinctively translate the deficiency in the cause into a deficiency in the men not wholly persuaded by the cause. Farnley, as we have seen, is irate over the way in which a malefactor can be saved by sentimental pleas in a court. Such pleas are made, he says, by "Osgood or Davies, or some other whining women" (87). The key phrase is "some other whining women." To men, that is, it seems effeminate to hesitate, inquire, or introduce conflicting evidence when the business at hand is the punishment of guilt. Gil Carter commands preacher Osgood, who argues against the expedition, "Shut up, gran'ma" (32). When Davies calls extralegal punishment a "sin against society," Winder picks up the phrase sneeringly, "imitating a woman with a lisp" (48). There is a steady flow of such passages. One significant word is used twice: "stomach." Tetley ironically asks Gil Carter, "is . . . your stomach for justice cooling?" The Mex, superficially the toughest of the victims, alludes to Gerald Tetley with similar irony: "without the stomach for the blood, eh?" (176). "Stomach," of course, is "guts," and guts, as we know, are a male organ, the erectile tissue of the man who makes war instead of love.

Within the western stereotype, then, Clark has caught the male lust for warlike adventure that is a human constant rather than a historical accident peculiar to hesperophilia. At the same time he has seen that adventure is not only an exercise of male quality but a test of it: a man's nature volunteers him, and then he finds out the quality of that nature. We have different terms for what is at stake: I shall use *manliness*, because it leads us to a certain duality in the concept.[3] Clark understands this ambiguity, and thus again he departs from the western convention. Whereas in the stereotype manliness is always a two-fisted virility that makes no moral errors, Clark sees that it may err grossly. Thus he implicitly moves toward the duality already grasped by Shakespeare, who often has two counterdefinitions of manliness in competition—manliness as aggressiveness and revengefulness, and manliness as forbearance and even forgiveness. Without overtly stressing the latter meaning, Clark has put his finger on human uncertainty as to what is manly, and thus he touches on an extremely interesting theoretical issue: the problem of distinguishing what we may call manly virtues, womanly virtues, and human virtues. He does not deal with the issue explicitly. But he makes doubly clear what Shakespeare brings out: the male fear of effeminacy, the concept of manliness as a persuader to action, the immense psychic force exerted by manliness as an ideal; above all, the begging of the definition, and hence the tendency to enthrone outrage as the only possible courage.

The impact of the ideal may cause anguish to men in solitude, but the immediate impact is greatest when the ideal is voiced by society. Clark catches the subtle strength of the male society that is forming about the nucleus of the quest; we can imagine ourselves half subdued by it. There is the sharp vignette of the woman, beside her husband's mount, "holding onto [his] leg with both hands" while he "wasn't answering, but just shaking his head short" (67). Despite his own doubts, Gil feels pressed enough to say, "I'll see this thing out as far as any man will" (111), with "man" as the pivotal word. The narrator makes a key remark: "Most men are more afraid of being thought cowards than anything else" (57). His words are not "being cowards," but "being thought cowards"; the fear is of condemnation by others, and I think the reader is taken along by the narrator when the latter assumes, though he never needs to say it outright, that withdrawal from the pursuit party would seem cowardly rather than prudent and rational. In the conduct and speech of man after man we feel the heavy, undefined power of the group. No man is an island, and we sense the almost unbreakable tie of membership.

Clark has got hold, then, of three powerful impulses to action of a certain kind: millennial justice, manliness, and membership. Combined, they can sway men to pursue ends even though their minds are troubled by doubts about the means. Clark is not doing anything nearly so simple as showing that direct action, a staple of westerns, is unjust; rather he shows the roots of unjust action in deep passions that may seek good and may lead to it. The story makes us feel, as it should, the almost irresistible pull, upon people not at all monstrous, of an action that we eventually see will be monstrous. Indeed, given the overwhelming trio of imperatives—millennial justice, manliness, and membership—we may well wonder why the hunt is so slow in pulling itself together, why it is impeded by a hesitancy that no one ever acknowledges. Here we get to the heart of the conflict: the men also feel, of course, the bonds of the community that long antedated the immediate crisis. The conflict is a great and potentially tragic one: it is between the customs and values of their normal community, and the pressures and values that seem to compel them to go outside it. If Clark had been writing a quarter of a century later, he might have made the men mouth a few clichés about "the system." But though momentarily disenchanted, they are not, as we have learned to say, alienated; they have a substitute for alienation, and that is our next subject.

iv

From the time they receive reports of increased cattle rustling and the murder of Kinkaid until the time they find and hang Martin and his two workmen, the men are sorely torn between two contrasting human styles. On the one hand there are the ways of the established community, which seems to have muddled along adequately if not gloriously; on the other hand there are certain basic drives, primitive and instinctual. On the one hand there are the received ways of dealing with errant behavior; on the other, a retaliatory and punitive spirit, a passion for quick death as the solvent of exceptional wrongdoing. On the one hand, there are the rational restraints to dam hot blood until a cool judgment can be made; on the other hand, hot blood, prejudgment, and cooling off only by cathartic violence. Within limits we can think of one side as classical, the other as romantic: the one committed to forms, balance, and measure; the other to compulsive inner voices that, divine or demonic, claim transcendence over form and balance.

Clark has presented in full the symbolic voices of the traditional community. We see virtually all its institutional forms. Osgood embodies the church, Tyler the law. Davies is the responsible citizen who has profound convictions about the value of the civilized order that society has slowly won. In the wife trying to restrain a departing husband we see the institution of the family. And finally, and I think more importantly than may be realized, there is Sparks, the black handyman and ex-parson. I suggest that he is essentially an old Shakespearean character, the special voice of human wisdom—the fool, the court jester. He says simply that the expedition means a "man takin' upon himself the Lohd's vengeance," and he adds, "Man . . . is full of error." The author makes a significant comment on this: "He said it jokingly, but he wasn't joking" (118)—a good working description of the fool's style. As the sole black man in the community, Sparks is an outsider, as the fool was. He is liked but is the object of jokes, as was the fool. Fools often spoke in verse; Sparks sings hymns. Above all, he has the kind of impact that Renaissance fools had. Note the words that Clark uses of him: "Sparks had given a kind of body . . . to an ideal which Davies' argument hadn't made clear and Osgood's self-doubt had even clouded" (75). He had "given a kind of body"—that is, by images, by nonlogical discourse, by a condensed statement of the heart of the matter: the essential style of the fool.

So we have what ought to be the triumphant word of the community delivered by all its voices—church, law, family, responsible citizenship, and the special corrector whom we might call prophet or seer or, as I have done, fool. But they are defeated. And by what? How shall we think of the twenty-eight men riding through night and cold and snow and dangerous terrain to punish thieves and murderers? Judge Tyler calls them "a lynching mob" (65), and we must find the term *mob* very tempting. Yet Art Croft objects to the term (65), and I believe we should shun it. When we are attempting to be critics, we should always avoid the quick clichés of condemnation. The word *mob* is too easy; it begets self-approval in the user, and it tends to conceal rather than reveal the inner life of the pursuing group. The word that Gerald Tetley uses repeatedly is *pack*; for Gerald it is a term of contempt, and yet it comes close, I think, to the truth that we need to grasp. For *pack* at least implies a group

with a certain center and principles of order, with a unity and instinctual bond. It implies a mode of being to which I will apply a term that I
now use for the first time of the Tetley group—the term *community*. It
is a community, and we miss the underlying life of the story if we do not
think of it in terms of community.

The basic tension of Clark's novel is the conflict within man between
two different modes of community that have powerful appeals to him.
On the one hand there is the central, continuing community to which
we have applied such terms as *normal* and *traditional*. On the other hand
there is the crisis-born community that we ought not to underestimate
by using the facile terms of denigration that we are all rather fond of.
The Tetley group is a community that has its own cohesive and hence
magnetic quality. It does not make a random attack on existent order; it
stands for a different conception of order. The seekers of millennial justice and the judges of manliness are other men, the group. The group
constrains the individual; no doubter really challenges its force. No one
can deny his membership—that is, they all belong to a community—a
community whose commitment to the just and the manly shames any
serious questioning of its authority.

The stature of the book is rooted in the author's sense of a profound
conflict between two communities or modes of community. The new
community resists efforts at definition. We can dig out the motives of
millennialism and manliness and still feel somewhat dissatisfied, for these
provide a rational form that does not encompass all the energizing irrationalities. Clark tries to identify these too—in such a phrase as Gerald
Tetley's "pack instincts" (101), but more strikingly in a description of
Davies's dilemma. Davies, he says, is using "something remote and mis-
trusted" in trying to combat "something that had immediacy and a
strong animal grip." He is finding out that what "shaped men's deeds" is
"not the big misty 'we,'" but the "small but present 'we'" (57). The word
"we" implies community, and the two uses of it reflect two different
senses of community: the inclusive, historical one, nonlocalized because reflected in all places, and the exclusive, local, present one mysteriously coercive in its "immediacy and strong animal grip." We might
think of one of them as the large Western one, the occidental heritage,
and of the other as the small western one, the limited blood brotherhood
that shrinks into the western stereotype.

What Clark gets hold of is the authentic threat of this latter community to the other one in which we ordinarily live and find security. Let us
risk a strained antithesis of terms and call them the community of the
Holy Ghost and the community of the unholy guts. *Holy Ghost* can
image the informing spirit of substantive human order; in Davies's terms,

law is the "conscience of society." *Unholy guts* hardly needs definition, but we can use *id* as a loose synonym for it—the force that precedes conscience and ever seeks to supplant it. Its universality and primacy give it a bonding strength of exceptional tenacity, the "animal grip" that makes the pack, or the pack-as-community—the inferior but dangerous rival community. There is a nice symbolic representation of the two communities in that Sheriff Risley speaks for one, and Deputy Sheriff Mapes automatically attaches himself to the other, and thus gives it a quasi legality.

It is this threat to the established community that is the source of what I have called "dread." Others may prefer other terms, but to do this book justice we need to have a sense, not simply of an unpleasant danger of a familiar kind, but of an ominous disruption and displacement of essential order. Clark is not describing a standard kind of dis-order—a private, noncommunal violation of rules, such as theft, injury, or crime of passion. Such events may create excitement, fear, or even anxiety, but they are mild affairs—small, curable wounds to some part of the community—compared with the taking over of power by a deviant, narrow community of faulty substance, and hence more ruthless methods and more merciless bonds. The situation, as Davies puts it, is "infinitely more deadly when the law is disregarded by men pretending to act for justice than when it's simply inefficient" (47).

One physical source of dread, we might notice, is movement from an open to a shut-in situation. Without ever using the word, Clark has forced us into a kind of claustrophobia in the key scene: we are shut in by the night, by the storm, by the mountains. The specific scene is a tight little enclosure within the larger enclosure of the mountains. It sets off exactly the ironic enclosure by hard facts (Martin has no receipt, the Mex is tricky), the moral enclosure of the prejudgment that shores up circumstantial evidence, of the exclusion of counterevidence, of sim-ulated ritual that only seals a predetermined doom, of emotional doors that cannot be opened to forces that might revise these emotions—in sum, of "normal" men acting "ab-normally."

Clark has found, it seems to me, an extraordinary narrative image for the experience of being taken over by the deviant or deformed commu-nity. He has said that he had in mind the Nazi takeover in Germany, and his conviction that it *could* happen here. But luckily he gave rein to his storyteller's imagination instead of mechanically inventing parallels to the Nazi acquisition of power (many events of his story are not at all parallel to the history of the 1930s), and he did far better than arbitrarily constructing a one-dimensional parable. Rather he discovered a para-digm of events of which the Nazi affair was only one variant. For instance, many of us can still remember the ominousness of the 1930s, and the dread that it evoked. Those of us who can do so could not help noticing remarkable similarities between German goings-on of the 1930s and the style of American violence from 1968 to 1971. Writing in 1940 Clark so interpreted a contemporary terror that he managed to anticipate a near-terror of three decades later. The dread that some of us felt in the late 1960s and early 1970s was the dread of feeling a true though imperfect community in danger of going under to a fake community promising to enforce perfection. As many people put it, the problem was whether the fringe destroyers with slogans would gain the ear of the middle. For a time they seemed to be doing it, and the community hung in balance. We had a new awareness of its frailty, and wondered whether the frailty meant disastrous vulnerability. That theme is what Clark had got hold of years before.

My phrase was "destroyers with slogans." The community of the unholy guts is a pretty wily affair. For all its universality, the id has limited organizing powers; hence it tricks itself out—almost anagrammatically, one might add—in the idea. The instincts simulate an institution; the pack comes up with a program, the id with an idea. It is always the same one: perfect justice. It is so simple that it can be proclaimed by rascals as well as by honest idealists, by sick men as well as by the pure id boys. In our day, the sick man often pretends to be, or actually mistakes himself for, the specialist in internal medicine. He prescribes perfect health for all—that is, his own compulsory health insurance.

I am trying to describe some of the complex working mechanics of the millennialism that Clark long ago detected in the western stereotype. The rival community[4] becomes menacingly effective because it looks simple and honest but mixes up two or three appeals that fuddle us. It is not easy for the unanalytical—the class to which all of us belong most of the time— to disentangle the mingled calls of the wild, of the sick, and of the ideal. It is hard to resist the fused and thus confused summons of the irrational force and the rational perfection, of the barbarous and the utopian, of the noble goal publicly proclaimed and the demonic leadership, of guts and dream, id and idea, of the simultaneous assault from below and above— the visceral fear that one may not be brutal enough to be manly, and the spiritual fear that one may lack the soul for a more nearly ideal justice. The final source of dread is the sinister marriage of the Platonic and the primitive, the ultimate coupling that begets the deviant community.

v

It takes a penetrating book to set us off on these meditations that can cross back and forth between literary and historical realities. The hardest problem is to clarify the combination of the insinuating and the tough in the rival community that we know is always on the periphery, waiting for some trouble in the circle of the going order that will mean vulnerability to destructive attack. I have spoken of the frailty of the established community; in this context it is a susceptibility to the blandishments that call simultaneously to its crude passions and its corrective instincts.

To pass now from the theoretical problem to the specific literary method: Clark makes us feel the force of these blandishments, but in a rather subtle way. It is not, of course, that our sympathies are drawn to the Tetley project. But we are compelled to know inwardly the power of the group, its strong magnetic field, its almost magical suasiveness. If we do not want to be in that community, we can nevertheless see how it tugs at people who are more like ourselves than they are like monsters, and we can sense the enormous difficulty of resisting its strenuous though unspoken membership drive. If the group were openly barbarous, we could simply flee; but these people are, in Art's words, "quiet, gentle men, and the most independent in the world too" (55). They are hard to draw away from for an opposition that could seem censorious or priggish. Clark also sees them as striving for a certain decorum, always a mark of the legitimate institution; they are upset by loudmouths, unseemly jesters, arrogant predetermined hangmen. Thus by various narrative devices Clark so positions us that we can almost feel ourselves being drawn in, however reluctantly.

The use of a first-person narrator is important. We always tend to go along with him and share his feelings unless, by some device within the fiction, he is repudiated or, like Gulliver, made ambiguous. We are not seriously separated from Art Croft and his friend Gil Carter. Art's human decency is established by the fact that Davies sees him as a possible ally and gets some help from him, that Gerald Tetley feels quite able to talk intimately to him, and that he keeps wrestling with the problems of the crisis. Initially he and Gil fall in with the manhunt because they need to overcome the unspoken but communicated suspicion of themselves as outsiders and to be at one with the power group. In their desire not to be suspect outsiders, they are not special cases different from ourselves; in the long absence that makes others unsure of them we see projected our own weaknesses or skeletons that could be damaging to us if we directly challenged a community with a salvationary program. So Art and Gil never really act on their occasional impulses to feel apart from it all, to criticize the affair, and to assure themselves, as Gil puts it several times, that "this ain't our picnic" (54, 140). If they are bothered by the style of the quest, they tend to accept its premises and the circumstantial evidence that spurs the group.

But though we instinctively go along with a first-person narrator who is not stupid or palpably self-deceiving or vicious, "go along with" does not mean "agree with"; obviously we do not share Art's conviction about the guilt of the prisoners. But we do understand why he feels it; we sense the deep pressures upon his belief and action. It is the paradoxical gift of Clark's novel to afford us two contradictory experiences. On the one hand it provides the aesthetic distance that makes it possible for us to judge. On the other hand it gives us a felt proximity of crisis that enables us to know the frightening difficulty of maintaining, in the ultimately close quarters of actuality, the judicial separateness of art. We judge others while we know how painfully difficult it would be not to join them if we were there. In the art form of fantasy we entertain images of heroic individualism that we do not often transmute into an actual risking of public scorn and humiliation. We know the force of Art Croft's phrase, "each man afraid to disagree with the rest" (48).

But now the next step: Suppose we do become bold and fight shy of the crime-hunters, where do we go? Here again Clark shows great skill, and I think more than may be apparent on the surface. He creates barriers, conspicuous or delicate, between us and almost everyone with whom we might ally ourselves. The minister's style puts us off; Osgood falls into homiletic truisms that gain no edge from his sincerity. We cannot join him. Judge Tyler's rhetoric spurts up and out in mechanical leaps, but it is more like Fourth of July fireworks than the D-day firepower that is needed. We might conclude that Clark is satirizing church and bench, but that, I think, is a too-easy reading. In my view, the stylistic shortcomings of both men symbolize the defective power of institutional order in this kind of crisis. What they say does not get hold of us, though we know it ought to. Then there is Sparks, but we could not hold hands with him, because an outcast cannot supply the alternative shelter that we need.

Why, however, not Davies, the good citizen, the passionate voice of the community conscience? All he says is right, but he remains impotent. What Clark catches hold of here is the insubstantialness of intellectual truth against the pseudo community of virility and instant justice. He presents the ineffectiveness of the right idea in various inconspicuous symbols that, in a real-life situation, would tend to push us away from Davies or at least make us diffident about allying ourselves with him. Davies *looks* ineffectual: "an old man, short and narrow and so round-shouldered he was nearly a hunchback" (31); he "would have been a good figure of a miser" (32); he is a shopkeeper, and he can be accused of the profit motive (37, 85). Art tries to duck him (38); his Socratic questions seem, in this atmosphere, a little pedantic (46–47); at one time he looks "as if he were going to cry" (48); after a while he "sounded . . . defeated" (78); Tetley's challenge makes him "confused" (88); he is a target for jokes. Surely Clark's most difficult feat was to make Davies right but not quite convincing, almost persuasive yet lacking in what we now call charisma; wholly worthy of respect and yet weaker than the Tetley whom no one likes.

Finally, there is Gerald Tetley, who balances Davies nicely in the story: Davies articulates the theoretical principles of the true community; Gerald excoriates the working principles of the deviant community. Gerald is utterly right, too. But we shrink from him. For he is weak, hysterical, even neurotic; we doubtless remember that he is a "sullen, sick boy" who looks like his mother (79); and he must remind us of another ailing son of a disciplinary Civil War officer, Orin Mannon in Eugene O'Neill's *Mourning Becomes Electra* of just a decade earlier. We fall away from him; he could never be a rallying point.

Clark has shown extraordinary ingenuity in leaving us, so to speak, nowhere to go—that is, as soon as the aesthetic stimulus draws us away from aesthetic distance and imaginatively into the interplay of actual society. In contemplation we can remain solitary; in participation we cannot be solitary unless we are saints or heroes. But when I say "we" I mean not saints and heroes but, in the familiar phrase, us average sensual men. Clark forces us to feel the pull of the deviant community, if not upon us as individuals, at least upon others like ourselves—the secret and unacknowledged attractiveness of the spirit of the new community, with its destructiveness clothed in a sense of mission and even of ironic decorousness.

But beyond our feeling the secret grip I think must lie another deep and unarticulated fear—namely, that under stress we might not be immune to the unwanted invitation. After all, we are the middle that may be drawn in by the devious, self-righteous, threatening, mesmeric fringe, which can always find an occasion and proclaim a virtue. The ultimate dread must be that of in some way being carried along by or consenting to the deformed society. If Clark has taken us to that point, then he has indeed met the ultimate obligation of art: to make us hold back the finger of accusation, and instead to look into a mirror—a clear mirror, neither flattering nor distorting, of ourselves. This is not the experience of satiric and melodramatic art and of their counterparts in societal art—politics and war—for in these we separate ourselves from the wrongdoers and condemn them. Rather it is the experience of comic art and of tragic art, for these must elicit from us the "there go I" of the no longer innocent.

vi

Clark completes the story with another action of deep significance: the reordering of the community after its lapse into the ways of the fringe community of the unholy guts. This is in chapter 5, which I am inclined to think of as act 5 of the drama. It is, however, more detailed than drama could be, for it observes nearly all the possible ways of responding to disaster, of the conscience trying to recover ground lost to guts and dreams, id-cum-idea.

Judge Tyler applies the law literally: he declares everybody under arrest. Sheriff Risley countermands the judge's order. The sheriff's realism confirms the view that Tetley's posse is a community and you cannot hang a whole community. The sheriff's decision thus raises the complex question of penance and atonement for the guilt of a whole community. In the place of formal legal action the group tends to apply what we may call folk-law: purgation by scapegoat. Clark has prepared us for this quite early in the story by having Davies declare that the group needs a leader whom it can, if need be, turn into a scapegoat. Clark is very shrewd in seeing the inner tie between leader and scapegoat: leadership depends on a singleness of will made possible by a freedom from common scruple; the followers' absence of will frees them from guilt, and the leader's freedom from scruple is just what can be blamed if things go wrong. Again, Clark is wonderfully perceptive in handling the inchoate move to lynch Tetley; though a number of men might like this way out, we see only one man pushing it—Smith. Early in the story Smith was defined as "the town bum, . . . balanced between begging and a conceited, nagging humor that made people afraid of him" (7). Purification by scapegoat is the special cleansing style of a spiritually unclean man who needs an execution as a retaliatory consolation for his own maculate condition. Smith provides the unsavory alternative to the dry, unsentimental morality of Sheriff Risley, who says to Davies: "there's nothing you or anybody else can do about it now" (192).

But individuals can do something about it; they can respond in different ways that reveal different spiritual potentialities. Beset by different attacks upon his selfhood—guilt, public humiliation, the shame of a sensibility that seems unmasculine—Gerald Tetley commits suicide: the response of despair. For different reasons, rather unclear ones, his father does too, in the old Roman style that befits a part of his personality, even if the act itself is, as I find it, a little too neat. In contrast with all the rest is Davies, whom Clark rightly makes the dominant figure of the final section. Davies's anguished, non-self-exonerating grasping for and grappling with self-knowledge is in the tragic mode, and to introduce the tragic is the final achievement of the book. Getting revenge, as Smith wants to do, or making a final exit, as the Tetleys do—these are in the style of melodrama, which is natural to the life of the western.[5] Yet Clark complicates the tone and actually gives us something of a tragic hero. Davies repeatedly makes an assertion that comes out of the tragic point of view: the others, especially Tetley, he says are not to "blame" (199, 202). Blaming is the spirit of satire and melodrama, modes of punishment and revenge; Davies blames only himself—the tragic style. Further, Clark makes the narrator say of Davies that "the flaw had been in him from the start" (211). "Flaw" is the ancient term for the error of being or doing that the tragic hero, in the final phase, comes to know about.

Through the admirably paced revelation by which, step by step, we go deeper and deeper into his personality, we learn that Davies's flaw is unused knowledge. Davies knew that a gun, to threaten with or actually kill, was necessary to keep Tetley from going on with the triple murder, but he did not take a gun along, because he could not face this ultimate act of preventive force. Hence his tragic anguish, so sharply different from the irremediable despair of killing oneself, or the scapegoat method of killing someone else, or the ordinary man's living uneasily, without further killing, with the killing done.

The tragic climax is remarkable in several ways. Clark not only makes another break with the western stereotype; he also breaks sharply from a basic element in tragic form. In the stereotype the hero—ready with gun, firm of hand, certain of what has to be done—comes up fearlessly with the needed direct action. Clark, on the other hand, presents a virtuous man who does not and perhaps cannot have it in him to be the cool triggerman of justice in an all-or-nothing confrontation. As for the tragic form: Clark simply turns a central feature of it upside down. The traditional tragic flaw is hubris, the arrogance or insolence that bursts forth in violence; Davies's flaw—he calls it fear—is an unwillingness or inability to use a violence that would be only technically arrogant.

Furthermore, in breaking with both melodramatic and tragic patterns Clark not only closes doors, so to speak, but opens up a very large door upon a philosophical scene that is fused with the dramatic scene. The philosophical scene has to do with a disturbing issue, a possible vulnerability at the heart of civilization: the paradox that this ultimate secular achievement may have a built-in self-destructiveness. The mark of civilization is the civilized person who uses civility in all modes of intercourse. This is Davies: the civilized man who has a grasp of the culture, a feeling for its patterns of order, a passion for the rational discipline of passionate irrationality. But can all that knowledge and sensitivity coexist with the toughness apparently indispensable for crisis politics? Does not the civilized man, of his own nature, always act with civility? Can he of his nature achieve an incivility upon which the survival of civil men and of a civil order may depend? That he literally cannot do this is one premise of all deliberate destroyers of order: their initial rule of battle is to immobilize civilized man with a barrage of effrontery, insolence, and brutality that they think him by nature lacking the resources to deal with. Tetley's lynchers do not want to destroy order, of course, but Winder's sneer at "law and order crap" (45) is remarkably like some battle cries of a later day.

Thus Clark's novel keeps expanding and reaching out; it keeps revealing bonds of meaning with historical events and with other works of literature. That is why we can say that Clark has transmuted a stereotype into a model, an exemplary shaping of reality whose presence we can see elsewhere in life and in art. In presenting the recurrent problem of the civilized man who shrinks, perhaps disastrously, from a critical confrontation, *The Ox-Bow Incident* inevitably takes us back two and a half decades to Conrad's *Victory*, which has the same theme (as does also Clark's *The Track of the Cat*, in a different way, in the treatment of Arthur). Conrad and Clark both make us wonder whether man must not deny something of his civilization to protect the rest of it. Beyond that, he may be subtly entrapped by a paradox of moral advancement: that the desirable state achieved contains within itself the virus of a pathological hypertrophy. That is to say, the process of becoming civilized may trigger a mechanism that, unless we brake it by some extraordinary act of will, inflates the civilized into the overcivilized which invites the undercivilized.

In *The City of Trembling Leaves* Clark can look at civilized society hopefully, at least in the sense that the troubled artist eventually finds himself—his way of living and of effectively using his talent—not in solitude or in a commune but within the ordered community. But Clark comes closer to achieving a model when he treats the crisis within the community. *The Track of the Cat*, recounting the family community in crisis, has some striking resemblances to O'Neill's *Long Day's Journey into Night*, which O'Neill was writing about the same time (1940; published, 1955). It even has an affiliation with O'Neill's *Emperor Jones*—in the effect of severe unwonted pressure by nature and solitude upon the personality accustomed to the ways of societal living. But *The Ox-Bow Incident* is the model of greatest usefulness. It provides, as we have seen, the essential pattern of historical events of three decades later. What is more, it anticipated by fifteen to twenty years a set of European plays that brilliantly dramatized disorder within the community and most of which, like the *Incident*, felt at least a partial impetus in the Nazi revelation of what could take place in an apparently sound community. Three of these are Friedrich Dürrenmatt's *The Visit* (1955) and Max Frisch's *The Firebugs* (1958) and *Andorra* (1962).[6]

The tone of "it *can* happen here" may be frightening or saddening. It is ominous and appalling when we occupy the role, not of defenseless victims, as in moments of grim light we know that we may be at any time, but of contributing to our own disaster, of having the tools and the talent for betraying ourselves. The final dread is of what one's own humanity may be capable of. Two brilliant plays use opposite technical ways of exploring this dark possibility: in the one we see a representative individual, and in the other the whole community, losing the right way and feeling the insidious pull of the deviant community. In Jean-Paul Sartre's *Les Séquestrés d'Altona* (1959) the central character, a young German officer, is driven virtually mad by the recognition that, in an episode in which Nazis tortured a Jew, he had actually felt "some strange kind of approval." In Eugène Ionesco's *Rhinoceros* (1960) we see a whole town throwing aside its communal bonds and, with various rational justifications, joining in a new, inferior, and indeed bestial community, grotesquely symbolized in the rhinoceroses that the people become.

All this, Clark had already caught: the precariousness of community because its members, people like us, choose the wrong act, the wrong bonds. It is not that we approve the new inadequate, shortcut, visceral order; it is simply that we recognize some part of ourselves in it. As we read, we experience a deep-feeling knowledge of the intense difficulty of facing down the deviant community, exerting an almost demonic pressure in its millennial appeal to conscience, its code of manliness that engages mysterious subconscious forces, its moral arrogance, and its call to membership that arouses our fear of solitude. Some part of ourselves has to fight another part. The new crisis-born order makes an appeal that is hypnotic because it is directed simultaneously to the higher man, the lower man, and the social man.

What an immensely embracing model of reaction to a crisis Clark has constructed from the rubble of the old stereotype! When *The Ox-Bow Incident* reached print, he was thirty-one years old. We wonder that a youth of so few years could know so much about humanity and could find so successful an artistic form for what he knew. In that knowing and that forming we see something of genius.

NOTES

Notes to Essay 4, "The Comedy of Conscience: Trollope's *The Warden*"

1. I mean, not that there are not excrescences, but that the materials in the novel are predominantly relevant and ordered. Too much has been made of the excrescences, real or apparent.

2. Quotations are from the Modern Library edition of *The Warden and Barchester Towers* (New York, 1950). They are identified by chapter number.

3. *An Autobiography* (Berkeley and Los Angeles, 1947), 80, 83.

4. Quoted by Monk Gibbon, *The Masterpiece and the Man: Yeats as I Knew Him* (New York, 1959), 93.

Notes to Essay 6, "*E Pluribus Unum*: Parts and Whole in *Pride and Prejudice*"

1. The themes and issues dealt with in this essay have been much discussed in articles and books. Various studies of *Pride and Prejudice* allude to the title themes, the centrality of irony, and the learning process that Elizabeth and Darcy undergo. The marriage theme has received considerable attention. When there is such a wealth of commentary, one may have missed something relevant to one's own argument. However, to the best of my knowledge the familiar aspects of *Pride and Prejudice* which I notice have not previously been combined and treated as they are here.

2. In some criticism there is a tendency to censure Austen for the stereotype and not to notice the major innovation by which she pushes the stereotype into the background.

Notes to Essay 7, "Charlotte Brontë, Reason, and the Moon"

1. "The White Goddess," *New Republic* 136 (June 24, 1957): 9 ff.

2. For Anne Brontë, too, the moon apparently took on more than pictorial meanings. In the poem "Fluctuations," according to recent biographers, the "moon's re-emergence" symbolizes "divine intervention." See Ada Harrison and Derek Stanford, *Anne Brontë: Her Life and Work* (New York, 1959), 189.

Notes to Essay 9, "Nomad, Monads, and the Mystique of the Soma: D. H. Lawrence's Art and Doctrine"

1. The materials in my essay were originally part of a review of Eliseo Vivas's *D. H. Lawrence: The Failure and the Triumph of Art*; the review appeared in *Sewanee Review* 68 (1960): 635–59. A section of the review dealing only with Lawrence's style appears as essay 18 of the present volume. I have omitted some parts of the review in which the discussion of Lawrence's work is secondary to a discussion of some of Vivas's aesthetic principles.

Notes to Essay 10, "Lemuel Gulliver and Tess Durbeyfield: Houyhnhnms, Yahoos, and Ambiguities"

1. Another interesting contrast between Austen and Hardy derives from the fact that both Mrs. Bennet in *Pride and Prejudice* and Mrs. Durbeyfield in *Tess* are assiduous marrying mothers. In the convention of comedy of manners, however, circumstances are amenable to character: one daughter put out as bait by Mrs. Bennet is loved by an honorable man; another daughter is content to marry her seducer, who can be bribed to marry her. In the naturalistic mode partly congenial to Hardy's temperament, circumstances rarely yield to character but more often conspire against men.

2. David J. De Laura, "'The Ache of Modernism' in Hardy's Later Novels," *English Literary History* 23 (1967): 390–99. De Laura also uses the term *ambiguity* with reference to Hardy's treatment of Angel.

3. The quotations are from the essays "The Symbolic Imagination" and "The Angelic Imagination" in Tate's *The Forlorn Demon* (Chicago, 1953), 37, 38, 77. While I was exploring the hypothesis that Angel is a figure of angelism, I found that it had already been expressed by De Laura (see note 2).

Notes to Essay 14, "Greene's Euphuism and Some Congeneric Styles"

1. There is an urbane description of the genre in A. C. Hamilton, "Elizabethan Prose Fiction and Some Trends in Recent Criticism," *Renaissance Quarterly* 37 (1984): 21–33.

2. All page references are to the 1587 text reprinted in *Shorter Novels: Elizabethan and Jacobean*, Everyman's Library 824 (London and New York, 1929). I give no page numbers for phrases often repeated. Since the spellings in the text are inconsistent, I regularize by modernizing.

3. The dominance of *f* in these quotations calls to mind Greene's thematic word *fancy*, which leads Hamilton to remark that the work "builds increasingly to an elaborate rhetorical fugue in F" ("Elizabethan Prose Fiction," 27).

4. Approaching the end, Greene tended to hurry things, as if he was getting weary of the double labors with style and plot. Indeed, a twelve-line paragraph at the end covers so much ground that one could read it as a consciously jesting dismissal of the project. A critic who wanted to pursue this argument could call attention to the generic terms that Greene uses: "this tragical comedy" (211), when Gwydonius is concerned about the apparent illness of Castania; "this tragedy" (246), when Orlanio has Castania and Melytta jailed because Castania loves Gwydonius, the son of a political enemy; and finally "this strange tragedy" (260), of a final solution happy for everybody. He may, of course, be using *tragedy* as a loose synonym for *drama*.

5. The table concludes my use of statistics, which I know are tedious, but which have seemed the only way to present, in relatively brief compass, the distribution of space as a significant reflector of the influence exerted by the euphuistic habit of mind.

6. References are to the text in Samuel Johnson, *"Rasselas," Poems, and Selected Prose*, ed. Bertrand H. Bronson (New York, 1952).

Notes to Essay 15, "Tulip-hood, Streaks, and Other Strange Bedfellows: Style in *Villette*"

1. Compare Mrs. G. B. Shaw's "sentimental people are always unkind. They think of their own sentiments, and not of the feelings of the other person" (Janet

Dunbar, *Mrs. G.B.S.: A Portrait* [New York, 1963], 276), which could apply to Lucy at times.

2. With such materials, statistics easily become laughable. But curiosity led me to a quick count, informal and uncomputerized: some seventy common nouns are made proper by type, and there are 130 instances of this. The words promoted three or four times are *Reason, Fate, Hope, Imagination, Destiny, Disappointment, Death,* and *Truth;* the two-time words are *Providence, Common Sense, Time, Life, Feeling, Power, Freedom, Renovation,* and *Fancy.* The long list of once-onlys includes *the Real, Temptation, Inclination, True Love, Substance, Hypochondria, Fact, Pity, Comparison, Rumour, Hate, Conception, Falsehood, Heresy,* and *Creative Impulse.*

3. Compare "The hag, Wisdom" in *The Ordeal of Richard Feverel,* ch. 31.

4. Brontë seems quite unable to imagine the particulars of the life of such a professional as Paul is said to be. He not only teaches an apparently daylong schedule at the girls' school, but seems to teach at will in almost all fields from literature to mathematics. But that is only the half of it; he is also a professor at the university, and in local mind-circles he is esteemed as both orator and thinker. When does he study? In some way Brontë may sense that there is a problem, for she sets limits in a way that fascinatingly anticipates a familiar twentieth-century situation: Lucy as the undergraduate adoring the don who does not sink to the commonplaceness of print—"M. Emanuel was not a man to write books; but I have heard him lavish, with careless, unconscious prodigality, such mental wealth as books seldom boast" (33). "Wealth" is one of her abstractions not made concrete by evidence.

5. Another form of concreteness is the slender but steady stream of allusions to mythic, literary, and historical characters (and sometimes objects, places, and events), nearly always as parallels to, or illustrations of, elements in her own narrative. In the classical realm she alludes to Aeschylus, Aphrodite, the Apple of Discord, Atlas, Charon, Hymettus, Juno, Nero, Phidias, Rhadamanthus, and Timon (Ginevra's playful name for Lucy); in the biblical—Baal, Babylonish furnace, Daniel, David, Esau, Jacob, Jael and Sisera, Meribah's waters, Methusaleh, Joseph, Nebo, Nebuchadnezzar, Rimmon, Samuel, Saul (a notable concentration on the Old Testament, possibly significant); in other myths and folklore—Azrael, Bedreddin Hassan, Cunegonde, Malevola, Undine. There are a few literary references—several to Bunyan and Burns, others to Scott, *The Vicar of Wakefield,* and *A Midsummer Night's Dream.*

6. Like Dickens she can make physical features emblematic of moral qualities. Miss Marchmont's heir is "an avaricious-looking man, with pinched nose and narrow temples," who indeed is a "thorough miser" (5). And one can imagine Dickens, when he was assembling the decor for Miss Havisham's quarters in *Great Expectations,* remembering the attic where Lucy learned her lines for the play: "Boxes and lumber filled it; old dresses draped its unstained wall—cobwebs its unswept ceiling. Well was it known to be tenanted by rats, by black beetles, and by cockroaches. A partial darkness obscured one end, across which, as for deeper mystery, an old russet curtain was drawn, by way of screen to a somber band of winter cloaks, pendant each from its pin—like a malefactor from his gibbet" (14).

7. Compare George Eliot's description of Ladislaw's smile: "a gush of inward light illuminating the transparent skin" (*Middlemarch,* bk. 2, ch. 21).

8. Beginning with "drooping draperies," the quoted passages, in the order in which they are arranged, are located in chapters as follows: 3, 14, 35, 14, 21, 26, 2, 4, 4, 25, 6, 3, 9, 35, 15, 33, 9, 11, 26.

9. Compare Elizabeth Bennet at the climactic moment of ch. 36 in *Pride and Prejudice:* "Till this moment I never knew myself."

Notes to Essay 17, "The Muddled and the Masterful: Style in *The Mayor of Casterbridge*"

1. Compare the line "I knew a woman, lovely in her bones" in Theodore Roethke's "I Knew a Woman."

2. Only after I completed the essay did I discover the following facts: the citations and references, numbering about 135, are distributed through forty-one of the forty-five chapters; there are two or more allusions to thirty-six chapters.

Notes to Essay 21, "The Dictatorial Idea: Hardy and Some Late Characters"

1. Occasionally there is an interesting interplay between folk action and major action: for example, Christian Cantle, as the man no woman will marry, is a sort of comic version of Wildeve and Clym, whom we might say no woman should marry. There is, of course, a much more overt relationship between Susan Nunsuch and Eustacia: the literal witchcraft used against the supposed witch whose emotional witchcraft is well dramatized.

2. The cycle has some interesting echoes in book VI. "No more Novembers" might be the principle of this section. The key occasion for Thomasin and Diggory is May Day, also a day of ritual festivities, and they are married in August—a blotting out, as it were, of that long August two years before in which everything went downhill for all the Yeobrights. Even in what we may call the outlying parts of the story Hardy uses regularities of dating. On the first November 5 we learn that Diggory had received a letter of refusal from Thomasin just two years before (I, 9) and that just one year ago Eustacia summoned Wildeve by a fifth of November fire (I, 6). It is just a year, too, since Mrs. Yeobright rejected Wildeve as a husband for Thomasin (I, 4). For four years running, then, November is a time of significant events. (In *Tess*, Hardy would use the months of May [hopeful starts] and October [subsequent troubles] similarly, several times with two-year intervals.) Hardy gives us one dating clue which, if we can assume that he was using an actual day of week and month, makes it possible to work out a complete calendar of events. In IV, 5, he identifies August 31 as a Thursday: this would put the main action in either 1843 or 1848, since in the preface dated July 1895 Hardy says that the date of the actions "may be set down as between 1840 and 1850."

3. Resemblances between episodes in Hardy and other novelists may be matters of chance—for example, the double drowning in *The Return* and in George Eliot's *Mill on the Floss* (1860). Still, it is a rather interesting coincidence when Clym and Dickens's Pip (*Great Expectations*, 1860) have identical ironic experiences: all passion spent, Pip decides to propose to Biddy, only to find her heart committed to Joe; Clym decides to propose to Thomasin, only to find her heart committed to Diggory—two somewhat complacent heroes in the same anticlimax. Eustacia's infatuation with Paris anticipates the longing for Moscow that appears repeatedly in Chekhov's women, especially in *The Three Sisters*.

Notes to Essay 23, "Trouble in Eden: James's *The Turn of the Screw*"

1. My impression is that the Freudian reading, first given wide currency by Edmund Wilson in 1938, no longer has the hold that it once had. For the argument against it, see my "The Freudian Reading of *The Turn of the Screw*," *Modern Language Notes* 62 (1947): 433–45. Criticism of the story is too vast to summarize here. The most profound analysis is that by Eric Voegelin, *Southern Review* n.s. 7.1 (Winter 1971): 9–48. I quote one significant sentence from it: "the employer, the

governess, and the housekeeper . . . symbolize, in this order, God, the soul, and the earthy, common-sense existence" (10). Ironic side-note on lost opportunities: some time after reading Voegelin, I came across a marginal inquiry in the edition of *The Turn* that I had once used in a course on the novel: "Is the uncle God?" I had dropped it there.

2. On the corruptibility of children, see "The Lure of the Demonic," essay 11, above.

Notes to Essay 26, "Clark's Western Incident: From Stereotype to Model"

1. As it appears in a devotion to westerns, hesperophilia may reflect a number of motives. In an intellectual it may be only a form of play, of escape from the critical rigors of life; it must be much the same thing as the passion for detective stories often professed by writers and scholars. Sometimes there is an element of pure or playful perversity in this: you expect me to be above this kind of thing, so I will make a point of being, not above it, but with it. I am so secure in my professional exercise of critical or creative intelligence that I can flaunt my privilege of acclaiming that which will not stand rigorous criticism. I can display my exemption from ordinary critical canons, or even go to the opposite extreme of implying that there is a subtle superiority of taste in my addiction to the popular art.

2. After writing this I learned from Robert Clark that Rose's appearance was historically an "intrusion"—a response to the publisher's fears that the story was deficient in sex appeal. However, the women's driving Rose out of town is struc-turally appropriate: it is an earlier, anticipatory instance of a special community's taking over an enforcement program to gratify its own needs, regardless of the well-being of the larger community.

3. D. H. Lawrence liked *maleness,* but his emphasis was different from that of the western. More familiar are *masculinity* and *virility,* terms that could apply to a per-manent Hemingway problem. *Virtue* is interesting in its etymological sense: the qualities of *vir,* or "man." The root meaning is perhaps best represented in *man-liness,* which I use.

4. Up to a point one might call it a community of the ill and injured, those who, having some psychic wound or moral trouble, or beset by a sense of injury, or lacking the normal person's ability to cope with actual injury, work off grievances in aggres-sive and retaliatory activities concealed under ennobling banners. Tetley's son is a severe disappointment to him, Winder is aggrieved by the decline of stagecoaching, Monty Smith is a spiritual defective, Farnley has lost heavily at cards. Tetley, as Robert Harvey has pointed out to me, may still be suffering from the Civil War defeat. The search for individual compensation and wholeness in a new order oper-ating through punitive violence but proclaiming virtuous ends is of course a familiar event on the twentieth-century political scene.

5. In spending all my time on interpretation I have ignored a subject that deserves considerable attention—the technical expertise of Clark as storyteller, especially in the melodramatic mode of authentic conflict. His skill appears in scene after scene—the card game, the visit to Judge Tyler's, the episodes that slow down and speed up the formation of the Tetley group, the incidents on the trail, the tension after the three innocent men are taken prisoner. The discovery that Kinkaid is not dead is handled with fine understatement, indeed masterfully "thrown away." The stagecoach episode, later addition though it is, functions as an excellent micro-cosmic symbolization of the larger community action: crisis, inadequate leadership (the driver and guard are at least partly drunk), panic, heroics, shooting in the dark,

the wounding of an innocent bystander, and, above all, the near self-destruction of the community (the occupants of the coach) rushing headlong to save itself.

6. In *The Firebugs* a citizen helps destroy his community—symbolized in the burning of his house by professional arsonists who have moved into it—by his inability to take necessary action against the destroyers; like Davies, he can call upon force but is reluctant to do so. In Frisch's *Andorra* a community allows itself to fall into an unwanted but somehow irresistible campaign against its single Jewish resident; his innocence is identical with that of the hanged men in *The Ox-Bow Incident*. In Dürrenmatt's *The Visit* we see a community taking on a distorted form by accepting an enormous bribe to commit murder and then using the bribe as the cornerstone of a new era of progress and prosperity. In both *The Visit* and *Andorra* there is a Davies character who protests and fails; in each play the Davies character is a schoolteacher, both teachers take to drink, and both commit suicide—one literally, the other symbolically by acquiescing in the sweep of destructive public action.

ACKNOWLEDGMENTS

THE AUTHOR AND THE PUBLISHER acknowledge the original publishers of essays that appear in this volume and the granting of permissions to reprint.

"Versions of Renunciation: Hardy and Waugh" originally appeared in *Accent* 7 (1947), under the title "Sue Bridehead Revisited"; "The Possessed Artist and the Ailing Soul" in *Canadian Literature* 8 (1961); "The Western Theme: Exploiters and Explorers" in *Northwest Review* 4 (1960), and "Lampedusa and Bulwer: *Sic Transit* in Different Keys" in *Northwest Review* 7 (1965–1966); "Hawthorne's 'The Birthmark': Science as Religion" in *South Atlantic Quarterly* 48 (1949); and "Lemuel Gulliver and Tess Durbeyfield: Houyhnhnms, Yahoos, and Ambiguities" in *Southern Review*, n.s. 6 (1970), under the title "*Gulliver* and Hardy's *Tess*: Houyhnhnms, Yahoos, and Ambiguities."

For permission to reprint, we are grateful to the University of California Press for "Charlotte Brontë, Reason, and the Moon," which appeared in *Nineteenth Century Fiction* 14 (1960); for "The Muddled and the Masterful: Style in *The Mayor of Casterbridge*," which appeared in *Nineteenth Century Fiction* 18 (1964), under the title "Hardy's *Mayor*: Notes on Style"; and for "Sue Bridehead: A Brilliant Portrait," which appeared in *Nineteenth Century Fiction* 20 (1966), under the title "Hardy's Sue Bridehead."

To the Cambridge University Press for "*E Pluribus Unum:* Parts and Whole in *Pride and Prejudice*," from *Jane Austen: Bicentenary Essays*, ed. John Halperin (1975); to *Comparative Literature* for "The Lure of the Demonic: James and Dürrenmatt," *CL* 13 (1961); to Cornell University Press for "Greene's Euphuism and Some Congeneric Styles," reprinted from *Unfolded Tales: Essays on Renaissance Romance*, ed. George M. Logan and Gordon Teskey, Copyright © 1989 by Cornell University; to Holt, Rinehart and Winston for "Tragic Unity in Conrad's *Lord Jim*," revised from the Introduction to *Lord Jim*, Introduction and Notes by Robert B. Heilman (1957).

To the Louisiana State University Press for "The Comedy of Conscience: Trollope's *The Warden*," which appeared in *Essays in Honor of*

Esmond Linworth Marilla, ed. T. A. Kirby and W. J. Olive (1970), under the title "Trollope's *The Warden:* Structure, Tone, Genre"; to Macmillan London for "'Stealthy Convergence' in *Middlemarch,"* from *George Eliot: A Centenary Tribute,* ed. Gordon S. Haight and Rosemary T. Van Arsdel (1982); to *New Letters* and the Curators of the University of Missouri–Kansas City for "Trouble in Eden: James's *The Turn of the Screw,"* which, under the title *"The Turn of the Screw* as Poem," originally appeared in the *University of Kansas City Review* 14 (1948); and to the University of Minnesota Press for the same essay, which appeared in *Forms of Modern Fiction,* ed. William Van O'Connor (1948), and for "Innovations in Gothic: Charlotte Brontë," which, under the title "Charlotte Brontë's 'New' Gothic," appeared in *From Jane Austen to Joseph Conrad: Essays Collected in Memory of James T. Hillhouse,* ed. Robert C. Rathburn and Martin Steinmann, Jr. (1958).

To the National Council of Teachers of English for *"Silas Marner:* The Explicit Style," which, under the title "Return to Raveloe: Thirty-Five Years Later," appeared in *The English Journal* 46, copyright 1957 by the National Council of Teachers of English; to the University of Nevada Press for "Clark's Western Incident: From Stereotype to Model," from *Walter Van Tilburg Clark: Critiques,* ed. Charlton Laird (1983); to Oxford University Press for "Two-Tone Fiction: Nineteenth-Century Types and Eighteenth-Century Problems," from *The Theory of the Novel: New Essays,* ed. John Halperin, copyright 1974 by Oxford University Press, Inc.; to *Studies in the Novel* for "Tulip-hood, Streaks, and Other Strange Bedfellows: Style in *Villette,"* published in vol. 14, copyright 1982 by North Texas State University; and to Wayne State University Press for "'Intentions' in *The Mayor,"* which originally appeared under the title "Hardy's *Mayor* and the Problem of Intention" in *Criticism* 5 (1963).

And to George Core, editor of *Sewanee Review,* for two articles which appeared originally in that review: "Variations on Picaresque: Mann's *Felix Krull,"* 66 (1958), and "Nomad, Monads, and the Mystique of the Soma: D. H. Lawrence's Art and Doctrine," and "A Singular Element in D. H. Lawrence's Style," both parts of one essay that appeared under the title "Nomad, Monads, and the Mystique of the Soma" in 68 (1960); copyright 1958, 1960, 1986, and 1988 by the University of the South.

CONCERNING NOVELS AND NOVELISTS
Essays and Reviews by Robert Bechtold Heilman

Contributions to Books

1. "Charlotte Brontë's 'New Gothic,'" in *From Jane Austen to Joseph Conrad: Essays Collected in Memory of James T. Hillhouse*, ed. Robert Rathburn and Martin Steinmann, Jr. (University of Minnesota Press, 1958), 118–32.

2. "Trollope's *The Warden*: Structure, Tone, Genre," in *Essays in Honor of Esmond Linworth Marilla*, ed. T. A. Kirby and W. J. Olive (Louisiana State University Press, 1970), 210–29.

3. "Two-Tone Fiction: Nineteenth-Century Types and Eighteenth-Century Problems," in *The Theory of the Novel: New Essays*, ed. John Halperin (Oxford University Press, 1974), 305–22.

4. "*E Pluribus Unum*: Part and Whole in *Pride and Prejudice*," in *Jane Austen: Bicentenary Essays*, ed. John Halperin (Cambridge University Press, 1975), 123–43.

5. "*The Return [of the Native]*: Centennial Observations," in *The Novels of Thomas Hardy*," ed. Anne Smith (Vision Press, 1979), 58–90.

6. "*Losing Battles* and Winning the War," in *Eudora Welty: Critical Essays*, ed. Peggy W. Prenshaw (University Press of Mississippi, 1979), 269–304.

7. "'Stealthy Convergence' in *Middlemarch*," in *George Eliot: A Centenary Tribute*, ed. Gordon S. Haight and Rosemary T. VanArsdel (London: Macmillan, 1982), 47–54.

8. "Clark's Western Incident: From Stereotype to Model," in *Walter Van Tilburg Clark: Critiques*, ed. Charlton Laird (University of Nevada Press, 1983), 79–104.

9. "Greene's Euphuism and Some Congeneric Styles," in *Unfolded Tales: Essays on Renaissance Romance*, ed. George M. Logan and Gordon Teskey (Cornell University Press, 1989), 49–73.

Journal Articles

1. "The New World in Charles Dickens' Writings," Part I, *The Trollopian* [later, *Nineteenth Century Fiction*] (1946): 25–43; Part II, *The Trollopian* (1947): 11–26.

2. "Sue Bridehead Revisited," *Accent* 7 (1947): 123–26.

3. "The Freudian Reading of *The Turn of the Screw,*" *Modern Language Notes* 62 (1947): 433–45.

4. "*The Turn of the Screw* as Poem," *University of Kansas City Review* 14 (1948): 277–89.

5. "Hawthorne's 'The Birthmark': Science as Religion," *South Atlantic Quarterly* 48 (1949): 575–83.

6. "Return to Raveloe: Thirty Five Years After," *English Journal* 46 (1957): 1–10.

7. "Variations on Picaresque (*Felix Krull*)," *Sewanee Review* 66 (1958): 547–77.

8. "Charlotte Brontë, Reason, and the Moon," *Nineteenth Century Fiction* 14 (1960): 283–302.

9. "The Possessed Artist and the Ailing Soul," *Canadian Literature* 8 (1961): 7–16.

10. "The Lure of the Demonic: James and Dürrenmatt," *Comparative Literature* 13 (1961): 346–57.

11. "*Ship of Fools* [by Katherine Anne Porter]: Notes on Style," *Four Quarters* 12 (1962): 46–55.

12. "Hardy's *Mayor* and the Problem of Intention," *Criticism* 5 (1963): 199–213.

13. "Hardy's *Mayor*: Notes on Style," *Nineteenth Century Fiction* 18 (1964): 307–29.

14. "Lampedusa and Bulwer: *Sic Transit* in Different Keys," *Northwest Review* 7 (1965–1966): 21–28.

15. "Hardy's Sue Bridehead," *Nineteenth Century Fiction* 20 (1966): 307–23.

16. "Salesmen's Deaths: Documentary and Myth," *Shenandoah Review* 21 (1969): 20–26.

17. "*Gulliver* and Hardy's *Tess*: Houyhnhnms, Yahoos, and Ambiguities," *Southern Review*, n.s. 6 (1970): 277–301.

18. "Tulip-hood, Streaks, and Other Strange Bedfellows: Style in *Villette,*" *Studies in the Novel* 14 (1982): 223–47.

Review Articles

1. "Melpomene as Wallflower; or, The Reading of Tragedy," *Sewanee Review* 55 (1947): 154–66. (On R. P. Warren, *All the King's Men*.)

2. "Four Novels," *Sewanee Review* 55 (1947): 483–92. (On Albert Idell, *The Sea Is Woman*; John Kelly, *All Souls' Night*; Jean Stafford, *The Mountain Lion*; Malcolm Lowry, *Under the Volcano*.)

3. "Recent Fiction," *Hudson Review* 1 (1948): 108–19. (On Theodore Dreiser, *The Stoic*; Lionel Trilling, *The Middle of the Journey*; Philip

Toynbee, *Prothalamium*; Jean-Paul Sartre, *The Age of Reason, The Reprieve.*)

4. "Versions of Documentary," *Sewanee Review* 56 (1948): 671–84. (On John Williams, *Nothing But the Night*; Arne Skouen, *Stoker's Mess*; Humphrey Slater, *Conspirator*; Maxence van der Meersch, *Bodies and Souls*; Ralph Ingersoll, *The Great Ones*; Ramon Sender, *The King and the Queen*; Ernst Juenger, *On the Marble Cliffs*; Feike Feikema, *The Chokecherry Tree*; Graham Greene, *The Heart of the Matter.*)

5. "Tangled Web," *Sewanee Review* 59 (1951): 107–19. (On R. P. Warren, *World Enough and Time.*)

6. "Schools for Girls," *Sewanee Review* 60 (1952): 299–309. (On William Faulkner, *Requiem for a Nun*; Caroline Gordon, *The Strange Children*; Shirley Jackson, *Hangsaman.*)

7. "Nomad, Monads, and the Mystique of the Soma," *Sewanee Review* 68 (1960): 635–59. (On Eliseo Vivas, *D. H. Lawrence: The Failure and the Triumph of Art*, and on Lawrence's fiction generally.)

8. "The Western Theme: Exploiters and Explorers," *Northwest Review* 4 (1960): 5–14; reprinted in *Partisan Review* 28 (1961): 286–97. (On John Williams, *Butcher's Crossing.*)

Critical Introductions to Editions

1. Joseph Conrad, *Lord Jim* (Rinehart, 1957), v–xxv.

2. Thomas Hardy, *The Mayor of Casterbridge* (Houghton Mifflin, 1962), v–xxxviii.

3. George Eliot, *Silas Marner* (Houghton Mifflin, 1962), vi–xi.

4. Thomas Hardy, *Jude the Obscure* (Harper, 1966), 1–46.

5. Jonathan Swift, *Gulliver's Travels* (Random House, 1969), vii–xxxiv.

6. Thomas Hardy, *Tess of the D'Urbervilles* (Bantam, 1971), vii–xxiv.

INDEX